21 世纪课程规划教材

| A Selected Reading from
Western Classics |

西方思想经典选读
（第二版）

乔国强 何辉斌 /主编

图书在版编目 (CIP) 数据

西方思想经典选读 / 乔国强，何辉斌主编 . —2 版 . —北京：北京大学出版社，2021.2
21 世纪课程规划教材
ISBN 978-7-301-31912-3

Ⅰ. ①西… Ⅱ. ①乔… ②何… Ⅲ. ①思想史—西方国家—高等学校—教材
Ⅳ. ① B5

中国版本图书馆 CIP 数据核字 (2020) 第 252402 号

书　　　名	西方思想经典选读（第二版）
	XIFANG SIXIANG JINGDIAN XUANDU（DI-ER BAN）
著作责任者	乔国强　何辉斌　主编
责任编辑	朱丽娜
标准书号	ISBN 978-7-301-31912-3
出版发行	北京大学出版社
地　　　址	北京市海淀区成府路 205 号　100871
网　　　址	http://www.pup.cn　新浪微博：@北京大学出版社
电子信箱	zln@pup.cn
电　　　话	邮购部 010-62752015　发行部 010-62750672　编辑部 010-62754382
印　刷　者	天津中印联印务有限公司
经　销　者	新华书店
	730 毫米 ×980 毫米　16 开本　21.25 印张　520 千字
	2007 年 4 月第 1 版
	2021 年 2 月第 2 版　2022 年 1 月第 2 次印刷
定　　　价	58.00 元

未经许可，不得以任何方式复制或抄袭本书之部分或全部内容。
版权所有，侵权必究
举报电话：010-62752024　电子信箱：fd@pup.pku.edu.cn
图书如有印装质量问题，请与出版部联系，电话：010-62756370

参与编写者：

乔国强　何辉斌　主　编

姜玉琴　陈　娴
卢燕飞　方环非　编　注
于凤宝　管海佳

前　言

《西方思想经典选读》在初版13年后终于再版了。北京大学出版社外语编辑部张冰主任在本教材的编写和再版过程中予以了热情的鼓励和支持，编辑朱丽娜同志也为本教材的再版编辑和校对做了大量的工作。在此一并表示最为诚挚的谢意。这次再版主要做了两项工作：一是增添了三位西方学者的选文，即节选了达马西奥的《笛卡尔的错误：情绪、推理和人脑》、道金斯的《自私的基因》以及伊格尔顿的《批评的功能》；二是对初版中出现的印刷和编排等问题做出了订正。

新选入的三位学者的作品分别讨论了理性与身体、生命与信仰以及批评与非批评等问题。达马西奥的代表作《笛卡尔的错误》主要阐述了情绪对于决策以及社会行为的意义。法国哲学家笛卡尔是唯心主义哲学观的代表人物，强调人的主体性与身心二元论。笛卡尔认为身体拥有运动的特性，但是却是被动的，而精神代表了纯粹的思维，是主动的。笛卡尔与康德皆认为人类依靠理性做出最佳决策，理性决策须将情绪排除在外。《笛卡尔的错误》一书否定了二人的观点，认为理性本身存在诸多缺陷，并且重新审视了情感的作用。道金斯的《自私的基因》是其所有著作中影响力最为强劲和持久的一部。无论在生物学等自然科学领域，还是在哲学、宗教等人文学科，抑或在非学术研究的普通读者中，《自私的基因》都因对达尔文的自然选择理论的重新阐释而激发了读者们极大的兴趣。它不仅系统性地改变了社会生物学的原有本质，也使芸芸众生以一种新的视角重新审视生命的存在和信仰的存在。伊格尔顿的《批评的功能》表达了对以英国为代表的欧洲现代批评现状的失望。伊格尔顿认为,现有的批评已经走上了非批评的道路,丧失了批评的原有功能,使批评家丧失了独立的批评立场,落入到文学产业的公共关系网中。

我们在长期的教学实践中发现,许多文科学生对西方的思想经典知之甚少,而能够潜心阅读西方思想经典原作的学生更是少之又少。因此,我们从两千多年间堆积起来的卷帙浩繁的西方思想宝库中精选了23位思想家的精品佳作,编辑了这本《西方思想经典选读》,以期能对文科学生学习和了解西方思想经典有所帮助。

西方思想源远流长、博大精深,对其进行简单的概括和分期并非易事。不过,为了便于学习,我们在此尝试做一个粗略的概括和梳理。古希腊、古罗马是西方思想的源头,这个时代的思想家不仅喜欢对现实中的一般性事物进行思考,而且还喜欢将其所思所想进行概括、升华,找到抽象的概念和原理,以探索何为世界的真正本原。米利都学派的"始基"、柏拉图的理念、亚里士多德的本体等都以寻求万物最后的本质为特征。这种对世界总体的最一般的概括的学问叫作"本体论"(ontology)。到了中世纪,西方人的本体论有了一定的变化,他们把神看作世界的本体,是把万物统一起来的绝对的最高的存在。古希腊罗马和中世纪的思想很复杂,具体的流派和观点非常多,但总体上看,他们有着重本体论的倾向。

文艺复兴之后直到19世纪,西方思想的核心转向了认识论的问题。他们更加关心认识的过程和方法、获取真理的途径以及知识的可靠性和真理性等。这一转向始自法国的笛卡尔,后被大陆的理性主义者和英国的经验主义者共同加以发展,并在德国古典主义时期达到了非常高的水平。英国经验主义者主要包括培根、霍布斯、洛克、休谟等。培根的《新工具》是经验主义的里程碑式著作。它强调了"归纳"在科学中的作用,突破了亚里士多德的《工具论》只重演绎推理的局限。霍布斯、洛克对理性主义的"天赋观念"说进行了批评,强调经验在认识过程中的作用,进一步完善了经验主义的思想。休谟认为,所谓的因果关系只是经验的重复,即两者经常在时间中相继出现,以至于使那些轻信的人断定,前者的出现肯定会引起后者的出现,把两者的关系看作是必然的,还会在将来保持不变。休谟认为这种现象并不意味着必然联系,因为相继出现过一万次的两件事情,完全有可能在一万零一次的时候停止相随,就是无数次升起过的太阳也不能保证明天还会升起,总要到来不升起的时刻,说不定在明天就会出现。

欧洲大陆理性主义思想的奠基人笛卡尔积极地寻求通向真理的途径,仔细考察了知识的可靠性、清晰性和明确性。为了找到准确无误的知识,他主张怀疑一切可以怀疑的东西。在不断地批评和否定之后,他发现原先被人们看作非常确定的知识都经不起推敲,只有那个能够怀疑一切的理性主体是不可怀疑的。欧洲大陆的理性主义者还包括斯宾诺莎、莱布尼茨、伏尔泰、卢梭等。到了德国古典主义时代,康德、黑格尔、费希特、谢林等把理性主义思想推向了高潮。与经验主义相比,理性主义更有深度和系统性,但没有经验主义那么接近现实,有时难免有教条主义的倾向。除了认识论之外,这一时期的思想家所关心的问题还有很多,如叔本华探讨了意志和表象的问题,尼采探索了超人意志,克尔凯郭尔批判了思辨哲学,研究了"生存境界"等。

概言之,西方思想历史悠久,涉及的流派和国家很多,伟大的思想家层出不穷,要做出合理的选择不是一件容易的事情。我们在筛选的时候,首先考虑到的是所选思想家在历史上的重要性。一些具有划时代意义的思想家,如柏拉图、亚里士多德、笛卡尔、康德等,都被列入了我们的范围;其次,我们还考虑要尽量涵盖各个历史时期,把古希腊、古罗马、中世纪、16—20世纪的部分学者的思想著作都包括进来。其次,我们在编选的过程中,尽可能地把多学科的内容包括进来,使哲学、伦理学、神学、逻辑学、政治学、社会学、历史学、文学批评等都能在这本书中有所体现;最后,我们尽可能地选入不同国别的思想经典作品,让希腊、罗马、意大利、英国、法国、德国、丹麦等主要欧洲国家都有自己的声音。但由于篇幅和水平所限,我们的选文也只能增加至现有的篇数,偏颇遗漏之处,敬请读者谅解。

本教材由乔国强和何辉斌主编,姜玉琴、陈娴、方环非、卢燕飞、于凤宝、管海佳同志参加编写。

目　录

柏拉图　/　1
Republic　/　4

亚里士多德　/　15
Nicomachean Ethics　/　17

卢克莱修　/　26
On the Nature of Things　/　28

奥古斯丁　/　39
Confessions　/　42

阿奎那　/　54
Summa Theologiae　/　56

马基雅维利　/　65
The Prince　/　67

培　根　/　76
The New Organon　/　78

霍布斯　/　90
Leviathan　/　93

笛卡尔　/　103
Meditations on First Philosophy　/　106

帕斯卡尔 / 119
Pensees / 122

洛　克 / 133
Two Treatises of Government / 135

休　谟 / 144
An Enquiry Concerning Human Understanding / 146

卢　梭 / 158
The Social Contract / 161

康　德 / 179
Foundations of the Metaphysics of Morals / 182

叔本华 / 191
The World as Will and Representation / 194

尼　采 / 204
Thus Spake Zarathustra / 207

克尔凯郭尔 / 218
Either—Or / 221

克罗齐 / 239
History: Its Theory and Practice / 242

韦　伯 / 252
The Protestant Ethic and the Spirit of Capitalism / 255

柯林武德 / 264
The Idea of History / 266

道金斯 / 275
Nice Guys Finish First / 277

伊格尔顿 / 291
Preface / 295
The Function of Criticism / 296

达马西奥 / 311
A Modern Phineas Gage / 314

柏拉图

柏拉图(Plato,前 427—前 347)出生在一个古老的雅典名门,是古希腊的百科全书式的思想家,在许多领域都有里程碑般的建树。他小时候喜欢绘画和文学创作。大约在 20 岁时成为苏格拉底的学生。40 岁时,他曾前往叙拉古,试图说服那里的统治者狄奥尼修一世采用他的政治主张,但惨遭失败。同年回到雅典,创立举世闻名的学园(Academy)。此后主要在学园里从事教育和研究,直到去世。有关他投师苏格拉底一事,有个美丽的传说。在第欧根尼·拉尔修的《著名哲学家的生平和学说》中有这样的记载:一天晚上,苏格拉底梦见一只小天鹅停在他的膝盖上,然后发出嘹亮美丽的声音并一飞冲天;第二天柏拉图前来投师,苏氏把柏拉图看作他梦见的那只天鹅。这个故事未必属实,但起码说明了这两位伟大思想家的关系非同一般,在希腊人心目中有着非常崇高的地位。他在公元前 387 年创办的学园,坐落在雅典城西北角的阿卡德摩(Academus),持续了九百多年,于公元 529 年被迫关闭。学园集中了当时在数学、动物学、植物学、地理学、哲学、政治学等领域的顶尖专家,培养出了大量的杰出人才,其中最有名的弟子为亚里士多德。学园的学术水平、社会影响、历史跨度等都是无与伦比的。

柏拉图的著作主要包括《理想国》(*Republic*)、《巴门尼德篇》(*Parmenides*)、《会饮篇》(*Symposium*)等 40 多篇对话,以及 13 封书信。柏拉图对西方文化的影响之大是无法估计的。黑格尔曾说:"哲学之作为科学是从柏拉图开始而由亚里士多德完成的。他们比起所有别的哲学家来应该可以叫作人类的导师。"①英国哲学家怀特海甚至说:"欧洲哲学传统的最没有争议的一般特征是:它由对柏拉图的一系列注释组成。"②

《理想国》是柏拉图最有名的著作。标题的希腊语为 politeia,指的是"关于城邦的学问",兼有"对城邦的研究"和"对人的研究"两层意思。很多研究哲学的专业人士都把这个题目译成《国家篇》,虽然比较忠于原意,但也只表达了前一种意思,却无法体现作者用了大量的篇幅阐述的有关人的教育问题。现在的英语名称来自拉丁译名 De Res Publica,但这里所谓的 republic 指的是古希腊的城邦,与现代意义上的"共和国"有很大的区别,不能望文生义。虽说这个标题本身并没有理想的意思,但柏拉图在对话中的确描绘了一个相当理想化的国家,所以最早翻译这本书的吴献书、郭斌和、张竹明都意译为《理想国》。这一译名已经被广泛地接受,所以我们仍然沿用这一名称。

《理想国》是当时的学术大全,各个领域的研究者,包括政治学、伦理学、教育学、心理学、诗学等学科的专家,纷纷把这部著作列为自己领域中的里程碑。由于当时的学术还没有明确的分科,所以这部著作的覆盖面很广。如要全面了解这本书,应当阅读全文。这里的片段选自《理想国》的第 7 卷,展现了柏拉图的著名的"洞穴"比喻。

柏拉图运用丰富的想象力,构思出一个如此奇特的地方。有一个很深的洞穴,洞中的人世世代代居住在这里,被铁链锁在固定的地点上,连脑袋都不能转动,眼睛只能看着洞穴最深处的洞壁。他们的后面有一堆火,在火和人之间,有一堵矮墙,墙的后面有人举着各种器物和雕像走来走去,火光将这些物体投影到囚徒面对的墙上。他们由于没有见过真实的东西,只能把影像当作事物本身。他们每天好像都在看皮影戏,已完全习惯于这种生活,没有人试图改变现状。洞穴的情况如下图所示。

---

① 黑格尔:《哲学史讲演录》第 2 册,北京:商务印书馆,1997 年,第 151 页。
② A. N. Whitehead, *Process and Reality: An Essay in Cosmology*, New York: Free Press, 1978, p.39.

如果有人把其中一个囚徒释放出来,并强迫他看火光和真实的东西,他肯定会感觉十分痛苦,在眼花缭乱的情况中无法看清实物,认为影子是更为真实的东西。如果有人硬将他拉出洞穴,在强光之下他必然感到眼睛疼痛,什么也看不清。若要他适应新的环境,需要一定的时间。柏拉图借用苏格拉底之口说:"首先他看影子最清楚,其次是人和其他物体在水中的倒影,然后才是真实的物体本身。接着他可以对着天体和天空本身大饱眼福,当然这种事情在晚上更容易做到:他将看月亮和星星的光,而不是在白天看太阳和阳光。"这个人一旦看清了太阳,他就会庆幸自己摆脱了原来的黑暗的洞穴,来到了阳光普照的世界。外面的世界象征着本质的世界,用柏拉图的话来说是理念(idea)的世界;太阳代表着善,是最高的理念,是万物的本原。柏拉图在这里所主张的就是撇开表面现象,看到事物本身,再上升到最为本质的理念。他的这种学术方法对西方国家产生了深远的影响,以至于怀特海把西方学术看作是对柏拉图的脚注。

柏拉图把理念的世界看作明显高于现象的世界,一旦步入这个世界,就不屑于回到原来的地方,因为"那些已经达到这种境界的人不愿俯身处理人类的事情:除了这个更高的世界之外,他们的灵魂哪儿也不想呆"。这就给柏拉图哲学带来了明显的出世的理想主义色彩。不过,他同时还有着非常入世的一面。这个摆脱了愚昧的人虽然很不愿意回到洞穴里,但还是要硬着头皮回到那里去。看到了光明和事物本身之后,他一下子还适应不了洞穴的生活,难以辨别洞穴里的影子,也有点不屑于那些囚徒所谓的智慧。但那些囚徒根本不能理解他,他们嘲笑他,甚至还威胁他,正如柏拉图所说的那样,"人们会说,难道他上去了一趟就把眼睛弄瞎了吗?难道不是根本不值得上去吗?如果可能的话,难道他们不会抓住并处死任何试图把他们释放并带到上面去的人吗?"(243)这是苏格拉底殉身真理的写照,也表现了柏拉图为理想而奋斗终生的精神。他曾三次前往叙拉古试图说服那里的僭主狄奥尼修一世和狄奥尼修二世采用他的政治主张。结果遭到了沉重的打击,一次被带到奴隶市场上出售,幸亏有人把他赎回来,另外两次也遇到了不同程度的危险。尽管如此,他对理想的追求并没有放弃,他坚信,"除非真正的哲学家获得政治权力,或者出于某种神迹,政治家成了真正的哲学家,否则人类就不会有好日子过"①。

柏拉图敢于为理想而奋斗的精神是非常可贵的。不过,在最愚昧的地方实践最前沿的理想是注定要失败的,也许折中一点更有现实意义。而且,所谓的本质往往是以牺牲丰富性为代价的,海德格尔认为这样的真理从另一个角度看是一种遮蔽。按照这样的观点去实践必然会有一定的弊端。此外,柏拉图过于

---

① 《柏拉图全集》第4卷,王晓朝译,北京:人民出版社,2003年,第80页。

强调哲学家的善意的屈就,把所有的希望都寄托在圣人的自我牺牲之上,完全否定政治家的功利主义的行为。他说:"不,事实是这样:将要执政的统治者越不愿意从政,其国家治理得越好,越没有分歧,但统治者越渴望从政,其管理最差。"政治家为自己的荣誉和利益而忙碌固然有不少弊病,但不考虑政治家的利益,只讲大思想家的奉献,可能是苍白无力的。在这个问题上面,黑格尔比他更有洞见,他把恶看作历史发展的杠杆,离开这种力量,历史的发展就失去了动力。

柏拉图的"洞穴"比喻包含着非常深刻的道理,而且形象鲜明,语言生动,是将哲学与文学熔为一炉的典范。我们应当从"洞穴"比喻中获得启发,不断地提高自己的修养,摆脱愚昧的状况。用我们中国话来说,就是不要做井底之蛙。

Republic

The final image, the Allegory of the Cave, is the longest and most famous of the three. It is introduced rather abruptly, but is meant to fit in with the preceding two images (517b—c, 532a—d). Further details of the fit are a matter of dispute, although the broad outlines are clear enough. Like all the great images of the world's greatest literature, Plato's Cave manages simultaneously to appear transparent and yet unexpectedly rich and surprising. Those readers who believe that philosophy is a dry academic pursuit will be surprised at its presentation here as a pursuit which frees us from terrible slavery; but for Plato and his peers philosophy was a way of life, not just a course of study.

"Next," I said, "here's a situation which you can use as an analogy for the human condition—for our education or lack of it. Imagine people living in a cavernous cell down under the ground; at the far end of the cave, a long way off, there's an entrance open to the outside world. They've been there since childhood, with their legs and necks tied up in a way which keeps them in one place and allows them to look only straight ahead, but not to turn their heads. There's firelight burning a long way further up the cave behind them, and up the slope between the fire and the prisoners there's a road, beside which you should imagine a low wall has been built—like the partition which conjurors place between themselves and their audience and above which they show their tricks."①

"All right," he said.

"Imagine also that there are people on the other side of this wall who are carrying all sorts of artefacts. These artefacts, human statuettes, and animal models carved in stone and wood and all kinds of materials stick out over the wall; and as you'd expect, some of the people talk as they carry these objects along, while others are silent."

"This is a strange picture you're painting," he said, "with strange prisoners."

"They're no different from us,"② I said. "I mean, in the first place, do you think they'd see anything of themselves and one another except the shadows cast by the fire on to the cave wall directly opposite them?"

"Of course not," he said. "They're forced to spend their lives without moving their heads."

"And what about the objects which were being carried along? Won't they only see their shadows as well?"

"Naturally."

"Now, suppose they were able to talk to one another: don't you think they'd assume that their words applied to what they saw passing by in front of them?"

"They couldn't think otherwise."

"And what if sound echoed off the prison wall opposite them? When any of the passers-by spoke, don't you think they'd be bound to assume that the sound came from a passing shadow?"

"I'm absolutely certain of it," he said.

"All in all, then," I said, "the shadows of artefacts would constitute the

---

① 以下对话在苏格拉底(Socrates)与格老孔(Glaucon)之间进行。这一段是苏格拉底的话,接着的是格老孔的回应,以此类推。在柏拉图的对话录中,作者本人没有亲自出场。一般来说,苏格拉底是他的代言人。但苏氏的话中有没有自己的观点?在多大的程度上他是在说自己的话?别的人物是否也会说一些代表柏拉图的观点的话?这些问题都不容易解决,需要仔细体会。

② 在苏格拉底看来,包括他自己在内的任何人都不可能完全摆脱身处"洞穴"的无知状态,所以这些囚徒"并不与我们不同"。

only reality people in this situation would recognize."

"That's absolutely inevitable," he agreed.

"What do you think would happen, then," I asked, "if they were set free from their bonds and cured of their inanity? What would it be like if they found that happening to them? Imagine that one of them has been set free and is suddenly made to stand up, to turn his head and walk, and to look towards the firelight. It hurts him to do all this and he's too dazzled to be capable of making out the objects whose shadows he'd formerly been looking at. And suppose someone tells him that what he's been seeing all this time has no substance, and that he's now closer to reality and is seeing more accurately, because of the greater reality of the things in front of his eyes—what do you imagine his reaction would be? And what do you think he'd say if he were shown any of the passing objects and had to respond to being asked what it was? Don't you think he'd be bewildered and would think that there was more reality in what he'd been seeing before than in what he was being shown now?"

"Far more," he said.

"And if he were forced to look at the actual firelight, don't you think it would hurt his eyes? Don't you think he'd turn away and run back to the things he could make out, and would take the truth of the matter to be that these things are clearer than what he was being shown?"

"Yes," he agreed.

"And imagine him being dragged forcibly away from there up the rough, steep slope," I went on, "without being released until he's been pulled out into the sunlight. Wouldn't this treatment cause him pain and distress? And once he's reached the sunlight, he wouldn't be able to see a single one of the things which are currently taken to be real, would he, because his eyes would be overwhelmed by the sun's beams?"

"No, he wouldn't," he answered, "not straight away."

"He wouldn't be able to see things up on the surface of the earth, I suppose, until he'd got used to his situation. At first, it would be shadows that he could most easily make out, then he'd move on to the reflections of people and so on in water, and later he'd be able to see the actual things themselves. Next, he'd feast his eyes on the heavenly bodies and the heavens themselves, which would be easier at night: he'd look at the light of the stars and the moon, rather than at the sun and sunlight during the daytime."

"Of course."

"And at last, I imagine, he'd be able to discern and feast his eyes on the sun—not the displaced image of the sun in water or elsewhere, but the sun on its own, in its proper place."

"Yes, he'd inevitably come to that," he said.

"After that, he'd start to think about the sun and he'd deduce that it is the source of the seasons and the yearly cycle, that the whole of the visible realm is its domain, and that in a sense everything which he and his peers used to see is its responsibility."

"Yes, that would obviously be the next point he'd come to," he agreed.

"Now, if he recalled the cell where he'd originally lived and what passed for knowledge there and his former fellow prisoners, don't you think he'd feel happy about his own altered circumstances, and sorry for them?"

"Definitely."

"Suppose that the prisoners used to assign prestige and credit to one another, in the sense that they rewarded speed at recognizing the shadows as they passed, and the ability to remember which ones normally come earlier and later and at the same time as which other ones, and expertise at using this as a basis for guessing which ones would arrive next. Do you think our former prisoner would covet these honours and would envy the people who had status and power there, or would he much prefer, as Homer describes it, 'being a slave labouring for someone else—someone without property',① and would put up with anything at all, in fact, rather than share their beliefs and their life?"

"Yes, I think he'd go through anything rather than live that way," he said.

"Here's something else I'd like your opinion about," I said. "If he went back underground and sat down again in the same spot, wouldn't the sudden transition from the sunlight mean that his eyes would be overwhelmed by darkness?"

---

① 这句话出自《奥德赛》,整句话的意思是:放弃信念和生活比给穷人当奴隶还难以忍受。

"Certainly," he replied.

"Now, the process of adjustment would be quite long this time, and suppose that before his eyes had settled down and while he wasn't seeing well, he had once again to compete against those same old prisoners at identifying those shadows. Wouldn't he make a fool of himself? Wouldn't they say that he'd come back from his upward journey with his eyes ruined, and that it wasn't even worth trying to go up there? And wouldn't they—if they could—grab hold of anyone who tried to set them free and take them up there and kill him?"

"They certainly would," he said.

"Well, my dear Glaucon," I said, "you should apply this allegory, as a whole, to what we were talking about before. The region which is accessible to sight should be equated with the prison cell, and the firelight there with the light of the sun. And if you think of the upward journey and the sight of things up on the surface of the earth as the mind's ascent to the intelligible realm, you won't be wrong—at least, I don't think you'd be wrong, and it's my impression that you want to hear. Only God knows if it's actually true, however. Anyway, it's my opinion that the last thing to be seen—and it isn't easy to see either—in the realm of knowledge is goodness; and the sight of the character of goodness leads one to deduce that it is responsible for everything that is right and fine, whatever the circumstances, and that in the visible realm it is the progenitor of light and of the source of light, and in the intelligible realm it is the source and provider of truth and knowledge. And I also think that the sight of it is a prerequisite for intelligent conduct either of one's own private affairs or of public business."

"I couldn't agree more," he said.

"All right, then," I said. "I wonder if you also agree with me in not finding it strange that people who've travelled there don't want to engage in human business: there's nowhere else their minds would ever rather be than in the upper region—which is hardly surprising, if our allegory has got this aspect right as well."

"No, it's not surprising," he agreed.

"Well, what about this?" I asked. "Imagine someone returning to the human world and all its misery after contemplating the divine realm. Do you think it's surprising if he seems awkward and ridiculous while he's still not seeing well, before he's had time to adjust to the darkness of his situation, and he's forced into a contest (in a lawcourt or wherever) about the shadows of morality or the statuettes which cast the shadows, and into a competition whose terms are the conceptions of morality held by people who have never seen morality itself?"

"No, that's not surprising in the slightest," he said.

"In fact anyone with any sense," I said, "would remember that the eyes can become confused in two different ways, as a result of two different sets of circumstances: it can happen in the transition from light to darkness, and also in the transition from darkness to light. If he took the same facts into consideration when he also noticed someone's mind in such a state of confusion that it was incapable of making anything out, his reaction wouldn't be unthinking ridicule. Instead, he'd try to find out whether this person's mind was returning from a mode of existence which involves greater lucidity and had been blinded by the unfamiliar darkness, or whether it was moving from relative ignorance to relative lucidity and had been overwhelmed and dazzled by the increased brightness. Once he'd distinguished between the two conditions and modes of existence, he'd congratulate anyone he found in the second state, and feel sorry for anyone in the first state. If he did choose to laugh at someone in the second state, his amusement would be less absurd than when laughter is directed at someone returning from the light above."

"Yes," he said, "you're making a lot of sense."

Since the Cave was expressly introduced as being relevant to education, its immediate educational implications are now drawn out. We all have the capacity for knowledge (in the Platonu sense, not just information), and education should develop that potential. But since it requires knowledge of goodness to manage a community well, then those who gain such knowledge have to "return to the cave": paradoxically, those who least want power are the ones who should have it.

"Now, if this is true," I said, "we must bear in mind that education is not capable of doing what some people promise. They claim to introduce knowledge into a mind which doesn't have it, as if they were introducing sight into eyes which are blind."①

"Yes, they do," he said.

"An implication of what we're saying at the moment, however," I pointed out, "is that the capacity for knowledge② is present in everyone's mind. If you can imagine an eye that can turn from darkness to brightness only if the body as a whole turns, then our organ of understanding is like that. Its orientation has to be accompanied by turning the mind as a whole away from the world of becoming③, until it becomes capable of bearing the sight of real being and reality at its most bright, which we're saying is goodness. Yes?"

"Yes."

"That's what education should be," I said, "the art of orientation. Educators should devise the simplest and most effective methods of turning minds around. It shouldn't be the art of implanting sight in the organ, but should proceed on the understanding that the organ already has the capacity, but is improperly aligned and isn't facing the right way."

"I suppose you're right," he said.

"So although the mental states which are described as good generally seem to resemble good physical states, in the sense that habituation and training do in fact implant them where they didn't use to be, yet understanding (as it turns out) is undoubtedly a property of something which is more divine: it never loses its power, and it is useful and beneficial, or useless and harmful, depending on its orientation. For example, surely you've noticed how the petty minds of those who are acknowledged to be bad, but clever, are sharp-eyed and perceptive enough to gain insights into matters they direct their attention towards. It's not as if they weren't sharp-sighted, but their minds are forced to serve evil, and consequently the keener their vision is, the greater the evil they accomplish."

"Yes, I've noticed this," he said.

"However," I went on, "if this aspect of that kind of person is hammered at from an early age, until the inevitable consequences of incarnation have been

---

① 柏拉图认为知识已经在人的灵魂中,学习只是一个回忆的过程。
② knowledge 在柏拉图著作中是与 opinion 相对的概念,前者指确定的本质的知识,后者指变化的表面的观点。
③ the world of becoming 指的是变化的表面的世界,real being 指的是本质的稳定的东西。

knocked off it—the leaden weights, so to speak, which are grafted on to it as a result of eating and similar pleasures and indulgences and which turn the sight of the mind downwards—if it sheds these weights and is reoriented towards the truth, then (and we're talking about the same organ and the same people) it would see the truth just as clearly as it sees the objects it faces at the moment."

"Yes, that makes sense," he said.

"Well, doesn't this make sense as well?" I asked. "Or rather, isn't it an inevitable consequence of what we've been saying that uneducated people, who have no experience of truth, would make incompetent administrators of a community, and that the same goes for people who are allowed to spend their whole lives educating themselves? The first group would be no good because their lives lack direction: they've got no single point of reference to guide them in all their affairs, whether private or public. The second group would be no good because their hearts wouldn't be in the business: they think they've been transported to the Isles of the Blessed even while they're still alive."①

"True," he said.

"Our job as founders, then," I said, "is to make sure that the best people come to that fundamental field of study (as we called it earlier): we must have them make the ascent we've been talking about and see goodness. And afterwards, once they've been up there and had a good look, we mustn't let them get away with what they do at the moment."

"Which is what?"

"Staying there," I replied, "and refusing to come back down again to those prisoners, to share their work and their rewards, no matter whether those rewards are trivial or significant."

"But in that case," he protested, "we'll be wronging them: we'll be making the quality of their lives worse and denying them the better life they could be living, won't we?"

"You're again forgetting, my friend," I said, "that the point of legislation is not to make one section of a community better off than the rest,

---

① 知识分子一旦进入自己的理想天地,就会自命清高,中西方都有这种现象。

but to engineer this for the community as a whole. Legislators should persuade or compel the members of a community to mesh together, should make every individual share with his fellows the benefit which he is capable of contributing to the common welfare, and should ensure that the community does contain people with this capacity; and the purpose of all this is not for legislators to leave people to choose their own directions, but for them to use people to bind the community together."

"Yes, you're right," he said. "I was forgetting."

"I think you'll also find, Glaucon," I said, "that we won't be wronging any philosophers who arise in our community. Our remarks, as we force them to take care of their fellow citizens and be their guardians,① will be perfectly fair. We'll tell them that it's reasonable for philosophers who happen to occur in other communities not to share the work of those communities, since their occurrence was spontaneous, rather than planned by the political system of any of the communities in question, and it's fair for anything which arises spontaneously and doesn't owe its nurture to anyone or anything to have no interest in repaying anyone for having provided its nourishment, 'we've bred *you*, however,' we'll say, 'to act, as it were, as the hive's leaders and kings, for your own good as well as that of the rest of the community. You've received a better and more thorough education than those other philosophers, and you're more capable of playing a part in both spheres. So each of you must, when your time comes, descend to where the rest of the community lives, and get used to looking at things in the dark. The point is that once you become acclimatized, you'll see infinitely better than the others there; your experience of genuine right, morality, and goodness will enable you to identify every one of the images and recognize what it is an image of. And then the administration of our community—ours as well as yours—will be in the hands of people who are awake, as distinct from the norm nowadays of communities being governed by people who shadow-box and fall out with one another in their dreams over who should rule, as if that were a highly desirable thing to do. No, the truth of the matter is this: the less keen the would-be rulers of a

---

① 知识分子喜欢待在自己的理想世界中，所以人们得强迫他们从政，正如《庄子·让王》所描写的情景一样。

community are to rule, the better and less divided the administration of that community is bound to be, but where the rulers feel the opposite, the administration is bound to be the opposite.'"

"Yes," he said.

"And do you think our wards will greet these views of ours with scepticism and will refuse to join in the work of government when their time comes, when they can still spend most of their time living with one another in the untainted realm?"

"No, they couldn't." he answered. "They're fair-minded people, and the instructions we're giving them are fair. However, they'll undoubtedly approach rulership as an inescapable duty—an attitude which is the opposite of the one held by the people who have power in communities at the moment."

"You're right, Glaucon," I said. "You'll only have a well-governed community if you can come up with a way of life for your prospective rulers that is preferable to ruling! The point is that this is the only kind of community where the rulers will be genuinely well off (not in material terms, but they'll possess the wealth which is a prerequisite of happiness—a life of virtue and intelligence), whereas if government falls into the hands of people who are impoverished and starved of any good things of their own, and who expect to wrest some good for themselves from political office, a well-governed community is an impossibility. I mean, when rulership becomes something to fight for, a domestic and internal war like this destroys not only the perpetrators, but also the rest of the community."

"You're absolutely right," he said.

"Apart from the philosophical life," I said, "is there any way of life, in your opinion, which looks down on political office?"

"No, definitely not," he answered.

"In fact, political power should be in the hands of people who aren't enamoured of it. Otherwise their rivals in love will fight them for it."

"Of course."

"There's no one you'd rather force to undertake the guarding of your community, then, than those who are experts in the factors which contribute towards the good government of a community, who don't look to politics for their rewards, and whose life is better than the political life. Agreed?"

"Yes," he said.

 选文出处

Plato. *Republic*. Translated by Robin Waterfield, Beijing: China Social Sciences Publishing House (reprinted from the English Edition by Oxford University Press, 1993), 1999, pp. 240—249.

 思考题

1. 柏拉图认为,在某种程度上每个人都处于无知的"洞穴"之中。如何评价这个"洞穴"比喻?
2. 谈谈你对哲学家国王的看法。

 阅读

参考书目

1. 范明生:《柏拉图哲学述评》,上海:上海人民出版社,1984年。
2. G. C. Field, *Plato and His Contemporaries: A Study in Fourth Centurary Life and Thought*, London: Metheun, 1967.

亚里士多德

亚里士多德(Aristotle,前384—前322)出生在一个医生的家庭,幼年父母双亡,由亲戚抚养成人。他17岁时来到雅典,在柏拉图的学园学习,后来在这里从事研究和教学,直到柏拉图去世,长达20年之久。他曾应马其顿国王菲利普的邀请,担任他的儿子亚历山大的老师。亚历山大征服雅典后,亚里士多德回到雅典并在吕克昂(Lyceum)建立了一所学校,逐渐形成了自己的学派——漫步学派(Peripatetics)。亚历山大大帝逝世后,亚里士多德离开雅典,并在次年去世。

亚里士多德的主要著作包括:《形而上学》(*Metaphysics*)、《尼各马科伦理学》(*Nicomachean Ethics*)、《政治学》(*Politics*)、《修辞学》(*Rhetoric*)、《诗学》(*Poetics*)、《物理学》(*Physics*)、《工具论》(*Organon*)等。罗素对亚里士多德有很高的评价,他认为亚里士多德"死之后一直过了两千年,世界才又产生出任何可以认为是大致能和他相匹敌的哲学家"[①]。罗素甚至认为,亚里士多德的影响之大,束缚了思想的进一步发展。他说:"直迄这个漫长时期的末尾,他的权威性差不多始终是和基督教教会的权威性一样地不容置疑,而且它在科学方面也正如在哲学方面一样,始终是对于进步的一个严重障碍。"[②]

《尼各马科伦理学》是亚里士多德的重要作品之一。尼各马科本

---

① 罗素:《西方哲学史》(上卷),何兆武、李约瑟译,北京:商务印书馆,1997年,第209页。
② 同上。

来是亚里士多德的儿子的名字,他用自己儿子的名字给自己的伦理学著作命名。这部著作探讨的最核心问题是,怎样培养出完人(perfect man),并让他获得至善(highest good),以便享受最大的幸福(happiness)。为了达到这个目的,亚里士多德分别探讨了勇敢(courage)、慷慨(magnificence)、机敏(wittiness)、友爱(friendship)、公平(justice)、理性(reason)等概念。

本书所选的内容出自该书的第3卷,探讨了什么是勇敢。亚里士多德在文章的开篇强调说,勇敢是"在恐惧和鲁莽之间的中间状态"。勇敢并不是什么都不怕,惧怕也不见得就是坏事,例如说,"一个人并不因为惧怕给妻子或者孩子带来侮辱,或者妒忌,或者如此之类的任何事情而成为懦夫,也不因为在挨鞭子时能忍耐而成为勇敢"。一个鲁莽的人虽然看起来很像勇敢的人,好像天不怕地不怕,可一旦意识到自己的盲目性,他在不可抵抗的势力面前还会退缩回来,与怯懦者殊途同归。怯懦的人的问题在于不该害怕的时候却没有足够的勇气。而勇敢的人却不一样,在该胆大的时候就胆大,在该害怕的时候就害怕。亚里士多德说:"所以怯懦的人、鲁莽的人和勇敢的人面对的对象完全相同,但与对象的关系不一样,前两者分别是过度和不及,后者则恰得中间,处在应该处的状态中。"可见过多和过少的勇气都不好,不如恰到好处的中间。

亚里士多德还接着分析了五种勇敢的方式。第一种是"公民的勇敢",尤其体现在自觉地为自己的国家战斗的行为。这种行为正是出于对荣誉的追求,对耻辱的不屑,是由德性促成的。当然打仗的时候,将领也常常采用强迫的手段来促使士兵投入战斗。亚里士多德虽然认为强迫本身与勇敢是相矛盾的,但他还是同意将这种行为列入勇敢的行列。在这一点上,亚里士多德的伦理观念有着明显的功利主义倾向,认为能够起到保卫祖国作用的被迫参与战斗的行为也是勇敢的表现。第二种勇敢在于"经验和技能"。许多人因为这方面的优势而不会害怕,用我们的谚语来说,就是"艺高人胆大"。但这种人一旦发现仅仅凭借以前的经验对付不了眼下的难题时,就会失去自信,从而变为胆怯,因为这种行为毕竟不是出自德性本身。第三种勇敢是出于"动物般的激情"的驱动。如果只靠激情未必能够导致勇敢,否则"饥饿的驴也是勇敢的,虽然遭到鞭打,却不肯停止吃草;渴欲也可使奸夫做出许多勇猛的事情"。所以激情还应当加上"道德的选择和恰当的动机",才能真正孕育出勇敢的行为。虽然激情本身和勇敢有一定的区别,但伟大的行为也往往需要借助于激情的作用,这样更有利于伟大目标的实现。此外,乐观的人和对危险无知的人也似乎挺勇敢,但他们一旦意识到了真实的危险,就难免逃跑。当然,无知者和乐观者的勇敢程度还是有着一定的区别,前者不如后者,"他们没有自知之明;乐观者有一定的自知,能够坚持战斗到一定的时候;但蒙在鼓里的无知者一旦知道情况不跟他们想象的一样就马上逃跑"。总的来看这两种人的勇敢都是比较有限的。

在这个选段中,亚里士多德提出了不少有意思的观点,其中最著名的是对勇敢的定义:勇敢是鲁莽和怯懦的中间状态。这是一种很成熟的智慧,不盲目地提倡胆大。这种智慧在古代中国也发展到了很高的水平,古人称之为"中庸"。孔子与子贡曾经有这么一段对话:"子贡问:'师与商也,属贤?'子曰:'师也过,商也不及。'曰:'然则师愈与?'子曰:'过犹不及。'"[①]根据孔子的意思,过贤与不贤是同样不符合中庸之道的。《论语》还有这样的记载:"吾有知乎哉?无知也。有鄙夫问于我,空空如也;我叩其两端而竭焉。"[②]"叩其两端而竭焉"指的是尽可能地把事物的两个极端探索出来,以便找到那个恰到好处的中庸。可见孔子的中庸之道与亚里士多德的 mean 有着相通的地方,真是英雄所见略同。中庸之道曾经遭到很多人的批评,有时甚至被当作平庸的同义词,但这种否定有简单化的嫌疑。最近中庸又受到了重视,其合理部分得到了肯定。

亚里士多德对勇敢的探讨采取了条分缕析的方法,精确地辨别了勇敢以及和勇敢相关的概念的含义。古希腊人非常精于分析,亚里士多德尤其如此。这种注重分析的方法一直影响到整个西方学术传统,并且不停地被后人加以发展。

Nicomachean Ethics

First, then, of Courage. Now that it is a mean state, in respect of fear and boldness, has been already said: further, the objects of our fears are obviously things fearful or, in a general way of statement, evils; which accounts for the common definition of fear, viz. "expectation of evil."

Of course we fear evils of all kinds: disgrace, for instance, poverty, disease, desolateness, death; but not all these seem to be the object-matter of the Brave man, because there are things which to fear is right and noble, and not to fear is base; disgrace, for example, since he who fears this is a good man and has a sense of honour, and he who does not fear it is shameless (though there are those who call him Brave by analogy, because he somewhat

---

① 《论语正义·先进》,《诸子集成》本,上海:上海书店出版社,1996 年,第 245—246 页。
② 《论语正义·子罕》,《诸子集成》本,上海:上海书店出版社,1996 年,第 179 页。

resembles the Brave man who agrees with him in being free from fear); but poverty, perhaps, or disease, and in fact whatever does not proceed from viciousness, nor is attributable to his own fault, a man ought not to fear: still, being fearless in respect of these would not constitute a man Brave in the proper sense of the term.

Yet we do apply the term in right of the similarity of the cases; for there are men who, though timid in the dangers of war, are liberal men and are stout enough to face loss of wealth.

And, again, a man is not a coward for fearing insult to his wife or children, or envy, or any such thing; nor is he a Brave man for being bold when going to be scourged.

What kind of fearful things then do constitute the object-matter of the Brave man? First of all, must they not be the greatest, since no man is more apt to withstand what is dreadful. Now the object of the greatest dread is death, because it is the end of all things, and the dead man is thought to be capable neither of good nor evil. Still it would seem that the Brave man has not for his object-matter even death in every circumstance; on the sea, for example, or in sickness: in what circumstances then? Must it not be in the most honourable? Now such is death in war, because it is death in the greatest and most honourable danger; and this is confirmed by the honours awarded in communities, and by monarchs.

He then may be most properly denominated Brave who is fearless in respect of honourable death and such sudden emergencies as threaten death; now such specially are those which arise in the course of war.

It is not meant but that the Brave man will be fearless also on the sea (and in sickness), but not in the same way as sea-faring men; for these are lighthearted and hopeful by reason of their experience, while landsmen though Brave are apt to give themselves up for lost and shudder at the notion of such a death: to which it should be added that Courage is exerted in circumstances which admit of doing something to help one's self, or in which death would be honourable; now neither of these requisites attach to destruction by drowning or sickness.

Again, fearful is a term of relation, the same thing not being so to all, and there is according to common parlance somewhat so fearful as to be beyond human endurance: this of course would be fearful to every man of sense, but those objects which are level to the capacity of man differ in magnitude and admit of degrees, so too the objects of confidence or boldness.

Now the Brave man cannot be frighted from his propriety (but of course only so far as he is man); fear such things indeed he will, but he will stand up against them as he ought and as right reason may direct, with a view to what is honourable, because this is the end of the virtue.

Now it is possible to fear these things too much, or too little, or again to fear what is not really fearful as if it were such. So the errors come to be either that a man fears when he ought not to fear at all, or that he fears in an improper way, or at a wrong time, and so forth; and so too in respect of things inspiring confidence. He is Brave then who withstands, and fears, and is bold, in respect of right objects, from a right motive, in right manner, and at right times: since the Brave man suffers or acts as he ought and as right reason may direct.

Now the end of every separate act of working is that which accords with the habit, and so to the Brave man Courage; which is honourable; therefore such is also the End, since the character of each is determined by the End.

So honour is the motive from which the Brave man withstands things fearful and performs the acts which accord with Courage.

Of the characters on the side of Excess, he who exceeds in utter absence of fear has no appropriate name (I observed before that many states have none), but he would be a madman or inaccessible to pain if he feared nothing, neither earthquake, nor the billows, as they tell of the Celts[①].

He again who exceeds in confidence in respect of things fearful is rash. He is thought moreover to be a braggart, and to advance unfounded claims to the character of Brave: the relation which the Brave man really bears to objects of fear this man wishes to appear to bear, and so imitates him in whatever points he can; for this reason most of them exhibit a curious mixture of rashness and cowardice; because, affecting rashness in these circumstances, they do not withstand what is truly fearful.

The man moreover who exceeds in feeling fear is a coward, since there

---

① Celt,凯尔特人,包括高卢人、不列颠人等。亚里士多德这里所提到的事情属于希腊人的偏见。

attach to him the circumstances of fearing wrong objects, in wrong ways, and so forth. He is deficient also in feeling confidence, but he is most clearly seen as exceeding in the case of pains; he is a fainthearted kind of man, for he fears all things: the Brave man is just the contrary, for boldness is the property of the light-hearted and hopeful.

So the coward, the rash, and the Brave man have exactly the same object-matter, but stand differently related to it: the two first-mentioned respectively exceed and are deficient, the last is in a mean state and as he ought to be. The rash again are precipitate, and, being eager before danger, when actually in it fall away, while the Brave are quick and sharp in action, but before are quiet and composed.

Well then, as has been said, Courage is a mean state in respect of objects inspiring boldness or fear, in the circumstances which have been stated, and the Brave man chooses his line and withstands danger either because to do so is honourable, or because not to do so is base. But dying to escape from poverty, or the pangs of love, or anything that is simply painful, is the act not of a Brave man but of a coward; because it is mere softness to fly from what is toilsome, and the suicide braves the terrors of death not because it is honourable but to get out of the reach of evil.

Courage proper is somewhat of the kind I have described, but there are dispositions, differing in five ways, which also bear in common parlance the name of Courage.

We will take first that which bears most resemblance to the true, the Courage of Citizenship, so named because the motives which are thought to actuate the members of a community in braving danger are the penalties and disgrace held out by the laws to cowardice, and the dignities conferred on the Brave; which is thought to be the reason why those are the bravest people among whom cowards are visited with disgrace and the Brave held in honour.

Such is the kind of Courage Homer exhibits in his characters; Diomed and Hector for example. The latter says,

Polydamas will be the first to fix

> Disgrace upon me.①

Diomed again,

> For Hector surely will hereafter say,
> Speaking in Troy, Tydides by my hand —

This I say most nearly resembles the Courage before spoken of, because it arises from virtue, from a feeling of shame, and a desire of what is noble (that is, of honour), and avoidance of disgrace which is base.

In the same rank one would be inclined to place those also who act under compulsion from their commanders; yet are they really lower, because not a sense of honour but fear is the motive from which they act, and what they seek to avoid is not that which is base but that which is simply painful: commanders do in fact compel their men sometimes, as Hector says (to quote Homer again),

> But whomsoever I shall find cowering afar from the fight,
> The teeth of dogs he shall by no means escape.

Those commanders who station staunch troops by doubtful ones, or who beat their men if they flinch, or who draw their troops up in line with the trenches, or other similar obstacles, in their rear, do in effect the same as Hector, for they all use compulsion.

But a man is to be Brave, not on compulsion, but from a sense of honour.

In the next place, Experience and Skill in the various particulars is thought to be a species of Courage: whence Socrates also thought that Courage was knowledge.

This quality is exhibited of course by different men under different circumstances, but in warlike matters, with which we are now concerned, it is exhibited by the soldiers ("the regulars"): for there are, it would seem, many things in war of no real importance which these have been constantly used to see; so they have a show of Courage because other people are not aware of the real nature of these things. Then again by reason of their skill they are better able than any others to inflict without suffering themselves,

---

① 这两个句子以及紧接着的那段引文都出自《伊利亚特》,这里提到的几个人物都是这部史诗中出现的英雄。

because they are able to use their arms and have such as are most serviceable both with a view to offence and defence: so that their case is parallel to that of armed men fighting with unarmed or trained athletes with amateurs, since in contests of this kind those are the best fighters, not who are the bravest men, but who are the strongest and are in the best condition.

In fact, the regular troops come to be cowards whenever the danger is greater than their means of meeting it; supposing, for example, that they are inferior in numbers and resources: then they are the first to fly, but the mere militia stand and fall on the ground (which as you know really happened at the Hermaeum), for in the eyes of these flight was disgraceful and death preferable to safety bought at such a price: while "the regulars" originally went into the danger under a notion of their own superiority, but on discovering their error they took to flight, having greater fear of death than of disgrace; but this is not the feeling of the Brave man.

Thirdly, mere Animal Spirit is sometimes brought under the term Courage: they are thought to be Brave who are carried on by mere Animal Spirit, as are wild beasts against those who have wounded them, because in fact the really Brave have much Spirit, there being nothing like it for going at danger of any kind; whence those frequent expressions in Homer, "infused strength into his spirit," "roused his strength and spirit," or again, "and keen strength in his nostrils," "his blood boiled:" for all these seem to denote the arousing and impetuosity of the Animal Spirit.

Now they that are truly Brave act from a sense of honour, and this Animal Spirit co-operates with them; but wild beasts from pain, that is because they have been wounded, or are frightened; since if they are quietly in their own haunts, forest or marsh, they do not attack men. Surely they are not Brave because they rush into danger when goaded on by pain and mere Spirit, without any view of the danger: else would asses be Brave when they are hungry, for though beaten they will not then leave their pasture: profligate men besides do many bold actions by reason of their lust. We may conclude then that they are not Brave who are goaded on to meet danger by pain and mere Spirit; but still this temper which arises from Animal Spirit appears to be most natural, and would be Courage of the true kind if it could have added to it moral choice and the proper motive.

So men also are pained by a feeling of anger, and take pleasure in revenge; but they who fight from these causes may be good fighters, but they are not truly Brave (in that they do not act from a sense of honour, nor as reason directs, but merely from the present feeling), still they bear some resemblance to that character.

Nor, again, are the Sanguine and Hopeful therefore Brave: since their boldness in dangers arises from their frequent victories over numerous foes. The two characters are alike, however, in that both are confident; but then the Brave are so from the afore-mentioned causes, whereas these are so from a settled conviction of their being superior and not likely to suffer anything in return (they who are intoxicated do much the same, for they become hopeful when in that state); but when the event disappoints their expectations they run away: now it was said to be the character of a Brave man to withstand things which are fearful to man or produce that impression, because it is honourable so to do and the contrary is dishonourable.

For this reason it is thought to be a greater proof of Courage to be fearless and undisturbed under the pressure of sudden fear than under that which may be anticipated, because Courage then comes rather from a fixed habit, or less from preparation: since as to foreseen dangers a man might take his line even from calculation and reasoning, but in those which are sudden he will do so according to his fixed habit of mind.

Fifthly and lastly, those who are acting under Ignorance have a show of Courage and are not very far from the Hopeful; but still they are inferior inasmuch as they have no opinion of themselves; which the others have, and therefore stay and contest a field for some little time; but they who have been deceived fly the moment they know things to be otherwise than they supposed, which the Argives① experienced when they fell on the Lacedaemonians②, taking them for the men of Sicyon③.

We have described then what kind of men the Brave are, and what they who are thought to be, but are not really, Brave.

---

① Argives 指希腊古城阿尔戈斯（Argos）的居民。
② Lacedaemonians 指斯巴达人。
③ Sicyon 是古希腊的一个城邦。

It must be remarked, however, that though Courage has for its object-matter boldness and fear it has not both equally so, but objects of fear much more than the former; for he that under pressure of these is undisturbed and stands related to them as he ought is better entitled to the name of Brave than he who is properly affected towards objects of confidence. So then men are termed Brave for withstanding painful things.

It follows that Courage involves pain and is justly praised, since it is a harder matter to withstand things that are painful than to abstain from such as are pleasant.

It must not be thought but that the End and object of Courage is pleasant, but it is obscured by the surrounding circumstances: which happens also in the gymnastic games; to the boxers the End is pleasant with a view to which they act, I mean the crown and the honours; but the receiving the blows they do is painful and annoying to flesh and blood, and so is all the labour they have to undergo; and, as these drawbacks are many, the object in view being small appears to have no pleasantness in it.

If then we may say the same of Courage, of course death and wounds must be painful to the Brave man and against his will: still he endures these because it is honourable to do so or because it is dishonourable not to do so. And the more complete his virtue and his happiness so much the more will he be pained at the notion of death: since to such a man as he is it is best worth while to live, and he with full consciousness is deprived of the greatest goods by death, and this is a painful idea. But he is not the less Brave for feeling it to be so, nay rather it may be he is shown to be more so because he chooses the honour that may be reaped in war in preference to retaining safe possession of these other goods. The fact is that to act with pleasure does not belong to all the virtues, except so far as a man realises the End of his actions.

But there is perhaps no reason why not such men should make the best soldiers, but those who are less truly Brave but have no other good to care for: these being ready to meet danger and bartering their lives against small gain.

Let thus much be accepted as sufficient on the subject of Courage; the true nature of which it is not difficult to gather, in outline at least, from what has been said.

选文出处

Aristotle. *Nicomachean Ethics*. Translated by D. P. Chase, Beijing: China Social Sciences Publishing House (reprinted from the English Edition by E. P. Dutton & Co., 1934), 1999, pp. 59—67.

思考题

1. 仔细研究亚氏的 mean 和孔子的中庸之道,并将两者加以比较。
2. 你赞同亚氏的勇敢观吗？为什么？

参考书目

1. 严群:《亚里士多德之伦理思想》,北京:商务印书馆,2003 年。
2. Ackrill, J. L., *Aristotle the Philosopher*, Oxford: Oxford University Press, 1981.

卢克莱修

卢克莱修（Titus Lucretius Carus，约前98—约前55）是古罗马时期著名的哲学家、诗人和无神论者。有关他的生平，我们所知不多。他的唯一传世之作《物性论》（De Rerum Natura）完成于约公元前60年。从作品内容看，他应是古希腊哲学家伊壁鸠鲁（Epicurus）的忠实追随者。《物性论》采用诗歌的形式，运用大量的自然科学知识，系统阐述了伊壁鸠鲁的原子论哲学，是唯物主义思想的集中体现。卢克莱修在其中所阐释的基本观点如下：一、"原子"与"虚空"。卢克莱修认为，一切事物均由物质构成，而构成物质的最基本粒子为"原子"。"虚空"是原子赖以存在的空间。原子在虚空中游走，以不同的方式组合，便产生了万物。二、感觉与推理。卢克莱修认为，感觉是原子作用于人的感官而产生的结果，所以是客观、可信的。而理性，即推理却是主观的。三、灵魂和精神。在卢克莱修看来，灵魂和精神也是由原子构成的。当死亡降临时，人的灵魂就与身体分离，构成灵魂与精神的原子也将随之消散。四、卢克莱修用"进化"的观点探讨了社会的发展，认为人类社会的发展是一个由低级到高级的过程。

这里所选取的片段《怕死的愚蠢》（Against the Fear of Death）选自《物性论》的第3卷，是针对人们对死亡的恐惧所做出的辩驳。全篇语言生动雄辩、例证丰富、循循善诱、步步进逼，被认为是整部作品的高潮，也是哲学与诗歌的完美结合。作品从原子论的观点出发，肯定灵魂是一种物质现象，因而是有死亡之说的。不过，所谓的死亡，不过是原子的分离解散，所以并不值得我们忧虑与害怕，因为"我们是在灵魂和身体的结合中活着"。换句话说,我们在死后没有知觉,正如人在出生之前没有知觉一样,所以死亡对我们而言无所谓感受与痛苦。即使当灵魂脱离身体而单独地存在时,还仍存留有感觉与记忆,那也没有任何关系,即等到灵魂与身体再度结合并形成生命之时,我们对于那些逝去的远古事情已经变得毫无记忆了。总之,卢克莱修认为,死亡就是灵魂与身体的分离,是感觉的丧失,当人活着时,死亡还没有到来;当死亡到来时,人已经不存在了,所以人们没有惧怕死亡的理由。

卢克莱修认为,人的生、老、病、死是一个自然的过程,没有谁可以永远地拥有生命。每个人都有义务传递生命的接力棒,从而使历史在生命的新陈代谢中得到发展与延续。他说:"许多代曾经过去了,将来也将要过去。这样,一物永远从他物中产生出来,生命并不无条件地给予任何一个人,给予所有人的,只是它的用益权。"也就是说,在历史的长河中,每个生命的存在不过是其中的一粒尘埃。自然(Nature)不会因你的贡献成就来决定你的生命长短。即便是那些功勋卓著的王者英雄以及那些为人类撒播思想火花的诗人、哲学家,也都无一例外地走向死亡。他认为生命是暂时的,死亡才是永恒的。因此,他说:"无论你活满多少代的时间,永恒的死仍然将在等候着你。"一个更长的生命也不会带给我们什么新的快乐,也不能减少半点死后所占的无限长的时间。他以自然(Nature)的口吻斥责那些贪恋生命,为死亡而悲苦的人们:"省点眼泪罢,丑东西,别再号啕大哭!你的皮也皱了,也享受过生命的一切赏赐……你就把不适合你年纪的东西放下,大大方方地让位给你的子孙们吧!"在短暂的生命历程中,他认为生命的质量远远高于生命的时间。他说:"你这个虽然还活着,还睁着眼,但活着和死去差不多已全无区别的人,你这把生命大部分时间浪费于睡眠中的人……难道还要踌躇,老是不肯走?"在他看来,没有质量的生命是羞辱的,与其痛苦地活着,不如坦然地接受死亡的结局。换言之,要满足于我们已经获得的,不要害怕死亡,"地狱"只不过是现世痛苦幻化而成的寓言,它并不是真实存在的。

卢克莱修关于死亡的哲学,强调的是幸福在于摆脱对神和死亡的恐惧,从而获得一种精神上的宁静。这对于那些生活在战乱不断的罗马士兵来说,无疑是一剂解除精神苦痛的良药。但是,他的哲学与基督教宣扬的灵魂不死,将一切美好置于死后的教义是相违背的。因此在古罗马,卢克莱修一直被视为异端。直到1473年仅存的一个《物性论》稿本被发现时,他的思想才被人们重新认识。卢克莱修《物性论》的发现和出版,扩大了伊壁鸠鲁学说对早期启蒙思想家的影响。

当然,站在科学高度发展的今天来看,卢克莱修的作品无疑存在着种种不足,譬如体系不够完整、论证缺乏依据等等。但他试图对宇宙、历史、宗教、疾病等做出合理解释的勇气是可嘉的。除此之外,诗人广阔而丰富的想象力以及雄浑善辩的语言,也让作品拥有别样的魅力。

On the Nature of Things

Against the Fear of Death

Is nothing to us, has no relevance
To our condition, seeing that the mind
Is mortal. Just as, long ago, we felt
Not the least touch of trouble when the wars
Were raging all around the shaken earth
And from all sides the Carthaginian hordes①
Poured forth to battle, and no man ever knew
Whose subject he would be in life or death,
Which doom, by land or sea, would strike him down,
So, when we cease to be, and body and soul,
Which joined to make us one, have gone their ways,
Their separate ways, nothing at all can shake
Our feelings, not if earth were mixed with sea
Or sea with sky. Perhaps the mind or spirit,
After its separation from our body,
Has some sensation; what is that to us?
Nothing at all, for what we knew of being,
Essence, identity, oneness, was derived
From body's union with spirit, so, if time,

---

① Carthaginian horde,迦太基游牧部落。Carthage 指迦太基,非洲北部一古代城邦,位于今突尼斯东北部突尼斯湾沿岸。罗马与迦太基为争夺地中海西部的控制权曾经进行过三次战争。诗中提到的应该是发生在公元前 218 至前 201 年间的第二次战争。

After our death, should some day reunite
All of our present particles, bring them back
To where they now reside, give us once more
The light of life, this still would have no meaning
For us, with our self-recollection gone.
As we are now, we lack all memory
Of what we were before, suffer no wound
From those old days. Look back on all that space
Of time's immensity, consider well
What infinite combinations there have been
In matter's ways and groupings. How easy, then,
For human beings to believe we are
Compounded of the very selfsame motes,
Arranged exactly in the selfsame ways
As once we were, our long-ago, our now
Being identical. And yet we keep
No memory of that once-upon-a time,
Nor can we call it back; somewhere between
A break occurred, and all our atoms went
Wandering here and there and far away
From our sensations. If there lies ahead
Tough luck for any man, he must be there,
Himself, to feel its evil, but since death
Removes this chance, and by injunction stops
All rioting of woes against our state,
We may be reassured that in our death
We have no cause for fear, we cannot be
Wretched in nonexistence. Death alone
Has immortality, and takes away
Our mortal life. It does not matter a bit
If we once lived before.

So, seeing a man

Feel sorry for himself, that after death
He'll be a rotting corpse, laid in a tomb,
Succumb to fire, or predatory beasts,
You'll know he's insincere, just making noise,
With rancor in his heart, though he believes,
Or tries to make us think so, that death ends all.
And yet, I'd guess, he contradicts himself,
He does not really see himself as gone,
As utter nothingness, but does his best—
Not really understanding what he's doing—
To have himself survive, for, in his life,
He will project a future, a dark day
When beast or bird will lacerate his corpse.
So he feels sorry for himself; he fails
To make the real distinction that exists
Between his castoff body and the man
Who stands beside it grieving, and imputes
Some of his sentimental feelings to it.
Resenting mortal fate, he cannot see
That in true death he'll not survive himself
To stand there as a mourner, stunned by grief
That he is burned or mangled. If in death
It's certainly no pleasure to be mauled
By beak of bird or fang of beast, I'd guess
It's no voluptuous revel to be laid
Over the flames, Or packed in honey and ice,
Stiff on the surface of a marble slab,
Or buried under a great mound of earth.

And men behave the same way at a banquet,
Holding the cups or garlanding the brows,

And sighing from the heart, "Ah, life is short
For puny little men, and when it goes
We cannot call it back," as if they thought
The main thing wrong, after their death, will be
That they are very thirsty, or may have
A passionate appetite for who knows what.
"No longer will you happily come home
To a devoted wife, or children dear
Running for your first kisses, while your heart
Is filled with sweet unspoken gratitude.
You will no longer dwell in happy state,
Their sword and shield. Poor wretch," men tell themselves,
"One fatal day has stolen all your gains."
But they don't add, "And all Your covetings."
If they could see this clearly, follow it
With proper reasoning, their minds would be
Free of great agony and fear, "As now
You lie asleep in death, forevermore
You will be quit of any sickening pain,
While we, who stood beside your funeral pyre,
Have, with no consolation, mourned your death
In sorrow time will never heal." Well, then,
Ask of your dead what bitterness he finds
In sleep and quiet; why should anyone
Wear himself out in everlasting grief?
No man, when body and soul are lost in sleep,
Finds himself missing, or conducts a search
For his identity; for all we know,
For all we care, that sleep might last forever
And we would never list ourselves as missing.
Yet, all this while, our motes, our atoms, wander
Not far from sense producing shift and stir,
And suddenly we come to wakefulness.
So we must think of death as being nothing,

As less than sleep, or less than nothing, even,
Since our array of matter never stirs
To reassemble, once the chill of death
Has taken over.

Hark! The voice of Nature

Is scolding us: "What ails you, little man,
Why this excess of self-indulgent grief,
This sickliness? Why weep and groan at death?
If you have any sense of gratitude
For a good life, if you can't claim her gifts
Were dealt you in some kind of riddled jar①
So full of cracks and holes they leaked away
Before you touched them, why not take your leave
As men go from a banquet, fed to the full
On life's good feast, come home, and lie at ease,
Free from anxiety? Alas, poor fool,
If, on the other hand, all of your joys
Are gone, and life is only wretchedness,
Why try to add more to it? Why not make
A decent end? There's nothing, it would seem,
My powers can contrive for your delight.
The same old story, always. If the years
Don't wear your body, don't corrode your limbs
With lassitude, if you keep living on
For centuries, if you never die at all,
What's in it for you but the same old story
Always, and always?" How could we reply
To this, except to say that Nature's case
Is argued to perfection? Now suppose

---

① riddled jar, 这里作者所指的是丹尼斯的女儿们, 她们因为谋杀丈夫而被罚在地狱里永远把水倒进有孔或无底的容器中。

Some older man, a senior citizen,
Were plaintiff, wretcheder than he ought to be,
Lamenting death, would Nature not be right
To cry him down, with even sharper voice,
"Why, you old scoundrel, take those tears of yours
Somewhere away from here, cut out the whining.
You have had everything from life, and now
You find you're going to pieces. You desire,
Always, what isn't there; what is, you scorn,
So life has slipped away from you, incomplete,
Unsatisfactory, and here comes death,
An unexpected summoner, to stand
Beside you, long before you want to leave,
Long, long, before you think you've had enough.
Let it all go, act as becomes your age.
Be a great man, composed; give in; you must."
Such a rebuke from Nature would be right,
For the old order yields before the new,
All things require refashioning from others.
No man goes down to Hell's black pit; we need
Matter for generations yet to come,
Who, in their turn, will follow you, as men
Have died before you and will die hereafter.
So one thing never ceases to arise
Out of another; life's a gift to no man
Only a loan to him. Look back at time—
How meaningless, how unreal! —before our birth.
In this way Nature holds before our eyes
The mirror of our future after death.
Is this so grim, so gloomy? Is it not
A rest more free from care than any sleep?

Now all those things which people say exist
In Hell, are really present in our lives.

The story says that Tantalus①, the wretch,
Frozen in terror, fears the massive rock
Balanced in air above him. It's not true.
What happens is that in our lives the fear,
The silly, vain, ridiculous fear of gods,
Causes our panic dread of accident.
No vultures feed on Tityos②, who lies
Sprawled out for them in Hell; they could not find
In infinite eternities of time
What they are searching for in that great bulk,
Nine acres wide, or ninety, or the spread
Of all the globe. No man can ever bear
Eternal pain, nor can his body give
Food to the birds forever. We do have
A Tityos in ourselves, and lie, in love,
Torn and consumed by our anxieties,
Our fickle passions. Sisyphus③, is here
In our own lives; we see him as the man
Bent upon power and office, who comes back
Gloomy and beaten after every vote.
To seek for power, such an empty thing,
And never gain it, suffering all the while,
This is to shove uphill the stubborn rock
Which over and over comes bouncing down again
To the flat levels where it started from.
Or take another instance: when we feed
A mind whose nature seems unsatisfied,
Never content, with all the blessings given
Through season after season, with all the charms
And graces of life's harvest, this, I'd say,

---

① Tantalus,希腊神话中人物,宙斯的儿子。因其犯过罪而被打入阴间并被罚站立在水中,当他想去饮水时水即流走;其头上挂有水果,但当他想拿时水果却退开。这里显然是用了不同的版本。
② Tityos,希腊神话中的巨人。
③ Sisyphus,西西弗斯,希腊神话中的人物。

Is to be like those young and lovely girls,
The Danaids, trying in vain to fill
Their leaky jars with water, Cerberus①,
The Furies, and the dark, and the grim jaws
Of Tartarus, belching blasts of heat—all these
Do not exist at all, and never could.
But here on earth we do fear punishment
For wickedness, and in proportion dread
Our dreadful deeds, imagining all too well
Being cast down from the Tarpeian Rock②,
Jail, flogging, hangmen, brands, the rack, the knout;
And even though these never touch us, still
The guilty mind is its own torturer
With lash and rowel, can see no end at all
To suffering and punishment, and fears
These will be more than doubled after death.
Hell does exist on earth—in the life of fools.

You well might think of saying to yourself:
"Even good Ancus closed his eyes on the light—
A better man than you will ever be,
You reprobate—and many lords and kings
Rulers of mighty nations, all have died.
Even that monarch, who once paved the way
Making the sea a highway for his legions
Where foot and horse alike could march dry-shod
While the deep foamed and thundered at the outrage,
Even he, great Xerxes, died and left the light,
And Scipio, the thunderbolt of war,
Terror of Carthage, gave his bones to earth
As does the meanest lackey. Add to these

---

① Cerberus,守护冥府入口的长有三头的狗。
② Tarpeian Rock,塔尔皮亚岩石,罗马的叛国者都从这里被扔下去。

Philosophers and artists, all the throng
Blessed by the Muses; Homer's majesty
Lies low in the same sleep as all the rest.
Democritus①, warned by a ripe old age
That, with his memory, his powers of mind
Were also failing, gave himself to death;
And Epicurus② perished, that great man
Whose genius towered over all the rest,
Making their starry talents fade and die
In his great sunlight. Who are you, forsooth,
To hesitate, resent, protest your death?
Your life is death already, though you live
And though you see, except that half your time
You waste in sleep, and the other half you snore
With eyes wide open, forever seeing dreams,
Forever in panic, forever lacking wit
To find out what the trouble is, depressed,
Or drunk, or drifting aimlessly around."

Men seem to feel some burden on their souls,
Some heavy weariness; could they but know
Its origin, its cause, they'd never live
The way we see most of them do, each one
Ignorant of what he wants, except a change,
Some other place to lay his burden down.
One leaves his house to take a stroll outdoors
Because the household's such a deadly bore,
And then comes back, in six or seven minutes—
The street is every bit as bad. Now what?
He has his horses hitched up for him, drives,
Like a man going to a fire, full-speed,

---

① Democritus,德谟克利特,古希腊哲学家,原子唯物论的创始人之一。
② Epicurus,伊壁鸠鲁,古希腊哲学家。卢克莱修的整部作品就是对伊壁鸠鲁哲学的系统阐述。

Off to his country-place, and when he gets there
Is scarcely on the driveway, when he yawns,
Falls heavily asleep, oblivious
To everything, or promptly turns around,
Whips back to town again. So each man flees
Himself, or tries to, but of course that pest
Clings to him all the more ungraciously.
He hates himself because he does not know
The reason for his sickness; if he did,
He would leave all this foolishness behind,
Devote his study to the way things are,
The problem being his lot, not for an hour,
But for all time, the state in which all men
Must dwell forever and ever after death.
Finally, what's this wanton lust for life
To make us tremble in dangers and in doubt?
All men must die, and no man can escape.
We turn and turn in the same atmosphere
In which no new delight is ever shaped
To grace out living; what we do not have
Seems better than everything else in all the world
But should we get it, we want something else.
Our gaping thirst for life is never quenched.
We have to know what luck next year will bring,
What accident, what end. But life, prolonged,
Subtracts not even one second from the term
Of death's continuance. We lack the strength
To abbreviate that eternity. Suppose
You could contrive to live for centuries,
As many as you will. Death, even so,
Will still be waiting for you; he who died
Early this morning has as many years
Interminably before him, as the man,
His predecessor, has, who perished months

Or years, or even centuries ago.

 选文出处

Lucretius. *On the Nature of Things*. in *The Norton Anthology of World Masterpieces*(Vol. 1), New York：W. W. Norton & Company, Inc.，pp. 564—571.

思考题

1. 试比较卢克莱修与伊壁鸠鲁的哲学思想。
2. 如何看卢克莱修对死亡的论述？它与柏拉图的灵魂不死论，以及斯多葛主义有关死亡的哲学有何异同？

阅读
参考书目

1. 尼古拉斯：《伊壁鸠鲁主义的政治哲学：卢克莱修的〈物性论〉》，溥林译，北京：华夏出版社，2004年。
2. 桑塔亚那：《诗与哲学：三位哲学诗人卢克莱修、但丁及歌德》，华明译，桂林：广西师范大学出版社，2002年。

奥古斯丁

奥古斯丁(Aurelius Augustinus,354—430)是欧洲中世纪基督教神学的著名大师,一位"将哲学引入基督教教义的研究"的集大成者①。他的神学思想和哲学、美学观念在基督教世界中一直占据着崇高而权威的地位。另外,他对基督教神学理论体系的研究和创建还对整个西方的思想与文化都产生了不可估量的影响。

奥古斯丁出生于北非的塔加斯特城(Tagaste)。母亲慕尼加(Monica)是基督教徒,而在城镇政府中任职的父亲巴特利西乌斯(Patricius)则是一位异教徒。也就是说,奥古斯丁自小生活在不同信仰的家庭中。由于母亲的影响,他开始对基督教有了感性的认识与了解。然而,望子成龙的父亲却一直坚持对他实行传统的异教教育,这又使奥古斯丁对基督教产生了轻视、怠慢的心理。由此我们也不难理解奥古斯丁为何绕了一个大圈子后,才皈依了基督教的内在心理轨迹。

在公元300多年以前,塔加斯特城便被划进了罗马帝国的版图,所以被父亲寄予厚望的奥古斯丁从小接受过良好且系统的罗马"三级制"式教育。在他7岁时,进入当地小学,学习拉丁文、初等算术和希腊文。他12岁时,前往马都拉城,学习文法、诗歌和历史等。在此阶段中,他还阅读了大量的拉丁文学作品,特别是维吉尔的诗给他留下了深刻的印象。16岁时,由于家境的原因,在家辍学一年。一年后,他

---

① 张秉真、章安祺、杨慧林:《西方文艺理论史》,北京:中国人民大学出版社,1994年,第111页。

被父亲送往北非的学术中心迦太基城读书,主修修辞学和哲学。修辞学即是雄辩术,经过这方面的专业训练,奥古斯丁的口才和逻辑思辨都得到了极好的锻炼。重要的是,这期间学校所列的一本必读书,即罗马作家西塞罗的《荷尔顿西乌斯》使奥古斯丁第一次对哲学产生了浓厚的兴趣。尽管经过一番比较与思考,他最终还是选择了推举善恶二元论的摩尼教,点燃了潜伏于他胸中的追求智慧与真理的愿望。毕业后,奥古斯丁曾先后在迦太基和罗马的米兰城任雄辩术教授,教授修辞与哲学课程。

应该说,奥古斯丁的一生是极其复杂、矛盾和富于戏剧性的一生:他既有过沉湎于情欲、肉欲的玩世不恭,又有过圣人般的虔诚与专注;他曾唾弃、反对基督教,但又倾其后半生的心血把基督教阐释为最符合真理的教派。若以时间为界标,公元387年是他生命的一个重大转折点。此时已经33岁,历经精神、信仰煎熬的奥古斯丁,在米兰城的基督教教主安布罗西乌斯(Ambrosius,339—397)以及新柏拉图派、怀疑派著作的影响和母亲无数次的含泪祈祷下,终于告别了以往轻薄、荒诞的生活和信奉了九年的摩尼教,正式接受了洗礼,成为一名虔诚、笃信与寻求上帝真理的基督教徒。之后,他返回家乡塔迦斯特城,以祈祷、读经、著述等隐居方式度日。3年后,奥古斯丁前往非洲的希波(Hippo)城,先是担任该城教会的长老,后担任副主教。公元396年,希波城主教瓦勒里去世后,他接任了主教的位置。在与其他异端教派的论战与争辩中,他把整个身心都献给了基督教,并写下了一系列的理论文章。公元430年8月28日,76岁高龄的奥古斯丁因病去世,进入了他所追随的永恒天国之中。

奥古斯丁一生著述甚丰,据本人晚年在《订正》中统计,他所写下的著作共计93种,多达232部,主要著作有《论自由意志》(*On Free Will*,386—388)、《忏悔录》(*Confessions*,397—401)、《论三位一体》(*On the Trinity*,399—422)、《上帝之城》(*City of God*,413—427)等。由于时间久远,能完整流传至今的只有《忏悔录》和《上帝之城》。

生活于两个时代之交的奥古斯丁,不论是在欧洲宗教思想史上,还是文学创作上都有着极为特殊的地位,他被誉为"一个时代的结束,同时也是另一个新纪元的开始。他是古代基督教作家中的最后一人,同时也是中世纪神学的开路先锋"[①]。这种评价本身意味着奥古斯丁的神学、美学体系具有两个时代的思想特征。具体地说,作为对古希腊、罗马文化的研究、反思与总结者,他的不少美学观点,如美与和谐、美与比例等的关系认识,就是对其传统文化的继承与发

[①] 转引自奥尔森:《基督教神学思想史》,吴瑞诚、徐成德译,北京:北京大学出版社,2003年,第268页。

扬。当然,奥古斯丁之所以能成为承前启后的里程碑式的人物,更在于他对自希腊以来文化传统的革新与颠覆。其主要标志是,他瓦解了自古希腊人以来的原有创世观念。如果说柏拉图、亚里士多德的"模仿说"意味着创造必须要以某种"'根据'为前提"的话,那么奥古斯丁对于上帝创世说则予以了重新的阐释,即他认为"真正的'创造',并不是对于先在物的模仿,而是创造者自身意志的结果"。① 显然,在奥古斯丁这里,上帝或者神被赋予了至高无上的特权,即宇宙中的万事、万物都是神根据其意志来创造的,"天地存在着,天地高呼说它们是受造的,因为它们在变化。……是你,主,创造了天地;你是美,因为它们是美丽的;你是善,因为它们是好的;你实在,因为它们存在,但它们的美、善、存在,并不和创造者一样;相形之下,它们并不美,并不善,并不存在。感谢你,这一切我们知道,但我们的知识和你的知识相较,还不过是无知"②。天地、美善、存在,知识和我们都是上帝,即"主"所亲手创造与赋予的。可见,构成奥古斯丁神学、美学思想体系核心的并不是看得见的人类和万物,而是形而上的"主"。有研究者就曾指出:"在奥古斯丁对于神圣照管与救恩的神恩独作观念中,神是独一无二的主动者与能力来源;而所有人类,无论是集体或个人,都是神施行恩典或忿怒的工具与方法。"③《上帝之城》就是这样的一首献给和捍卫神的颂歌。

在奥古斯丁的所有著作中,《忏悔录》一书占有非常独特的地位。该书不但详细记录了他一生的经历,而且还忠实记录下了他的灵魂转变过程以及写作此书时的思想状况。为我们研究奥古斯丁本人及其那个遥远的时代提供了一份难得的资料。

《忏悔录》的原名是"Confessiones",这个词原本有两层含义:一是指承认、认罪,从这个意义上说,翻译成"忏悔录"是恰如其分的。在转向基督教之前,奥古斯丁曾有过一段漫长迷惘、痛苦和迷失的日子。他和家乡的孩子们一起以偷盗为乐;在迦太基雄辩学校读书时,他被疯狂燃烧的情欲笼罩着,曾和一个女人同居,并生有一个儿子。而且,后来抛弃了这个女人,又和别人订婚,但在等待婚礼的过程中,因耐不住寂寞又与其他女人有染等。该书就是奥古斯丁对自己的前半生沉湎于荒诞、罪恶世俗生活的解剖与忏悔。然而,这个拉丁文除了有"忏悔"之意外,还另含歌功颂德的意思。阅读全书,不难发现,除了自责、忏悔以外,该书的另一重心是表达对"天主"的崇信与膜拜,如"我的好天主,万有中最美善的,万有的创造者,我的至善,我真正的至宝"。书中这类歌颂上帝恩德的话比比皆是。从这一层面看,翻译成"忏悔录"只凸现了前者,而忽略了后一

---

① 张秉真、章安祺、杨慧林:《西方文艺理论史》,北京:中国人民大学出版社,1994年,第119—120页。
② 奥古斯丁:《忏悔录》,周士良译,北京:商务印书馆,1997年,第234—235页。
③ 奥尔森:《基督教神学思想史》,吴瑞诚、徐成德译,北京:北京大学出版社,2003年,第268—269页。

种意义上的写作。

《忏悔录》共有 13 卷。由于该书是一部自传体作品,所以在写作上严格按照时间的线索,即从出生、到求学、父亲、母亲病逝,再到皈依天主、交代撰写此书的目的等。该书所选出的"卷 2",就是作者对往昔自己"污秽""纵情肉欲"以及"以地狱的快乐为满足"和"各式各样的黑暗恋爱"进行忏悔。在该部分中,作者主要围绕 16 岁时的一次"偷盗"事件来写。从马都拉城毕业后,按计划奥古斯丁本应继续到迦太基去读书,但由于家中经济拮据不得不停学一年。就在这一年中,已发育成熟,有了青春苦闷的奥古斯丁与伙伴们到处游荡,听着同伴们竞相夸耀自己的"丑史",他为自己的"天真"和"纯洁"感到前所未有的羞愧。为了不使自己显得太无知,他开始为学坏而学坏。在一个深夜,他与闲游浪荡的同伴把梨树上的所有果子都摇晃了下来,不是为了吃,而只是为了证明敢于去做违禁的事情。

偷果之事本是微不足道的事件,奥古斯丁为何念念不忘,还把当时的动机与感受慢慢道来,细细分析。应该说,这与他对自我的认识有关,即他认为果树事件是其背离上帝,踏上歧途的开始。为了获得上帝的谅解和爱怜,他必须要向上帝如实地坦白一切。正如作者在本卷的开篇即言明回忆过去,并不是"流连以往,而是为了爱你,我的天主"①。《忏悔录》就是对自己前半生荒诞、罪恶生活的忏悔。

《忏悔录》虽然写作的时间久远,但由于作者采取敞开胸怀与灵魂的祷告方式,所以在事件的讲述与语言的使用上都具有情感真挚、文字通达、神采飞扬、一气呵成的特点。这种写法不但使读者阅读起来没有什么障碍,重要的是,还开创了西方忏悔文学的先河,后来卢梭、托尔斯泰的《忏悔录》都与这本书有着不解的渊源。

Confessions

I

I PROPOSE NOW to set down my past wickedness and the carnal

---

① 奥古斯丁:《忏悔录》,周士良译,北京:商务印书馆,1997 年,第 25 页。

corruptions of my soul, not for love of them but that I may love Thee, O my God. I do it for love of Thy love, passing again in the bitterness of remembrance over my most evil ways that Thou mayest thereby grow ever lovelier to me, O Loveliness that dost not deceive, Loveliness happy and abiding: and I collect my self out of that broken state in which my very being was torn asunder because I was turned away from Thee, the One, and wasted myself upon the many.

Arrived now at adolescence I burned for all the satisfactions of hell, and I sank to the animal in a succession of dark lusts: *my beauty consumed away*, and I stank in Thine eyes, yet was pleasing in my own and anxious to please the eyes of men.

II

My one delight was to love and to be loved. But in this I did not keep the measure of mind to mind, which is the luminous line of friendship; but from the muddy concupiscence of the flesh and the hot imagination of puberty mists steamed up to becloud and darken my heart so that I could not distinguish the white light of love from the fog of lust. Both love and lust boiled within me, and swept my youthful immaturity over the precipice of evil desires to leave me half drowned in a whirlpool of abominable sins. Your wrath had grown mighty against me and I knew it not. I had grown deaf from the clanking of the chain of my mortality, the punishment for the pride of my soul: and I departed further from You, and You left me to myself: and I was tossed about and wasted and poured out and boiling over in my fornications: and You were silent, O my late-won Joy. You were silent, and I, arrogant and depressed, weary and restless, wandered further and further from You into more and more sins which could bear no fruit save sorrows.

If only there had been some one then to bring relief to the wretchedness of my state, and turn to account the fleeting beauties of these new temptations and bring within bounds their attractions for me: so that the tides of my youth might have driven in upon the shore of marriage: for then they might have been brought to calm with the having of children as Your law prescribes, O Lord, for in this way You form the offspring of this our death, able with gentle hand to blunt the thorns that You would not have in Your paradise. For Your omnipotence is not far from us, even when we are far from You. Or, on the other hand, I might well have listened more heedfully to the voice from the clouds: "*Nevertheless such [as marry] shall have tribulation of the flesh; but I spare you*"; and "*It is good for a man not to touch a woman*"; and "*He that is without a wife is solicitous for the things that belong to the Lord, how he may please God: but he that is with a wife is solicitous for the things of the world, how he may please his wife.*" I should have listened more closely to these words and made myself a eunuch for the kingdom of heaven; and so in all tranquillity awaited Your embraces. Instead I foamed in my wickedness, following the rushing of my own tide, leaving You and going beyond all Your laws. Nor did I escape Your scourges. No mortal can. You were always by me, mercifully hard upon me, and besprinkling all my illicit pleasures with certain elements of bitterness, to draw me on to seek for pleasures in which no bitterness should be. And where was I to find such pleasures save in You O Lord, You who use sorrow to teach, and wound us to heal, and kill us lest we die to You. Where then was I, and how far from the delights of Your house, in that sixteenth year of my life in this world, when the madness of lust—needing no licence from human shamelessness, receiving no licence from Your laws—took complete control of me, and I surrendered wholly to it? My family took no care to save me from this moral destruction by marriage: their only concern was that I should learn to make as fine and persuasive speeches as possible.

III

In that year my studies were interrupted. I had come back from Madaura, a neighboring city to which I had been sent to study grammar and rhetoric, and the money was being got together for the longer journey to Carthage①, where I was to go because my father was set upon it—not that he was rich, for

---

① Carthage,迦太基,古代腓尼基人在北非今突尼斯一带建立的国家。在腓尼基时期,迦太基是罗马最难缠的敌手。在罗马人重建下,它成为大城市,并成为早期基督教深具意义之中心,在商业与政治上始终占有极重要的地位。

he was only a poor citizen of Tagaste. But to whom am I telling this? Not to Thee, O my God, but in Thy presence I am telling it to my own kind, to the race of men, or rather to that small part of the human race that may come upon these writings. And to what purpose do I tell it? Simply that I and any other who may read may realise out of what depths we must cry to Thee. For nothing is more surely heard by Thee than a heart that confesses Thee and a life in Thy faith.

Everyone of course praised my father because, although his means did not allow it, he had somehow provided the wherewithal for his son to travel so far for the sake of his studies. Many a very much richer citizen did no such thing for his children. Yet this same father never bothered about how I was growing towards You or how chaste or unchaste I might be, so long as I grew in eloquence, however much I might lack of Your cultivation O God, who are the one true and good Lord of your field, my heart.

But during that sixteenth year between Madaura and Carthage, owing to the narrowness of the family fortunes I did not go to school, but lived idly at home with my parents. The briars of unclean lusts grew so that they towered over my head, and there was no hand to root them out. On the contrary my father saw me one day in the public baths, now obviously growing towards manhood and showing the turbulent signs of adolescence. The effect upon him was that he had already began to look forward to grandchildren, and went home in happy excitement to tell my mother. He rejoiced, indeed, through that intoxication in which the world forgets You its Creator and loves what You have created instead of You, the intoxication of the invisible wine of a will perverted and turned towards baseness. But in my mother's breast You had already laid the foundation of Your temple and begun Your holy habitation: whereas my father was still only a catechumen, and a new catechumen at that. So that she was stricken with a holy fear. And though I was not as yet baptised, she was in terror of my walking in the crooked ways of those who walk with their backs towards You and not their faces.

I have dared to say that You were silent, my God, when I went afar from You. But was it truly so? Whose but Yours were the words You dinned into my ears through the voice of my mother, Your faithful servant? Not that at that time any of it sank into my heart to make me do it. I still remember her anxiety and how earnestly she urged upon me not to sin with women, above all not with any man's wife. All this sounded to me womanish and I should have blushed to obey. Yet it was from You, though I did not know it and thought that You were silent and she speaking: whereas You were speaking to me through her, and in ignoring her I was ignoring You: I, her son, the son of Your handmaid, Your servant. But I realised none of this and went headlong on my course, so blinded that I was ashamed among the other youths that my viciousness was less than theirs; I heard them boasting of their exploits, and the viler the exploits the louder the boasting; and I set about the same exploits not only for the pleasure of the act but for the pleasure of the boasting.

Nothing is utterly condemnable save vice: yet I grew in vice through desire of praise; and when I lacked opportunity to equal others in vice, I invented things I had not done, lest I might be held cowardly for being innocent, or contemptible for being chaste. With the basest companions I walked the streets of Babylon①[the city of this World as opposed to the city of God] and wallowed in its filth as if it had been a bed of spices and precious ointments. To make me cleave closer to that city's very center, the invisible Enemy trod me down and seduced me, for I was easy to seduce. My mother had by now fled out of the center of Babylon, but she still lingered in its outskirts. She had urged me to chastity but she did not follow up what my father had told her of me: and though she saw my sexual passions as most evil now and full of peril for the future, she did not consider that if they could not be pared down to the quick, they had better be brought under control within the bounds of married love. She did not want me married because she feared that a wife might be a hindrance to my prospects—not those hopes of the world to come which my mother had in You, O God, but my prospects as a student. Both my parents were unduly set upon the success of my studies, my father because he had practically no thought of You and only vain ambition for me, my mother because she thought that the usual course of studies would be not only no hindrance to my coming to You but an actual help. Recalling the

---

① Babylon,巴比伦,古巴比伦首都,位于现巴格达幼发拉底河南部。公元前2150至前1740年间,巴比伦国王在汉谟拉比(Hammurabi)的统治下,曾武力统一美索不达米亚地区,实行中央集权统治,巴比伦国开始兴盛。公元前539年,巴比伦国战败,向波斯居鲁士大帝(Cyrus the Great)投降。

past as well as I can, that is how I read my parents' characters. Anyhow, I was left to do pretty well as I liked, and go after pleasure not only beyond the limit of reasonable discipline but to sheer dissoluteness in many kinds of evil. And in all this, O God, a mist hung between my eyes and the brightness of Your truth: *and mine iniquity had come forth as it were from fatness.*

IV

Your law, O Lord, punishes theft; and this law is so written in the hearts of men that not even the breaking of it blots it out: for no thief bears calmly being stolen from—not even if he is rich and the other steals through want. Yet I chose to steal, and not because want drove me to it—unless a want of justice and contempt for it and an excess of iniquity. For I stole things which I already had in plenty and of better quality. Nor had I any desire to enjoy the things I stole, but only the stealing of them and the sin. There was a pear tree near our vineyard, heavy with fruit, but fruit that was not particularly tempting either to look at or to taste. A group of young blackguards, and I among them, went out to knock down the pears and carry them off late one night, for it was our bad habit to carry on our games in the streets till very late. We carried off an immense load of pears, not to eat—for we barely tasted them before throwing them to the hogs. Our only pleasure in doing it was that it was forbidden. Such was my heart, O God, such was my heart: yet in the depth of the abyss You had pity on it. Let that heart now tell You what it sought when I was thus evil for no object, having no cause for wrongdoing save my wrongness. The malice of the act was base and I loved it—that is to say I loved my own undoing, I loved the evil in me—not the thing for which I did the evil, simply the evil: my soul was depraved, and hurled itself down from security in You into utter destruction, seeking no profit from wickedness but only to be wicked.

V

There is an appeal to the eye in beautiful things, in gold and silver and all such; the sense of touch has its own powerful pleasures; and the other senses find qualities in things suited to them. Worldly success has its glory, and the power to command and to overcome: and from this springs the thirst for revenge. But in our quest of all these things, we must not depart from You, Lord, or deviate from Your Law. This life we live here below has its own attractiveness, grounded in the measure of beauty it has and its harmony with the beauty of all lesser things. The bond of human friendship is admirable, holding many souls as one. Yet in the enjoyment of all such things we commit sin if through immoderate inclination to them—for though they are good, they are of the lowest order of good—things higher and better are forgotten, even You, O Lord our God, and Your Truth and Your Law. These lower things have their delights but not such as my God has, for He made them all: *and in Him doth the righteous delight, and He is the joy of the upright of heart.*

Now when we ask why this or that particular evil act was done, it is normal to assume that it could not have been done save through the desire of gaining or the fear of losing some one of these lower goods. For they have their own charm and their own beauty, though compared with the higher values of heaven they are poor and mean enough. Such a man has committed a murder. Why? He wanted the other man's wife or his property; or he had chosen robbery as a means of livelihood; or he feared to lose this or that through his victim's act; or he had been wronged and was aflame for vengeance. Would any man commit a murder for no cause, for the sheer delight of murdering? The thing would be incredible. There is of course the case of the man [Catiline]① who was said to be so stupidly and savagely cruel that he practised cruelty and evil even when he had nothing to gain by them. But even there a cause was stated—he did it, he said, lest through idleness his hand or his resolution should grow slack. And why did he want to prevent that? So that one day by the multiplication of his crimes the city should be his, and he would have gained honors and authority and riches, and would no longer be in fear of the law or in the difficulties that want of money and the awareness of his crimes had brought him. So that not even Catiline loved his crimes as crimes; he loved some other thing which was his reason for

---

① Catiline,喀提林(拉丁名为 Lucius Sergius Catilina,前 108—前 62),罗马政客。因公元前 63 年所筹划的流产政变而声名狼藉。

committing them.

VI

What was it then that in my wretched folly I loved in You, O theft of mine, deed wrought in that dark night when I was sixteen? For you were not lovely: you were a theft. Or are you anything at all, that I should talk with you? The pears that we stole were beautiful for they were created by Thee, Thou most Beautiful of all, Creator of all, Thou good God, my Sovereign and true Good. The pears were beautiful but it was not pears that my empty soul desired. For I had any number of better pears of my own, and plucked those only that I might steal. For once I had gathered them I threw them away, tasting only my own sin and savouring that with delight; for if I took so much as a bite of any one of those pears, it was the sin that sweetened it. And now, Lord my God, I ask what was it that attracted me in that theft, for there was no beauty in it to attract. I do not mean merely that it lacked the beauty that there is in justice and prudence, or in the mind of man or his senses and vegetative life: or even so much as the beauty and glory of the stars in the heavens, or of earth and sea with their oncoming of new life to replace the generations that pass. It had not even that false show or shadow of beauty by which sin tempts us.

[For there *is* a certain show of beauty in sin.] Thus pride wears the mask of loftiness of spirit, although You alone, O God, are high over all. Ambition seeks honor and glory, although You alone are to be honored before all and glorious forever. By cruelty the great seek to be feared, yet who is to be feared but God alone: from His power what can be wrested away, or when or where or how or by whom? The caresses by which the lustful seduce are a seeking for love: but nothing is more caressing than Your charity, nor is anything more healthfully loved than Your supremely lovely, supremely luminous Truth. Curiosity may be regarded as a desire for knowledge, whereas You supremely know all things. Ignorance and sheer stupidity hide under the names of simplicity and innocence: yet no being has simplicity like to Yours: and none is more innocent than You, for it is their own deeds that harm the wicked. Sloth pretends that it wants quietude: but what sure rest is there save the Lord? Luxuriousness would be called abundance and completeness; but You are the fullness and inexhaustible abundance of incorruptible delight. Wastefulness is a parody of generosity: but You are the infinitely generous giver of all good. Avarice wants to possess overmuch: but You possess all. Enviousness claims that it strives to excel: but what can excel before You? Anger clamors for just vengeance: but whose vengeance is so just as Yours? Fear is the recoil from a new and sudden threat to something one holds dear, and a cautious regard for one's own safety: but nothing new or sudden can happen to You, nothing can threaten Your hold upon things loved, and where is safety secure save in You? Grief pines at the loss of things in which desire delighted: for it wills to be like to You from whom nothing can be taken away.

Thus the soul is guilty of fornication when she turns from You and seeks from any other source what she will nowhere find pure and without taint unless she returns to You. Thus even those who go from You and stand up against You are still perversely imitating You. But by the mere fact of their imitation, they declare that You are the creator of all that is, and that there is nowhere for them to go where You are not.

So once again what did I enjoy in that theft of mine? Of what excellence of my Lord was I making perverse and vicious imitation? Perhaps it was the thrill of acting against Your law—at least in appearance, since I had no power to do so in fact, the delight a prisoner might have in making some small gesture of liberty—getting a deceptive sense of omnipotence from doing something forbidden without immediate punishment. I was that slave, who fled from his Lord and pursued his Lord's shadow. O rottenness, O monstrousness of life and abyss of death! Could you find pleasure only in what was forbidden, and only because it was forbidden?

VII

What shall I render unto the Lord, that I can recall these things and yet not be afraid! *I shall love Thee, Lord, and shall give thanks to Thee and confess Thy Name*, because Thou hast forgiven me such great sins and evil deeds. I know that it is only by Thy grace and mercy that Thou hast melted away the ice of my sins. And the evil I have not done, that also I know is by Thy grace: for what might I not have done, seeing that I loved evil solely because it was evil? I confess that Thou hast forgiven all alike—the sins I committed of my own motion: the sins I would have committed but for Thy grace.

Would any man, considering his own weakness, dare to attribute his chastity or his innocence to his own powers and so love Thee less—as if he did not need the same mercy as those who return to Thee after sin. If any man has heard Thy voice and followed it and done none of the things he finds me here recording and confessing, still he must not scorn me: for I am healed by the same doctor who preserved him from falling into sickness, or at least into such grievous sickness. But let him love Thee even more: seeing me rescued out of such sickness of sin, and himself saved from falling into such sickness of sin, by the one same Saviour.

VIII

What fruit therefore had I (in my vileness) *in those things of which I am now ashamed?* Especially in that piece of thieving, in which I loved nothing except the thievery—though that in itself was no *thing* and I only the more wretched for it. Now—as I think back on the state of my mind then—I am altogether certain that I would not have done it alone. Perhaps then what I really loved was the companionship of those with whom I did it. If so, can I still say that I loved nothing over and above the thievery? Surely I can; that companionship was nothing over and above, because it was nothing. What is the truth of it? Who shall show me, unless He that illumines my heart and brings light into its dark places? What is the thing that I am trying to get at in all this discussion? If I had liked the pears that I stole and wanted to enjoy eating them, I might have committed the offence alone. if that had been sufficient, to get me the pleasure I wanted; I should not have needed to inflame the itch of my desires by rubbing against accomplices. But since the pleasure I got was not in the pears, it must have been in the crime itself, and put there by the companionship of others sinning with me.

IX

What was my feeling in all this? Depraved, undoubtedly, and woe is me that I had it. But what exactly was it? *Who can understand sins*? We laughed together as if our hearts were tickled to be playing a trick upon the owners, who had no notion of what we were doing and would very strongly have objected. But what delight did I find in that, which I should not equally have found if I had done it alone? Because we are not much given to laughing when we are alone? Not much given, perhaps, but laughter does sometimes overcome a man when no one else is about, if something especially ridiculous is seen or heard or floats into the mind. Yet I would not have done this by myself: quite definitely I would not have done it by myself.

Here, then, O God, is the memory still vivid in my mind. I would not have committed that theft alone: my pleasure in it was not what I stole but that I stole: yet I would not have enjoyed doing it, I would not have done it, alone. O friendship unfriendly, unanalysable attraction for the mind, greediness to do damage for the mere sport and jest of it, desire for another's loss with no gain to oneself or vengeance to be satisfied! Someone cries "Come on, let's do it" —and we would be ashamed to be ashamed!

X

Who can unravel that complex twisted knottedness? It is unclean, I hate to think of it or look at it. I long for Thee, O Justice and Innocence; Joy and Beauty of the clear of sight, I long for Thee with unquenchable longing. There is sure repose in Thee and life untroubled. He that enters into Thee, enters into the joy of his Lord and shall not fear and shall be well in Him who is the Best. I went away from Thee, my God, in my youth I strayed too far from Thy sustaining power, and I became to myself a barren land.

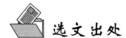选文出处

St. Augustine. *Confessions*. Translated by F. J. Sheed, Beijing: China

Social Sciences Publishing House (reprinted from the English Edition by Hackett Publishing Co., 1993), 1999, pp. 23—31.

思考题

1. 试论"天主"在奥古斯丁的宗教哲学思想中占据着怎样的位置?
2. 有人评价奥古斯丁说,他是"一个时代的结束,同时也是另一个新纪元的开始。他是古代基督教作家中的最后一人,同时也是中世纪神学的开路先锋"。应该怎样理解这段话?请结合奥古斯丁的生平背景、思想主张做出相关评述。

阅读

参考书目

1. 奥古斯丁:《忏悔录》,周士良译,北京:商务印书馆,1997年。
2. 沙伦·M. 凯、保罗·汤姆森:《奥古斯丁》,周伟驰译,北京:中华书局,2002年。
3. Bonner, Gerald, *Augustine of Hippo: Life and Controversies*, London: Canterbury Press, 1986.
4. Gilson, Etienne, *The Christian Philosophy of Saint Augustine*, translated by L. E. M. Lynch, London: Random House, 1967.

阿奎那

托马斯·阿奎那（Thomas Aquinas，约 1224—1274）是中世纪的著名哲学家和神学家。阿奎那 5 岁时被父母送入本笃会（Benedictine order）①卡西诺山修道院，20 岁加入多明我修会（Dominican order）②，曾先后就读于那不勒斯大学和巴黎大学，师从大阿尔伯特（Albertus Magnus）③。由于受其老师的影响，阿奎那对亚里士多德有着浓厚的兴趣。通过注释大量亚里士多德的著作，他吸收了亚里士多德理论的精髓，并以此为基础构建了基督教神学体系。

阿奎那认为，神学是一门学问。神不仅是信仰的对象，也可以成为理智把握的对象。他承认哲学的独立地位，认为哲学是理性的，而

---

① 本笃会是天主教隐修会之一，一译本尼狄克派，529 年由贵族出身的意大利人本笃所创。他手定会规，规定会士不可婚娶，不可有私财，一切服从长上，称此为"发三愿"。本笃会会士每日必须按时进经堂诵经，咏唱"大日课"，余暇时从事各种劳动。会规要求祈祷不忘工作，视游手好闲为罪恶。后来该会规成为天主教修会制度的范本。

② 天主教托钵修会之一，布道兄弟会，1215 年由西班牙贵族 Dominic 创立于法国图卢兹。其会士戴黑色风帽，被称为黑衣修士。多明我修会坚持纯朴和贫穷的生活。会士都是乞丐，不能拥有财产，过着边工作边乞讨的生活。多明我修会以布道为宗旨，着重劝化异教徒和排斥异端。由于在反对卡特里派等异端的斗争中的成功，教皇洪诺留三世于 1217 年批准其合法地位并将其置于自己管辖之下。受教皇委托，多明我修会主持异端裁判所，执掌教会法庭及教徒诉讼事宜。至今罗马教廷的信理部及教会最高法庭仍由其会士掌握。多明我修会重视教育，提倡学术研究。他们开办大学，设立专门研究机构从事教育和学术研究。由于多明我修会的演讲活动对公众开放，它对于提高欧洲的教育水平发挥了重要作用。

③ 主教，罗马天主教会圣徒和博士，德国多明我修会的缔造者之一，知识渊博，以深入研究亚里士多德学派和新柏拉图主义者的传统而享有盛名。主要著作有：《受造物论》《伦巴特箴言四书》评注》及《神学手册》。

神学则是启示与信仰。无论是理性还是启示，它们的最终源泉均为上帝，二者不相矛盾。但总的来说，信仰高于理性，神学高于哲学，哲学必须服务于神学。通过阐明神学与哲学之间的关系，阿奎那在信仰和理性之间找到了一种平衡，架起了一座桥梁。

托马斯·阿奎那一生著作颇丰，主要包括《反异教大全》(*Summa Contra Gentiles*)、《神学大全》(*Summa Theologiae*)、《哲学大全》(*Summa Philsophica contra Gentiles*)等。其中的《神学大全》被许多人认为是他一生中最伟大的著作。全书包括3个部分。第一部分探讨如何看待上帝以及上帝造物的过程；第二部分揭示人类向上帝的道德复归，涉及美德与邪恶的讨论；第三部分讨论了救世主及圣礼问题。

在某种程度上，《神学大全》的伟大主要应归功于它的结构。整部作品不分章节，而是由论题与论文构成。每个论题都通过一系列独立的论文进行论证。每篇论文分5个部分，分别是：问题的设定；对问题的异议；与异议相对立的权威性陈述；阿奎那提出的结论；以及他对异议所做的回答。这种先提问，后论述，最后得出结论的论证方式充分保留了辩论的形式。它步步深入，循循善诱，引人思考，适合用作神职人员的教材，这与阿奎那写作的初衷是相吻合的。

本文节选的是《神学大全》第1部分的第2个问题，其论题是上帝的存在与本质。在这里阿奎那设定了"上帝的存在是否直接自明"，"上帝的存在是否能被证明"，"上帝是否存在"这三个问题，并通过上述几个步骤，对每个问题进行了论证。其中最为经典的当属阿奎那针对最后一个问题"上帝是否存在"所做的五种论证。这五种论证如下：第一，上帝是一切运动的始发者。这个观点以亚里士多德关于运动的论证为基础，认为凡是运动的事物都为他物所推动，而这一"他物"的背后必然还存在着另一推动它的事物，由此构成一条不断延伸的链条。但因为不可能漫无止境地往上追溯始动者，所以我们断定在这个链条的某一点上必定会有一个始动而非受动的事物。这个非受动的始动者只能是上帝；第二，上帝是一切事物存在的第一原因。这个观点认为，任何事物的存在，都无法通过自身对其进行解释，因此，任何事物的存在都需要某种原因。原因一旦消失，结果亦即随之消失。但我们显然不可能无穷无尽地追溯上一级原因，所以我们不得不假定有第一个有效原因的存在，而这便是大家熟知的上帝；第三，上帝是必然的存在。日常经验告诉我们，万物都是有生有灭的，也就是说，它们的存在并不是必然的。因此，某类事物在某一时间可能并不存在。如果是这样，那么就有可能在历史的某一时刻，世间并无任何事物存在。但这显然是荒谬的，如果曾经有一个时刻，世间空无一物，那么现在世上事物又来自哪里？显然任何事物都不可能横空出世。如果这样的逻辑成立，所有事物的存在都只是一种可能性的说法显然是不对的。这世上必须有某种东西，它具有必要的存在，这就是所谓的上帝；第四，上帝是完美的存在。如果承认事物都有不同的完善程度，那么必然存在某种完美的东西，而这就是人人皆知的上帝；第五，上帝是秩序的支配者。在这个世界上，即便是没有生命的自然物体，也总是朝着一定的方向发展，仿佛存在着某种目的。但我们都知道，只有有生事物才能有内在的目的。所以我们推测可能有某种外在智力在操纵着世界的秩序，而这就是所谓的上帝。阿奎那著名的五大论证在逻辑上是牵强的，它的目的是维护基督教的信仰。但有趣的是，在阿奎那的时代，他的观点并没有得到正统神学家的认同，甚至被视为异端。在他死后的三年内，他的一些观点受到巴黎大学和牛津大学某些权威人士的公开谴责。直到阿奎那去世五十年后，他的学说才被公开承认。随着教会权威的没落，阿奎那的地位不断上升。阿奎那被教皇封为圣徒。他的《神学大全》曾经被置于和《圣经》同等的位置。

Summma Theologiae

Because the chief aim of sacred doctrine is to teach the knowledge of God not only as He is in Himself, but also as He is the beginning of things and their last end, and especially of rational creatures, as is clear from what has been already said, therefore, in our endeavor to expound this science, we shall treat: (1) of God; (2) of the rational creature's movement towards God; (3) of Christ Who as man is our way to God.

In treating of God there will be a threefold division:—

For we shall consider (1) whatever concerns the divine essence. (2) Whatever concerns the distinctions of Persons. (3) Whatever concerns the procession of creatures from Him.

Concerning the divine essence, we must consider:—

(1) Whether God exists? (2) The manner of His existence, or, rather, what is *not* the manner of His existence. (3) Whatever concerns His operations—namely, His knowledge, will, power.

Concerning the first, there are three points of inquiry:—

(1) Whether the proposition *God exists* is self-evident? (2) Whether it is demonstrable? (3) Whether God exists?

First Article
WHETHER THE EXISTENCE OF GOD IS SELF-EVIDENT?

We proceed thus to the First Article:—

Objection 1. It seems that the existence of God is self-evident. For those things are said to be self-evident to us the konwledge of which exists naturally in us, as we can see in regard to first principles. But as Damascene① says, *the knowledge of God is naturally implanted in all*. Therefore the existence of God is self-evident.

Obj. 2. Further, those things are said to be self-evident which are known as soon as the terms are known, which the Philosopher says is true of the first principles of demonstration. Thus, when the nature of a whole and of a part is known, it is at once recognized that every whole is greater than its part. But as soon as the signification of the name *God* is understood, it is at once seen that God exists. For by Luis name is signified that thing than which nothing greater can be conceived. But that which exists actually and mentally is greater than that which exists only mentally. Therefore, since as soon as the name *God* is understood it exists mentally, it also follows that it exists actually. Therefore the proposition God *exists* is self-evident.

Obj. 3. Further, the existence of truth is self-evident. For whoever denies the existence of truth grants that truth does not exist: and, if truth does not exist, then the proposition *Truth does not exist* is true: and if there is anything true, there must be truth. But God is truth itself: *I am the way*, *the truth*, *and the life* (*Jo*. xiv. 6). Therefore God *exists* is self-evident.

On the contrary, No one can mentally admit the opposite of what is self-evident, as the Philosopher states concerning the first principles of demonstration. But the opposite of the proposition God is can be mentally

---

① St. John Damascene(约 675—749),东方教会最后一位教父,著名的系统神学家,其神学代表作为《知识之源》(*Fountain of Knowledge*)。

admitted: *The fool said in his heart, There is no God* (*Ps.* lii. I). Therefore, that God exists is not self-evident.

I answer that, A thing can be self-evident in either of two ways: on the one hand, self-evident in itself, though not to us; on the other, self-evident in itself, and to us. A proposition is self-evident because the predicate is included in the essence of the subject: *e. g.*, *Man is an animal*, for animal is contained in the essence of man. If, therefore, the essence of the predicate and subject be known to all, the proposition will be self-evident to all; as is clear with regard to the first principles of demonstration, the terms of which are certain common notions that no one is ignorant of, such as being and non-being, whole and part, and the like. If, however, there are some to whom the essence of the predicate and subject is unknown, the proposition will be self-evident in itself, but not to those who do not know the meaning of the predicate and subject of the proposition. Therefore, it happens, as Boethius① says, that there are some notions of the mind which are common and self-evident only to the learned, as that incorporeal substances are not in space. Therefore I say that this proposition, *God exists*, of itself is self-evident, for the predicate is the same as the subject, because God is His own existence as will be hereafter shown. Now because we do not know the essence of God, the proposition is not self-evident to us, but needs to be demonstrated by things that are more known to us, though less known in their nature—namely, by His effects.

Reply Obj. 1. To know that God exists in a general and confused way is implanted in us by nature, inasmuch as God is man's beatitude. For man naturally desires happiness, and what is naturally desired by man is naturally known by him. This, however, is not to know absolutely that God exists; just as to know that someone is approaching is not the same as to know that Peter is approaching, even though it is Peter who is approaching; for there are many who imagine that man's perfect good, which is happiness, consists in riches, and others in pleasures, and others in something else.

Reply Obj. 2. Perhaps not everyone who hears this name *God*

---

① Boethius(470—524),罗马哲学家,被误判叛国罪处死,在狱中写成以柏拉图思想为理论依据的名著《哲学的慰藉》(*The Consolation of Philosophy*)。

understands it to signify something than which nothing greater can be thought, seeing that some have believed God to be a body. Yet, granted that everyone understands that by this name *God* is signified something than which nothing greater can be thought, nevertheless, it does not therefore follow that he understands that what the name signifies exists actually, but only that it exists mentally. Nor can it be argued that it actually exists, unless it be admitted that there actually exists something than which nothing greater can be thought; and this precisely is not admitted by those who hold that God does not exist.

Reply Obj. 3. The existence of truth in general is self-evident, but the existence of a Primal Truth is not self-evident to us.

Second Article
WHETHER IT CAN BE DEMONSTRATED THAT GOD EXISTS?

We proceed thus to the Second Article:—

Objection 1. It seems that the existence of God cannot be demonstrated. For it is an article of faith that God exists. But what is of faith cannot be demonstrated, because a demonstration produces scientific knowledge, whereas faith is of the unseen, as is clear from the Apostle (*Heb.* xi. 1). Therefore it cannot be demonstrated that God exists.

Obj. 2. Further, essence is the middle term of demonstration. But we cannot know in what God's essence consists, but solely in what it does not consist, as Damascene says. Therefore we cannot demonstrate that God exists.

Obj. 3. Further, if the existence of God were demonstrated, this could only be from His effects. But His effects are not proportioned to Him, since He is infinite and His effects are finite, and between the finite and infinite there is no proportion. Therefore, since a cause cannot be demonstrated by an effect not proportioned to it, it seems that the existence of God cannot be demonstrated.

On the contrary, The Apostle says: *The invisible things of Him are clearly seen, being understood by the things that are made* (*Rom.* i. 20). But this would not be unless the existence of God could be demonstrated through the things that are made; for the first thing we must know of anythis is, whether it exists.

I answer that, Demonstration can be made in two ways: One is through the cause, and is called *propter quid*①, and this is to argue from what is prior absolutely. The other is through the effect, and is called a demonstration *quia*; this is to argue from what is prior relatively only to us. When an effect is better known to us than its cause, from the effect we proceed to the knowledge of the cause. And from every effect the existence of its proper cause can be demonstrated, so long as its effects are better known to us; because, since every effect depends upon its cause, if the effect exists, the cause must preexist. Hence the existence of God, in so far as it is not self-evident to us, can be demonstrated from those of His effects which are known to us.

Reply Obj. 1. The existence of God and other like truths about God, which can be known by natural reason, are not articles of faith, but are preambles to the articles; for faith presupposes natural knowledge, even as grace presupposes nature and perfection the perfectible. Nevertheless, there is nothing to prevent a man, who cannot grasp a proof, from accepting, as a matter of faith, something which in itself is capable of being scientifically known and demonstrated.

Reply Obj. 2. When the existence of a cause is demonstrated from an effect, this effect takes the place of the definition of the cause in proving the cause's existence. This is especially the case in regard to God, because, in order to prove the existence of anything, it is necessary to accept as a middle term the meaning of the name, and not its essence, for the question of its essence follows on the question of its existence. Now the names given to God are derived from His effects, as will be later shown. Consequently, in demonstrating the existence of God from His effects, we may take for the middle term the meaning of the name *God*.

Reply Obj. 3. From effects not proportioned to the cause no perfect

---

① 阿奎那认为论证有归纳与演绎两种途径。演绎又有先天演绎与后天演绎之分。所谓的先天演绎是指由原因推出结果,即这里的"propter quid";而后天演绎是指由可以感知的结果,推出导致这一结果的原因,也即后面提到的"quia"。阿奎那认为关于上帝的证明应该是后天演绎。文章后面提出的五种关于上帝存在的证明就是建立在后天演绎的基础之上的。

knowledge of that cause can be obtained. Yet from every effect the existence of the cause can be clearly demonstrated, and so we can demonstrate the existence of God from His effects; though from them we cannot know God perfectly as He is in His essence.

Third Article
WHETHER GOD EXISTS?

We proceed thus to the Third Article:—

Objection 1. It seems that God does not exist; because if one of two contraries be infinite, the other would be altogether destroyed. But the name *God* means that He is infinite goodness. If, therefore, God existed, there would be no evil discoverable; but there is evil in the world. Therefore God does not exist.

Obj. 2. Further, it is superfluous to suppose that what can be accounted for by a few principles has been produced by many. But it seems that everything we see in the world can be accounted for by other principles, supposing God did not exist. For all natural things can be reduced to one principle, which is nature; and all voluntary things can be reduced to one principle, which is human reason, or will. Therefore there is no need to suppose God's existence.

On the contrary, It is said in the person of God: *I am Who am* (*Exod*. iii. 14).

I answer that, The existence of God can be proved in five ways.

The first and more manifest way is the argument from motion. It is certain, and evident to our senses, that in the world some things are in motion. Now whatever is moved is moved by another, for nothing can be moved except it is in potentiality to that towards which it is moved; whereas a thing moves inasmuch as it is in act. For motion is nothing else than the reduction of something from potentiality to actuality. But nothing can be reduced from potentiality to actuality, except by something in a state of actuality. Thus that which is actually hot, as fire, makes wood, which is potentially hot, to be actually hot, and thereby moves and changes it. Now it is not possible that the same thing should be at once in actuality and potentiality in the same respect, but only in different respects. For what is actually hot cannot simultaneously be potentially hot; but it is simultaneously potentially cold. It is therefore impossible that in the same respect and in the same way a thing should be both mover and moved, *i. e.*, that it should move itself. Therefore, whatever is moved must be moved by another. If that by which it is moved be itself moved, then this also must needs be moved by another, and that by another again. But this cannot go on to infinity, because then there would be no first mover, and, consequently, no other mover, seeing that subsequent movers move only inasmuch as they are moved by the first mover; as the staff moves only because it is moved by the hand. Therefore it is necessary to arrive at a first mover, moved by no other; and this everyone understands to be God.

The second way is from the nature of efficient causes. In the world of sensible things we find there is an order of efficient causes. There is no case known (neither is it, indeed, possible) in which a thing is found to be the efficient cause of itself; for so it would be prior to itself, which is impossible. Now in efficient causes it is not possible to go on to infinity, because in all efficient causes following in order, the first is the cause of the intermediate cause, and the intermediate is the cause of the ultimate cause, whether the intermediate cause be several, or one only. Now to take away the cause is to take away the effect. Therefore, if there be no first cause among efficient causes, there will be no ultimate, nor any intermediate, cause. But if in efficient causes it is possible to go on to infinity, there will be no first efficient cause, neither will there be an ultimate effect, nor any intermediate efficient causes; all of which is plainly false. Therefore it is necessary to admit a first efficient cause, to which everyone gives the name of God.

The third way is taken from possibility and necessity, and runs thus. We find in nature things that are possible to be and not to be, since they are found to be generated, and to be corrupted, and consequently, it is possible for them to be and not to be. But it is impossible for these always to exist, for that which can not-be at some time is not. Therefore, if everything can not-be, then at one time there was nothing in existence. Now if this were true, even now there would be nothing in existence, because that which does not exist begins to exist only through something already existing. Therefore, if at one time nothing was in existence, it would have been impossible for anything to have begun to exist; and thus even now nothing would be in existence—which is absurd. Therefore, not all beings are merely possible, but there must exist something the existence of which is necessary. But every necessary thing either has its necessity caused by another, or not. Now it is impossible to go on to infinity in necessary things which have their necessity caused by another, as has been already proved in regard to efficient causes. Therefore we cannot but admit the existence of some being having of itself its own necessity, and not receiving it from another, but rather causing in others their necessity. This all men speak of as God.

The fourth way is taken from the gradation to be found in things. Among beings there are some more and some less good, true, noble, and the like. But *more* and *less* are predicated of different things according as they resemble in their different ways something which is the maximum, as a thing is said to be hotter according as it more nearly resembles that which is hottest; so that there is something which is truest, something best, something noblest, and, consequently, something which is most being, for those things that are greatest in truth are greatest in being, as it is written in *Metaph*. ii. Now the maximum in any genus is the cause of all in that genus, as fire, which is the maximum of heat, is the cause of all hot things, as is said in the same book. Therefore there must also be something which is to all beings the cause of their being, goodness, and every other perfection; and this we call God.

The fifth way is taken from the governance of the world. We see that things which lack knowledge, such as natural bodies, act for an end, and this is evident from their acting always, or nearly always, in the same way, so as to obtain the best result. Hence it is plain that they achieve their end, not fortuitously, but designedly. Now whatever lacks knowledge cannot move towards an end, unless it be directed by some being endowed with knowledge and intelligence; as the arrow is directed by the archer. Therefore some intelligent being exists by whom all natural things are directed to their end; and this being we call God.

Reply Obj. 1. As Augustine says: *Since God is the highest good, He would not allow any evil to exist in His works, unless His omnipotence and goodness were such as to bring good even out of evil*. This is part of the infinite goodness of God, that He should allow evil to exist, and out of it produce good.

Reply Obj. 2. Since nature works for a determinate end under the direction of a higher agent, whatever is done by nature must be traced back to God as to its first cause. So likewise whatever is done voluntarily must be traced back to same higher cause other than human reason and will, since these can change and fail; for all things that are changeable and capable of defect must be traced back to an immovable and self-necessary first principle, as has been shown.

 选文出处

Thomas Aquina. *Summa Theologica*. in *Basic Writings of Saint Thomas Aquina*（Vol. One－I）, Beijing: China Social Sciences Publishing House (reprinted from the English Edition by Random House, Inc., 1945), 1999, pp. 18－24.

 思考题

1. 简要叙述阿奎那的五大论证。
2. 请说明阿奎那的《神学大全》在基督教历史上的地位。

阅读

参考书目

1. 约翰·英格利斯:《阿奎那》,刘中民译,北京:中华书局,2002年。
2. 赵敦华:《基督教哲学1500年》,北京:商务印书馆,2004年。

马基雅维利

尼科洛·马基雅维利（Niccolo Machiavelli，1469—1527）是文艺复兴时期意大利佛罗伦萨的政治家、外交家、历史学家、军事学家、诗人和剧作家。马基雅维利出生在一个显赫的贵族家庭。这个家族产生过几十名重要的官员。他父亲贝尔纳多是法学博士、律师；他母亲也有着良好的教育，能诗会文。马基雅维利7岁入学，约在12岁时就能用拉丁语作文。他熟习拉丁文和意大利的古典文学、史学。在1494年到1512年间，他为佛罗伦萨共和国效力，是一位出色的政治家。1512年，佛罗伦萨共和国覆灭，他的14年政治生涯随之结束。不过，他没有因为仕途的失意而自暴自弃，而是将精力投入到著书立说中去，为后人留下了丰厚的财富。主要著作有《君主论》(*The Prince*)、《李维史论》(*Discourses on Livy*)、《战争的艺术》(*The Art of War*)、《曼陀罗花》(*La Mandragola*)等。

本书所选的第一篇文章是《君主论》的第16章。马基雅维利在这里探讨的问题是君主花钱应当慷慨还是吝啬。马基雅维利发现慷慨和吝啬的关系是辩证的，一个大方的君主，往往容易把自己的财力耗尽，最后只能面临两难的选择——要么收回慷慨，并在巨大落差之中显得特别吝啬；要么横征暴敛，成为人民眼中的暴君。他发现，很多成功的国王，如法国的路易十二、西班牙的费尔迪南多等都是通过节约而成就大业的，因为节约的国王不会给国人增加负担，在需要钱的关键时刻可以做到出手大方。马基雅维利还这样评价吝啬的国君："这样他对于大多数人来说就是慷慨的，因为他没有增加他们的负担，对于没有被施与的人来说是吝啬的,但这些人毕竟为数甚少。"可见吝啬不是什么坏事。当然,君主不是在任何情况下都越吝啬越好,例如说,想当君主而尚未当上的人应当尽量显得大方,否则就不能获得支持,而一旦当上了君主,就是另外一回事了。还有,如果所花的钱是掠夺来的,既不是自己的,也不是本国人民的,那就应当越大方越好。所以马基雅维利清楚地看到了慷慨和吝啬之间的辩证关系:慷慨必然耗尽财力,最后走向吝啬;而吝啬能够集聚财力,最后在成就一些伟大事业的时候,不会增加人民的负担,结果反而显得慷慨。

第二篇是该书的第17章。马基雅维利在这里谈论的是君主应当被爱戴好,还是被畏惧好。爱戴和畏惧的关系也是辩证的。切萨雷·博尔贾是人们公认的残酷君主,但是"他的残酷却恢复了罗马尼阿的秩序,把它统一起来,并且迎来了和平与忠诚"。相比之下,佛罗伦萨的统治者为了避免残酷,对国内的派系斗争采取容忍的态度,结果酿成流血、掠夺的惨局。前者虽然残酷,结果比后者所谓的仁慈更有利于国家。通过残酷的手段而取得伟大成就的人比比皆是,但残酷也应当注意分寸,不能激起民众的憎恨。在详细探讨了吝啬和慷慨的利弊之后,他给君主提出了一个很著名的建议:"由于人们爱戴君主,基于他们自己的方便,而畏惧则基于君主的方便,因此一位明智的君主应当立足于自己控制的范围之内,而不应当立足于他人控制的范围之内。"在马氏看来,君主只有这样才能把握自己的命运,更好地管理自己的国家。

第三篇选自该书的第18章,谈的是君主是否应该守信用的问题。马基雅维利认为君主不应该局限于法律的手段来治理国家,还应使用野兽的方法,即运用武力。在各种野兽中,他所推崇的是狐狸和狮子:"君主既然必须懂得运用野兽的方法,他就应该效法狐狸和狮子,因为狮子不能防止自己落入陷阱,而狐狸不能抵御狼。"他认为用兽性武装起来的君主在必要的时候不应当守信用:"因此,一个审慎的君主不能守信用,也不应该守信用,当这样做反而对自己不利的时候,或者原来使自己做出诺言的理由不复存在的时候。"这种不守信用的君主往往取得成功,例如说,亚历山大六世就是这么一个君王,"世界上从来不曾有过一个人比他更加有力地做出保证,比他更加信誓旦旦地肯定一件事情,而同时没有一个人比他更加食言而肥;然而他的欺骗总是如愿成功,因为他深知人世的这一面"。像亚历山大六世一样的君主还很多;纵观历史上所有的君主,往往是那些诡计多端的战胜重信用的。所以聪明的君主不应该重信用。但公开承认自己不守信用是愚蠢的,君主总是需要装作很忠厚的样子,其原因在于,"如果具备这些品质并且常常本着这些品质行事,那是有害的;可是如果显得具备这一切品质,那却是有益的"。马基雅维利所揭示的道理是很深刻的,但也的确让人感到非常胆战心寒。

马基雅维利是一个充满争议的人物。在英语中 Machiavellian 这个词与狡猾、不择手段等意思相联系。也许在世界上的很多语言当中都是如此。马基雅维利死后受到了激烈的抨击。莎士比亚称他为"凶残的马基雅维利",有的神学家把《君主论》看作"邪恶的圣经",道德家简提利特指责他的政治思想为"一种邪恶的学说"。但他所遭到的这些批评有着很不合理的地方。马基雅维利撰写这部书的重要目的在于谋求意大利的统一。在战乱的年代,作者希望有一位强大的君主来拯救国家,当然是情理之中的。而且这种观点并不是马基雅维利思想的全部。如果我们读一读他的另一部著作《李维史论》就会发现,里面充满了自由主义的思想。当然也有人充分肯定马基雅维利的成就。马克思曾说:"从马基雅弗利……以及近代其他许多思想家谈起,权力都是作为法的基础的,由此,政治的理论观念摆脱了道德,所剩下的是独立地研究政治的主张,其他没有别的了。"[1]马基雅维利最早把政治与道德、宗教完全区分开来,使政治学成为一门独立的科学。哲学家罗素在评论马基雅维利时曾说:"'成功'意思指达到你的目的,不管是什么目的。假若世间有一门'成功学',按恶人的成功去研究,可以和按善人的成功去研究同样研究得好——实际上更好,因为成功的罪人实例比成功的圣贤实例尤其繁多。"[2]可见马氏的这种研究方法有着自身的意义,我们不能因此就认为马基雅维利这个人本身是邪恶的。他的政治学思想对欧洲政治学产生了深远的影响,"霍布士、洛克、休谟、孟德斯鸠都在某种程度上是他的学徒"。[3] 在政治实践方面他的影响更大,英国女王伊丽莎白一世、西班牙国王腓力二世等伟大的政治家都深深地领会了马基雅维利学说的真谛。当然不少暴君,如希特勒,也很好地利用了马基雅维利的学问。但学问本身并没有错,我们不能因为恐怖分子会用高科技就认为高科技是不好的。

The Prince

Of Liberality and Parsimony

Beginning, then, with the first of the above-mentioned qualities, I say

---

[1] 《马克思恩格斯全集》第 3 卷,北京:人民出版社,1956 年,第 368 页。
[2] 罗素:《西方哲学史》(下卷),何兆武、李约瑟译,北京:商务印书馆,1996 年,第 24 页。
[3] 《美国哲学百科全书》,转引自邹永贤:《国家学说史》(上册),福州:福建人民出版社,1987 年,第 278 页。

that it would be good to be held liberal; nonetheless, liberality, when used so that you may be held liberal, harms you. For if it is used virtuously and as it should be used, it may not be recognized, and you will not escape the infamy of its contrary. And so, if one wants to maintain a name for liberality among men, it is necessary not to leave out any kind of lavish display, so that a prince who has done this will always consume all his resources in such deeds. In the end it will be necessary, if he wants to maintain a name for liberality, to burden the people extraordinarily, to be rigorous with taxes, and to do all those things that can be done to get money. This will begin to make him hated by his subjects, and little esteemed by anyone as he becomes poor; so having offended the many and rewarded the few with this liberality of his, he feels every least hardship and runs into risk at every slight danger. When he recognizes this, and wants to draw back from it, he immediately incurs the infamy of meanness.

Thus, since a prince cannot, without damage to himself, use the virtue of liberality so that it is recognized, he should not, if he is prudent, care about a name for meanness. For with time he will always be held more and more liberal when it is seen that with his parsimony his income is enough for him, that he can defend himself from whoever makes war on him, and that he can undertake campaigns without burdening the people. So he comes to use liberality with all those from whom he does not take, who are infinite, and meanness with all those to whom he does not give, who are few. In our times we have not seen great things done except by those who have been considered mean; the others have been eliminated. Pope Julius II[①], while he made use of a name for liberality to attain the papacy, did not think of maintaining it later, so as to be able to make war. The present king of France has carried on many wars without imposing an extraordinary tax on his subjects, because the extra expenses were administered with his long-practiced parsimony. If the present king of Spain had been held liberal, he would not have been able to make or win so many campaigns.

Therefore, so as not to have to rob his subjects, to be able to defend himself, not to become poor and contemptible, nor to be forced to become

---

① Pope Julius II,教皇朱利奥二世(1443—1513),不仅善战,还资助过一些艺术家。

rapacious, a prince should esteem it little to incur a name for meanness, because this is one of those vices which enable him to rule. And if someone should say: Caesar attained empire with liberality, and many others, because they have been and have been held to be liberal, have attained very great rank, I respond: either you are already a prince or you are on the path to acquiring it: in the first case this liberality is damaging; in the second it is indeed necessary to be held liberal. And Caesar was one of those who wanted to attain the principate of Rome; but if after he had arrived there, had he remained alive and not been temperate with his expenses, he would have destroyed that empire. And if someone should reply: many have been princes and have done great things with their armies who have been held very liberal, I respond to you: either the prince spends from what is his own and his subjects' or from what belongs to someone else. In the first case he should be sparing; in the other, he should not leave out any part of liberality. And for the prince who goes out with his armies, who feeds on booty, pillage, and ransom and manages on what belongs to someone else, this liberality is necessary; otherwise he would not be followed by his soldiers. And of what is not yours or your subjects' one can be a bigger giver, as were Cyrus[①], Caesar, and Alexander, because spending what is someone else's does not take reputation from you but adds it to you; only spending your own is what hurts you. And there is nothing that consumes itself as much as liberality: while you use it, you lose the capacity to use it; and you become either poor and contemptible or, to escape poverty, rapacious and hateful. Among all the things that a prince should guard against is being contemptible and hated, and liberality leads you to both. So there is more wisdom in maintaining a name for meanness, which begets infamy without hatred, than in being under a necessity, because one wants to have a name for liberality, to incur a name for rapacity, which begets infamy with hatred.

---

① Cyrus 指的是 Cyrus the Great（前 580—前 529），古代波斯的居鲁士大帝。

Of Cruelty and Mercy, and Whether It Is Better to Be Loved than Feared, or the Contrary

Descending next to the other qualities set forth before, I say that each prince should desire to be held merciful and not cruel; nonetheless he should take care not to use this mercy badly. Cesare Borgia① was held to be cruel; nonetheless his cruelty restored the Romagna, united it, and reduced it to peace and to faith. If one considers this well, one will see that he was much more merciful than the Florentine people, who so as to escape a name for cruelty, allowed Pistoia to be destroyed. A prince, therefore, so as to keep his subjects united and faithful, should not care about the infamy of cruelty, because with very few examples he will be more merciful than those who for the sake of too much mercy allow disorders to continue, from which come killings or robberies; for these customarily harm a whole community, but the executions that come from the prince harm one particular person. And of all princes, it is impossible for the new prince to escape a name for cruelty because new states are full of dangers. And Virgil says in the mouth of Dido: "The harshness of things and the newness of the kingdom force me to contrive such things, and to keep a broad watch over the borders."

Nonetheless, he should be slow to believe and to move, nor should he create fear for himself, and he should proceed in a temperate mode with prudence and humanity so that too much confidence does not make him incautious and too much diffidence does not render him intolerable.

From this a dispute arises whether it is better to be loved than feared, or the reverse. The answer is that one would want to be both the one and the other; but because it is difficult to put them together, it is much safer to be feared than loved, if one has to lack one of the two. For one can say this generally of men: that they are ungrateful, fickle, pretenders and dissemblers, evaders of danger, eager for gain. While you do them good, they are yours, offering you their blood, property, lives, and children, as I said

---

① Cesare Borgia (1475—1507),教皇亚历山大六世的私生子,曾任巴伦西亚大主教,枢机主教,为教皇的主要顾问。

above, when the need for them is far away; but, when it is close to you, they revolt. And that prince who has founded himself entirely on their words, stripped of other preparation, is ruined; for friendships that are acquired at a price and not with greatness and nobility of spirit are bought, but they are not owned and when the time comes they cannot be spent. And men have less hesitation to offend one who makes himself loved than one who makes himself feared; for love is held by a chain of obligation, which, because men are wicked, is broken at every opportunity for their own utility, but fear is held by a dread of punishment that never forsakes you.

The prince should nonetheless make himself feared in such a mode that if he does not acquire love, he escapes hatred, because being feared and not being hated can go together very well. This he will always do if he abstains from the property of his citizens and his subjects, and from their women; and if he also needs to proceed against someone's life, he must do it when there is suitable justification and manifest cause for it. But above all, he must abstain from the property of others, because men forget the death of a father more quickly than the loss of a patrimony. Furthermore, causes for taking away property are never lacking, and he who begins to live by rapine always finds cause to seize others' property; and, on the contrary, causes for taking life are rarer and disappear more quickly.

But when the prince is with his armies and has a multitude of soldiers under his control, then it is above all necessary not to care about a name for cruelty, because without this name he never holds his army united, or diposed to any feat. Among the admirable actions of Hannibal[①] is numbered this one: that when he had a very large army, mixed with infinite kinds of men, and had led it to fight in alien lands, no dissension ever arose in it, neither among themselves nor against the prince, in bad as well as in his good fortune. This could not have arisen from anything other than his inhuman cruelty which, together with his infinite virtues, always made him venerable and terrible in the sight of his soldiers; and without it, his other virtues would not have sufficed to bring about this effect. And the writers, having considered little in

---

① Hannibal,汉尼拔(前247—前183或182),迦太基统帅,曾率大军远征意大利,三次重创罗马军队。

this, on the one hand admire this action of his but on the other condemn the principal cause of it.

And to see that it is true that his other virtues would not have been enough, one can consider Scipio①, who was very rare not only in his times but also in the entire memory of things known—whose armies in Spain rebelled against him. This arose from nothing but his excessive mercy, which had allowed his soldiers more license than is fitting for military discipline. Scipio's mercy was reproved in the Senate by Fabius Maximus②, who called him the corruptor of the Roman military. After the Locrians had been destroyed by an officer of Scipio's, they were not avenged by him, nor was the insolence of that officer corrected—all of which arose from his agreeable nature, so that when someone in the Senate wanted to excuse him, he said that there were many men who knew better how not to err than how to correct errors. Such a nature would in time have sullied Scipio's fame and glory if he had continued with it in the empire; but while he lived under the government of the Senate, this damaging quality of his not only was hidden, but made for his glory.

I conclude, then, returning to being feared and loved, that since men love at their convenience and fear at the convenience of the prince, a wise prince should found himself on what is his, not on what is someone else's; he should only contrive to avoid hatred, as was said.

In What Mode Faith Should Be Kept by Princes

How laudable it is for a prince to keep his faith, and to live with honesty and not by astuteness, everyone understands. Nonetheless one sees by experience in our times that the princes who have done great things are those who have taken little account of faith and have known how to get around men's brains with their astuteness; and in the end they have overcome those who have founded themselves on loyalty.

Thus, you must know that there are two kinds of combat: one with laws,

---

① Scipio,大西庇阿(前234—前183),罗马部队统帅,曾在西班牙战胜汉尼拔。
② Fabius Maximus,费比乌斯·马克西姆斯(约前280—前203),古罗马统帅,曾五次任执政官(公元前233、前228、前215、前214、前209)。

the other with force. The first is proper to man, the second to beasts; but because the first is often not enough, one must have recourse to the second. Therefore it is necessary for a prince to know well how to use the beast and the man. This role was taught covertly to princes by ancient writers, who wrote that Achilles, and many other ancient princes, were given to Chiron① the centaur to be raised, so that he would look after them with his discipline. To have as teacher a half-beast, half-man means nothing other than that a prince needs to know how to use both natures; and the one without the other is not lasting.

Thus, since a prince is compelled of necessity to know well how to use the beast, he should pick the fox and the lion, because the lion does not defend itself from snares and the fox does not defend itself from wolves. So one needs to be a fox to recognize snares and a lion to frighten the wolves. Those who stay simply with the lion do not understand this. A prudent lord, therefore, cannot observe faith, nor should he, when such observance turns against him, and the causes that made him promise have been eliminated. And if all men were good, this teaching would not be good; but because they are wicked and do not observe faith with you, you also do not have to observe it with them. Nor does a prince ever lack legitimate causes to color his failure to observe faith. One could give infinite modern examples of this, and show how many peace treaties and promises have been rendered invalid and vain through the infidelity of princes; and the one who has known best how to use the fox has come out best. But it is necessary to know well how to color this nature, and to be a great pretender and dissembler; and men are so simple and so obedient to present necessities that he who deceives will always find someone who will let himself be deceived.

I do not want to be silent about one of the recent examples, Alexander VI never did anything, nor ever thought of anything, but how to deceive men, and he always found a subject to whom he could do it. And there never was a man with greater efficacy in asserting a thing, and in affirming it with greater oaths, who observed it less; nonetheless, his deceits succeeded at his will, because he well knew this aspect of the world.

---

① Chiron,喀戎,希腊神话中半人半马的怪物,博学多智,以医技闻名,是多位英雄的老师。

Thus, it is not necessary for a prince to have all the above-mentioned qualities in fact, but it is indeed necessary to appear to have them. Nay, I dare say this, that by having them and always observing them, they are harmful; and by appearing to have them, they are useful, as it is to appear merciful, faithful, humane, honest, and religious, and to be so; but to remain with a spirit built so that, if you need not to be those things, you are able and know how to change to the contrary. This has to be understood: that a prince, and especially a new prince, cannot observe all those things for which men are held good, since he is often under a necessity, to maintain his state, of acting against faith, against charity, against humanity, against religion. And so he needs to have a spirit disposed to change as the winds of fortune and variations of things command him, and as I said above, not depart from good, when possible, but know how to enter into evil, when forced by necessity.

A prince should thus take great care that nothing escape his mouth that is not full of the above-mentioned five qualities and that, to see him and hear him, he should appear all mercy, all faith, all honesty, all humanity, all religion. And nothing is more necessary to appear to have than this last quality. Men in general judge more by their eyes than by their hands, because seeing is given to everyone, touching to few. Everyone sees how you appear, few touch what you are; and these few dare not oppose the opinion of many, who have the majesty of the state to defend them; and in the actions of all men, and especially of princes, where there is no court to appeal to, one looks to the end. So let a prince win and maintain his state: the means will always be judged honorable, and will be praised by everyone. For the vulgar are taken in by the appearance and the outcome of a thing, and in the world there is no one but the vulgar; the few have a place there when the many have somewhere to lean on. A certain prince of present times, whom it is not well to name, never preaches anything but peace and faith, and is very hostile to both. If he had observed both, he would have had either his reputation or his state taken from him many times.

Niccolo Machiavelli. *The Prince*. Translated by Harvey C. Mansfield, Jr.,

Beijing：China Social Sciences Publishing House（reprinted from the English Edition by The University of Chicago Press，1974），1999，pp. 62—71.

思考题

1. 你喜欢、同意马基雅维利的观点吗？为什么？
2. 能否在中国古代思想中找到类似的观点？

阅读
参考书目

1. 昆廷·斯金那：《马基雅维利》，王锐生、张阳译，北京：工人出版社，1986年。
2. Leo Strauss, *Thoughts on Machiavelli*, Chicago：The University of Chicago Press，1995.

培　根

弗朗西斯·培根(Francis Bacon，1561—1626)生于一个贵族家庭，父亲是掌玺大臣，母亲也出自贵族之家。他从小见多识广，而且受过良好的教育。他21岁开始当律师，23岁当选议员，最后一直升为大法官(仅次于国王的重要职位)。3年后，他因受贿罪被剥夺一切官职，永远不得从政。培根一生虽然十分忙碌，但他一直没有放弃学术研究。从政治舞台退出后，他把最后五年全部献给科学研究，给人类留下了丰富的精神遗产。他在哲学、文学、法学、宗教、历史、政治等方面都有很大的贡献。罗素曾高度评价这位思想家，认为他是"近代归纳法的创始人，又是科学研究程序进行组织化的先驱"[1]。他的主要著作包括《伟大的复兴》(*The Great Instauration*)、《新工具》(*Novum Organum*)、《新大西岛》(*New Atlantis*)、《学术的进步》(*Advancement of Learning*)、《随笔》(*Essays*)等。

培根的《新工具》是相对于亚里士多德的《工具论》(*Organon*)而写的。培根认为，亚里士多德的三段论主要是对概念进行推演，只追求论证形式的精确性，只能使人们对推理的程序满意，却不能保证前提和结论的真理性。培根反其道而行之，特别强调归纳在逻辑学中的作用，认为"归纳是那种维护感觉、贴近自然、几乎与活动相接(即使它并

---

[1] 罗素：《西方哲学史》(下卷)，何兆武、李约瑟译，北京：商务印书馆，1996年，第61页。

不实际涉及活动)的证明形式"①。培根改变了自亚里士多德以来对演绎推理的过多依赖,并且使重归纳的经验主义成为和重演绎推理的理性主义相抗衡的学术流派。当然他的这种方法也有其自身的问题。罗素曾这样批评培根:"培根的归纳法由于对假说不够重视,以致带有缺点。培根希望仅只把观察材料加以整理,正确的假说就会显明必露,但事实很难如此。"②事实上完全离开了假说,就无法收集资料,更无法整理资料,假说应该是研究的出发点和指导原则。

本书的选读是《新工具》的第 1 卷的 45 至 65 章。培根认为,人要认识客观世界就应该摆脱各种假象。他把假象分为四类,第一类假象为"族类的假象"(Idols of the Tribe),指普遍地存在于人类本性中的假象。人难以客观地反映世界,因为"人类理解力正如一面凹凸镜,它接受光线既不规则,于是就因在反映事物时掺入了它自己的性质而使得事物的性质变形和褪色"③。可见作为主体的人总是把主观的东西投射到客体上面,不可能完全真实地反映世界。这类假象主要表现在以下几个方面:(一)人类易于给世界设想出比实际更多的秩序和规则;(二)人们一旦接受了某一观点,常常死守这一观点,忽视相反的事例;(三)人类理解力总是不断进取、无休无止,永远无法形成定论,最终徒劳无益;(四)人类的理解力容易受到自身的意志和情感的影响,将主观的色彩强加给对象;(五)由于感观的迟钝、无能和欺骗的阻碍,人们难以认识不直接打动感观的事物;(六)人们容易片面地注重抽象的形式,忽视物质的结构、变化、活动及其规律。可见人类的本性中有着不利于客观认识的因素,只有不停地从这些方面进行批评,才能减少错误。

"洞穴的假象"(Idols of the Cave)是由于个人不同的具体情况而引起的假象。这个比喻来自柏拉图的《理想国》所描写的"洞穴"。培根曾解释说:"这个洞穴的形成,或是由于这个人自己固有的独特的本性;或是由于他所受的教育和别人的交往;或是由于他阅读一些书籍而对其权威性发生崇敬和赞美;又或是由于各种感印,这些感印又是依人心之不同(如有的人是'心怀成见'和'胸有成竹',有的人是'漠然无所动于中')而作用各异的;以及类此等等。"④这类假象的数目很大,以下便是几种重要的形式:(一)对特定的科学格外留恋,而且倾向于不适当地将这一领域的学问扩大到其他领域;(二)有的人适合于观察事物的相似之点,有的则适合于观察不同之点;(三)有的人崇古,有的

---

① 培根:《伟大的复兴》,转引自周晓亮主编:《西方哲学史》(第 4 卷),南京:江苏人民出版社,2004 年,第 245 页。
② 罗素:《西方哲学史》(下卷),何兆武、李约瑟译,北京:商务印书馆,1996 年,第 65 页。
③ 培根:《新工具》,许宝骙译,北京:商务印书馆,1997 年,第 19 页。
④ 同上书,第 20 页。

爱新；（四）有的人只对事物的个别形式感兴趣，有的对事物的一般组合和结构感兴趣。这类假象还有很多其他形式，造成假象的原因都是因人而异的。每个人只有根据自己的特点对症下药，才能纠正错误。

"市场的假象"（Idols of the Market-place）是人们在交往的过程中由于语言文字的使用引起的。"市场"是人们交往的场所，必须通过语言来达到交流的目的，但这种语言的使用也会给准确的交流造成了一定的混乱。这类假象主要可分为两种：第一种表现为只有名称而没有实存；第二种在于语义的混乱。第一种情况比较容易对付，只要将这个不存在的东西揭露出来，这个名称就不容易存在。但语义的混乱很难廓清，就算经常使用"定义"的方法也不容易做到。培根对语言的分析很有前瞻性，在20世纪具有重大影响的分析哲学就是顺着这个方向发展出来的。

"剧场的假象"（Idols of the Theatre）不是人性固有的，"而是被虚构的理论和败坏的论证规律灌输进来并得到巩固的"。各种理论体系无非是一些"舞台剧"，表现的是理论家根据自己的"假布景"创造的"世界"。理论的剧场"正如在诗歌的剧场中一样，为舞台而创造的情节总比真实的历史中的事件更为前后一致，更为雅致，更合乎人们的愿望"。虽说理论体系的完善是件好事，但实际上体系越完美虚构性就越强，距离客观现实就越远。这些体系主要有三种：只重形式推演的诡辩哲学（理性主义哲学），其中亚里士多德是这类假象的典型代表；只以少数试验为根据的经验哲学，如炼金术等；与神学和迷信相联系的迷信哲学，如毕达哥拉斯、柏拉图等的哲学。

在培根看来，前三种假象是人性本身所固有的，而最后一种假象是外在获得的。人们如果想更加客观地认识世界，就应该经常地运用培根的假象理论来批评自己的认识活动。虽说我们不可能通过这种批评摆脱所有的错误，但我们可以更加接近真理。培根的假象说对近代以来的西方认识论产生了深远的影响。

The New Organon

The human understanding, from its peculiar nature, easily supposes a greater degree of order and equality in things than it really finds; and although many things in nature be sui generis① and most irregular, will yet invent parallels and conjugates and relatives, where no such thing is. Hence the fiction, that all celestial bodies move in perfect circles, thus rejecting entirely spiral and serpentine lines (except as explanatory terms). Hence also the element of fire② is introduced with its peculiar orbit, to keep square with those other three which are objects of our senses. The relative rarity of the elements (as they are called) is arbitrarily made to vary in tenfold progression, with many other dreams of the like nature. Nor is this folly confined to theories, but it is to be met with even in simple notions.

The human understanding, when any proposition has been once laid down (either from general admission and belief, or from the pleasure it affords), forces everything else to add fresh support and confirmation; and although most cogent and abundant instances may exist to the contrary, yet either does not observe or despises them, or gets rid of and rejects them by some distinction, with violent and injurious prejudice, rather than sacrifice the authority of its first conclusions. It was well answered by him who was shown in a temple the votive tablets suspended by such as had escaped the peril of shipwreck, and was pressed as to whether he would then recognize the power of the gods, by an inquiry. But where are the portraits of those who have perished in spite of their vows? All superstition is much the same, whether it be that of astrology, dreams, omens, retributive judgment, or the like, in all of which the deluded believers observe events which are fulfilled, but neglect and pass over their failure, though it be much more common. But this evil insinuates itself still more craftily in philosophy and the sciences, in which a settled maxim vitiates and governs every other circumstance, though the latter be much more worthy of confidence. Besides, even in the absence of that eagerness and want of thought (which we have mentioned), it is the peculiar and perpetual error of the human understanding to be more moved and excited by affirmatives than negatives, whereas it ought duly and regularly to be impartial; nay, in establishing any true axiom the negative instance is the most

---

① sui generis,拉丁语,意思为独特的、特有的。
② the element of fire,古代的西方人相信四大元素构成了这个世界,自下而上分别为土、水、空气、火,四者的密度逐层等差下降,比例为 10 比 1。他们在土、水和空气之外想象出了一层火。

powerful.

The human understanding is most excited by that which strikes and enters the mind at once and suddenly, and by which the imagination is immediately filled and inflated. It then begins almost imperceptibly to conceive and suppose that everything is similar to the few objects which have taken possession of the mind, whilst it is very slow and unfit for the transition to the remote and heterogeneous instances by which axioms are tried as by fire, unless the office be imposed upon it by severe regulations and a powerful authority.

The human understanding is active and cannot halt or rest, but even, though without effect, still presses forward. Thus we cannot conceive of any end or external boundary of the world, and it seems necessarily to occur to us that there must be something beyond. Nor can we imagine how eternity has flowed on down to the present day, since the usually received distinction of an infinity, a parte ante and a parte post cannot hold good; for it would thence follow that one infinity is greater than another, and also that infinity is wasting away and tending to an end. There is the same difficulty in considering the infinite divisibility of lines arising from the weakness of our minds, which weakness interferes to still greater disadvantage with the discovery of causes; for although the greatest generalities in nature must be positive, just as they are found, and in fact not causable, yet the human understanding, incapable of resting, seeks for something more intelligible. Thus, however, whilst aiming at further progress, it falls back to what is actually less advanced, namely, final causes; for they are clearly more allied to man's own nature, than the system of the universe, and from this source they have wonderfully corrupted philosophy. But he would be an unskilful and shallow philosopher who should seek for causes in the greatest generalities, and not be anxious to discover them in subordinate objects.

The human understanding resembles not a dry light[①], but admits a tincture of the will and passions, which generate their own system accordingly; for man always believes more readily that which he prefers. He, therefore, rejects difficulties for want of patience in investigation; sobriety,

---

① dry light, 古希腊哲学家赫拉克利特有一句名言:"最聪明的心乃是一种干燥的光。"在他看来潮湿的东西是混乱而松散的,干燥的却相反,代表着聪明。

because it limits his hope; the depths of nature, from superstition; the light of experiment, from arrogance and pride, lest his mind should appear to be occupied with common and varying objects; paradoxes, from a fear of the opinion of the vulgar; in short, his feelings imbue and corrupt his understanding in innumerable and sometimes imperceptible ways.

But by far the greatest impediment and aberration of the human understanding proceeds from the dullness, incompetency, and errors of the senses; since whatever strikes the senses preponderates over everything, however superior, which does not immediately strike them. Hence contemplation mostly ceases with sight, and a very scanty, or perhaps no regard is paid to invisible objects. The entire operation, therefore, of spirits enclosed in tangible bodies is concealed, and escapes us. All that more delicate change of formation in the parts of coarser substances (vulgarly called alteration, but in fact a change of position in the smallest particles) is equally unknown; and yet, unless the two matters we have mentioned be explored and brought to light, no great effect can be produced in nature. Again, the very nature of common air, and all bodies of less density (of which there are many) is almost unknown; for the senses are weak and erring, nor can instruments be of great use in extending their sphere or acuteness. All the better interpretations of nature are worked out by instances, and fit and apt experiments, where the senses only judge of the experiment, the experiment of nature and the thing itself.

The human understanding is, by its own nature, prone to abstraction, and supposes that which is fluctuating to be fixed. But it is better to dissect than abstract nature; such was the method employed by the school of Democritus, which made greater progress in penetrating nature than the rest. It is best to consider matter, its conformation, and the changes of that conformation, its own action, and the law of this action or motion; for forms are a mere fiction of the human mind, unless you will call the laws of action by that name.

Such are the idols of the tribe, which arise either from the uniformity of the constitution of man's spirit, or its prejudices, or its limited faculties or restless agitation, or from the interference of the passions, or the incompetency of the senses, or the mode of their impressions.

The idols of the den derive their origin from the peculiar nature of each individual's mind and body, and also from education, habit, and accident; and although they be various and manifold, yet we will treat of some that require the greatest caution, and exert the greatest power in polluting the understanding.

Some men become attached to particular sciences and contemplations, either from supposing themselves the authors and inventors of them, or from having bestowed the greatest pains upon such subjects, and thus become most habituated to them. If men of this description apply themselves to philosophy and contemplations of a universal nature, they wrest and corrupt them by their preconceived fancies, of which Aristotle affords us a signal instance, who made his natural philosophy completely subservient to his logic, and thus rendered it little more than useless and disputatious. The chemists, again, have formed a fanciful philosophy with the most confined views, from a few experiments of the furnace. Gilbert[①], too, having employed himself most assiduously in the consideration of the magnet, immediately established a system of philosophy to coincide with his favorite pursuit.

The greatest and, perhaps, most radical distinction between different men's dispositions for philosophy and the sciences is this, that some are more vigorous and active in observing the differences of things, others in observing their resemblances; for a steady and acute disposition can fix its thoughts, and dwell upon and adhere to a point, through all the refinements of differences, but those that are sublime and discursive recognize and compare even the most delicate and general resemblances; each of them readily falls into excess, by catching either at nice distinctions or shadows of resemblance.

Some dispositions evince an unbounded admiration of antiquity, others eagerly embrace novelty, and but few can preserve the just medium, so as neither to tear up what the ancients have correctly laid down, nor to despise the just innovations of the moderns. But this is very prejudicial to the sciences and philosophy, and instead of a correct judgment we have but the factions of the ancients and moderns. Truth is not to be sought in the good fortune of any

---

① Gilbert,全名为 William Gilbert of Colchester,是英国伊丽莎白女王和詹姆士一世的御医,著有《磁论》(*De Magnete*)。

particular conjuncture of time, which is uncertain, but in the light of nature and experience, which is eternal. Such factions, therefore, are to be abjured, and the understanding must not allow them to hurry it on to assent.

The contemplation of nature and of bodies in their individual form distracts and weakens the understanding; but the contemplation of nature and of bodies in their general composition and formation stupefies and relaxes it. We have a good instance of this in the school of Leucippus[①] and Democritus compared with others, for they applied themselves so much to particulars as almost to neglect the general strutcture of things, whilst the others were so astounded whilst gazing on the structure that they did not penetrate the simplicity of nature. These two species of contemplation must, therefore, be interchanged, and each employed in its turn, in order to render the understanding at once penetrating and capacious, and to avoid the inconveniences we have mentioned, and the idols that result from them.

Let such, therefore, be our precautions in contemplation, that we may ward off and expel the idols of the den, which mostly owe their birth either to some predominant pursuit, or, secondly, to an excess in synthesis and analysis, or, thirdly, to a party zeal in favor of certain ages, or, fourthly, to the extent or narrowness of the subject. In general, he who contemplates nature should suspect whatever particularly takes and fixes his understanding, and should use so much the more caution to preserve it equable and unprejudiced.

The idols of the markert are the most troublesome of all, those namely which have entwined themselves round the understanding from the associations of words and names. For men imagine that their reason governs words, whilst, in fact, words react upon the understanding; and this has rendered philosophy and the sciences sophistical and inactive. Words are generally formed in a popular sense, and define things by those broad lines which are most obvious to the vulgar mind; but when a more acute understanding, or more diligent observation is anxious to vary those lines, and to adapt them more accurately to nature, words oppose it. Hence the great and solemn disputes of learned men often terminate in controversies about

---

① Leucippus,留基伯(约前500—前440),古希腊哲学家,原子论的支持者之一。

words and names, in regard to which it would be better (imitating the caution of mathematicians) to proceed more advisedly in the first instance, and to bring such disputes to a regular issue by definitions. Such definitions, however, cannot remedy the evil in natural and material objects, because they consist themselves of words, and these words produce others; so that we must necessarily have recourse to particular instances, and their regular series and arrangement, as we shall mention when we come to the mode and scheme of determining notions and axioms.

The idols imposed upon the understanding by words are of two kinds. They are either the names of things which have no existence (for as some objects are from inattention left without a name, so names are formed by fanciful imaginations which are without an object), or they are the names of actual objects, but confused, badly defined, and hastily and irregularly abstracted from things. Fortune, the primum mobile, the planetary orbits, the element of fire, and the like fictions, which owe their birth to futile and false theories, are instances of the first kind. And this species of idols is removed with greater facility, because it can be exterminated by the constant refutation or the desuetude of the theories themselves. The others, which are created by vicious and unskilful abstraction, are intricate and deeply rooted. Take some word for instance, as moist, and let us examine how far the different significations of this word are consistent. It will be found that the word moist is nothing but a confused sign of different actions admitted of no settled and defined uniformity. For it means that which easily diffuses itself over another body; that which is indeterminable and cannot be brought to a consistency; that which yields easily in every direction; that which is easily divided and dispersed; that which is easily united and collected; that which easily flows and is put in motion; that which easily adheres to, and wets another body; that which is easily reduced to a liquid state though previously solid. When, therefore, you come to predicate or impose this name, in one sense flame is moist, in another air is not moist, in another fine powder is moist, in another glass is moist; so that it is quite clear that this notion is hastily abstracted from water only, and common ordinary liquors, without any due verification of it.

There are however, different degrees of distortion and mistake in words.

One of the least faulty classes is that of the names of substances, particularly of the less abstract and more defined species (those then of chalk and mud are good, of earth bad); words signifying actions are more faulty, as to generate, to corrupt, to change; but the most faulty are those denoting qualities (except the immediate objects of sense), as heavy, light, rare, dense. Yet in all of these there must be some notions a little better than others, in proportion as a greater or less number of things come before the senses.

The idols of the theatre are not innate, nor do they introduce themselves secretly into the understanding, but they are manifestly instilled and cherished by the fictions of theories and depraved rules of demonstration. To attempt, however, or undertake their confutation would not be consistent with our declarations. For since we neither agree in our principles nor our demonstrations, all argument is out of the question. And it is fortunate that the ancients are left in possession of their honors. We detract nothing from them, seeing our whole doctrine relates only to the path to be pursued. The lame (as they say) in the path outstrip the swift who wander from it, and it is clear that the very skill and swiftness of him who runs not in the right direction must increase his aberration.

Our method of discovering the sciences is such as to leave little to the acuteness and strength of wit, and indeed rather to level wit and intellect. For as in the drawing of a straight line, or accurate circle by the hand, much depends on its steadiness and practice, but if a ruler or compass be employed there is little occasion for either; so it is with our method. Although, however, we enter into no individual confutations, yet a little must be said, first, of the sects and general divisions of these species of theories; secondly, something further to show that there are external signs of their weakness; and, lastly, we must consider the causes of so great a misfortune, and so long and general an unanimity in error, that we may thus render the access to truth less difficult, and that the human understanding may the more readily be purified, and brought to dismiss its idols.

The idols of the theatre, or of theories, are numerous, and may, and perhaps will, be still more so. For unless men's minds had been now occupied for many ages in religious and theological considerations, and civil governments (especially monarchies) had been averse to novelties of that nature even in theory (so that men must apply to them with some risk an injury to their own fortunes, and not only without reward, but subject to contumely and envy), there is no doubt that many other sects of philosophers and theorists would have been introduced, like those which formerly flourished in such diversified abundance amongst the Greeks. For as many imaginary theories of the heavens can be deduced from the phenomena of the sky, so it is even more easy to found many dogmas upon the phenomena of philosophy; and the plot of this our theatre resembles those of the poetical, where the plots which are invented for the stage are more consistent, elegant, and pleasurable than those taken from real history.

In general, men take for the groundwork of their philosophy either too much from a few topics, or too little from many; in either case their philosophy is founded on too narrow a basis of experiment and natural history, and decides on too scanty grounds. For the theoretic philosopher seizes various common circumstances by experiment, without reducing them to certainty or examining and frequently considering them, and relies for the rest upon meditation and the activity of his wit.

There are other philosophers who have diligently and accurately attended to a few experiments, and have thence presumed to deduce and invent systems of philosophy, forming everything to conformity with them.

A third set, from their faith and religious veneration, introduce theology and traditions; the absurdity of some among them having proceeded so far as to seek and derive the sciences from spirits and genii. There are, therefore, three sources of error and three species of false philosophy; the sophistic, empiric, and superstitious.

Aristotle affords the most eminent instance of the first; for he corrupted natural philosophy by logic. Thus he formed the world of categories, assigned to the human soul, the noblest of substances, a genus determined by words of secondary operation, treated of density and rarity (by which bodies occupy a greater or lesser space), by the frigid distinctions of action and power, asserted that there was a peculiar and proper motion in all bodies, and that if they shared in any other motion, it was owing to an external moving cause, and imposed innumerable arbitrary distinctions upon the nature of things; being everywhere more anxious as to definitions in teaching and the accuracy of the wording of his propositions, than the internal truth of things. And this is best shown by a comparison or of his philosophy with the others of greatest repute among the Greeks. For the simiar parts of Anaxagoras①, the atoms of Leucippus and Democritus, the heaven and earth of Parmenides②, the discord and concord of Empedocles③, the resolution of bodies into the common nature of fire, and their condensation according to Heraclitus, exhibit some sprinkling of natural philosophy, the nature of things, and experiment; whilst Aristotle's physics are mere logical terms, and he remodelled the same subject in his metaphysics under a more imposing title, and more as a realist than a nominalist. Nor is much stress to be laid on his frequent recourse to experiment in his books on animals, his problems, and other treatises; for he had already decided, without having properly consulted experience as the basis of his decisions and axioms, and after having so decided, he drags experiment along as a captive constrained to accommodate herself to his decisions; so that he is even more to be blamed than his modern followers (of the scholastic school) who have deserted her altogether.

The empiric school produces dogmas of a more deformed and monstrous nature than the sophistic or theoretic school; not being founded in the light of common notions (which however poor and superstitious, is yet in a manner universal and of a general tendency), but in the confined obscurity of a few experiments. Hence this species of philosophy appears probable, and almost certain to those who are daily practised in such experiments, and have thus corrupted their imagination, but incredible and futile to others. We have a strong instance of this in the alchemists and their dogmas; it would be difficult to find another in this age, unless perhaps in the philosophy of Gilbert. We could not, however, neglect to caution others against this school, because we already foresee and argue, that if men be hereafter induced by our exhortations to apply seriously to experiments (bidding farewell to the sophistic doctrines), there will then be imminent danger frow empirics; owing to the premature and forward haste of the understanding, and its jumping or flying to generalities

---

① Anaxagoras,阿那克萨哥拉(前500—前428),古希腊哲学家。
② Parmenides,巴门尼德斯(前515—前5世纪中叶后),古希腊哲学家。
③ Empedocles,恩培多克勒(约前490—前430),古希腊哲学家,曾提出宇宙是由水、火、气、土"四原质"构成的。

and the principles of things. We ought, therefore, already to meet the evil.

The corruption of philosophy by the mixing of it up with superstition and theology, is of a much wider extent, and is most injurious to it both as a whole and in parts. For the human understanding is no less exposed to the impressions of fancy than to those of vulgar notions. The disputatious and sophistic school entraps the understanding, whilst the fanciful, bombastic, and, as it were, poetical school, rather flatters it. There is a clear example of this among the Greeks, especially in Pythagoras①, where, however, the superstition is coarse and overcharged, but it is more dangerous and refined in Plato and his school. This evil is found also in some branches of other systems of philosophy, where it introduces abstracted forms, final and first causes, omitting frequently the intermediate and the like. Against it we must use the greatest caution; for the apotheosis of error is the greatest evil of all, and when folly is worshipped, it is, as it were, a plague spot upon the understanding. Yet some of the moderns have indulged this folly with such consummate inconsiderateness, that they have endeavored to build a system of natural philosophy on the first chapter of Genesis, the book of Job, and other parts of Scripture; seeking thus the dead amongst the living. And this folly is the more to be prevented and restrained, because not only fantastical philosophy, but heretical religion spring from the absurd mixture of matters divine and human. It is therefore most wise soberly to render unto faith the things that are faith's.

 选文出处

Francis Bacon. *The Novum Organum*. in *Great Books of the Western World · Francis Bacon*, Chicago: Encyclopaedia Britannica, Inc., 1980, pp. 110—114.

---

① Pythagoras,毕达哥拉斯(约前580—约前500),古希腊著名学者。

思考题

1. 简单地描述一下四种假象的特点。
2. 你有没有自己的特殊的"洞穴假象"? 如果有,请尝试谈谈其特征。

阅读

参考书目

1. 余丽嫦:《培根及其哲学》,北京:人民出版社,1987年。
2. 陈修斋:《欧洲哲学史上的经验主义和理性主义》,北京:人民出版社,2007年。

霍布斯

托马斯·霍布斯(Thomas Hobbes，1588—1679)，生于一个英国牧师家庭。他自小非常聪明，14 岁时就已经熟练地掌握了古希腊语和拉丁语，成功地将欧里庇得斯的悲剧《美狄亚》从希腊文译成拉丁文。要知道，在这两门古典语言之间进行翻译绝非易事，可这位思想家在短时间内就做到了。霍布斯在 14 岁那年到牛津大学学习，并于 5 年后获得了学士学位。后来他当了德文郡伯爵威廉·卡文迪许(William Cavendish)儿子的家庭教师，并得到了这位伯爵的赏识，进而认识了许多重要人物，特别是学界的知名人士。他还当过培根的秘书，被培根看作是最能理解他的思想的人。他的主要著作包括《人性》(*Human Nature*)、《论国家》(*De Corpore Politico*)、《论公民》(*De Cive*)、《论物体》(*De Corpore*)、《论人》(*De Homine*)、《利维坦》(*Leviathan*)等。霍布斯既具有培根、休谟等英国经验主义者的特点，即注重从实际出发，同时又具有欧洲大陆的理性主义者的优点，非常欣赏数学的方法。从这个角度来说，霍布斯是很了不起的，避免了这两个流派的不少缺点。

《利维坦》是一部非常优秀的政治哲学著作。霍布斯的政治思想建立于他对人性的研究之上。在他看来，人的本性是自私自利的，如果不加以控制，就会陷入你争我夺的可怕的"自然状态"，而这样一来必然会给社会带来灾难。为了避免这种麻烦，人们只能依靠一个像"利维坦"一样强有力的政府来维持秩序。"利维坦"是《圣经》里描写的海中巨兽，力量无比，极度可怕，没有动物敢与之较量。利维坦式的政府,拥有绝对的权力,没有人可以与之对抗,社会因此获得安宁。霍布斯还认为,君主制是各种政权中最好的体制,因为君主把大权握在一个人的手中,能够高效地决策和指挥,可以避免内耗与混乱。

　　本书的第一个选段是《利维坦》的第 13 章,探讨了什么是"人的自然状态"。霍布斯的"自然状态"指的是没有公共权力来维持秩序的混乱状态,他说:"这就显而易见,在没有一个共同权力使大家慑服的时候,人们便处在所谓的战争状态之下。这种战争是每一个人对每一个人的战争。"在霍布斯看来,这种状态是人在体力和脑力方面没有多少差距所造成的。霍布斯认为,在体力方面,最弱小的人通过运用密谋或者与其他处在同一种危险下的人联合起来,就具有足够的力量来杀死最强大的人。在智力方面差距也不是太大,而且人们一般从近处看自己的智慧,从远处看他人的智慧,往往自恃才华出众,而不是感到不如别人。从某个角度看,这倒是平等的表现,因为,"通常来说,分配平均的最大证据莫过于人人都满足于自己的一份"。但霍布斯认为这种平等不是好事,能力的平等就会产生希望的平等。如果两个或者更多的人想得到同样的东西,就会彼此为敌,陷入混乱的自然状态之中。人类不但在天赋方面如此平等,而且还热衷于竞争、猜疑和荣誉的获得,所以难以避免相互为敌的战争状态。当然这种状态并没有真的存在过,毕竟一般的情况下都有公共权力约束着人们,所以这只是一种假设的状态。不过应该意识到,这种状态还是局部地存在着,在一些原始部落之中,由于缺乏公共的权力,还是处在这种自然状态之中。例如,美洲许多地方的原始部落只依靠小家族的管理,而小家族中的协调又完全取决于自然欲望,除此之外完全没有政府;他们今天还生活于上文所说的那种野蛮、残忍的状态中。在文明社会中,虽然每个国家的内部往往有公共权力来保证和平,但由于国家与国家之间一直没有这样的权力,"国王和最高主权者由于具有独立的地位,始终是互相猜疑的,保持着格斗的状态和姿势"。所以人类历史上国与国之间的战争从来就没有停止过。而且,在战争中,没有什么是不正义的,暴力和欺骗是战争中的两种主要美德。如果换个角度看,很多爱国英雄可能都具有这两个特点。

　　由于"自然状态"会给人们的生活带来如此多的不幸,所以就得摆脱这种状态。第 2 篇选读是《利维坦》的第 17 章,探讨的就是如何通过建立国家来摆脱"自然状态"的问题。

　　天生爱好自由和统治他人的人类,为了摆脱可怕的"自然状态",就得联合起来,组成国家。霍布斯认为国家应当有一定的规模,他说:"少数人联合也不能使人们得到安全保障;因为在数量少的人群中,这边或者那边人数稍微有所增加就可以使优势扩大到足以决定胜负的程度;因而鼓励人们进行侵略。"但是光有庞大的群体还不够,"就算有一个这么大的群体;如果大家的行动都以各人的判断和各人的欲望作指导,那就不能期待这种群体能对外抵御共同的敌人和对内制止人们之间的伤害"。这就必然需要一个有威力的机构来管理。

为什么只有人类有这个问题,而动物却没有呢?蜜蜂、蚂蚁等也被亚里士多德列为政治动物,同样在集体中生存,却不会受到这个困扰。霍布斯是这样解释这一现象的:因为动物没有荣誉和地位的概念;没有共同利益和个体利益的区分;不会运用理智来攻击公共事务中的缺点;不会花言巧语;不会区分无形的侵害和有形的损失。也就是说,动物的协同是出于自然,所以,不需要协约来维持秩序。而人类则相反,因此需要政府的干涉。他通过人和动物的对比,揭示出了对于人类而言,一个强有力的政府的必要性。

如果要抵御外来侵略,制止内部的相互残害,只有一个办法,那就是将大家的权力集中起来交给一个人或者集体来管理公共事务,强有力的国家因此而建立了起来。在这样的国家中,人们把自己的权力交出来,并相互订契约,"我承认这个人或者集体,并放弃管理自己的权利,把它授予这个人或者集体,其条件是你也把自己的权利拿出来授予他,并以同样方式承认他的一切行为"。大家一旦把权利交了出来,统治者就有着绝对的权力按"契约"统治国家,每个个体都应绝对地服从。这样的国家就像那头怪兽利维坦一样可怕,尽管有人可能不喜欢,但与无政府的"自然状态"相比,利还是远远大于弊。所以霍布斯愿意拥抱这样的政府,特别是具有绝对权力的君主制。但是如果过于强调政权的集中,也会产生一些弊端。正如美国学者米斯纳所说:"在20世纪,我们已经感受到了像希特勒那样的统治者,足以使我们对霍布斯的主张产生疑惑。"[1]

一切社会都面临着无政府和专制的危险。霍布斯经历了各种狂热的战争,所以就特别地强调政权的重要性。比他稍晚的洛克恰恰相反,认为政治学的关键在于如何制约统治者,使权力分开。历史的经验证明,在处理复杂的国际、国内的事物中,任何一种极端都会带来一定的负面影响。

---

[1] 马歇尔·米斯纳:《霍布斯》,于涛译,北京:中华书局,2002年,第68页。

Leviathan

Of the Naturall Condition of Mankind, as Concerning Their Felicity, and Misery

Nature hath made men so equall, in the faculties of body, and mind; as that though there bee① found one man sometimes manifestly stronger in body, or of quicker mind than another; yet when all is reckoned together, the difference between man, and man, is not so considerable, as that one man can thereupon claim to himselfe any benefit, to which another may not pretend, as well as he. For as to the strength of body, the weakest has strength enough to kill the strongest, either by secret machination, or by confederacy with others, that are in the same danger with himselfe.

And as to the faculties of the mind, (setting aside the arts grounded upon words, and especially that skill of proceeding upon generall, and infallible rules, called Science; which very few have, and but in few things; as being not a native faculty, born with us; nor attained, (as Prudence,) while we look after somewhat els,) I find yet a greater equality amongst men, than that of strength. For Prudence, is but Experience; which equall time, equally bestowes on all men, in those things they equally apply themselves unto. That which may perhaps make such equality incredible, is but a vain conceit of ones owne wisdome, which almost all men think they have in a greater degree, than the Vulgar; that is, than all men but themselves, and a few others, whom by Fame, or for concurring with themselves, they approve. For such is the nature of men, that howsoever they may acknowledge many others to be more witty, or more eloquent, or more learned; Yet they will hardly believe there be many so wise as themselves: For they see their own wit at hand, and

---

① bee 在现代英语中拼作 be,这篇选读中有很多单词的拼写与现代英语有些区别,其中一个最显著的特征是,许多单词后面都加了一个"e",如 againe, griefe 等。

other mens at a distance. But this proveth rather that men are in that point equall, than unequall. For there is not ordinarily a greater signe of the equall distribution of any thing, than that every man is contented with his share.

From this equality of ability, ariseth equality of hope in the attaining of our Ends. And therefore if any two men desire the same thing, which neverthelesse they cannot both enjoy, they become enemies; and in the way to their End, (which is principally their owne conservation, and sometimes their delectation only,) endeavour to destroy, or subdue one an other. And from hence it comes to passe, that where an Invader hath no more to feare, than an other mans single power; if one plant, sow, build, or possesse a convenient Seat①, others may probably be expected to come prepared with forces united, to dispossesse, and deprive him, not only of the fruit of his labour, but also of his life, or liberty. And the Invader again is in the like danger of another.

And from this diffidence of one another, there is no way for any man to secure himselfe, so reasonable, as Anticipation②; that is, by force, or wiles, to master the persons of all men he can, so long, till he see no other power great enough to endanger him: And this is no more than his own conservation requireth, and is generally allowed. Also because there be some, that taking pleasure in contemplating their own power in the acts of conquest, which they pursue farther than their security requires; if others, that otherwise would be glad to be at ease within modest bounds, should not by invasion increase their power, they would not be able, long time, by standing only on their defence, to subsist. And by consequence, such augmentation of dominion over men, being necessary to a mans conservation, it ought to be allowed him.

Againe, men have no pleasure, (but on the contrary a great deale of griefe) in keeping company, where there is no power able to over-awe them all. For every man looketh that his companion should value him, at the same rate he sets upon himselfe: And upon all signes of contempt, or undervaluing, naturally endeavours, as far as he dares (which amongst them that have no common power to keep them in quiet, is far enough to make them destroy each other,) to extort a greater value from his contemners, by dommage; and from

---

① seat,这里不是指座位,而是位置、地点的意思。
② Anticipation,指先发制人。

others, by the example.

So that in the nature of man, we find three principall causes of quarrell. First, Competition; Secondly, Diffidence; Thirdly, Glory.

The first, maketh men invade for Gain; the second, for Safety; and the third, for Reputation. The first use Violence, to make themselves Masters of other mens persons, wives, children, and cattell; the second, to defend them; the third, for trifles, as a word, a smile, a different opinion, and any other signe of undervalue, either direct in their Persons, or by reflexion in their Kindred, their Friends, their Nation, their Profession, or their Name.

Hereby it is manifest, that during the time men live without a common Power to keep them all in awe, they are in that condition which is called Warre; and such a warre, as is of every man, against every man. For WARRE, consisteth not in Battell① onely, or the act of fighting; but in a tract of time, wherein the Will to contend by Battell is suffciently known: and therefore the notion of *Time*, is to be considered in the nature of Warre; as it is in the nature of Weather. For as the nature of Foule weather, lyeth not in a showre or two of rain; but in an inclination thereto of many dayes together: So the nature of War, consisteth not in actuall fighting; but in the known disposition thereto, during all the time there is no assurance to the contrary. All other time is PEACE.

Whatsoever therefore is consequent to a time of Warre, where every man is Enemy to every man; the same is consequent to the time, wherein men live without other security, than what their own strength, and their own invention shall furnish them withall. In such condition, there is no place for Industry; because the fruit thereof is uncertain: and consequently no Culture of the Earth; no Navigation, nor use of the commodities that may be imported by Sea; no commodious Building; no Instruments of moving, and removing such things as require much force; no Knowledge of the face of the Earth; no account of Time; no Arts; no Letters; no Society; and which is worst of all, continuall feare, and danger of violent death; And the life of man, solitary, poore, nasty, brutish, and short.

It may seem strange to some man, that has not well weighed these

---

① Battell,即现代英语中的 battle。

things; that Nature should thus dissociate, and render men apt to invade, and destroy one another: and he may therefore, not trusting to this Inference, made from the Passions, desire perhaps to have the same confirmed by Experience. Let him therefore consider with himselfe, when taking a journey, he armes himselfe, and seeks to go well accompanied; when going to sleep, he locks his dores; when even in his house he locks his chests; and this when he knowes there bee Lawes, and publike Officers, armed, to revenge all injuries shall bee done him; what opinion he has of his fellow subjects, when he rides armed; of his fellow Citizens, when he locks his dores; and of his children, and servants, when he locks his chests. Does he not there as much accuse mankind by his actions, as I do by my words? But neither of us accuse mans nature in it. The Desires, and other Passions of man, are in themselves no Sin. No more are the Actions, that proceed from those Passions, till they know a Law that forbids them: which till Lawes be made they cannot know: nor can any Law be made, till they have agreed upon the Person that shall make it.

It may peradventure be thought, there was never such a time, nor condition of warre as this; and I believe it was never generally so, over all the world: but there are many places, where they live so now. For the savage people in many places of *America*, except the government of small Families, the concord whereof dependeth on naturall lust, have no government at all; and live at this day in that brutish manner, as I said before. Howsoever, it may be perceived what manner of life there would be, where there were no common Power to feare; by the manner of life, which men that have formerly lived under a peacefull government, use to degenerate into, in a civill Warre.

But though there had never been any time, wherein particular men were in a condition of warre one against another; yet in all times, Kings, and Persons of Soveraigne authority, because of their Independency, are in continuall jealousies, and in the state and posture of Gladiators; having their weapons pointing, and their eyes fixed on one another; that is, their Forts, Garrisons, and Guns upon the Frontiers of their Kingdomes; and continuall Spyes upon their neighbours; which is a posture of War. But because they uphold thereby, the Industry of their Subjects; there does not follow from it, that misery, which accompanies the Liberty of particular men.

To this warre of every man against every man, this also is consequent; that nothing can be Unjust. The notions of Right and Wrong, Justice and Injustice have there no place. Where there is no common Power, there is no Law: where no Law, no Injustice. Force, and Fraud, are in warre the two Cardinall vertues. Justice, and Injustice are none of the Faculties neither of the Body, nor Mind. If they were, they might be in a man that were alone in the world, as well as his Senses, and Passions. They are Qualities, that relate to men in Society, not in Solitude. It is consequent also to the same condition, that there be no Propriety, no Dominion, no *Mine* and *Thine* distinct; but onely that to be every mans, that he can get; and for so long, as he can keep it. And thus much for the ill condition, which man by meer Nature is actually placed in; though with a possibility to come out of it, consisting partly in the Passions, partly in his Reason.

The Passions that encline men to Peace, are Feare of Death; Desire of such things as are necessary to commodious living; and a Hope by their Industry to obtain them. And Reason suggesteth convenient Articles of Peace, upon which men may be drawn to agreement. These Articles, are they, which otherwise are called the Lawes of Nature: whereof I shall speak more particularly, in the two following Chapters.

Of the Causes, Generation, and Definition of a COMMON-WEALTH

The finall Cause, End, or Designe of men, (who naturally love Liberty, and Dominion over others,) in the introduction of that restraint upon themseives, (in which wee see them live in Common-wealths①,) is the foresight of their own preservation, and of a more contented life thereby; that is to say, of getting themselves out from that miserable condition of Warre, which is necessarily consequent (as hath been shewn) to the naturall Passions of men, when there is no visible Power to keep them in awe, and tye them by feare of punishment to the performance of their Covenants, and observation of those Lawes of Nature set down in the fourteenth and fifteenth Chapters.

---

① Common-wealth,这里指独立的政治实体、国家。

For the Lawes of Nature (as *Justice*, *Equity*, *Modesty*, *Mercy*, and (in summe) *doing to others, as wee would be done to*,①) of themselves, without the terrour of some Power, to cause them to be observed, are contrary to our naturall Passions, that carry us to Partiality, Pride, Revenge, and the like. And Covenants, without the Sword, are but Words, and of no strength to secure a man at all. Therefore notwithstanding the Lawes of Nature, (which every one hath then kept, when he has the will to keep them, when he can do it safely,) if there be no Power erected, or not great enough for our security; every man will, and may lawfully rely on his own strength and art, for caution against all other men. And in all places, where men have lived by small Families, to robbe and spoyle one another, has been a Trade, and so farre from being reputed against the Law of Nature, that the greater spoyles they gained, the greater was their honour; and men observed no other Lawes therein, but the Lawes of Honour; that is, to abstain from cruelty, leaving to men their lives, and instruments of husbandry. And as small Familyes did then; so now do Cities and Kingdomes which are but greater Families (for their own security) enlarge their Dominions, upon all pretences of danger, and fear of Invasion, or assistance that may be given to Invaders, endeavour as much as they can, to subdue, or weaken their neighbours, by open force, and secret arts, for want of other Caution, justly; and are remembred for it in after ages with honour.

Nor is it the joyning together of a small number of men, that gives them this security; because in small numbers, small additions on the one side or the other, make the advantage of strength so great, as is sufficient to carry the Victory; and therefore gives encouragement to an Invasion. The Multitude sufficient to confide in for our Security, is not determined by any certain number, but by comparison with the Enemy we feare; and is then sufficient, when the odds of the Enemy is not of so visible and conspicuous moment, to determine the event of warre, as to move him to attempt.

And be there never so great a Multitude; yet if their actions be directed according to their particular judgements, and particular appetites, they can

---

① 这句话可翻译为"己所欲，施于人"，与孔子的"己所不欲，勿施于人"相反。但孔子也有类似的观点，他曾说："己欲立而立人，己欲达而达人。"

expect thereby no defence, nor protection, neither against a Common enemy, nor against the injuries of one another. For being distracted in opinions concerning the best use and application of their strength, they do not help, but hinder one another; and reduce their strength by mutuall opposition to nothing: whereby they are easily, not onely subdued by a very few that agree together; but also when there is no common enemy, they make warre upon each other, for their particular interests. For if we could suppose a great Multitude of men to consent in the observation of Justice, and other Lawes of Nature, without a common Power to keep them all in awe; we might as well suppose all Man-kind to do the same; and then there neither would be, nor need to be any Civill Government, or Common-wealth at all; because there would be Peace without subjection.

Nor is it enough for the security, which men desire should last all the time of their life, that they be governed, and directed by one judgement, for a limited time; as in one Battell, or one Warre. For though they obtain a Victory by their unanimous endeavour against a forraign enemy; yet afterwards, when either they have no common enemy, or he that by one part is held for an enemy, is by another part held for a friend, they must needs by the difference of their interests dissolve, and fall again into a Warre amongst themselves.

It is true, that certain living creatures, as Bees, and Ants, live sociably one with another, (which are therefore by *Aristotle* numbred amongst Politicall creatures;) and yet have no other direction, than their particular judgements and appetites; nor speech, whereby one of them can signifie to another, what he thinks expedient for the common benefit: and therefore some man may perhaps desire to know, why Man-kind cannot do the same. To which I answer,

First, that men are continually in competition for Honour and Dignity, which these creatures are not; and consequently amongst men there ariseth on that ground, Envy and Hatred, and finally Warre; but amongst these not so.

Secondly, that amongst these creatures, the Common good differeth not from the Private; and being by nature enclined to their private, they procure thereby the common benefit. But man, whose Joy consisteth in comparing himselfe with other men, can relish nothing but what is eminent.

Thirdly, that these creatures, having not (as man) the use of reason, do not see, nor think they see any fault, in the administration of their common businesse: whereas amongst men, there are very many, that thinke themselves wiser, and abler to govern the Publique better than the rest; and these strive to reforme and innovate, one this way, another that way; and thereby bring it into Distraction and Civill warre.

Fourthly, that these creatures, though they have some use of voice, in making knowne to one another their desires, and other affections; yet they want that art of words, by which some men can represent to others, that which is Good, in the likenesse of Evill; and Evill, in the likenesse of Good; and augment, or diminish the apparent greatnesse of Good and Evill; discontenting men, and troubling their Peace at their pleasure.

Fiftly, irrationall creatures cannot distinguish betweene *Injury*, and *Dammage*; and therefore as long as they be at ease, they are not offended with their fellowes: whereas Man is then most troublesome, when he is most at ease: for then it is that he loves to shew his Wisdome, and controule the Actions of them that governe the Common-wealth.

Lastly, the agreement of these creatures is Naturall; that of men, is by Covenant only, which is Artificiall: and therefore it is no wonder if there be somwhat else required (besides Covenant) to make their Agreement constant and lasting; which is a Common Power, to keep them in awe, and to direct their actions to the Common Benefit.

The only way to erect such a Common Power, as may be able to defend them from the invasion of Forraigners, and the injuries of one another, and thereby to secure them in such sort, as that by their owne industrie, and by the fruites of the Earth, they may nourish themselves and live contentedly; is, to conferre all their power and strength upon one Man, or upon one Assembly of men, that may reduce all their Wills, by plurality of voices, unto one Will: which is as much as to say, to appoint one Man, or Assembly of men, to beare their Person; and every one to owne, and acknowledge himselfe to be Author of whatsoever he that so beareth their Person, shall Act, or cause to be Acted, in those things which concerne the Common Peace and Safetie; and therein to submit their Wills, every one to his Will, and their Judgements, to his Judgment. This is more than Consent, or Concord; it is a reall Unitie of them all, in one and the same Person, made by Covenant of every man with every man, in such manner, as if every man should say to every man, *I Authorise and give up my Right of Governing my selfe, to this Man, or to this Assembly of men, on this condition, that thou give up thy Right to him, and Authorise all his Actions in like manner.* This done, the Multitude so united in one Person, is called a COMMON-WEALTH, in latine CIVITAS. This is the Generation of that great LEVIATHAN①, or rather (to speake more reverently) of that *Mortall God*, to which wee owe under the *Immortall God*, our peace and defence. For by this Authoritie, given him by every particular man in the Common-Wealth, he hath the use of so much Power and Strength conferred on him, that by terror thereof, he is inabled to forme the wills of them all, to Peace at home, and mutuall ayd against their enemies abroad. And in him consisteth the Essence of the Common-wealth; which (to define it,) is *One Person, of whose Acts a great Multitude, by mutuall Covenants one with another, have made themselves every one the Author, to the end he may use the strength and means of them all, as he shall think expedient, for their Peace and Common Defence.*

And he that carryeth this Person, is called SOVERAIGNE, and said to have *Soveraigne Power*; and every one besides, his SUBJECT.

The attaining to this Soveraigne Power, is by two wayes. One, by Naturall force; as when a man maketh his children, to submit themselves, and their children to his government, as being able to destroy them if they refuse; or by Warre subdueth his enemies to his will, giving them their lives on that condition. The other, is when men agree amongst themselves, to submit to some Man, or Assembly of men, voluntarily, on confidence to be protected by him against all others. This later, may be called a Politicall Common-wealth, or Common-wealth by *Institution*; and the former, a Common-wealth by *Acquisition*. And first, I shall speak of a Common-wealth by Institution.

---

① Leviathan 是《圣经》中描述的力大无比的水中怪物，在中文版本《圣经》中译为"鳄鱼"。霍布斯用这个形象比拟具有巨大威力的国家机器。

选文出处

Thomas Hobbes. *Leviathan*. Beijing：China Social Sciences Publishing House（reprinted from the English Edition by Oxford University Press，1943），1999，pp. 94—98，128—132.

1. 专制和无政府的混乱，哪种状态更为可怕？为什么？
2. 谈一谈权力集中于一个或一群领导的危害和优点。

阅读 参考书目

1. 列奥·施特劳斯：《霍布斯的政治哲学》，申彤译，南京：译林出版社，2004年。
2. Samuel Mintz，*The Hunting of Leviathan*，Cambridge：Cambridge University Press，1969.

笛卡尔[①]

笛卡尔(Rene Descartes，1596—1650)是法国著名哲学家,西方近代理性主义哲学的奠基人,对西方近代思想的形成和发展起到了极为重要的作用。笛卡尔的座右铭是:隐居得越深,生活得越好。或许正是出于这样的一种信念,他曾在法国的普罗旺斯断断续续地隐居了20年,长期苦思冥想。笛卡尔的那个年代充满了发明和创新,新旧思想的交锋特别激烈。1600年布鲁诺由于持有异端邪说而被教会施以火刑;1633年伽利略因证实了哥白尼的假说而遭到审判,背上了坚持异端邪说和不服从教会的罪名。面对这些事件,笛卡尔相当谨慎,不过他的理性主义精神还是引起了教会的警觉,他的书曾被罗马教廷列为禁书。

笛卡尔的主要著作包括《方法谈》(*Discourse on the Method*)、《第一哲学沉思集》(*Meditations on First Philosophy*)、《论世界》(*The World*)、《哲学原理》(*Principles of Philosophy*)、《灵魂的激情》(*Passions of the Soul*)等。他的怀疑论方法,拒绝接受任何教条主义,全面挑战了各种思考习惯和自然而然的看法,把先哲和神学也搁置一边。哲学史专家尚杰认为,笛卡尔的主要贡献在于,他是"理性启蒙道路的开创者",促使了"哲学问题的转变:从古代的本体论过渡到近代

[①] 旧译"笛卡儿",现在多译为"笛卡尔",为便于阅读及保持连贯性,在具体篇章的行文中使用该篇章所引用的译著的译名。

的认识论或知识论"。① 黑格尔曾这样评价:"这个人对他的时代以及对近代的影响,我们决不能以为已经得到了充分的发挥。从古希腊到中世纪的哲学以本体论为核心,研究的中心问题为什么是世界的本原。他是一个彻底从头做起、带头重建哲学的基础的英雄人物,哲学在奔波了一千年之后,现在才回到这个基础上面。"②

笛卡尔在第一个沉思中提出了普遍怀疑的新方法。他认为,如果要建立起可靠的科学,"在我有生之日,有必要对一切来一次彻底的清除,再从根基上重新开始"。就要把不是完全确定无疑的东西和完全荒谬的东西一样彻底否定掉。而且,他不是一项一项地论证以前观点的错误,而是将知识大厦的整个基础拆掉,使所有的旧见解全部倒塌。在他看来,旧见解都来自感官。而感官是不可靠的,不但无法准确掌握不明显的和遥远的东西,甚至连最简单、最明显的东西,"比如说,我在这里,坐在炉火旁边,穿着冬季的晨衣,两只手拿着这张纸,以及诸如此类的事情",也有把握不准的可能性。为什么呢?笛卡尔说:"在夜晚的睡梦中,我多少次以为见到这些熟悉的事情——我在这个地方,穿着衣服,在火炉旁边——虽然我是一丝不挂地躺在我的被窝里!……当我更仔细地思考,就明显地看到从来没有什么相当可靠的迹象能够把清醒和睡梦分别出来。结果使我开始感到大吃一惊,这种感觉只能加强这个念头,我也许正在睡眠之中。"除了这些直接来自感觉的、好像显然正确的东西之外,那些经过多次推敲的观点是否可靠呢?例如说,物体总有广延性、形状、量,二加三等于五,正方形总不会有四条以上的边等,这些是不是不可推翻的真理呢?反思一下历史就会发现,许许多多的科学定论后来都被推翻了,谁能保证这些结论是正确的呢?于是笛卡尔假设有一个狡诈的妖怪,其本领不亚于上帝本身,总是欺骗人们:"我要认为天、空气、地、颜色、形状、声音以及我们所看到的一切外界事物都不过是梦中幻觉,是他设计出来骗取我的判断的。我要把自己看成是本来就没有手,或者眼睛,或者肉,或者血,或者感官,却错误地相信我有这些东西。"到此为止,笛卡尔已经把一切已有知识的根基拆除了,人们因此可以带着怀疑的目光审视万物。这种思想方法对于西方人走出中世纪的教条主义有着极大的意义。当然,怀疑一切的方法也会带来自身的问题,不停地追问下去就会把信仰、人生意义等都否定掉,从而使自己陷入更大的困惑之中。

在第二个沉思中,笛卡尔终于找到了一种无法怀疑的东西。笛卡尔认为,

---

① 尚杰:《大陆理性主义哲学》,周晓亮主编:《西方哲学史》第 4 卷,南京:凤凰出版社,2004 年,第 81 页。

② 黑格尔:《哲学史讲演录》第 4 卷,贺麟、王太庆译,北京:商务印书馆,1996 年,第 63 页。

思想可以怀疑一切外在的对象，也可以怀疑内在的对象，却不可能怀疑自身的存在。否则，怀疑就会失去怀疑的主体，从而导致怀疑本身的不可能。所以笛卡尔肯定地说："如果我曾说服我自己相信什么东西，那么毫无疑问我是存在的。"就是在自我遭到欺骗的时候，也照样意味着一个被欺骗的主体的存在。那么这个自我究竟是什么呢？是一个在思维的东西。什么是在思维的东西呢？就是一个在怀疑、领会、肯定、否定、愿意、不愿意、也在想象和感觉的东西。但这些功能的作用并不是平等的，笛卡尔认为理性高于感官。他举了一个有趣的例子：例如，这是一块刚从蜂房里取出来的蜡。它还没有失去蜜的甜味，还保存着一点香气，因为是从花里采来的。它的颜色、形状、大小明显可见。它是硬的、凉的、形状触摸可辨。如果用指关节敲它一下，它就发出一点声音。但这些通过感官认识到的东西并不是最本质的，因为，一旦拿到火旁边，剩下的味道发散了，香气消失了，它的颜色变了，它的形状和原来不一样了，它的体积增大了。它变成液体了，而且是热的。无法触摸出它的形状了。如果这时敲击它，也发不出声音了。也就是说，现在所感知到的东西已经完全不同了，可我们还是知道这是蜡，关键就在于我们能够运用理性来判断。他说："我现在知道，严格地说，就是物体也不是通过感官或者想象来认识的，而只能依靠理智，而且这种认知不是由于事物被看见了或者摸到了，而只是由于被领会了；考虑到这点，我显然知道，认识我的心灵比任何别的东西更容易更明白。"把一切旧知识通过怀疑加以否定了之后，最后找到了不可否定的东西，那就是作为理性主体的自我。人的理性成了万物的试金石，西方的启蒙大门从此打开了。

笛卡尔是一个二元论者，他把灵魂和肉体看作是完全独立的两种实体，而且灵魂比肉体更容易认识，纵使没有肉体，灵魂也照样存在。这就引起了一些人的非议。英国哲学家霍布斯反驳过他的观点，认为笛卡尔混淆了两个不同的概念。霍布斯指出："说我是在思维的，因而我是一个思维，或者说，我是有理智的，因而我是一个理智，这样的推理是不正确的。"[①]霍布斯认为思维只是"我"的一种功能，不能将两者等同起来。他还说："没有主体[体]，我们就不能领会其任何行为[用]，就像没有一个在思维的东西就不能领会思维，没有一个在知道的东西就不能领会知道，没有一个散步的东西就不能领会散步。"[②]霍布斯认为思维活动必须依附于一个物质主体。从某个角度看，他的观点似乎更为合理。

---

① 霍布斯：《第三组反驳》，笛卡尔：《第一哲学沉思集》，庞景仁译，北京：商务印书馆，1998 年，第 173 页。
② 同上书，第 174 页。

Meditations on First Philosophy

What can be called into doubt

Some years ago I was struck by the large number of falsehoods that I had accepted as true in my childhood, and by the highly doubtful nature of the whole edifice that I had subsequently based on them. I realized that it was necessary, once in the course of my life, to demolish everything completely and start again right from the foundations if I wanted to establish anything at all in the sciences that was stable and likely to last. But the task looked an enormous one, and I began to wait until I should reach a mature enough age to ensure that no subsequent time of life would be more suitable for tackling such inquiries. This led me to put the project off for so long that I would now be to blame if by pondering over it any further I wasted the time still left for carrying it out. So today I have expressly rid my mind of all worries and arranged for myself a clear stretch of free time. I am here quite alone, and at last I will devote myself sincerely and without reservation to the general demolition of my opinions.

But to accomplish this, it will not be necessary for me to show that all my opinions are false, which is something I could perhaps never manage. Reason now leads me to think that I should hold back my assent from opinions which are not completely certain and indubitable just as carefully as I do from those which are patently false. So, for the purpose of rejecting all my opinions, it will be enough if I find in each of them at least some reason for doubt. And to do this I will not need to run through them all individually, which would be an endless task. Once the foundations of a building are undermined, anything built on them collapses of its own accord; so I will go straight for the basic principles on which all my former beliefs rested.

Whatever I have up till now accepted as most true I have acquired either from the senses or through the senses. But from time to time I have found that the senses deceive, and it is prudent never to trust completely those who have deceived us even once.

Yet although the senses occasionally deceive us with respect to objects which are very small or in the distance, there are many other beliefs about which doubt is quite impossible, even though they are derived from the senses—for example, that I am here, sitting by the fire, wearing a winter dressing-gown, holding this piece of paper in my hands, and so on. Again, how could it be denied that these hands or this whole body are mine? Unless perhaps I were to liken myself to madmen, whose brains are so damaged by the persistent vapours of melancholia that they firmly maintain they are kings when they are paupers, or say they are dressed in purple① when they are naked, or that their heads are made of earthenware, or that they are pumpkins, or made of glass. But such people are insane, and I would be thought equally mad if I took anything from them as a model for myself.

A brilliant piece of reasoning! As if I were not a man who sleeps at night, and regularly has all the same experiences while asleep as madmen do when awake—indeed sometimes even more improbable ones. How often, asleep at night, am I convinced of just such familiar events—that I am here in my dressing-gown, sitting by the fire—when in fact I am lying undressed in bed! Yet at the moment my eyes are certainly wide awake when I look at this piece of paper; I shake my head and it is not asleep; as I stretch out and feel my hand I do so deliberately, and I know what I am doing. All this would not happen with such distinctness to someone asleep. Indeed! As if I did not remember other occasions when I have been tricked by exactly similar thoughts while asleep! As I think about this more carefully, I see plainly that there are never any sure signs by means of which being awake can be distinguished from being asleep. The result is that I begin to feel dazed, and this very feeling only reinforces the notion that I may be asleep.

Suppose then that I am dreaming, and that these particulars—that my eyes are open, that I am moving my head and stretching out my hands—are not true. Perhaps, indeed, I do not even have such hands or such a body at all. Nonetheless, it must surely be admitted that the visions which come in

---

① purple,在古代的西方国家,紫色为皇帝、国王所创的高贵的颜色。

sleep are like paintings, which must have been fashioned in the likeness of things that are real, and hence that at least these general kinds of things—eyes, head, hands and the body as a whole—are things which are not imaginary but are real and exist. For even when painters try to create sirens① and satyrs② with the most extraordinary bodies, they cannot give them natures which are new in all respects; they simply jumble up the limbs of different animals. Or if perhaps they manage to think up something so new that nothing remotely similar has ever been seen before—something which is therefore completely fictitious and unreal—at least the colours used in the composition must be real. By similar reasoning, although these general kinds of things—eyes, head, hands and so on—could be imaginary, it must at least be admitted that certain other even simpler and more universal things are real. These are as it were the real colours from which we form all the images of things, whether true or false, that occur in our thought.

This class appears to include corporeal nature in general, and its extension; the shape of extended things; the quantity, or size and number of these things; the place in which they may exist, the time through which they may endure, and so on.

So a reasonable conclusion from this might be that physics, astronomy, medicine, and all other disciplines which depend on the study of composite things, are doubtful; while arithmetic, geometry and other subjects of this kind, which deal only with the simplest and most general things, regardless of whether they really exist in nature or not, contain something certain and indubitable. For whether I am awake or asleep, two and three added together are five, and a square has no more than four sides. It seems impossible that such transparent truths should incur any suspicion of being false.

And yet firmly rooted in my mind is the long-standing opinion that there is an omnipotent God who made me the kind of creature that I am. How do I know that he has not brought it about that there is no earth, no sky, no extended thing, no shape, no size, no place, while at the same time ensuring

---

① Siren,译作"塞壬",是古希腊神话中的半人半鸟的女海妖,以美妙的歌声诱惑过往的海员,使靠近的船只触礁沉没。

② Satyr,译作"萨梯",是希腊神话中的森林之神,具人形而有羊的尾、耳、角等,喜欢嬉戏,好色。

that all these things appear to me to exist just as they do now? What is more, since I sometimes believe that others go astray in cases where they think they have the most perfect knowledge, may I not similarly go wrong every time I add two and three or count the sides of a square, or in some even simpler matter, if that is imaginable? But perhaps God would not have allowed me to be deceived in this way, since he is said to be supremely good. But if it were inconsistent with his goodness to have created me such that I am deceived all the time, it would seem equally foreign to his goodness to allow me to be deceived even occasionally; yet this last assertion cannot be made.

Perhaps there may be some who would prefer to deny the existence of so powerful a God rather than believe that everything else is uncertain. Let us not argue with them, but grant them that everything said about God is a fiction. According to their supposition, then, I have arrived at my present state by fate or chance or a continuous chain of events, or by some other means; yet since deception and error seem to be imperfections, the less powerful they make my original cause, the more likely it is that I am so imperfect as to be deceived all the time. I have no answer to these arguments, but am finally compelled to admit that there is not one of my former beliefs about which a doubt may not properly be raised; and this is not a flippant or ill-considered conclusion, but is based on powerful and well thought-out reasons. So in future I must withhold my assent from these former beliefs just as carefully as I would from obvious falsehoods, if I want to discover any certainty.

But it is not enough merely to have noticed this; I must make an effort to remember it. My habitual opinions keep coming back, and, despite my wishes, they capture my belief, which is as it were bound over to them as a result of long occupation and the law of custom. I shall never get out of the habit of confidently assenting to these opinions, so long as I suppose them to be what in fact they are, namely highly probable opinions—opinions which, despite the fact that they are in a sense doubtful, as has just been shown, it is still much more reasonable to believe than to deny. In view of this, I think it will be a good plan to turn my will in completely the opposite direction and deceive myself, by pretending for a time that these former opinions are utterly false and imaginary. I shall do this until the weight of preconceived opinion is counter-balanced and the distorting influence of habit no longer prevents my judgement from perceiving things correctly. In the meantime, I know that no danger or error will result from my plan, and that I cannot possibly go too far in my distrustful attitude. This is because the task now in hand does not involve action but merely the acquisition of knowledge.

I will suppose therefore that not God, who is supremely good and the source of truth, but rather some malicious demon of the utmost power and cunning has employed all his energies in order to deceive me. I shall think that the sky, the air, the earth, colours, shapes, sounds and all external things are merely the delusions of dreams which he has devised to ensnare my judgement. I shall consider myself as not having hands or eyes, or flesh, or blood or senses, but as falsely believing that I have all these things. I shall stubbornly and firmly persist in this meditation; and, even if it is not in my power to know any truth, I shall at least do what is in my power, that is, resolutely guard against assenting to any falsehoods, so that the deceiver, however powerful and cunning he may be, will be unable to impose on me in the slightest degree. But this is an arduous undertaking, and a kind of laziness brings me back to normal life. I am like a prisoner who is enjoying an imaginary freedom while asleep; as he begins to suspect that he is asleep, he dreads being woken up, and goes along with the pleasant illusion as long as he can. In the same way, I happily slide back into my old opinions and dread being shaken out of them, for fear that my peaceful sleep may be followed by hard labour when I wake, and that I shall have to toil not in the light, but amid the inextricable darkness of the problems I have now raised.

The nature of the human mind, and how it is better known than the body

So serious are the doubts into which I have been thrown as a result of yesterday's meditation that I can neither put them out of my mind nor see any way of resolving them. It feels as if I have fallen unexpectedly into a deep whirlpool which tumbles me around so that I can neither stand on the bottom nor swim up to the top. Nevertheless I will make an effort and once more attempt the same path which I started on yesterday. Anything which admits of the slightest doubt I will set aside just as if I had found it to be wholly false; and I will proceed in this way until I recognize something certain, or, if nothing else, until I at least recognize for certain that there is no certainty. Archimedes① used to demand just one firm and immovable point in order to shift the entire earth; so I too can hope for great things if I manage to find just one thing, however slight, that is certain and unshakeable.

I will suppose then, that everything I see is spurious. I will believe that my memory tells me lies, and that none of the things that it reports ever happened. I have no senses. Body, shape, extension, movement and place are chimeras. So what remains true? Perhaps just the one fact that nothing is certain.

Yet apart from everything I have just listed, how do I know that there is not something else which does not allow even the slightest occasion for doubt? Is there not a God, or whatever I may call him, who puts into me the thoughts I am now having? But why do I think this, since I myself may perhaps be the author of these thoughts? In that case am not I, at least, something? But I have just said that I have no senses and no body. This is the sticking point: what follows from this? Am I not so bound up with a body and with senses that I cannot exist without them? But I have convinced myself that there is absolutely nothing in the world, no sky, no earth, no minds, no bodies. Does it now follow that I too do not exist? No: if I convinced myself of something then I certainly existed. But there is a deceiver of supreme power and cunninge who is deliberately and constantly deceiving me. In that case I too undoubtedly exist, if he is deceiving me; and let him deceive me as much as he can, he will never bring it about that I am nothing so long as I think that I am something. So after considering everything very thoroughly, I must finally conclude that this proposition, *I am, I exist*, is necessarily true whenever it is put forward by me or conceived in my mind.

But I do not yet have a sufficient understanding of what this "I" is, that now necessarily exists. So I must be on my guard against carelessly taking something else to be this "I", and so making a mistake in the very item of

---

① Archimedes,阿基米德(前287—前212),古希腊数学家、物理学家和发明家,提出了阿基米德原理和杠杆定律。

knowledge that I maintain is the most certain and evident of all. I will therefore go back and meditate on what I originally believed myself to be, before I embarked on this present train of thought. I will then subtract anything capable of being weakened, even minimally, by the arguments now introduced, so that what is left at the end may be exactly and only what is certain and unshakeable.

What then did I formerly think I was? A man. But what is a man? Shall I say "a rational animal"? No; for then I should have to inquire what an animal is, what rationality is, and in this way one question would lead me down the slope to other harder ones, and I do not now have the time to waste on subtleties of this kind. Instead I propose to concentrate on what came into my thoughts spontaneously and quite naturally whenever I used to consider what I was. Well, the first thought to come to mind was that I had a face, hands, arms and the whole mechanical structure of limbs which can be seen in a corpse, and which I called the body. The next thought was that I was nourished, that I moved about, and that I engaged in sense-perception and thinking; and these actions I attributed to the soul. But as to the nature of this soul, either I did not think about this or else I imagined it to be something tenuous, like a wind or fire or ether, which permeated my more solid parts. As to the body, however, I had no doubts about it, but thought I knew its nature distinctly. If I had tried to describe the mental conception I had of it, I would have expressed it as follows: by a body I understand whatever has a determinable shape and a definable location and can occupy a space in such a way as to exclude any other body; it can be perceived by touch, sight, hearing, taste or smell, and can be moved in various ways, not by itself but by whatever else comes into contact with it. For, according to my judgement, the power of self-movement, like the power of sensation or of thought, was quite foreign to the nature of a body; indeed, it was a source of wonder to me that certain bodies were found to contain faculties of this kind.

But what shall I now say that I am, when I am supposing that there is some supremely powerful and, if it is permissible to say so, malicious deceiver, who is deliberately trying to trick me in every way he can? Can I now assert that I possess even the most insignificant of all the attributes which I have just said belong to the nature of a body? I scrutinize them, think about them, go over them again, but nothing suggests itself; it is tiresome and pointless to go through the list once more. But what about the attributes I assigned to the soul? Nutrition or movement? Since now I do not have a body, these are mere fabrications. Sense-perception? This surely does not occur without a body, and besides, when asleep I have appeared to perceive through the senses many things which I afterwards realized I did not perceive through the senses at all. Thinking? At last I have discovered it—thought; this alone is inseparable from me. I am, I exist—that is certain. But for how long? For as long as I am thinking. For it could be that were I totally to cease from thinking, I should totally cease to exist. At present I am not admitting anything except what is necessarily true. I am, then, in the strict sense only a thing that thinks; that is, I am a mind, or intelligence, or intellect, or reason—words whose meaning I have been ignorant of until now. But for all that I am a thing which is real and which truly exists. But what kind of a thing? As I have just said—a thinking thing.

What else am I? I will use my imagination. I am not that structure of limbs which is called a human body. I am not even some thin vapour which permeates the limbs—a wind, fire, air, breath, or whatever I depict in my imagination; for these are things which I have supposed to be nothing. Let this supposition stand; for all that I am still something. And yet may it not perhaps be the case that these very things which I am supposing to be nothing, because they are unknown to me, are in reality identical with the "I" of which I am aware? I do not know, and for the moment I shall not argue the point, since I can make judgements only about things which are known to me. I know that I exist; the question is, what is this "I" that I know? If the "I" is understood strictly as we have been taking it, then it is quite certain that knowledge of it does not depend on things of whose existence I am as yet unaware; so it cannot depend on any of the things which I invent in my imagination. And this very word "invent" shows me my mistake. It would indeed be a case of fictitious invention if I used my imagination to establish that I was something or other; for imagining is simply contemplating the shape or image of a corporeal thing. Yet now I know for certain both that I exist and at the same time that all such images and, in general, everything relating to the nature of body, could be mere dreams (and chimeras①). Once this point has been grasped, to say "I will use my imagination to get to know more distinctly what I am" would seem to be as silly as saying "I am now awake, and see some truth; but since my vision is not yet clear enough, I will deliberately fall asleep so that my dreams may provide a truer and clearer representation." I thus realize that none of the things that the imagination enables me to grasp is at all relevant to this knowledge of myself which I possess, and that the mind must therefore be most carefully diverted from such things if it is to perceive its own nature as distinctly as possible.

But what then am I? A thing that thinks. What is that? A thing that doubts, understands, affirms, denies, is willing, is unwilling, and also imagines and has sensory perceptions.

This is a considerable list, if everything on it belongs to me. But does it? Is it not one and the same "I" who is now doubting almost everything, who nonetheless understands some things, who affirms that this one thing is true, denies everything else, desires to know more, is unwilling to be deceived, imagines many things even involuntarily, and is aware of many things which apparently come from the senses? Are not all these things just as true as the fact that I exist, even if I am asleep all the time, and even if he who created me is doing all he can to deceive me? Which of all these activities is distinct from my thinking? Which of them can be said to be separate from myself? The fact that it is I who am doubting and understanding and willing is so evident that I see no way of making it any clearer. But it is also the case that the "I" who imagines is the same "I". For even if, as I have supposed, none of the objects of imagination are real, the power of imagination is something which really exists and is part of my thinking. Lastly, it is also the same "I" who has sensory perceptions, or is aware of bodily things as it were through the senses. For example, I am now seeing light, hearing a noise, feeling heat. But I am asleep, so all this is false. Yet I certainly *seem* to see, to hear, and to be warmed. This cannot be false; what is called "having a sensory perception" is strictly just this, and in this restricted sense of the term it is simply thinking.

---

① chimera,译作"客迈拉",希腊神话中的怪物,长着狮头、羊身、蛇尾的吐火女妖,这里指虚构的怪物。

From all this I am beginning to have a rather better understanding of what I am. But it still appears—and I cannot stop thinking this—that the corporeal things of which images are formed in my thought, and which the senses investigate, are known with much more distinctness than this puzzling "I" which cannot be pictured in the imagination. And yet it is surely surprising that I should have a more distinct grasp of things which I realize are doubtful, unknown and foreign to me, than I have of that which is true and known—my own self. But I see what it is: my mind enjoys wandering off and will not yet submit to being restrained within the bounds of truth. Very well then; just this once let us give it a completely free rein, so that after a while, when it is time to tighten the reins, it may more readily submit to being curbed.

Let us consider the things which people commonly think they understand most distinctly of all; that is, the bodies which we touch and see. I do not mean bodies in general—for general perceptions are apt to be somewhat more confused—but one particular body. Let us take, for example, this piece of wax. It has just been taken from the honeycomb; it has not yet quite lost the taste of the honey; it retains some of the scent of the flowers from which it was gathered; its colour, shape and size are plain to see; it is hard, cold and can be handled without difficulty; if you rap it with your knuckle it makes a sound. In short, it has everything which appears necessary to enable a body to be known as distinctly as possible. But even as I speak, I put the wax by the fire, and look: the residual taste is eliminated, the smell goes away, the colour changes, the shape is lost, the size increases; it becomes liquid and hot; you can hardly touch it, and if you strike it, it no longer makes a sound. But does the same wax remain? It must be admitted that it does; no one denies it, no one thinks otherwise. So what was it in the wax that I understood with such distinctness? Evidently none of the features which I arrived at by means of the senses; for whatever came under taste, smell, sight, touch or hearing has now altered—yet the wax remains.

Perhaps the answer lies in the thought which now comes to my mind; namely, the wax was not after all the sweetness of the honey, or the fragrance of the flowers, or the whiteness, or the shape, or the sound, but was rather a body which presented itself to me in these various forms a little while ago, but which now exhibits different ones. But what exactly is it that I am now imagining? Let us concentrate, take away everything which does not belong to the wax, and see what is left: merely something extended, flexible and changeable. But what is meant here by "flexible" and "changeable"? Is it what I picture in my imagination: that this piece of wax is capable of changing from a round shape to a square shape, or from a square shape to a triangular shape? Not at all; for I can grasp that the wax is capable of countless changes of this kind, yet I am unable to run through this immeasurable number of changes in my imagination, from which it follows that it is not the faculty of imagination that gives me my grasp of the wax as flexible and changeable. And what is meant by "extended"? Is the extension of the wax also unknown? For it increases if the wax melts, increases again if it boils, and is greater still if the heat is increased. I would not be making a correct judgement about the nature of wax unless I believed it capable of being extended in many more different ways than I will ever encompass in my imagination. I must therefore admit that the nature of this piece of wax is in no way revealed by my imagination, but is perceived by the mind alone. (I am speaking of this particular piece of wax; the point is even clearer with regard to wax in general.) But what is this wax which is perceived by the mind alone? It is of course the same wax which I see, which I touch, which I picture in my imagination, in short the same wax which I thought it to be from the start. And yet, and here is the point, the perception I have of it is a case not of vision or touch or imagination—nor has it ever been, despite previous appearances—but of purely mental scrutiny; and this can be imperfect and confused, as it was before, or clear and distinct as it is now, depending on how carefully I concentrate on what the wax consists in.

But as I reach this conclusion I am amazed at how (weak and) prone to error my mind is. For although I am thinking about these matters within myself, silently and without speaking, nonetheless the actual words bring me up short, and I am almost tricked by ordinary ways of talking. We say that we see the wax itself, if it is there before us, not that we judge it to be there from its colour or shape; and this might lead me to conclude without more ado that knowledge of the wax comes from what the eye sees, and not from the scrutiny of the mind alone. But then if I look out of the window and see men crossing the square, as I just happen to have done, I normally say that I see the men themselves, just as I say that I see the wax. Yet do I see any more than hats and coats which could conceal automatons? I *judge* that they are men. And so something which I thought I was seeing with my eyes is in fact grasped solely by the faculty of judgement which is in my mind.

However, one who wants to achieve knowledge above the ordinary level should feel ashamed at having taken ordinary ways of talking as a basis for doubt. So let us proceed, and consider on which occasion my percetion of the nature of the wax was more perfect and evident. Was it when I first looked at it, and believed I knew it by my external senses, or at least by what they call the "common" sense—that is, the power of imagination? Or is my knowledge more perfect now, after a more careful investigation of the nature of the wax and of the means by which it is known? Any doubt on this issue would clearly be foolish; for what distinctness was there in my earlier perception? Was there anything in it which an animal could not possess? But when I distinguish the wax from its outward forms—take the clothes off, as it were, and consider it naked—then although my judgement may still contain errors, at least my perception now requires a human mind.

But what am I to say about this mind, or about myself? (So far, remember, I am not admitting that there is anything else in me except a mind.) What, I ask, is this "I" which seems to perceive the wax so distinctly? Surely my awareness of my own self is not merely much truer and more certain than my awareness of the wax, but also much more distinct and evident. For if I judge that the wax exists from the fact that I see it, clearly this same fact entails much more evidently that I myself also exist. It is possible that what I see is not really the wax; it is possible that I do not even have eyes with which to see anything. But when I see, or think I see(I am not here distinguishing the two), it is simply not possible that I who am now thinking am not something. By the same token, if I judge that the wax exists from the fact that I touch it, the same result follows, namely that I exist. If I judge that it exists from the fact that I imagine it, or for any other reason, exactly the same thing follows. And the result that I have grasped in the case of the wax may be applied to everything else located outside me. Moreover, if my perception of the wax seemed more distinct after it was established not just by sight or touch but by many other considerations, it must be admitted that I now know myself even more distinctly. This is because every consideration whatsoever which contributes to my perception of the wax, or of any other body, cannot but establish even more effectively the nature of my own mind. But besides this, there is so much else in the mind itself which can serve to make my knowledge of it more distinct, that it scarcely seems worth going through the contributions made by considering bodily things.

I see that without any effort I have now finally got back to where I wanted. I now know that even bodies are not strictly perceived by the senses or the faculty of imagination but by the intellect alone, and that this perception derives not from their being touched or seen but from their being understood; and in view of this I know plainly that I can achieve an easier and more evident perception of my own mind than of anything else. But since the habit of holding on to old opinions cannot be set aside so quickly, I should like to stop here and meditate for some time on this new knowledge I have gained, so as to fix it more deeply in my memory.

选文出处

Rene Descartes. *Meditations on First Philosophy*. Translated by Bernard Williams, Beijing: China Social Sciences Publishing House (reprinted from the English Edition by Cambridge University Press, 1993), 1999, pp. 12—23.

思考题

1. 用笛卡尔的怀疑主义方法重新反思以前的各种观点，看看能否找到一些破绽。
2. 理性真的比感观更可靠吗？为什么？

阅读

参考书目

1. 冯俊：《开启理性之门——笛卡儿哲学研究》，北京：中国人民大学出版社，2005年。
2. Cottingham, John. (ed.) *The Cambridge Companion to Descartes*, Cambridge: Cambridge University Press, 1992.

帕斯卡尔

帕斯卡尔(Blaise Pascal,1623—1662)是17世纪法国著名的数学家、物理学家和思想家,近代概率论的创始人。他设计并制造出世界上第一台计算机。帕斯卡尔一直体弱多病,3岁时不幸失去母亲。他的父亲艾蒂安(Etienne)是一位拉丁学者,也是一位杰出的数学家,非常喜欢自然科学。艾蒂安没有把儿子送到学校,而是在家里进行教育。这位父亲按照当时法国绅士的标准教育儿子,希望帕斯卡尔成为品味雅致且具有敏锐判断力的文化贵族。起初他只让儿子学习拉丁文和希腊文,不过,帕斯卡尔很快就在数学方面展露出自己的天赋。据帕斯卡尔的姐姐回忆,在12岁那年,父亲突然发现没有受过相关训练的儿子,独自推导出欧几里得几何23条定理。从此,父亲对其加强了数学教育,使他在这个领域取得惊人的进步。帕斯卡尔在16岁的时候,就发表了一篇重要的数学论文《论圆锥曲线》(*Essai pour les Coniques*)。19岁那年,帕斯卡尔发明了世界上第一台加法器,这也是科学史上的第一台计算机。Pascal语言就是用来纪念他的。而作为一个思想家,帕斯卡尔的成就则主要体现在《思想录》中。

《思想录》是帕斯卡尔思想片段的记录,大部分内容写于1656年到1658年底,其中相当大的篇幅是讨论宗教的。帕斯卡尔去世时年仅39岁。尽管虚弱的身体和短暂的生命使这位天才难以将所有的才华发挥出来,但他还是成功地跻身一流科学家和思想家的行列,成为历史上的一个奇迹。帕斯卡尔曾说:"人只不过是一根苇草,是自然界最脆弱的东西;但他是一根能思想的苇草。"①人在宇宙面前是那么脆弱,但这并不影响人是宇宙的精华,因为只有人才具有思想的能力。帕斯卡尔这根苇草是脆弱的,可他的思想却是十分深刻的。

本书从帕斯卡尔的《思想录》中选取了两大部分,前面一部分是该书的第1篇至第15篇,后面一部分是第233篇。第1篇至第5篇探讨的是数学精神和直觉精神的区别。在帕斯卡尔看来,数学精神的特点在于总是建立在少数明确无误的原则之上,只要受过训练就能准确地进行推算,不容易出现错误,但是这些原则是远离日常运用的。直觉的精神就在日常应用之中。正如帕斯卡尔所说的那样,"人们只需看一看,而并不需要勉强用力;问题只在于有良好的洞见能力,但这一洞见能力却必须良好,因为这些原则是那么细微,而数量又是那么繁多,以至人们几乎不可能不错过一些。"可见数学精神和直觉精神有很大的区别:"所以很少数学家是敏感的,或者敏感的人是数学家;这是由于数学家企图数学式地对待那些敏感的事物,他们试图从定义出发,然后继之以定理,而这根本不是这类推论的活动方式,于是他们把自己弄得荒唐可笑。"另一方面,重直觉的人也难以理解数学的推理:"相反,直觉的精神既已习惯于这样一眼看去就下判断,当人们提出他们毫不理解的命题,他们就会惊愕失措,甚至望而却步并且感到灰心丧气,因为深入这些命题要经过许多如此之枯燥的定义和原理,而他们根本不习惯于那样仔细地加以观察。"帕斯卡尔还以手表为比喻来说明两种人的区别。一个戴着手表的人和两个没有戴手表的人讨论时间。一个认为已经过了两个小时,另一个还以为才过三刻钟。于是这个有手表的人就嘲笑他们,认为第一个人疲倦了,第二个人的时间在飞跑,因为手表显示的时间为一个半小时。在帕斯卡尔看来,三者都有正确的一面,有手表的人代表着数学式的理性思维,另外两个体现的是直觉思维,虽然各自的答案不同,但从自身的角度看是正确的。

帕斯卡尔生活在以理性主义为主要特色的欧洲大陆,但他没有把自己封闭在理性主义传统之中,而是超越于理性主义之上。一方面,他是著名的数学家,在理性思维方面非常出众;另一方面,他也看到了理性思维的局限性,非常重视直觉的作用。他既有思辨的深度,又有直觉的敏锐。从这个角度看他是更为了不起的天才。作为思想家的帕斯卡尔是重直觉的,他的《思想录》不是按照数学的从概念到体系的方法写成的,而是由很多不同的感悟组成的,颇有启发意义。如在第9篇中,他认为,如果要指出别人的错误,应先肯定别人从他自己的角度看问题的正确性,再指出其片面性,这样别人就很容

---

① 帕斯卡尔:《思想录》,何兆武译,北京:商务印书馆,1997年,第157—158页。

易接受批评。

《思想录》中第 233 篇是最长的篇章之一,主要讨论的是著名的上帝之赌。帕斯卡尔把人类、无限和上帝做了一个比较。他说:"我们认识有限的存在及其本性,因为我们也像它一样是有限的和广延的;我们认识无限的存在而不知道它的本性,因为它像我们一样具有广延性,却又不和我们一样有限;但我们既不认识上帝的存在也不认识上帝的本性,因为它既不具有广延性,也没有限度。"通过这段话我们可以看出,上帝是无法论证的,因为没有广延和限度,但上帝的存在还是可以想象的,正如我们可以想象无限一样。如果我们打个赌,就可以看到,相信上帝存在对人生更为有利。有人可能会说,为什么要赌呢?不赌不可以吗?但不赌其实就是在赌上帝不存在,所以我们并没有其他选择。在帕斯卡尔看来,上帝之赌的利弊是显而易见的:"假如你赢了,你就赢得了一切;假如你输了,你却一无所失。"帕斯卡尔还说:"然而,这里确乎是有着无限幸福的无限生命可赢,与这一场赢局的机遇相对的是有限的输局机遇,你所赌的又是有限的。输赢两边已经分配好了;凡是无限存在的地方,凡是不存在无限输局机遇的地方,就没有犹豫的余地,而是应该孤注一掷。"基督教与相信生死轮回的佛教不一样,基督教徒认为,人死后要么打入地狱永远受苦,要么升入天堂永远快乐,所以赌上帝存在就有可能赢得无限的幸福和生命。这种信仰之赌比日常生活中的赌更有利,因为一般意义上的赌不可能赢得无限的东西,而信仰之赌可能赢得无限。但所有的这些论证并不能解决信仰问题,最后还得靠自己的心去领悟,帕斯卡尔说:"你不应该努力增加对上帝的证明,而要减少你自己的感情,以便使自己信服。"这就是说,理性不能最终解决信仰的问题,还得从内心的情感着手,减少抵制情绪。这个上帝之赌建立于非常理性的概率原理之上,但作者认为这只是辅助手段,最终应当通过心去体会。

帕斯卡尔曾说:"有关外物的科学不会在我痛苦的时候安慰我在道德方面的愚昧无知;然而有关德行的科学却永远可以安慰我对外界科学的愚昧无知。"[①]作为一名科学家,他没有被科学主义的偏见所蒙蔽,而是强调人的问题的优先性。

---

① 帕斯卡尔:《思想录》,何兆武译,北京:商务印书馆,1997 年,第 26 页。

Pensees

1

The difference between the mathematical and the intuitive mind.[①]—In the one the principles are palpable, but removed from ordinary use; so that for want of habit it is difficult to turn one's mind in that direction: but if one turns it thither ever so little, one sees the principles fully, and one must have a quite inaccurate mind who reasons wrongly from principles so plain that it is almost impossible they should escape notice.

But in the intuitive mind the principles are found in common use, and are before the eyes of everybody. One has only to look, and no effort is necessary; it is only a question of good eyesight, but it must be good, for the principles are so subtle and so numerous, that it is almost impossible but that some escape notice. Now the omission of one principle leads to error; thus one must have very clear sight to see all the principles, and in the next place an accurate mind not to draw false deductions from known principles.

All mathematicians would then be intuitive if they had clear sight, for they do not reason incorrectly from principles known to them; and intuitive minds would be mathematical if they could turn their eyes to the principles of mathematics to which they are unused.

The reason, therefore, that some intuitive minds are not mathematical is that they cannot at all turn their attention to the principles of mathematics. But the reason that mathematicians are not intuitive is that they do not see what is before them, and that, accustomed to the exact and plain principles of mathematics, and not reasoning till they have well inspected and arranged their principles, they are lost in matters of intuition where the principles do

---

① the intuitive mind,在法文版中为l'esprit de finesse,《思想录》的中文翻译者何兆武把它译为"敏感性精神"。因为我们用的是英文版,所以直接将这个短语译为"直觉精神"。

not allow of such arrangement. They are scarcely seen; they are felt rather than seen; there is the greatest difficulty in making them felt by those who do not of themselves perceive them. These principles are so fine and so numerous that a very delicate and very clear sense is needed to perceive them, and to judge rightly and justly when they are perceived, without for the most part being able to demonstrate them in order as in mathematics; because the principles are not known to us in the same way, and because it would be an endless matter to undertake it. We must see the matter at once, at one glance, and not by a process of reasoning, at least to a certain degree. And thus it is rare that mathematicians are intuitive, and that men of intuition are mathematicians, because mathematicians wish to treat matters of intuition mathematically, and make themselves ridiculous, wishing to begin with definitions and then with axioms, which is not the way to proceed in this kind of reasoning. Not that the mind does not do so, but it does it tacitly, naturally, and without technical rules; for the expression of it is beyond all men, and only a few can feel it.

Intuitive minds, on the contrary, being thus accustomed to judge at a single glance, are so astonished when they are presented with propositions of which they understand nothing, and the way to which is through definitions and axioms so sterile, and which they are not accustomed to see thus in detail, that they are repelled and disheartened.

But dull minds are never either intuitive or mathematical.

Mathematicians who are only mathematicians have exact minds, provided all things are explained to them by means of definitions and axioms; otherwise they are inaccurate and insufferable, for they are only right when the principles are quite clear.

And men of intuition who are only intuitive cannot have the patience to reach to first principles of things speculative and conceptual, which they have never seen in the world, and which are altogether out of the common.

2

There are different kinds of right understanding; some have right understanding in a certain order of things, and not in others, where they go astray. Some draw conclusions well from a few premises, and this displays an acute judgment.

Others draw conclusions well where there are many premises.

For example, the former easily learn hydrostatics[①], where the premises are few, but the conclusions are so fine that only the greatest acuteness can reach them.

And in spite of that these persons would perhaps not be great mathematicians, because mathematics contain a great number of premises, and there is perhaps a kind of intellect that can search with ease a few premises to the bottom, and cannot in the least penetrate those matters in which there are many premises.

There are then two kinds of intellect: the one able to penetrate acutely and deeply into the conclusions of given premises, and this is the precise intellect; the other able to comprehend a great number of premises without confusing them, and this is the mathematical intellect. The one has force and exactness, the other comprehension. Now the one quality can exist without the other; the intellect can be strong and narrow, and can also be comprehensive and weak.

3

Those who are accustomed to judge by feeling do not understand the process of reasoning, for they would understand at first sight, and are not used to seek for principles. And others, on the contrary, who are accustomed to reason from principles, do not at all understand matters of feeling, seeking principles, and being unable to see at a glance.

4

Mathematics, intuition. —True eloquence makes light of eloquence, true morality makes light of morality; that is to say, the morality of the judgment, which has no rules, makes light of the morality of the intellect.

---

① hydrostatics, 流体静力学。

For it is to judgment that perception belongs, as science belongs to intellect. Intuition is the part of judgment, mathematics of intellect.

To make light of philosophy is to be a true philosopher.

5

Those who judge of a work by rule are in regard to others as those who have a watch are in regard to others. One says, "It is two hours ago"; the other says, "It is only three-quarters of an hour." I look at my watch, and say to the one, "You are weary," and to the other, "Time gallops with you"; for it is only an hour and a half ago, and I laugh at those who tell me that time goes slowly with me, and that I judge by imagination. They do not know that I judge by my watch.

6

Just as we harm the understanding, we harm the feelings also.

The understanding and the feelings are moulded by intercourse; the understanding and feelings are corrupted by intercourse. Thus good or bad society improves or corrupts them. It is, then, all-important to know how to choose in order to improve and not to corrupt them; and we cannot make this choice, if they be not already improved and not corrupted. Thus a circle is formed, and those are fortunate who escape it.

7

The greater intellect one has, the more originality one finds in men. Ordinary persons find no difference between men.

8

There are many people who listen to a sermon in the same way as they listen to vespers①.

9

When we wish to correct with advantage, and to show another that he errs, we must notice from what side he views the matter, for on that side it is usually true, and admit that truth to him, but reveal to him the side on which it is false. He is satisfied with that, for he sees that he was not mistaken, and that he only failed to see all sides. Now, no one is offended at not seeing everything; but one does not like to be mistaken, and that perhaps arises from the fact that man naturally cannot see everything, and that naturally he cannot err in the side he looks at, since the perceptions of our senses are always true.

10

People are generally better persuaded by the reasons which they have themselves discovered than by those which have come into the mind of others.

11

All great amusements are dangerous to the Christian life; but among all those which the world has invented there is none more to be feared than the theatre. It is a representation of the passions so natural and so delicate that it excites them and gives birth to them in our hearts, and, above all, to that of love, principally when it is represented as very chaste and virtuous. For the more innocent it appears to innocent souls, the more they are likely to be touched by it. Its violence pleases our self-love, which immediately forms a desire to produce the same effects which are seen so well represented; and, at the same time, we make ourselves a conscience founded on the propriety of the feelings which we see there, by which the fear of pure souls is removed, since they imagine that it cannot hurt their purity to love with a love which seems to them so reasonable.

---

① vespers,晚祷曲。

So we depart from the theatre with our heart so filled with all the beauty and tenderness of love, the soul and the mind so persuaded of its innocence, that we are quite ready to receive its first impressions, or rather to seek an opportunity of awakening them in the heart of another, in order that we may receive the same pleasures and the same sacrifices which we have seen so well represented in the theatre.

12

Scaramouch[①], who only thinks of one thing.

The doctor, who speaks for a quarter of an hour after he has said everything, so full is he of the desire of talking.

13

One likes to see the error, the passion of Cleobuline[②], because she is unconscious of it. She would be displeasing, if she were not deceived.

14

When a natural discourse paints a passion or an effect, one feels within oneself the truth of what one reads, which was there before, although one did not know it. Hence one is inclined to love him who makes us feel it, for he has not shown us his own riches, but ours. And thus this benefit renders him pleasing to us, besides that such community of intellect as we have with him necessarily inclines the heart to love.

15

Eloquence, which persuades by sweetness, not by authority; as a tyrant, not as a king.

---

① Scaramouch,当时意大利的著名喜剧演员。
② Cleobuline,传说中的古希腊公主,长期爱着名叫 Myrinthe 的臣子而不自觉。

233

Infinite—nothing. —Our soul is cast into a body, where it finds number, time, dimension. Thereupon it reasons, and calls this nature, necessity, and can believe nothing else.

Unity joined to infinity adds nothing to it, no more than one foot to an infinite measure. The finite is annihilated in the presence of the infinite, and becomes a pure nothing. So our spirit before God, so our justice before divine justice. There is not so great a disproportion between our justice and that of God, as between unity and infinity.

The justice of God must be vast like His compassion. Now justice to the outcast is less vast, and ought less to offend our feelings than mercy towards the elect.

We know that there is an infinite, and are ignorant of its nature. As we know it to be false that numbers are finite, it is therefore true that there is an infinity in number. But we do not know what it is. It is false that it is even, it is false that it is odd; for the addition of a unit can make no change in its nature. Yet it is a number, and every number is odd or even (this is certainly true of every finite number). So we may well know that there is a God without knowing what He is. Is there not one substantial truth, seeing there are so many things which are not the truth itself?

We know then the existence and nature of the finite, because we also are finite and have extension. We know the existence of the infinite, and are ignorant of its nature, because it has extension like us, but not limits like us. But we know neither the existence nor the nature of God, because He has neither extension nor limits.

But by faith we know His existence; in glory we shall know His nature. Now, I have already shown that we may well know the existence of a thing, without knowing its nature.

Let us now speak according to natural lights[①].

If there is a God. He is infinitely incomprehensible, since, having neither

---

① natural lights,指天赋的知识。

parts nor limits, He has no affinity to us. We are then incapable of knowing either what He is or if He is. This being so, who will dare to undertake the decision of the question? Not we, who have no affinity to Him.

Who then will blame Christians for not being able to give a reason for their belief, since they profess a religion for which they cannot give a reason? They declare, in expounding it to the world, that it is a foolishness, *stultitiam*[①]; and then you complain that they do not prove it! If they proved it, they would not keep their word; it is in lacking proofs, that they are not lacking in sense. "Yes, but although this excuses those who offer it as such, and takes away from them the blame of putting it forward without reason, it does not excuse those who receive it." Let us then examine this point, and say, "God is, or He is not." But to which side shall we incline? Reason can decide nothing here. There is an infinite chaos which separated us. A game is being played at the extremity of this infinite distance where heads or tails will turn up. What will you wager? According to reason, you can do neither the one thing nor the other; according to reason, you can defend neither of the propositions.

Do not then reprove for error those who have made a choice; for you know nothing about it. "No, but I blame them for having made, not this choice, but a choice; for again both he who chooses heads and he who chooses tails are equally at fault, they are both in the wrong. The true course is not to wager at all."

Yes; but you must wager. It is not optional. You are embarked. Which will you choose then? Let us see. Since you must choose, let us see which interests you least. You have two things to lose, the true and the good; and two things to stake, your reason and your will, your knowledge and your happiness; and your nature has two things to shun, error and misery. Your reason is no more shocked in choosing one rather than the other, since you must of necessity choose. This is one point settled. But your happiness? Let us weigh the gain and the loss in wagering that God is. Let us estimate these two chances. If you gain, you gain all; if you lose, you lose nothig. Wager, then, without hesitation that He is. —"That is very fine. Yes, I must wager;

---

① stultitiam,愚拙。

but I may perhaps wager too much." —Let us see. Since there is an equal risk of gain and of loss, if you had only to gain two lives, instead of one, you might still wager. But if there were three lives to gain, you would have to play (since you are under the necessity of playing), and you would be imprudent, when you are forced to play, not to chance your life to gain three at a game where there is an equal risk of loss and gain. But there is an eternity of life and happiness. And this being so, if there were an infinity of chances, of which one only would be for you, you would still be right in wagering one to win two, and you would act stupidly, being obliged to play, by refusing to stake one life against three at a game in which out of an infinity of chances there is one for you, if there were an infinity of an infinitely happy life to gain. But there is here an infinity of an infinitely happy life to gain, a chance of gain against a finite number of chances of loss, and what you stake is finite. It is all divided; wherever the infinite is and there is not an infinity of chances of loss against that of gain, there is no time to hesitate, you must give all. And thus, when one is forced to play, he must renounce reason to preserve his life, rather than risk it for infinite gain, as likely to happen as the loss of nothingness.

For it is no use to say it is uncertain if we will gain, and it is certain that we risk, and that the infinite distance between the *certainty* of what is staked and the *uncertainty* of what will be gained, equals the finite good which is certainly staked against the uncertain infinite. It is not so, as every player stakes a certainty to gain an uncertainty, and yet he stakes a finite certainty to gain a finite uncertainty, without transgressing against reason. There is not an infinite distance between the certainty staked and the uncertainty of the gain; that is untrue. In truth, there is an infinity between the certainty of gain and the certainty of loss. But the uncertainty of the gain is proportioned to the certainty of the stake according to the proportion of the chances of gain and loss. Hence it comes that, if there are as many risks on one side as on the other, the course is to play even; and then the certainty of the stake is equal to the uncertainty of the gain, so far is it from fact that there is an infinite distance between them. And so our proposition is of infinite force, when there is the finite to stake in a game where there are equal risks of gain and of loss, and the infinite to gain. This is demonstrable; and if men are capable of any truths, this is one.

"I confess it, I admit it. But, still, is there no means of seeing the faces of the cards?" —Yes, Scripture and the rest, etc. "Yes, but I have my hands tied and my mouth closed; I am forced to wager, and am not free. I am not released, and am so made that I cannot believe. What, then, would you have me do?"

True. But at least learn your inability to believe, since reason brings you to this, and yet you cannot believe. Endeavour then to convince yourself, not by increase of proofs of God, but by the abatement of your passions. You would like to attain faith, and do not know the way; you would like to cure yourself of unbelief, and ask the remedy for it. Learn of those who have been bound like you, and who now stake all their possessions. These are people who know the way which you would follow, and who are cured of an ill of which you would be cured. Follow the way by which they began; by acting as if they believed, taking the holy water, having masses said, etc. Even this will naturally make you believe, and deaden your acuteness. —"But this is what I am afraid of." —And why? What have you to lose?

But to show you that this leads you there, it is this which will lessen the passions, which are your stumbling-blocks.

The end of this discourse. —Now, what harm will befall you in taking this side? You will be faithful, honest, humble, grateful, generous, a sincere friend, truthful. Certainly you will not have those poisonous pleasures, glory and luxury; but will you not have others? I will tell you that you will thereby gain in this life, and that, at each step you take on this road, you will see so great certainty of gain, so much nothingness in what you risk, that you will at last recognise that you have wagered for something certain and infinite, for which you have given nothing.

"Ah! This discourse transports me, charms me," etc.

If this discourse pleases you and seems impressive, know that it is made by a man who has knelt, both before and after it, in prayer to that Being, infinite and without parts, before whom he lays all he has, for you also to lay before Him all you have for your own good and for His glory, that so strength may be given to lowliness.

选文出处

Blaise Pascal. *Pascal's Pensées*. Translated by W. F. Trotter, Beijing: China Social Sciences Publishing House (reprinted from the English Edition by J. M. Dent & Sons Ltd. And E. P. Dutton & Co. Inc.,), 1999, pp. 1—5, 65—69.

 思考题

1. 分析一下自己的心智的特点,看看自己是以数学推理为特长还是以直觉见长。
2. 生活中需要上帝吗?为什么?

阅读

参考书目

1. Morris Bishop, *Blaise Pascal*, New York: Dell Publishers Co., 1966.
2. Thomas Morris, *Making Sense of It All: Pascal and the Meaning of Life*, Michigan: Willian B. Eerdmans Publishing Company, 1992.

洛 克

约翰·洛克(John Locke，1632—1704)，出生于英国萨默塞特郡威灵顿，1656 年毕业于牛津大学，获得医学学士学位，1658 年获硕士学位，36 岁被选入英国皇家学会。1666 年，洛克与库珀(Anthony Ashley Cooper)相识，并进入政坛担任各种公职，后因受政治斗争的牵连而被迫迁居荷兰，直至 1689 年回国。洛克的主要著述包括《人类理解论》(*An Essay Concerning Human Understanding*)、《政府论两篇》(*Two Treatises of Government*)、《教育漫话》(*Some Thoughts Concerning Education*)、《宽容书笺》(*Letters on Toleration*)等。

洛克建树颇多，成就斐然。他是教育家、医生，也是哲学家，更是 1688 年英国"光荣革命"的倡导者和理论家。然而，洛克的声誉主要还是来自在哲学领域所取得的成就。洛克是经验主义哲学的开创者。他奠定了英国经验主义思想的传统，在哲学史上产生了巨大的影响。洛克是全面系统阐述宪政民主基本思想的第一人，被誉为自由主义学说的始祖。他的经典自由主义论述，对美国革命的产生乃至美国宪政的产生有着巨大的影响。在现当代哲学中，洛克所提出的有关心智、自由以及权力、权威等概念，仍然是讨论和研究的重要内容。因此说，洛克诸多理论的影响一直持续到了今天，并且还未见衰退的迹象。

洛克的《政府论两篇》发表于 1688 年，被视为最重要的政治学经典著作之一。它第一次比较系统地阐述了分权学说，对西方政治制度的建立产生了深远的影响。《政府论两篇》的上篇是对菲尔默爵士(Sir Robert Filmer)的《先祖论，即论国王之自然权》(*Patriarcha*：*or The*

Natural Power of Kings)的回应,驳斥了君权神授、君权世袭及其将父权转变为君主专制权力的谬说。《政府论两篇》的下篇在政治思想史上影响深远。洛克从"自然状态"的概念入手,阐述了自然法、天赋权利、财产权、社会契约等学说,进而论证了政府权力的真正起源、范围和目的,以及政府形式和权力分立等方面的政治理论。下篇的核心内容有两点:一是政府的目的是保护私有财产;二是最好的政府形式是议会具有最高主权的制度。[①]

在节选的《论国家权力的统属》中,论及了国家的形式、立法权范围以及国家的立法权、执行权和对外权。洛克认为,立法权是制定和公布法律的权力;执法权是对法律的执行;对外权主要包括宣战、媾和以及订条约等权力。这三者构成了国家政权,也是洛克阐述"国家权力的统属"的基础和对象。洛克明确指出,一个国家只能有一个最高权力,即立法权,其他权力包括执行权和对外权都是从属的。针对立法权,洛克强调人们的一致同意是联合成为一个政治社会和组成一个国家的必要条件,也是法律得以确立、政府得以正常运行以及民众服从政府的持久条件,社会和政治权力都只能建立在民众同意的基础上。

根据民众同意所设立的立法权,是最高的国家统治权力,但这种统治权力不是专制的权力,它源于人民、保护人民财产且制约其他国家权力。这种统治权具有委托性质,立法机关不能把权力转让给其他任何人或机构,只有民众才能处理和决定权力的归属与转移。立法机关必须通过长期有效的法律和得到授权的法官来主持公正和保护私有财产。

洛克认为,正因为立法权的委托性质,在最高立法机关之后还有民众的更高权力。因此,"当民众发现立法机关违背所赋予它的委托时,民众仍然拥有罢免或更换立法机关的最高权力"。从这个意义上说,共同体(community)是最高的,能决定其权力的委托对象。当然,"并不能认为在任何政体下都是这样,因为民众的这种最高权力到政府解体时才能表现出来"。那么,只有在立法机关或执行机关违背其所承担的权力委托时,才会出现民众革命的权力。

洛克认为,立法机关不是常设性的,因为法律并不需要经常制定或更新;执行机关却有必要长期存在,它既是政府有效运行的基本条件,也是法律的具体执行机构。立法机关和执行机关是相互分离的,唯有如此,才能使法律制定和执行达到保护民众各项权利的目标。对于立法机关和执行机关之间的协调性问题,洛克认为,在立法机关把制定的法律交给相关执行人之后,仍有可能在认为有必要时将执行权收回,并处罚不良执法行为。立法权与对外权的关系和立法权与执行权的关系是类似的。

[①] 洛克:《政府论》(下篇),叶启芳、瞿菊农译,北京:商务印书馆,1964年,VIII。

洛克指出，作为最高国家权力的立法权是民众授予的，这种授权通过有任期限制的民选代表来实现。立法机关中的民选代表，任期满就归于民众，除非能重新当选；然而一旦他们被赋予立法权，也就掌握了最高权力。在立法权的运作上，洛克也提出了相对具体的操作方式，比如"根据他们最初的宪法所规定的时间或在他们休会时所指定的时间，召开会议和行使他们的立法权"，"或者如果两者都没有指定任何时间或没有规定其他方法召集他们开会"，由他们自己确定合适的时间。

洛克还特别指出，"超越职权和违背所受的委托而对民众使用武力，就是和民众处于战争状态。"在这种情况下，民众有权恢复立法机关、使立法机关正常行使权力的权利；如果情况紧急，并关系到民众安全和权利保障，民众有权使用武力予以清除。以武力对付武力也是一种真正的纠正超权、越权的方式。民众的至高无上的权力在这个时候就显示了出来。

洛克一再强调民众的福利是最高的法律；遵循这一原则就不会犯危险的错误。政府的行为只要是依据正义、持久的法规，就必然是有利于社会和民众的。这样一来，社会就是民众的社会，民众也就是社会的民众。民众选出的代表在立法机关的行为就是一种社会的意志和行动。

洛克既支持"以暴制暴"的原则，又认为"暴力只可用来反对不公不法的暴力"。不过，"不公不法"是很难界定的，根本不存在客观的检验标准来证明革命的权利是否正当。尽管理论上民众可以撤销权力委托，但洛克"不曾提出也不可能提出任何以合法的方式这样做（指撤销权力委托）的明确办法"。[①] 洛克把民主构想为一种精神而不是一种政府形式，那么只要承认统治者是民众权力的受托者，任何一种政治制度都是合法的。洛克的理论作为一种政治哲学，经过孟德斯鸠的发展，不仅为美国、法国的革命提供了基本思想，为制定成文宪法提供了准则，而且至今仍然在一定领域内发挥着重要的作用。

Two Treatises of Government

Though in a Constituted Commonwealth, standing upon its own Basis, and acting according to its own Nature, that is, acting for the preservation of

---

① 鲍桑葵：《关于国家的哲学理论》，汪淑钧译，北京：商务印书馆，1995年，第126—127页。

the Community, there can be but *one Supream Power*, which is *the Legislative*, to which all the rest are and must be subordinate, yet the Legislative being only a Fiduciary Power to act for certain ends, there remains still *in the People a Supream Power*① to remove or *alter the Legislative*, when they find the *Legislative* act contrary to the trust reposed in them. For all *Power given with trust* for the attaining an *end*, being limited by that end, whenever that *end* is manifestly neglected, or opposed, the *trust* must necessarily be *forfeited*, and the Power devolve into the hands of those that gave it, who may place it anew where they shall think best for their safety and security. And thus the *Community*② perpetually *retains a Supream Power* of saving themselves from the attempts and designs of any Body, even of their Legislators, whenever they shall be so foolish, or so wicked, as to lay and carry on designs against the Liberties and Properties of the Subject. For no Man, or Society of Men, having a Power to deliver up their *Preservation*, or consequently the means of it, to the Absolute Will and arbitrary Dominion of another; whenever any one shall go about to bring them into such a Slavish Condition, they will always have a right to preserve what they have not a Power to part with; and to rid themselves of those who invade this Fundamental, Sacred, and unalterable Law of *Self-Preservation*, for which they enter'd into Society. And thus the *Community* may be said in this respect to be *always the Supream Power*, but not as considered under any Form of Government, because this Power of the People can never take place till the Government be dissolved.

In all Cases, whilst the Government subsists, the *Legislative is the Supream Power*.③ For what can give Laws to another, must needs be

---

① 可以看出，本段中前面部分出现的"one Supream Power"与此处用到"a Supream Power"表达形式基本相同，但意义却相矛盾。兰普勒希特(K. Lamprecht)曾解释说，这种最高立法权在一种条件下是完整的，而在另一种条件下则完全不存在。洛克既承认立法机关在法律上的最高权力，但又认为民众享有罢免或更换立法机关的最高权力。

② 这里的共同体(Community)实际上是社会或者民众的同义语，在不同的语境中表示由人民或民众共同组成的阵线或群体；托马斯·库恩(T. S. Kuhn)的共同体概念是指以相同或不同方式应用共有价值的团体，两者有一定的相同之处。

③ 立法权(the Legislative)是国家的最高权力(the Supream Power)，是洛克理论的重要特征之一，也是他的整个政治思想的关键概念。文中有些地方，"the Legislative"表示立法机关，立法权则是"Legislature"。

superiour to him: and since the Legislative is no otherwise Legislative of the Society, but by the right it has to make Laws for all the parts and for every Member of the Society, prescribing Rules to their actions, and giving power of Execution, where they are transgressed, the *Legislative* must needs be the *Supream*, and all other Powers in any Members or parts of the Society, derived from and subordinate to it.

In some Commonwealths where the *Legislative* is not always in being, and the *Executive* is vested in a single Person, who has also a share in the Legislative; there that single Person in a very tolerable sense may also be called *Supream*, not that he has in himself all the Supream Power, which is that of Law-making: But because he has in him the *Supream Execution*, from whom all inferiour Magistrates derive all their several subordinate Powers, or at least the greatest part of them: having also no Legislative superiour to him, there being no Law to be made without his consent, which cannot be expected should ever subject him to the other part of the Legislative, *he is* properly enough in this sense *Supream*. But yet it is to be observed, that though *Oaths of Allegiance* and Fealty are taken to him, 'tis not to him as Supream Legislator, but as *Supream Executor* of the Law, made by a joint Power of him with others; *Allegiance* being nothing but an *Obedience according to Law*, which when he violates, he has no right to Obedience, nor can claim it otherwise than as the publick Person vested with the Power of the Law, and so is to be consider'd as the Image, Phantom, or Representative① of the Commonwealth, acted by the will of the Society, declared in its Laws; and thus he has no Will, no Power, but that of the Law. But when he quits this Representation, this publick Will, and acts by his own private Will, he degrades himself, and is but a single private Person without Power, and without Will, that has any Right to *Obedience*; the Members owing no *Obedience* but to the publick Will of the Society.

---

① 洛克这里所用的"代表"(Representative)以及本段后文中的"Representation",仍然是霍布斯意义上的授权的对象,或者是根据国家法律所表示的社会意志而行动的国家的象征(Image)或标志(Phantom)。按照霍布斯的主张,代表的过程就是授权的过程,被代表的可以是"人",不一定是天、神和上帝。而在第158段中,洛克使用的"Representation"则不同,有关学者对此的理解为,洛克的理论无意将权力归给多数人或大众,洛克将没有财产的人排除在享有参政权的群体之外,甚至有人得出洛克主张限制公民权的结论。

The *Executive Power* placed any where but in a Person, that has also a share in the Legislative, is visibly subordinate and accountable to it, and may be at pleasure changed and displaced; so that it is not the *supream Executive Power* that is exempt from *Subordination*, but the *Supream Executive Power* vested in one, who having a share in the Legislative, has no distinct superiour Legislative to be subordinate and accountable to, farther than he himself shall joyn and consent: so that he is no more subordinate than he himself shall think fit, which one may certainly conclude will be but very little. Of other *Ministerial* and *subordinate Powers* in a Commonwealth, we need not speak, they being so multiply'd with infinite variety, in the different Customs and Constitutions of distinct Commonwealths, that it is impossible to give a particular account of them all. Only thus much, which is necessary to our present purpose, we may take notice of concerning them, that they have no manner of Authority any of them, beyond what is, by positive Grant, and Commission, delegated to them, and are all of them accountable to some other Power in the Commonwealth.

It is not necessary, no nor so much as convenient, that the *Legislative* should be *always in being*. But absolutely necessary that the *Executive Power* should, because there is not always need of new Laws to be made, but always need of Execution of the Laws that are made. When the *Legislative* hath put the *Execution* of the Laws, they make, into other hands, they have a power still to resume it out of those hands, when they find cause, and to punish for any mall-administration against the Laws. The same holds also in regard of the *Federative* Power, that and the Executive being both *Ministerial and subordinate to the Legislative*, which as has been shew'd in a Constituted Commonwealth, is the Supream. The *Legislative* also in this Case being suppos'd to consist of several Persons (for if it be a single Person, it cannot but be always in being, and so will as Supream, naturally have the Supream Executive Power, together with the Legislative) *may assemble and exercise their Legislature*, at the times that either their original Constitution, or their own Adjournment appoints, or when they please; if neither of these hath appointed any time, or there be no other way prescribed to convoke them. For the supream Power being placed in them by the People, 'tis always in them, and they may exercise it when they please, unless by their original

Constitution they are limited to certain Seasons, or by an Act of their Supream Power they have Adjourned to a certain time, and when that time comes, they have a right to *Assemble* and *act* again.

If the *Legislative*, or any part of it be made up of Representatives chosen for that time by the People, which afterwards return into the ordinary state of Subjects, and have no share in the Legislature but upon a new choice, this power of chusing must also be exercised by the People, either at certain appointed Seasons, or else when they are summon'd to it: and in this latter Case, the power of convoking the Legislative, is ordinarily placed in the Executive, and has one of these two limitations in respect of time: That either the Original Constitution requires their *assembling* and *acting* at certain intervals, and then the Executive Power does nothing but Ministerially issue directions for their Electing and Assembling, according to due Forms: Or else it is left to his Prudence to call them by new Elections, when the Occasions or Exigencies of the publick require the amendment of old, or making of new Laws, or the redress or prevention of any inconveniencies, that lie on, or threaten the People.

It may be demanded here, What if the Executive Power being possessed of the Force of the Commonwealth, shall make use of that force to hinder the *meeting* and *acting of the Legislative*, when the Original Constitution, or the publick Exigencies require it? I say using Force upon the People without Authority, and contrary to the Trust put in him, that does so, is a state of War with the People, who have a right to *reinstate* their *Legislative in the Exercise* of their Power. For having erected a Legislative, with an intent they should exercise the Power of making Laws, either at certain set times, or when there is need of it; when they are hindr'd by any force from, what is so necessary to the Society, and wherein the Safety and preservation of the People consists, the People have a right to remove it by force. In all States and Conditions the true remedy of *Force* without Authority, is to oppose *Force* to it. The use of *force* without Authority, always puts him that uses it into a *state of War*, as the Aggressor, and renders him liable to be treated accordingly.

The Power *of Assembling and dismissing the Legislative*, placed in the Executive, gives not the Executive a superiority over it, but is a Fiduciary

Trust, placed in him, for the safety of the People, in a Case where the uncertainty, and variableness of humane affairs could not bear a steady fixed rule. For it not being possible, that the first Framers of the Government should, by any foresight, be so much Masters of future Events, as to be able to prefix so just periods of return and duration to the *Assemblies of the Legislative*, in all times to come, that might exactly answer all the Exigencies of the Commonwealth; the best remedy could be found for this defect, was to trust this to the prudence of one, who was always to be present, and whose business it was to watch over the publick good. Constant *frequent meetings of the Legislative*, and long Continuations of their Assemblies, without necessary occasion, could not but be burthensome to the People, and must necessarily in time produce more dangerous inconveniences, and yet the quick turn of affairs might be sometimes such as to need their present help: Any delay of their *Convening* might endanger the publick; and sometimes too their business might be so great, that the limited time of their sitting might be too short for their work, and rob the publick of that benefit, which could be had only from their mature deliberation. What then could be done, in this Case, to prevent the Community, from being exposed sometime or other to eminent hazard, on one side, or the other, by fixed intervals and periods, set to the *meeting and acting of the Legislative*, but to intrust it to the prudence of some, who being present, and acquainted with the state of publick affairs, might make use of this Prerogative for the publick good? And where else could this be so well placed as in his hands, who was intrusted with the Execution of the Laws, for the same end? Thus supposing the regulation of times for the *Assembling and Sitting of the Legislative*, not settled by the original Constitution, it naturally fell into the hands of the Executive, not as an Arbitrary Power depending on his good pleasure, but with this trust always to have it exercised only for the publick Weal, as the Occurrences of times and change of affairs might require. Whether *settled periods of their Convening*, or a *liberty* left to the Prince *for Convoking the Legislative*, or perhaps a mixture of both, hath the least inconvenience attending it, 'tis not my business here to inquire, but only to shew, that though the Executive Power may have the Prerogative of *Convoking* and *dissolving* such *Conventions of the Legislative*, yet it is not thereby superiour to it.

Things of this World are in so constant a Flux, that nothing remains long in the same State. Thus People, Riches, Trade, Power, change their Stations; flourishing mighty Cities come to ruine, and prove in time neglected desolate Corners, whilst other unfrequented places grow into populous Countries, fill'd with Wealth and Inhabitants. But things not always changing equally, and private interest often keeping up Customs and Priviledges, when the reasons of them are ceased, it often comes to pass, that in Governments, where part of the Legislative consists of *Representatives* chosen by the People, that in tract of time this *Representation* becomes very *unequal* and disproportionate to the reasons it was at first establish'd upon. To what gross absurdities the following of Custom, when Reason has left it, may lead, we may be satisfied when we see the bare Name of a Town, of which there remains not so much as the ruines, where scarce so much Housing as a Sheep-coat; or more Inhabitants than a Shepherd is to be found, sends *as many Representatives* to the grand Assembly of Law-makers, as a whole County numerous in People, and powerful in riches. This Strangers stand amazed at, and every one must confess needs a remedy. Though most think it hard to find one, because the Constitution of the Legislative being the original and supream act of the Society, antecedent to all positive Laws in it, and depending wholly on the People, no inferiour Power can alter it. And therefore the *People*, when the *Legislative* is once Constituted, *having* in such a Government as we have been speaking of, *no Power* to act as long as the Government stands; this inconvenience is thought incapable of a remedy.

*Salus Populi Suprema Lex*①, is certainly so just and fundamental a Rule, that he, who sincerely follows it, cannot dangerously err. If therefore the Executive, who has the power of Convoking the Legislative, observing rather the true proportion, than fashion of *Representation*, regulates, not by old custom, but true reason, the *number of Members*, in all places, that have a right to be distinctly represented, which no part of the People however incorporated can pretend to, but in proportion to the assistance, which it

---

① "Salus Populi Suprema Lex",这里意在表明人民的福利才是最高的法律和最根本的准则。无论是法律的制定,还是其有效执行,一切须以民众的福利、利益为准,均要维护、保护人民的利益和意愿,也唯有如此,才是公正的和平等的,说明洛克所主张的社会是民众的社会,民众就是社会的政治内涵。

affords to the publick, it cannot be judg'd, to have set up a new Legislative, but to have restored the old and true one, and to have rectified the disorders, which succession of time had insensibly, as well as inevitably introduced. For it being the interest, as well as intention of the People, to have a fair and *equal Representative*; whoever brings it nearest to that, is an undoubted Friend, to, and Establisher of the Government, and cannot miss the Consent and Approbation of the Community. *Prerogative* being nothing, but a Power in the hands of the Prince to provide for the publick good, in such Cases, which depending upon unforeseen and uncertain Occurrences, certain and unalterable Laws could not safely direct, whatsoever shall be done manifestly for the good of the People, and the establishing the Government upon its true Foundations, is, and always will be just *Prerogative*. The Power of Erecting new Corporations, and therewith *new Representatives*, carries with it a supposition, that in time the *measures of representation* might vary, and those places have a just right to be represented which before had none; and by the same reason, those cease to have a right, and be too inconsiderable for such a Priviledge, which before had it. 'Tis not a change from the present State, which perhaps Corruption, or decay has introduced, that makes an Inroad upon the Government, but the tendency of it to injure or oppress the People, and to set up one part, or Party, with a distinction from, and an unequal subjection of the rest. Whatsoever cannot but be acknowledged to be of advantage to the Society, and People in general, upon just and lasting measures, will always, when done, justifie it self; and whenever the People shall chuse their *Representatives upon* just and undeniably *equal measures* suitable to the original Frame of the Government, it cannot be doubted to be the will and act of the Society, whoever permitted, or caused them so to do.

选文出处

John Locke. *Two Treatises of Government*. Beijing: China Social Sciences Publishing House (reprinted from the English Edition by Cambridge University Press, 1988), 1999, pp. 366—374.

思考题

1. 根据洛克的观点，最高权力属于共同体或民众。在西方世界，它是否只是一种理想，甚至是梦想？它能变成现实吗？
2. 当代西方政治制度与洛克的理论有何相似之处？根据节选部分体现的洛克的观点做适当的评论。

阅读

参考书目

1. 鲍桑葵:《关于国家的哲学理论》,汪淑钧译,北京:商务印书馆,1995年。
2. 杰弗里·托马斯:《政治哲学导论》,顾肃、刘雪梅译,北京:中国人民大学出版社,2006年。
3. 列奥·施特劳斯:《自然权利与历史》,彭刚译,北京:生活·读书·新知三联书店,2003年。

休　谟

大卫·休谟（David Hume，1711—1776），是英国经验主义的主要代表。休谟出生于苏格兰的爱丁堡，祖上为名门，父亲是律师，母亲是贵族之女，但休谟出生时家境已经衰落。在童年时代，休谟从母亲和家庭教师那里得到很好的教育。他 11 岁的时候进爱丁堡大学学习，后来由于家庭原因辍学，未获学位。休谟是个早熟的哲人，他的主要哲学思想在 18 岁时已经初步形成。他的最重要的著作《人性论》（A Treatise of Human Nature）在 26 岁时就已完成。不过，休谟的学术生涯充满坎坷，《人性论》出版之后，学术界几乎没有任何反应。休谟曾特地匿名写了一本介绍这本书的小册子《最近出版的题为〈人性论〉一书的概要》（An Abstract of a Book Lately Published Entitled, A Treatise of Human Nature）来推广自己的著作，但也没有什么收效。更为不幸的是，他后来还因为这部著作而被指责为反宗教、反道德，致使申请爱丁堡大学的道德哲学系教授的职位失败。1748 年，他把《人性论》的第 1 卷改写为《人类理解研究》（An Enquiry Concerning Human Understanding），出版后获得了很大的成功。他的主要著作还有《道德原理研究》（Enquiry Concerning the Principles of Morals）、《论文四篇》（Four Dissertations）、《自然宗教对话录》（Dialogues Concerning Natural Religion）、《英国史》（History of Great Britain）等。

这篇选读是《人类理解研究》中的第 7 章第 1 节，体现了休谟比较极端的经验主义观点。休谟否定因果关系的存在。在他看来，所谓的因果只是经验的重复，即两者经常在时间中相继出现。但轻信的人常常就因此断定,前者的出现肯定会引起后者的出现,把两者的关系看作是必然的,还会在将来保持不变。休谟认为这种现象并不意味着必然联系,因为相继出现过一万次的两件事情,完全有可能在一万零一次的时候停止相随,就是无数次升起过的太阳也不能保证明天还会升起,即不升起的那一天总是存在的。所以知识只不过是经验的重复,无论重复了多少次,并不能保证下一次还会重复,所谓的因果律不值得信任。

为了说明他的观点,休谟对各种因果现象进行了研究。休谟在探讨外在的事物时说:"在观察周围的外物并且思考原因的作用时,我们从不能在单一的事例中,发现任何能量或必然联系;从不能发现出任何性质可以把结果系于原因之上,可以使结果必然跟原因而来。"假如外在事物之间有什么必然联系,仅仅研究单独的事例就能够知道结果是什么。但事实上这是不可能的,只有不停地观察到两个事物相继出现才能找到所谓的因果关系。所以这种关系不是内在的,而是外在地根据经验连接起来的,随时都可能失去作用。在休谟看来,就是最为显而易见的真理也没有必然的依据。例如,就算你接触过一万种发热的火,也不能保证下一种火也是热的,就好像守在一个曾经有兔子撞死在上面的树桩旁边,不见得等得到另一只兔子来一样。

休谟接着探讨了内心的因果现象。他说:"可以这么说,我们在每时每刻都意识到自己的内部的能量;因为我们感觉到,单凭借我们意志的命令,我们就可以活动各个器官,并且指导心中的各种官能。"从表面上看,好像人的意志是促使自己运动的原因。但是,休谟却不这么认为。他首先研究了意志对肉体的指挥,并且从三个方面否定了这里的因果关系。第一,这种观点的支持者往往假设一种精神的实体借心灵和肉体的联合来影响物质的实体,使最精细的思想促动最粗重的物质,但心灵和肉体到底如何联合是一个难以解开的谜。这个谜无法解开就不可能真正找到它们之间的因果关系;第二,意志为什么不能使心脏和肝等随便活动,而只能指挥舌头和手指等,为什么不能指挥得病的器官,等等,都不能从意志本身是否明确得到解释,都得通过经验来判断;"第三,我们根据解剖学知道,在由意志发起的动作中,能量的直接对象不是那个运动的肢体自身,而是通过一些肌肉、神经和元精,或者是更微妙、更不为我们所知晓的一种东西,把运动相继传递过去,直到意志直接指挥的肢体。"这一现象说明了从精神上的指挥到肉体的运动是很复杂的,难以得到解释,不可能找到明确的因果关系。总之,意志能否指挥肉体以及如何指挥属于经验领域的问题,两者之间没有什么必然的因果关系。

接着休谟考察了人对心灵本身的控制。我们可以仅仅凭借意志的命令,使一个新观念产生出来,并把注意力集中于这个观念。在全面思考之后,可以自由地离开这个问题,再思考别的问题。在这个过程中,意志是不是思想的明确原因呢?休谟同样否认这种可能性。首先,人对灵魂的本性、观念的本性以及两者的关系知之甚少,所以不能断言其中有因果关系。其次,人心对于自己的控制能力也很有限;为什么人能够这样思考而不能那样思考,两者之间的界限不是理性所能弄明白的,只有依靠经验和观察才能知道。最后,这种自主的能力在不同的时候是很不相同的,人在生病等情况下控制思想的能力较差。这种变化只有通过经验才能观察到,而不是通过分析意志本身所能证明的。

有的哲学家认为,不可认识的因果律是神的意志的体现。他们认为:"普通所谓原因的那些事物,实际上只是一些机缘;各种结果的真正直接的原则,并不是自然中任何力量或威力,只是最高神明的一种意志,因为那种神明的意愿让某一些特殊的物象永久联合在一起。"但是,休谟并不认同这种观点。在休谟看来,主张最高神明有普遍能力和作用的这种学说,过于大胆;只要明白人类理性的脆弱,以及它的作用所能及的狭窄范围,就难以相信这种学说。另外,这种学说所依靠的论证没有什么力量。因果关系本来就难以认识,假如再把神牵涉进来可能只会让这个问题更加复杂化。

总之,休谟通过以上四个方面的探讨,阐明了作为一切知识的基础的因果律并不可靠,所谓的必然联系基本上是经验的重复。大哲学家康德曾说:"我坦率地承认,就是休谟的提示在多年以前首先打破了我教条主义的迷梦,并且在我对思辨哲学的研究上给我指出了一个完全不同的方向。"[1]哲学家罗素曾这样评论:"从某种意义上讲,他代表着一条死胡同:沿他的方向,不可能再往前进。自他著书以来,反驳他一向是形而上学家中间的一种时兴消遣。对我来说,我觉得他们的反驳没有一点是足以信服的。"[2]休谟的观点似乎既可爱又可恨,可爱的是他揭示了一个很深刻的问题;可恨的是任何一个想建立系统学问的人想反驳却又无能为力。

An Enquiry Concerning Human Understanding

The great advantage of the mathematical sciences above the moral consists

---

[1] 康德:《任何一种能够作为科学出现的未来形而上学导论》,庞景仁译,北京:商务印书馆,1997年,第9页。

[2] 罗素:《西方哲学史》(下卷),何兆武、李约瑟译,北京:商务印书馆,1996年,第196页。

in this, that the ideas of the former, being sensible, are always clear and determinate, the smallest distinction between them is immediately perceptible, and the same terms are still expressive of the same ideas, without ambiguity or variation. An oval is never mistaken for a circle, nor an hyperbola for an ellipsis. The isosceles and scalenum are distinguished by boundaries more exact than vice and virtue, right and wrong. If any term be defined in geometry, the mind readily, of itself, substitutes, on all occasions, the definition for the term defined: Or even when no definition is employed, the object itself may be presented to the senses, and by that means be steadily and clearly apprehended. But the finer sentiments of the mind, the operations of the understanding, the various agitations of the passions, though really in themselves distinct, easily escape us, when surveyed by reflection; nor is it in our power to recal the original object, as often as we have occasion to contemplate it. Ambiguity, by this means, is gradually introduced into our reasonings: Similar objects are readily taken to be the same: And the conclusion becomes at last very wide of the premises.

One may safely, however, affirm, that, if we consider these sciences in a proper light, their advantages and disadvantages nearly compensate each other, and reduce both of them to a state of equality. If the mind, with greater facility, retains the ideas of geometry clear and determinate, it must carry on a much longer and more intricate chain of reasoning, and compare ideas much wider of each other, in order to reach the abstruser truths of that science. And if moral ideas are apt, without extreme care, to fall into obscurity and confusion, the inferences are always much shorter in these disquisitions, and the intermediate steps, which lead to the conclusion, much fewer than in the sciences which treat of quantity and number. In reality, there is scarcely a proposition in Euclid[①] so simple, as not to consist of more parts, than are to be found in any moral reasoning which runs not into chimera and conceit. Where we trace the principles of the human mind through a few steps, we may be very well satisfied with our progress; considering how soon nature throws a bar to all our enquiries concerning causes, and reduces us to an acknowledgment of our ignorance. The chief obstacle, therefore, to our

---

① Euclid,欧几里得(约前 330—前 275),古希腊著名的数学家,公认的"几何之父"。

improvement in the moral or metaphysical sciences is the obscurity of the ideas, and ambiguity of the terms. The principal difficulty in the mathematics is the length of inferences and compass of thought, requisite to the forming of any conclusion. And, perhaps, our progress in natural philosophy is chiefly retarded by the want of proper experiments and phaenomena, which are often discovered by chance, and cannot always be found, when requisite, even by the most diligent and prudent enquiry. As moral philosophy seems hitherto to have received less improvement than either geometry or physics, we may conclude, that, if there be any difference in this respect among these sciences, the difficulties, which obstruct the progress of the former, require superior care and capacity to be surmounted.

There are no ideas, which occur in metaphysics, more obscure and uncertain, than those of *power*, *force*, *energy* or *necessary connexion*, of which it is every moment necessary for us to treat in all our disquisitions. We shall, therefore, endeavour, in this section, to fix, if possible, the precise meaning of these terms, and thereby remove some part of that obscurity, which is so much complained of in this species of philosophy.

It seems a proposition, which will not admit of much dispute, that all our ideas are nothing but copies of our impressions, or, in other words, that it is impossible for us to *think* of anything, which we have not antecedently *felt*, either by our external or internal senses. I have endeavoured to explain and prove this proposition, and have expressed my hopes, that, by a proper application of it, men may reach a greater clearness and precision in philosophical reasonings, than what they have hitherto been able to attain. Complex ideas may, perhaps, be well known by definition, which is nothing but an enumeration of those parts or simple ideas, that compose them. But when we have pushed up definitions to the most simple ideas, and find still some ambiguity and obscurity; what resource are we then possessed of? By what invention can we throw light upon these ideas, and render them altogether precise and determinate to our intellectual view? Produce the impressions or original sentiments, from which the ideas are copied. These impressions are all strong and sensible. They admit not of ambiguity. They are not only placed in a full light themselves, but may throw light on their correspondent ideas, which lie in obscurity. And by this means, we may, perhaps, attain a new microscope or species of optics, by which, in the moral sciences, the most minute, and most simple ideas may be so enlarged as to fall readily under our apprehension, and be equally known with the grossest and most sensible ideas, that can be the object of our enquiry.

To be fully acquainted, therefore, with the idea of power or necessary connexion, let us examine its impression; and in order to find the impression with greater certainty, let us search for it in all the sources, from which it may possibly be derived.

When we look about us towards external objects, and consider the operation of causes, we are never able, in a single instance, to discover any power or necessary connexion; any quality, which binds the effect to the cause, and renders the one an infallible consequence of the other. We only find, that the one does actually, in fact, follow the other. The impulse of one billiard-ball is attended with motion in the second. This is the whole that appears to the *outward* senses. The mind feels no sentiment or *inward* impression from this succession of objects: Consequently, there is not, in any single, particular instance of cause and effect, anything which can suggest the idea of power or necessary connexion.

From the first appearance of an object, we never can conjecture what effect will result from it. But were the power or energy of any cause discoverable by the mind, we could foresee the effect, even without experience; and might, at first, pronounce with certainty concerning it, by mere dint of thought and reasoning.

In reality, there is no part of matter, that does ever, by its sensible qualities, discover any power or energy, or give us ground to imagine, that it could produce any thing, or be followed by any other object, which we could denominate its effect. Solidity, extension, motion; these qualities are all complete in themselves, and never point out any other event which may result from them. The scenes of the universe are continually shifting, and one object follows another in an uninterrupted succession; but the power of force, which actuates the whole machine, is entirely concealed from us, and never discovers itself in any of the sensible qualities of body. We know, that, in fact, heat is a constant attendant of flame; but what is the connexion between them, we have no room so much as to conjecture or imagine. It is impossible, therefore, that the idea of power can be derived from the contemplation of bodies, in single instances of their operation; because no bodies ever discover any power, which can be the original of this idea.

Since, therefore, external objects as they appear to the senses, give us no idea of power or necessary connexion, by their operation in particular instances, let us see, whether this idea be derived from reflection on the operations of our own minds, and be copied from any internal impression. It may be said, that we are every moment conscious of internal power; while we feel, that, by the simple command of our will, we can move the organs of our body, or direct the faculties of our mind. An act of volition produces motion in our limbs, or raises a new idea in our imagination. This influence of the will we know by consciousness. Hence we acquire the idea of power or energy; and are certain, that we ourselves and all other intelligent beings are possessed of power. This idea, then, is an idea of reflection, since it arises from reflecting on the operations of our own mind, and on the command which is exercised by will, both over the organs of the body and faculties of the soul.

We shall proceed to examine this pretension; and first with regard to the influence of volition over the organs of the body. This influence, we may observe, is a fact, which, like all other natural events, can be known only be experience, and can never be foreseen from any apparent energy or power in the cause, which connects it with the effect, and renders the one an infallible consequence of the other. The motion of our body follows upon the command of our will. Of this we are every moment conscious. But the means, by which this is effected; the energy, by which the will performs so extraordinary an operation; of this we are so far from being immediately conscious, that it must for ever escape our most diligent enquiry.

For *first*, is there any principle in all nature more mysterious than the union of soul with body; by which a supposed spiritual substance acquires such an influence over a material one, that the most refined thought is able to actuate the grossest matter? Were we empowered, by a secret wish, to remove mountains, or control the planets in their orbit; this extensive authority would not be more extraordinary, nor more beyond our comprehension. But if by consciousness we perceived any power or energy in the will, we must know this power; we must know its connexion with the effect; we must know the secret union of soul and body, and the nature of both these substances; by which the one is able to operate, in so many instances, upon the other.

Secondly, We are not able to move all the organs of the body with a like authority; though we cannot assign any reason besides experience, for so remarkable a difference between one and the other. Why has the will an influence over the tongue and fingers, not over the heart or liver? This question would never embarrass us, were we conscious of a power in the former case, not in the latter. We should then perceive, independent of experience, why the authority of will over the organs of the body is circumscribed within such particular limits. Being in that case fully acquainted with the power or force, by which it operates, we should also know, why its influence reaches precisely to such boundaries, and no farther.

A man, suddenly struck with palsy in the leg or arm, or who had newly lost those members, frequently endeavours, at first to move them, and employ them in their usual offices. Here he is as much conscious of power to command such limbs, as a man in perfect health is conscious of power to actuate any member which remains in its natural state and condition. But consciousness never deceives. Consequently, neither in the one case nor in the other, are we ever conscious of any power. We learn the influence of our will from experience alone. And experience only teaches us, how one event constantly follows another; without instructing us in the secret connexion, which binds them together, and renders them inseparable.

Thirdly, We learn from anatomy, that the immediate object of power in voluntary motion, is not the member itself which is moved, but certain muscles, and nerves, and animal spirits, and, perhaps, something still more minute and more unknown, through which the motion is successively propagated, ere it reach the member itself whose motion is the immediate object of volition. Can there be a more certain proof, that the power, by which this whole operation is performed, so far from being directly and fully known by an inward sentiment or consciousness, is, to the last degree, mysterious and unintelligible? Here the mind wills a certain event: Immediately another event, unknown to ourselves, and totally different from the one intended, is produced: This event produces another, equally unknown: Till at last, through a long succession, the desired event is produced. But if the original power were felt, it must be known: Were it known, its effect also must be known; since all power is relative to its effect. And *vice versa*, if the effect be not known, the power cannot be known nor felt. How indeed can we be conscious of a power to move our limbs, when we have no such power; but only that to move certain animal spirits, which, though they produce at last the motion of our limbs, yet operate in such a manner as is wholly beyond our comprehension?

We may, therefore, conclude from the whole, I hope, without any temerity, though with assurance; that our idea of power is not copied from any sentiment or consciousness of power within ourselves, when we give rise to animal motion, or apply our limbs to their proper use and office. That their motion follows the command of the will is a matter of common experience, like other natural events: But the power or energy by which this is effected, like that in other natural events, is unknown and inconceivable.

Shall we then assert, that we are conscious of a power or energy in our own minds, when, by an act or command of our will, we raise up a new idea, fix the mind to the contemplation of it, turn it on all sides, and at last dismiss it for some other idea, when we think that we have surveyed it with sufficient accuracy? I believe the same arguments will prove, that even this command of the will gives us no real idea of force or energy.

Firstly, it must be allowed, that, when we know a power. we know that every circumstance in the cause, by which it is enabled to produce the effect: For these are supposed to be synonimous. We must, therefore, know both the cause and effect, and the relation between them. But do we pretend to be acquainted with the nature of the human soul and the nature of an idea, or the aptitude of the one to produce the other? This is a real creation; a production of something out of nothing: Which implies a power so great, that it may seem, at first sight, beyond the reach of any being, less than infinite. At least it must be owned, that such a power is not felt, nor known, nor even conceivable by the mind. We only feel the event, namely, the existence of an idea, consequent to a command of the will: But the manner, in which this operation is performed, the power by which it is produced, is entirely beyond our comprehension.

Secondly, the command of the mind over itself is limited, as well as its command over the body; and these limits are not known by reason, or any acquaintance with the nature of cause and effect, but only by experience and observation, as in all other natural events and in the operation of external objects. Our authority over our sentiments and passions is much weaker than that over our ideas; and even the latter authority is circumscribed within very narrow boundaries. Will any one pretend to assign the ultimate reason of these boundaries, or show why the power is deficient in one case, not in another.

Thirdly, this self-command is very different at different times. A man in health possesses more of it than one languishing with sickness. We are more master of our thoughts in the morning than in the evening: Fasting, than after a full meal. Can we give any reason for these variations, except experience? Where then is the power, of which we pretend to be conscious? Is there not here, either in a spiritual or material substance, or both, some secret mechanism or structure of parts, upon which the effect depends, and which, being entirely unknown to us, renders the power or energy of the will equally unknown and incomprehensible?

Volition is surely an act of the mind, with which we are sufficiently acquainted. Reflect upon it. Consider it on all sides. Do you find anything in it like this creative power, by which it raises from nothing a new idea, and with a kind of *Fiat*①, imitates the omnipotence② of its Maker, if I may be allowed so to speak, who called forth into existence all the various scenes of nature? So far from being conscious of this energy in the will, it requires as certain experience as that of which we are possessed, to convince us that such extraordinary effects do ever result from a simple act of volition.

The generality of mankind never find any difficulty in accounting for the more common and familiar operations of nature—such as the descent of heavy bodies, the growth of plants, the generation of animals, or the nourishment of bodies by food: But suppose that, in all these cases, they perceive the very force or energy of the cause, by which it is connected with its effect, and is for ever infallible in its operation. They acquire, by long habit, such a turn of

---

① Fiat,正规的命令。
② omnipotence,全能。基督教徒认为,上帝是全能的(omnipotent)、全知的(omniscient)、无所不在的(omnipresent)。

mind, that, upon the appearance of the cause, they immediately expect with assurance its usual attendant, and hardly conceive it possible that any other event could result from it. It is only on the discovery of extraordinary phaenomena, such as earthquakes, pestilence, and prodigies of any kind, that they find themselves at a loss to assign a proper cause, and to explain the manner in which the effect is produced by it. It is usual for men, in such difficulties, to have recourse to some invisible intelligent principle as the immediate cause of that event which surprises them, and which, they think, cannot be accounted for from the common powers of nature. But philosophers, who carry their scrutiny a little farther, immediately perceive that, even in the most familiar events, the energy of the cause is as unintelligible as in the most unusual, and that we only learn by experience the frequent *Conjunction* of objects, without being ever able to comprehend anything like *Connexion* between them.

Here, then, many philosophers think themselves obliged by reason to have recourse, on all occasions, to the same principle, which the vulgar never appeal to but in cases that appear miraculous and supernatural. They acknowledge mind and intelligence to be, not only the ultimate and original cause of all things, but the immediate and sole cause of every event which appears in nature. They pretend that those objects which are commonly denominated *causes*, are in reality nothing but *occasions*; and that the true and direct principle of every effect is not any power or force in nature, but a volition of the Supreme Being, who wills that such particular objects should for ever be conjoined with each other. Instead of saying that one billiard-ball moves another by a force which it has derived from the author of nature, it is the Deity himself, they say, who, by a particular volition, moves the second ball, being determined to this operation by the impulse of the first ball, in consequence of those general laws which he has laid down to himself in the government of the universe. But philosophers advancing still in their inquiries, discover that, as we are totally ignorant of the power on which depends the mutual operation of bodies, we are no less ignorant of that power on which depends the operation of mind on body, or of body on mind; nor are we able, either from our senses or consciousness, to assign the ultimate principle in one case more than in the other. The same ignorance, therefore, reduces them to the same conclusion. They assert that the Deity is the immediate cause of the union between soul and body; and that they are not the organs of sense, which, being agitated by external objects, produce sensations in the mind; but that it is a particular volition of our omnipotent Maker, which excites such a sensation, in consequence of such a motion in the organ. In like manner, it is not any energy in the will that produces local motion in our members: It is God himself, who is pleased to second our will, in itself impotent, and to command that motion which we erroneously attribute to our own power and efficacy. Nor do philosophers stop at this conclusion. They sometimes extend the same inference to the mind itself, in its internal operations. Our mental vision or conception of ideas is nothing but a revelation made to us by our Maker. When we voluntarily turn our thoughts to any object, and raise up its image in the fancy, it is not the will which creates that idea: It is the universal Creator, who discovers it to the mind, and renders it present to us.①

Thus, according to these philosophers, every thing is full of God. Not content with the principle, that nothing exists but by his will, that nothing possesses any power but by his concession: They rob nature, and all created beings, of every power, in order to render their dependence on the Deity still more sensible and immediate. They consider not that, by this theory, they diminish, instead of magnifying, the grandeur of those attributes, which they affect so much to celebrate. It argues surely more power in the Deity to delegate a certain degree of power to inferior creatures than to produce every thing by his own immediate volition. It argues more wisdom to contrive at first the fabric of the world with such perfect foresight that, of itself, and by its proper operation, it may serve all the purposes of providence, than if the great Creator were obliged every moment to adjust its parts, and animate by his breath all the wheels of that stupendous machine.

But if we would have a more philosophical confutation of this theory, perhaps the two following reflections may suffice.

First, it seems to me that this theory of the universal energy and operation of the Supreme Being is too bold ever to carry conviction with it to a

---

① 这一段所谈论的观点出自巴克莱(George Berkeley)的哲学。

man, sufficiently apprized of the weakness of human reason, and the narrow limits to which it is confined in all its operations. Though the chain of arguments which conduct to it were ever so logical, there must arise a strong suspicion, if not an absolute assurance, that it has carried us quite beyond the reach of our faculties, when it leads to conclusions so extraordinary, and so remote from common life and experience. We are got into fairy land, long ere we have reached the last steps of our theory; and *there* we have no reason to trust our common methods of argument, or to think that our usual analogies and probabilities have any authority. Our line is too short to fathom such immense abysses. And however we may flatter ourselves that we are guided, in every step which we take, by a kind of verisimilitude and experience, we may be assured that this fancied experience has no authority when we thus apply it to subjects that lie entirely out of the sphere of experience. But on this we shall have occasion to touch afterwards.

Secondly, I cannot perceive any force in the arguments on which this theory is founded. We are ignorant, it is true, of the manner in which bodies operate on each other: Their force or energy is entirely incomprehensible: But are we not equally ignorant of the manner or force by which a mind, even the supreme mind, operates either on itself or on body? Whence, I beseech you, do we acquire any idea of it? We have no sentiment or consciousness of this power in ourselves. We have no idea of the Supreme Being but what we learn from reflection on our own faculties. Were our ignorance, therefore, a good reason for rejecting anything, we should be led into that principle of denying all energy in the Supreme Being as much as in the grossest matter. We surely comprehend as little the operations of one as of the other. Is it more difficult to conceive that motion may arise from impulse than that it may arise from volition? All we know is our profound ignorance in both cases.

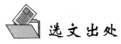 选文出处

David Hume. *An Enquiry Concerning Human Understanding*. in *Great Books of the Western World • David Hume*, Chicago: Encyclopaedia Britannica, Inc., 1980, pp. 470—475.

思考题

1. 在现实中,是否能够找到绝对、必然的知识?
2. 用休谟的论点反思以前的各种思想观点,看看有什么启发意义。

阅读参考书目

1. 周晓亮:《休谟哲学研究》,北京:人民出版社,1999年。
2. Barry Stroud, *Hume*, London: Routledge & Kegan Paul, 1977.

卢　梭

让-雅克·卢梭(Jean-Jacques Rousseau，1712—1778)是法国18世纪启蒙主义时期著名的思想家、哲学家和文学家。作为一位法国大革命思想的奠基者，他为现代民主观念和平等理想的确立和推进做出了杰出的贡献。

卢梭1712年6月29日出生于瑞士日内瓦，父亲伊萨克·卢梭是一位靠手艺维生的钟表匠。出身于牧师家庭的母亲苏萨娜·贝纳尔在生下他后，因难产离开了人世。由于家境贫寒，童年时期的卢梭并没有去学校读书。他最初接受的教育是与父亲一起通宵达旦地阅读母亲和外祖父留下来的小说。在他10岁时，父亲和一位法国陆军上尉发生了纠纷，结果不得不远走异国他乡。年幼的卢梭被舅父送到一个名叫包塞的乡村去学习拉丁文，这两年的乡村生活不但使卢梭爱上了淳朴、自然的田园风光，还养成了追求自由、不服强暴的叛逆性格。1728年，年满16岁的卢梭因不满被奴役的学徒生涯，最终选择离开日内瓦，开始了当仆人、随从、家庭教师、秘书等漂泊、流浪的生活。在这段日子中，华伦夫人给他在生活、学习和社交方面提供了无私的援助，为卢梭日后的成功奠定了基础。1741年，卢梭来到巴黎寻求发展，认识了著名的大哲学家狄德罗。1750年，卢梭在第戎科学院的一次社会征文中，以《论科学与艺术》("Discourse on the Arts and Sciences")一文而一举成名。1755年，卢梭出版了另一部政治学名著《论人类不平等的起源和基础》(*Discourse on the Origin of Inequality*)。

1756 到 1762 年是卢梭在巴黎近郊埋头思考与写作的一个重要时期,他完成并出版了《致达朗贝论戏剧书》(Letter to D'Alembert on the Theater,1758)、《新爱洛伊丝》(Julie or the New Heloise,1761)、《社会契约论》(The Social Contract,1762)、《爱弥儿》(Emile or On Education,1762)等多部具有划时代意义的作品。然而,《爱弥儿》这部本是讨论教育问题,即主张对儿童实行"自然教育",反对禁锢孩子天性的哲理小说却被法庭列为禁书。① 大理院下令逮捕作者,焚毁该小说。事先接到消息的卢梭先是逃到了瑞士,后又逃到了普鲁士的属地莫蒂业等地,可不管走到哪里,这位已被教会宣布为上帝的"敌人"的人都面临着被冷落、驱赶的尴尬。更为不幸的是,由于艺术观点上的分歧,卢梭与一直交往合作的百科全书派的朋友也分道扬镳了。政府当局的通缉、迫害以及来自朋友的攻击、揭短,使卢梭身心疲惫,几乎走向了崩溃的边缘。在这样一种内外交困的双重压力之下,卢梭萌生出了要捍卫尊严的决心。于是,便有了自传体小说《忏悔录》(Confessions,1766—1770)。我们在明白这样的一种写作背景后,便可理解小说中为何总是透出强烈的辩解和抗争意味:"不管末日审判的号角什么时候吹响,我都敢拿着这本书走到至高无上的审判者面前,果敢地大声说:'请看!这就是我所做过的,这就是我所想过的,我当时就是那样的人。'"② 换言之,要向世人证明自己到底是怎样的一个人,是卢梭写这部小说的主要内在动因。这之后,他又完成了《一个孤独的散步者的遐想》(Reveries of the Solitary Walker)、《山中书信》(Letters Written from the Mountain,1764)、《公民的情感》等著作。1778 年 7 月 2 日,卢梭因病去世,被安葬于巴黎先贤祠。

卢梭虽没有接受过系统的专业训练,但是其成就斐然,而且分布在哲学、政治、教育、音乐和文学等多个领域中。其中,文学与政治学的影响更为深远。在文学思想方面,卢梭崇尚大自然的美好,讴歌平民百姓的善良天性,使 18 世纪的欧洲文学增加了浓郁的人间烟火气息。尤其是他在作品中对情感、个性的崇尚与张扬更是开辟了一代文风,成为 19 世纪欧洲浪漫主义文学的重要先驱者之一。值得注意的是,卢梭的文学理论与创作实践有矛盾之处,即在理论上他是反对文学艺术的存在的,认为艺术中的奢侈淫逸之风会败坏社会风气,使人的道德沦丧。他的早期论文《论科学与艺术》就是围绕着这一思想展开的,"随着科学与艺术的光芒在我们的天边上升起,德行也就消逝了"。③ 显然,卢梭把

---

① 卢梭认为在对儿童的培养教育上,应充分尊重与发挥其天性,主张以实行情感培养为主,倡导通过体验而非书本学习的意义。
② 卢梭:《忏悔录》第一部,黎星译,北京:人民文学出版社,1982 年,第 1—2 页。
③ 伍蠡甫主编:《西方文论选》(上卷),上海:译文出版社,1979 年,第 332 页。

"德性"与"科学""艺术"对立了起来。可同时他又以自己的创作实践,证明了文学艺术非但不是腐蚀社会和人类精神的麻醉剂,相反还具有净化社会和心灵的作用。纵观卢梭复杂而艰辛的一生,会发现在不同阶段他的思考重心虽有所不同,可贯穿其思想始终的是反对专制,要求平等的观念,即面对社会上的不平等现象,他把自由与平等视为人的天然本性。这一思想不但在卢梭的文学创作中展现得淋漓尽致,而且他的政治、法律主张也是建立在这一认识基础上的。发表于1762年的《社会契约论》便是一部集中反映卢梭民主思想的著作。

《社会契约论》(*The Social Contract*),也译为《民约论》。该书共由四卷构成,每一卷又分成若干章。大致说来,这部著作涉及的内容较为广泛,既论述到了社会状态、国家立法、政府的形成,又讨论了巩固国家体制的方法与措施等,但贯穿全书的核心思想实际有两个:一个是"天赋人权",另一个是"主权在民"。正如前面所说,卢梭一直坚守着人生是自由、平等的理念。不过,他的自由、平等观念也有一个前、后的转换过程。简单说,卢梭早期把荒蛮的原始社会视为自由、平等的乐园,把不平等的根源归结为私有制的出现。所以,他曾在文章中激烈地抨击现代文明社会。卢梭后来意识到一味地追思人类远古的自然状态是无助于解决现实问题的。更为值得探讨的是,在一个既定的社会、国家中,应该制定、采用一些什么样的措施来维护、保证这种自由、平等的实施,即承认文明社会存在的合理性,进而寻找规范其正常运转的规则。事实上,卢梭在《社会契约论》的开篇就点明了其研究的宗旨:"我要探讨在社会秩序之中,从人类的实际情况与法律的可能情况着眼,能不能有某种合法的而又确切的政权规则。"那么,卢梭给人类所开出的这种"合法的而又确切的政权规则"是什么呢?是"契约",也就是采用"协议"的形式来确保每个社会成员的权利与地位。值得说明的是,卢梭是以一位国家的"公民",而非"君主"或"立法者"的身份来谈论政治、法律的,这就决定了《社会契约论》中的某些主张具有乌托邦的性质。

本书所选的"第一卷"便是对全书内容的一个纲领性概要。卢梭在"第一卷的题旨"中首先说出了那句"人是生而自由的,但却无往不在枷锁之中"的著名命题,即重点强调了自由是人类的一项天赋权利。接下来,他论述了人类由原始社会过渡到政权社会后所面临的诸如"权利""国家""主权者""政权""人民""公民""臣民"以及"财产权"等系列的相关问题。在这些关系中,卢梭把矛头对准了能对自由、平等与公正直接产生作用的权利,他认为"强力并不构成权利,而人们只是对合法的权力才有服从的义务",而又唯有"约定才可以成为人间一切合法权威的基础"。显然,卢梭认为国家是自由的人们自由协议的结果,任何人,包括"主权者"都没有高于他人的特权。为了能保障这一社会"契约"的顺利进行,卢梭还规定了"任何人拒不服从公意的,全体就要迫使他服从公意"。亦是说,一旦权力被某个人所篡夺、控制,人民就有权利用武力夺回所失去的自由,即国家的立法权属于人民。

《社会契约论》尽管还有不够完善之处,但是它已成为世界思想史上最重要的经典著作之一。卢梭在该书中所表达出的政治主张,不但为资产阶级推翻封建专制提供了思想武器,而且还对法国以及整个欧洲民主运动的推进做出了巨大的贡献。

The Social Contract

MY purpose is to consider if, in political society, there can be any legitimate and sure principle of government, taking men as they are and laws as they might be. In this inquiry I shall try always to bring together what right permits with what interest prescribes so that justice and utility are in no way divided.

I start without seeking to prove the importance of my subject. I may be asked whether I am a prince or a legislator that I should be writing about politics. I answer no: and indeed that that is my reason for doing so. If I were a prince or a legislator I should not waste my time saying what ought to be done; I should do it or keep silent.

Born as I was the citizen of a free state and a member of its sovereign body, the very right to vote imposes on me the duty to instruct myself in public affairs, however little infuence my voice may have in them. And whenever I reflect upon governments, I am happy to find that my studies always give me fresh reasons for admiring that of my own country.

CHAPTER 1
The Subject of Book I

MAN was born free, and he is everywhere in chains. Those who think themselves the masters of others are indeed greater slaves than they. How did this transformation come about? I do not know. How can it be made legitimate? That question I believe I can answer.

If I were to consider only force and the effects of force, I should say: "So long as a people is constrained to obey, and obeys, it does well; but as soon as it can shake off the yoke, and shakes it off, it does better; for since it regains its freedom by the same right as that which removed it, a people is either justified in taking back its freedom, or there is no justifying those who took it away." But the social order is a sacred right which serves as a basis for all other rights. And as it is not a natural right, it must be one founded on covenants. The problem is to deterimine what those covenants are. But before we pass on to that question, I must substantiate what I have so far said.

CHAPTER 2
The First Societies

The oldest of all societies, and the only natural one, is that of the family; yet children remain tied to their father by nature only so long as they need him for their preservation. As soon as this need ends, the natural bond is dissolved. Once the children are freed from the obedience they owe their father, and the father is freed from his responsibilities towards them, both parties equally regain their independencc. If they continue to remain united, it is no longer nature, but their own choice, which unites them; and the family as such is kept in being only by agreement.

This common liberty is a consequence of man's nature. Man's first law is to watch over his own preservation; his first care he owes to himself; and as soon as he reaches the age of reason, he becomes the only judge of the best means to preserve himself; he becomes his own master.

The family may therefore perhaps be seen as the first model of political societies: the head of the state bears the image of the father, the people the image of his children, and all, being born free and equal, surrender their freedom only when they see advantage in doing so. The only difference is that in the family, a father's love for his clildren repays him for the care he bestows on them, while in the state, where the ruler can have no such feeling for his people, the pleasure of commanding must take the place of love.

Grotius① denies that all human government is established for the benefit of the governed, and he cites the example of slavery. His characteristic method of reasoning is always to offer fact as a proof of right. It is possible to imagine a more logical method, but not one more favourable to tyrants.

According to Grotius, therefore, it is doubtful whether humanity belongs to a hundred men, or whether these hundred men belong to humanity, though he seems throughout his book to lean to the first of these views which is also that of Hobbes. These authors show us the human race divided into herds of cattle, each with a master who preserves it only in order to devour its members.

Just as a shepherd possesses a nature superior to that of his flock, so do those shepherds of men, their rulers, have a nature superior to that of their people. Or so, we are told by Philo, the Emperor Caligula argued, concluding, reasonably enough on this same analogy, that kings were gods or alternatively that the people were animals.

The reasoning of Caligula② coincides with that of Hobbes and Grotius. Indeed Aristotle, before any of them, said that men were not at all equal by nature, since some were born for slavery and others born to be masters.

Aristotle was right; but he mistook the effect for the cause. Anyone born in slavery is born for slavery—nothing is more certain. Slaves, in their bondage, lose everything, even the desire to be free. They love their servitude even as the companions of Ulysses③ loved their life as brutes. But if there are slaves by nature, it is only because there has been slavery against nature. Force made the first slaves; and their cowardice perpetuates their slavery.

I have said nothing of the King Adam④ or of the Emperor Noah⑤, father of the three great monarchs who shared out the universe among them, like the

---

① Grotius, H. 格鲁特(1583—1645), 荷兰学者、人道主义者、政治家。1621年至1631年间曾生活在法国;1634年至1644年间, 受瑞典政府派遣, 出使法国。著有大量政论文章和文学作品。
② Caligula, 卡利古拉(12—41), 罗马皇帝(37—41), 专横残暴, 处决将他扶上皇位的禁卫军长官, 屠杀犹太人等, 后被刺杀。
③ Ulysses, 尤利西斯, 古希腊史诗《奥德赛》中的英雄。他的同伴们在归途中遇险, 被变为猪。
④ Adam, 亚当, 据《圣经》记载, 亚当是上帝创造的第一个人。
⑤ Noah, 诺亚(又译挪亚), 据《圣经》记载, 洪水泛滥时, 只有诺亚一家听从上帝的安排, 在方舟中躲避了洪水, 成为洪水灭世后人类的新世祖。

children of Saturn①, with whom some authors have identified them. I hope my readers will be grateful for this moderation, for since I am directly descended from one of those princes, and perhaps in the eldest line, how do I know that if the deeds were checked, I might not find myself the legitimate king of the human race? However that may be, there is no gainsaying that Adam was the king of the world, as was Robinson Crusoe② of his island, precisely because he was the sole inhabitant; and the great advantage of such an empire was that the monarch, secure upon his throne, had no occasion to fear rebellions, wars or conspirators.

CHAPTER 3
The Right of the Strongest

The strongest man is never strong enough to be master all the time, unless he transforms force into right and obedience into duty. Hence "the right of the strongest" —a "right" that sounds like something intended ironically, but is actually laid down as a principle. But shall we never have this phrase explained? Force is a physical power; I do not see how its effects could produce morality. To yield to force is an act of necessity, not of will; it is at best an act of prudence. In what sense can it be a moral duty?

Let us grant, for a moment, that this so-called right exists. I suggest it can only produce a tissue of bewildering nonsense; for once might is made to be right, cause and effect are reversed, and every force which overcomes another force inherits the right which belonged to the vanquished. As soon as man can disobey with impunity, his disobedience becomes legitimate; and as the strongest is always right, the only problem is how to become the strongest. But what can be the validity of a right which perishes with the force on which it rests? If force compels obedience, there is no need to invoke a duty to obey, and if force ceases to compel obedience, there is no longer any obligation. Thus the word "right" adds nothing to what is said by "force"; it

---

① Saturn,萨图恩,罗马神话中的农神,即希腊神话中的克洛诺斯。据说,萨图恩曾与蒂但有约,生子之后要亲自吃掉自己的儿子。后来,他的儿子朱庇特篡位,将他逐出天庭。

② Robinson Grusoe,鲁滨逊·克鲁索,英国小说家笛福所著小说《鲁滨逊漂流记》(*Robinson Crusoe*,1719)中的主人公。

is meaningless.

"Obey those in power." If this means "yield to force" the precept is sound, but superfluous; it has never, I suggest, been violated. All power comes from God, I agree; but so does every disease, and no one forbids us to summon a physician. If I am held up by a robber at the edge of a wood, force compels me to hand over my purse. But if I could somehow contrive to keep the purse from him, would I still be obliged in conscience to surrender it? After all, the pistol in the robber's hand is undoubtedly a *power*.

Surely it must be admitted, then, that might does not make right, and that the duty of obedience is owed only to legitimate powers. Thus we are constantly led back to my original question.

CHAPTER 4
Slavery

SINCE no man has any natural authority over his fellows, and since force alone bestows no right, all legititmate authority among men must be based on covenants.

Grotius says: "If an individual can alienate his freedom and become the slave of a master, why may not a whole people alienate its freedom and become the subject of a king?" In this remark there are several ambiguous words which call for explanation; but let us confine ourselves to one—to "alienate". To alienate is to give or sell. A man who becomes the slave of another does not give himself, he sells himself in return for at least a subsistence. But in return for what could a whole people be said to sell itself? A king, far from nourishing his subjects, draws his nourishment from them; and kings, according to Rabelais[①], need more than a little nourishment. Do subjects, then, give their persons to the king on condition that he will accept their property as well? If so, I fail to see what they have left to preserve.

It will be said that a despot gives his subjects the assurance of civil tranquillity. Very well, but what does it profit them, if those wars against

---

① Rabelais,拉伯雷（1483—1553），法国作家，著有《卡冈都亚与庞大固埃》（*Gargantua and Pantagruel*，1532，或译《巨人传》）。

other powers which result from a despot's ambition, if his insatiable greed, and the oppressive demands of his administration, cause more desolation than civil strife would cause? What do the people gain if their very condition of civil tranquillity is one of their hardships? There is peace in dungeons, but is that enough to make dungeons desirable? The Greeks lived in peace in the cave of Cyclops① awaiting their turn to be devoured.

To speak of a man giving himself in return for nothing is to speak of what is absurd, unthinkable; such an action would be illegitimate, void, if only because no one who did it could be in his right mind. To say the same of a whole people is to conjure up a nation of lunatics; and right cannot rest on madness.

Even if each individual could alienate himself, he cannot alienate his children. For they are born men; they are born free; their liberty belongs to them; no one but they themselves has the right to dispose of it. Before they reach the years of discretion, their father may, in their name, make certain rules for their protection and their welfare, but he cannot give away their liberty irrevocably and unconditionally, for such a gift would be contrary to the natural order and an abuse of paternal rigt. Hence, an arbitrary government would be legitimate only if every new generation were free to accept or reject it, and in that case the government would cease to be arbitrary.

To renounce freedom is to renounce one's humanity, one's rights as a man and equally one's duties. There is no possible *quid pro quo* for one who renounces everything; indeed such renunciation is contrary to man's very nature; for if you take away all freedom of the will, you strip a man's actions of all moral significance. Finally, any covenant which stipulated absolute dominion for one party and absolute obedience for the other would be illogical and nugatory. Is it not evident that he who is entitled to demand everything owes nothing? And does not the single fact of there being no reciprocity, no mutual obligation, nullify the act? For what right can my slave have against me? If everything he has belongs to me, his right is *my* right, and it would be nonsense to speak of my having a right *against* myself.

---

① Cyclops,西克洛普(又译库克罗普斯),希腊神话中的巨人。

Grotius and the rest claim to find in war another justification for the so-called right of slavery. They argue that the victor's having the right to kill the vanquished implies that the vanquished has the right to purchase his life at the expense of his liberty—a bargain thought to be the more legitimate because it is advantageous to both parties.

But it is clear that this so-called right to kill the vanquished cannot be derived from the state of war. For this reason alone, that men living in their primitive condition of independence have no intercourse regular enough to constitute either a state of peace or a state of war; and men are not naturally enemies. It is conflicts over things, not quarrels between men which constitute war, and the state of war cannot arise from mere personal relations, but only from property relations. Private wars between one man and another can exist neither in a state of nature, where there is no fixed property, nor in society, where everything is under the authority of law.

Private fights, duels, encounters, do not constitute any kind of state; and as for the private wars that were permitted by the ordinances of Louis IX[①], King of France, and suspended by the Peace of God[②], these were no more than an abuse of feudal government, all irrational system if there ever was one, and contrary both to natural justice and to all sound polity.

War, then, is not a relation between men, but between states; in war individuals are enemies wholly by chance, not as men, not even as citizens, but only as soldiers; not as members of their country, but only as its defenders. In a word, a state can have as an enemy only another state, not men, because there can be no real relation between things possessing different intrinsic natures.

This principle conforms to the established rules of all times and to the constant practice of every political society. Declarations of war are warnings not so much to governments as to their subjects. The foreigner—whether he is a king, a private person or a whole people—who robs, kills or detains the subjects of another prince without first declaring war against that prince, is not an enemy but a brigand. Even in the midst of war, a just prince, seizing

---

① Louis IX,法国国王路易第九(1226—1270年在位),即法国历史上的圣路易。
② 1035年,基督教教会规定,每星期四至下星期一晨不得进行战争,称为"上帝的和平。"

what he can of public property in the enemy's territory, nevertheless respects the persons and possessions of private individuals; he respects the principles on which his own rights are based. Since the aim of war is to subdue a hostile state, a combatant has the right to kill the defenders of that state while they are armed; but as soon as they lay down their arms and surrender, they cease to be either enemies or instruments of the enemy; they become simply men once more, and no one has any longer the right to take their lives. It is sometimes possible to destroy a state without killing a single one of its members, and war gives no right to inflict any more destruction than is necessary for victory. These principles were not invented by Grotius, nor are they founded on the authority of the poets; they are derived from the nature of things; they are based on reason.

The right of conquest has no other foundation than the law of the strongest. And if war gives the conqueror no right to massacre a conquered people, no such right can be invoked to justify their enslavement. Men have the right to kill their enemies only when they cannot enslave them, so the right of enslaving cannot be derived from the right to kill. It would therefore be an iniquitous barter to make the vanquished purchase with their liberty the lives over which the victor has no legitimate claim. An argument basing the right over life and death on the right to enslave, and the right to enslave on the right over life and death, is an argument trapped in a vicious circle.

Even if we assumed that this terrible right of massacre did exist, then slaves of war, or a conquered people, would be under no obligation to obey their master any further than they were forced to do so. By taking an equivalent of his victim's life, the victor shows him no favour; instead of destroying him unprofitably, he destroys him by exploiting him. Hence, far from the victor having acquired some further authority beside that of force over the vanquished, the state of war between them continues; their mutual relation is the effect of war, and the continuation of the rights of war implies that there has been no treaty of peace. An agreement has assuredly been made, but that agreement, far from ending the state of war, presupposes its continuation.

Thus, however we look at the question, the "right" of slavery is seen to be void; void, not only because it cannot be justified, but also because it is nonsensical, because it has no meaning. The words "slavery" and "right" are contradictory, they cancel each other out. Whether as between one man and another, or between one man and a whole people, it would always be absurd to say: "I hereby make a covenant with you which is wholly at your expense and wholly to my advantage; I will respect it so long as I please and you shall respect it so long as I wish."

CHAPTER 5
That We Must Always Go Back to an Original Covenant

EVEN if I were to concede all that I have so far refuted, the champions of despotism would be no better off. There will always be a great difference between subduing a multitude and ruling a society. If one man successively enslaved many separate individuals, no matter how numerous, he and they would never bear the aspect of anything but a master and his slaves, not at all that of a people and their ruler; an aggregation, perhaps, but certainly not an association, for they would neither have a common good nor be a body politic. Even if such a man were to enslave half the world, he would remain a private individual, and his interest, always at variance with that of the others, would never be more than a personal interest. When he died, the empire he left would be scattered for lack of any bond of union, even as an oak crumbles and falls into a heap of ashes when fire has consumed it.

"A people," says Grotius, "may give itself to a king." Therefore, according to Grotius a people is *a people* even before the gift to the king is made. The gift itself is a civil act; it presupposes public deliberation. Hence, before considering the act by which a people submits to a king, we ought to scrutinize the act by which people become *a people*, for that act, being necessarily antecedent to the other, is the real foundation of society.

Indeed, if there were no earlier agreement, then how, unless the election were unanimous, could there be any obligation on the minority to accept the decision of the majority? What right have the hundred who want to have a master to vote on behalf of the ten who do not? The law of majority-voting itself rests on a covenant, and implies that there has been on at least one occasion unanimity.

CHAPTER 6
The Social Pact

I ASSUME that men reach a point where the obstacles to their preservation in a state of nature prove greater than the strength that each man has to preserve himself in that state. Beyond this point, the primitive condition cannot endure, for then the human race will perish if it does not change its mode of existence.

Since men cannot create new forces, but merely combine and control those which already exist, the only way in which they can preserve themselves is by uniting their separate powers in a combination strong enough to overcome any resistance, uniting them so that their powers are directed by a single motive and act in concert.

Such a sum of forces can be produced only by the union of separate men, but as each man's own strength and liberty are the chief instruments of his preservation, how can he merge his with others' without putting himself in peril and neglecting the care he owes to himself? This difficulty, which brings me back to my present subject, may be expressed in these words:

"How to find a form of association which will defend the person and goods of each member with the collective force of all, and under which each individual, while uniting himself with the others, obeys no one but himself, and remains as free as before." This is the fundamental problem to which the social contract holds the solution.

The articles of this contract are so precisely determined by the nature of the act, that the slightest modification must render them null and void; they are such that, though perhaps never formally stated, they are everywhere the same, everywhere tacitly admitted and recognized; and if ever the social pact is violated, every man regains his original rights and, recovering his natural freedom, loses that social freedom for which he exchanged it.

These articles of association, rightly understood, are reducible to a single one, namely the total alienation by each associate of himself and all his rights to the whole community. Thus, in the first place, as every individual gives himself absolutely, the conditions are the same for all, and precisely because they are the same for all, it is in no one's interest to make the conditions onerous for others.

Secondly, since the alienation is unconditional, the union is as perfect as it could be, and no individual associate has any longer any rights to claim; for if rights were left to individuals, in the absence of any higher authority to judge between them and the public, each individual, being his own judge in some causes, would soon demand to be his own judge in all; and in this way the state of nature would be kept in being, and the association inevitably become either tyrannical or void.

Finally, since each man gives himself to all, he gives himself to no one; and since there is no associate over whom he does not gain the same rights as others gain over him, each man recovers the equivalent of everything he loses, and in the bargain he acquires more power to preserve what he has.

If, then, we eliminate from the social pact everything that is not essential to it, we find it comes down to this: "Each one of us puts into the community his person and all his powers under the supreme direction of the general will; and as a body, we incorporate every member as an indivisible part of the whole."

Immediately, in place of the individual person of each contracting party, this act of association creates an artificial and collective body composed of as many members as there are voters in the assembly, and by this same act that body acquires its unity, its common *ego*, its life and its will. The public person thus formed by the union of all other persons was once called the *city*①, and is now known as the *republic* or the *body politic*. In its passive role it is called the *state*, when it plays an active role it is the *sovereign*; and when it is compared to others of its own kind, it is a *power*. Those who are associated in it take collectively the name of *a people*, and call themselves individually *citizens*, in so far as they share in the sovereign power, and *subjects*, in so far as they put themselves under the laws of the state. However, these words are often confused, each being mistaken for another;

---

① 此处为作者的原注。原注的内容可简略如下:"city"这个词语的真正含义在现代社会中几乎消失了。这个词语常被人们认为与"town"是同一个意思,即把市民与公民视为同一个意思。这些人不知道构成城市的是家庭,而构成城邦的是公民。

but the essential thing is to know how to recognize them when they are used in their precise sense.

CHAPTER 7
The Sovereign

THIS formula shows that the act of association consists of a reciprocal commitment between society and the individual, so that each person, in making a contract, as it were, with himself, finds himself doubly committed, first, as a member of the sovereign body in relation to individuals, and secondly as a member of the state in relation to the sovereign. Here there can be no invoking the principle of civil law which says that no man is bound by a contract with himself, for there is a great difference between having an obligation to oneself and having an obligation to something of which one is a member.

We must add that a public decision can impose an obligation on all the subjects towards the sovereign, by reason of the two aspects under which each can be seen, while, contrariwise, such decisions cannot impose an obligation on the sovereign towards itself; and hence it would be against the very nature of a political body for the sovereign to set over itself a law which it could not infringe. The sovereign, bearing only one single and identical aspect, is in the position of a private person making a contract with himself, which shows that there neither is, nor can be, any kind of fundamental law binding on the people as a body, not even the social contract itself. This does not mean that the whole body cannot incur obligations to other nations, so long as those obligations do not infringe the contract; for in relation to foreign powers, the body politic is a simple entity, an individual.

However, since the body politic, or sovereign, owes its being to the sanctity of the contract alone, it cannot commit itself, even in treaties with foreign powers, to anything that would derogate from the original act of association; it could not, for example, alienate a part of itself or submit to another sovereign. To violate the act which has given it existence would be to annihilate itself; and what is nothing can produce nothing.

As soon as the multitude is united thus in a single body, no one can injure any one of the members without attacking the whole, still less injure the whole without each member feeling it. Duty and self-interest thus equally oblige the two contracting parties to give each other mutual aid; and the same men should seek to bring together in this dual relationship, all the advantages that flow from it.

Now, as the sovereign is formed entirely of the individuals who compose it, it has not, nor could it have, any interest contrary to theirs; and so the sovereign has no need to give guarantees to the subjects, because it is impossible for a body to wish to hurt all of its members, and, as we shall see, it cannot hurt any particular member. The sovereign by the mere fact that it is, is always all that it ought to be.

But this is not true of the relation of subject to sovereign. Despite their common interest, subjects will not be bound by their commitment unless means are found to guarantee their fidelity.

For every individual as a man may have a private will contrary to, or different from, the general will that he has as a citizen. His private interest may speak with a very different voice from that of the public interest; his absolute and naturally independent existence may make him regard what he owes to the common cause as a gratuitous contribution, the loss of which would be less painful for others than the payment is onerous for him; and fancying that the artificial person which constitutes the state is a mere rational entity (since it is not a man), he might seek to enjoy the rights of a citizen without doing the duties of a subject. The growth of this kind of injustice would bring about the ruin of the body politic.

Hence, in order that the social pact shall not be an empty formula, it is tacitly implied in that commitment—which alone can give force to all others—that whoever refuses to obey the general will shall be constrained to do so by the whole body, which means nothing other than that he shall be forced to be free; for this is the condition which, by giving each citizen to the nation, secures him against all personal dependence, it is the condition which shapes both the design and the working of the political machine, and which alone bestows justice on civil contracts—without it, such contracts would be absurd, tyrannical and liable to the grossest abuse.

CHAPTER 8
Civil Society

THE passing from the state of nature to the civil society produces a remarkable change in man; it puts justice as a rule of conduct in the place of instinct, and gives his actions the moral quality they previously lacked. It is only then, when the voice of duty has taken the place of physical impulse, and right that of desire, that man, who has hitherto thought only of himself, finds himself compelled to act on other principles, and to consult his reason rather than study his inclinations. And although in civil society man surrenders some of the advantages that belong to the state of nature, he gains in return far greater ones; his faculties are so exercised and developed, his mind is so enlarged, his sentiments so ennobled, and his whole spirit so elevated that, if the abuse of his new condition did not in many cases lower him to something worse than what he had left, he should constantly bless the happy hour that lifted him for ever from the state of nature and from a narrow, stupid animal made a creature of intelligence and a man.

Suppose we draw up a balance sheet, so that the losses and gains may be readily compared. What man loses by the social contract is his natural liberty and the absolute right to anything that tempts him and that he can take; what he gains by the social contract is civil liberty and the legal right of property in what he possesses. If we are to avoid mistakes in weighing the one side against the other, we must clearly distinguish between *natural* liberty, which has no limit but the physical power of the individual concerned, and *civil* liberty, which is limited by the general will; and we must distinguish also between *possession*, which is based only on force or "the right of the first occupant", and *property*, which must rest on a legal title.

We might also add that man acquires with civil society, moral freedom, which alone makes man the master of himself; for to be governed by appetite alone is slavery, while obedience to a law one prescribes to oneself is freedom. However, I have already said more than enough on this subject, and the philosophical meaning of the word "freedom" is no part of my subject here.

CHAPTER 9
Of Estate

EVERY member of the community gives himself to it at the moment it is brought into being just as he is—he himself, with all his resources, including all his goods. This is not to say that possession by this act changes its nature in changing hands and becomes property in the grasp of the sovereign; but rather, that as the resources of the nation are incomparably greater than those of an individual, public possession is in simple fact more secure and more irrevocable than private possession, without being any more legitimate—at any rate, in the eyes of foreigners; for the state, *vis-à-vis* its own members, becomes master of all their goods by virtue of the social contract, which serves, within the state, as the basis of all other rights; while *vis-à-vis* other nations, the state has only the "right of the first occupant", which it derives from individuals.

The "right of the first occupant", although more real than the "right of the strongest", does not become a true right until the institution of property. Every man has a natural right to what he needs; but the positive act which makes a man the proprietor of any estate excludes him from everything else. His share having once been settled, he must confine himself to it, and he has no further right against the community. Thus we see how "the right of the first occupant", weak as it is in the state of nature, compels in political society the respect of all men. What this right makes one aware of is less what belongs to others than what does *not* belong to oneself.

As a general rule, to justify the right of the first occupant to any piece of land whatever, the following conditions must obtain: first, that the land shall not already be inhabited by anyone else; secondly, that the claimant occupies no more than he needs for subsistence; thirdly, that he takes possession, not by an idle ceremony, but by actually working and cultivating the soil—the only sign of ownership which need be respected by other people in the absence of a legal title.

It can, indeed, be said that tying "the right of the first occupant" to need and work is stretching it as far as it will go. Can one really avoid setting limits on the right? Is it enough to put one's feet on a piece of common land in order to claim it at once as one's own? Is it enough to have the power to keep other men off for one moment in order to deprive them of the right ever to return? How could a man or a people seize a vast territory and keep out the rest of the human race except by a criminal usurpation—since the action would rob the rest of mankind of the shelter and the food that nature has given them all in common? When Nunez Balbao① stood on the shore and took possession of the southern seas and of South America in the name of the crown of Castille②, was that enough to dispossess all the inhabitants and to exclude all the other princes of the world? If so, such idle ceremonies would have had no end; and the Catholic King might without leaving his royal chamber have taken possession of the whole universe, only excepting afterwards those parts of his empire already belonging to other princes.

We can see how the lands of private persons, when they are united and contiguous, become public territory; and how the right of sovereignty, extending from the subjects to the soil they occupy, covers both property and persons; it makes the owners all the more dependent, and turns their own strength into the guarantee of their fidelity. This advantage seems to have eluded the ancient monarchs, who, in calling themselves simply the King of the Persians or the Scythians or the Macedonians, appear to have regarded themselves rather as rulers of men than as masters of their countries. Monarchs of the present day call themselves more shrewdly the King of France, or of Spain, or of England and so on; in holding thus the land, they are very sure of holding the inhabitants.

What is unique about the alienation entailed by the social contract is that the community in accepting the goods of an individual is far from depriving him of them; on the contrary it simply assures him of their lawful possession; it changes usurpation into valid right and mere enjoyment into legal ownership. Since every owner is regarded as a trustee of the public property, his rights are respected by every other member of the state, and protected with its collective force

---

① Nunez Balbao, N. 巴尔波(1475—1517),西班牙航海家,于 1513 年发现南美洲和太平洋,并以卡斯提王斐迪南五世的名义宣布占有。
② Castille,此处指卡斯提王斐迪南五世。

against foreigners; men have, by a surrender which is advantageous to the public and still more to themselves, acquired, so to speak, all that they have given up—a paradox which is easily explained by the distinction between the rights which the soverign has and which the owner has over the same property, as will be seen later.

It may also happen that men begin to unite before they possess anything, and spreading over a territory large enough for them all, proceed to enjoy it in common, or, alternatively, divide it among themselves either equally or in shares determined by the sovereign. In whatever manner this acquisition is made, the right of any individual over his own estate is always subordinate to the right of the community over everything; for without this there would be neither strength in the social bond nor effective force in the exercise of sovereignty.

I shall end this chapter—and Book I—with an observation which might serve as a basis for the whole social system: namely, that the social pact, far from destroying natural equality, substitutes, on the contrary, a moral and lawful equality for whatever physical inequality that nature may have imposed on mankind; so that however unequal in strength and intelligence, men become equal by covenant and by right.

 选文出处

Jean-Jacques Rousseau. *The Social Contract*. Translated by Maurice Cranston, Beijing: China Social Sciences Publishing House (reprinted from the English Edition by Penguin Books Ltd., 1974), 1999, pp. 49－68.

思考题

1. 《社会契约论》中的"契约"是什么意思？卢梭利用"契约"试图实现一种怎样的社会模式？
2. 构成《社会契约论》的主导思想是什么？它们为资产阶级推翻封建专制以及整个欧洲的民主运动做出了哪些贡献？
3. 卢梭在理论上反对文学艺术的存在，认为会导致人类的腐化堕落，可他又以其创作证明了文学艺术具有净化人类精神的作用,这种理论与实际的反差应该怎样理解?

阅读
参考书目

1. 卢梭:《社会契约论》,何兆武译,北京:商务印书馆,2003年。
2. 卢梭:《忏悔录》,黎星译,北京:人民文艺出版社,1980年。
3. Maurice Cranston, *Jean-Jacques*: *The Early Life and Work of Jean-Jacques Rousseau*, *1712—1754*, Chicago: University of Chicago Press, 1991.
4. Maurice Cranston, *The Noble Savage*: *Jean-Jacques Rousseau*, *1754—1762*, Chicago: University of Chicago Press, 1991.
5. Maurice Cranston, *The Solitary Self*: *Jean-Jacques Rousseau in Exile and Adversity*, Chicago: University of Chicago Press, 1997.

康　德

伊曼努尔·康德(Immanuel Kant,1724—1804)出生在德国东普鲁士哥尼斯堡的一个工匠家庭,家中经济条件较差,而且兄弟姐妹很多。他16岁入哥尼斯堡大学学习,7年后获硕士学位,然后回到乡下做了将近9年的家庭教师。他31岁那年获博士学位,并取得了哥尼斯堡大学的"编外讲师"的职位。在这个职位上,康德非常忙碌,同时讲授逻辑学、形而上学、数学、物理、地理、伦理学等多门课程,每周得上16至28学时。但由于收入有限,他还在图书馆兼任助理馆员的职务。这种繁忙而清贫的生活持续了15年之久。他在46岁时升为教授,直到59岁才拥有自己的房子。

康德是一个生活十分有规律的人。据说,人们习惯根据他有规律的散步路程校对钟表。不过,有一次他的时间表被打乱了,那是因为被卢梭的《爱弥儿》迷住了。因为他初读这部作品时被优美的文笔所吸引而无法很好地理解书中的内容。他索性反复读了好几遍,结果忘记了时间。康德晚年的名气很大,几所著名的大学都想请他去当教授或校长,不过,他更喜欢自己的家乡,一辈子没有离开过这个小镇。他最重要的著作是著名的三大批判:《纯粹理性批判》(*Critique of Pure Reason*)、《实践理性批判》(*Critique of Practical Reason*)、《判断力批判》(*Critique of Judgment*)。康德在西方哲学史上地位非常高,日本学者安培能成认为,康德"在近代哲学上恰似一个处于贮水池地位的人。可以这样说,康德以前的哲学皆流向康德,而康德以后的哲学又是从康德这里流出的"。①

这篇选文选自康德的《道德形而上学的基础》(Foundations of the Metaphysics of Morals),集中探讨了他的道德哲学说中的重要概念——意志自律与他律。他把自律和他律作了一个比较:"那种情况下意志不给予自身规律,而是由对象通过它与意志的关系给予。这种关系,不管它依赖于爱好还是理性概念,只允许假设命令:因为我希望其他事情,所以我应该做某件事情。相反地,因道德而成为绝对的命令则说:即使我不希望任何事情,我也应该这样或者那样行动。例如,前者会说,如果我要维护我的名声就不应该撒谎;后者则说,即使一点也不会使我丧失名誉,我也不应该撒谎。"自律的特点在于作为主体的人,通过理性主动地选择具有普遍意义的道德标准,并以此为准则来指导自己的行动。这种行为使意志自律者独立于物理性质的一切规律,只遵守那些他自己制定的规律。正是由于意志自律使人与别的任何事物区别开来,创造出由自己的意志决定行动的自由空间,不同于完全受制于因果律的物理世界。这样的话,人才有真正的尊严,正如康德所说的那样:"但由于他同样是规律的立法者,并且只是由于这个原因才服从它,他才具有崇高性。"由于自己既是立法者,又是守法者,"我必须"和"我愿意"因此统一了起来。假如不是从自己的意志出发,而是外在地建立律令,必然需要某种利益,采取吸引或者压抑的方式来实现。这种行为虽然对社会也有一定的好处,但不是真正的道德命令,因为就服从道德规律而言,并没有什么崇高性可言。例如说,一个商人为了顾全自己的信誉,使自己的经济利益不至于减少,他可能会采取童叟无欺的经营方法。但这样的行为只能说明这个商人懂得经商之道,而不能真正体现道德的尊严。真正的道德在于,不管是否对自己有利,也要采取童叟无欺的方法,因为心中选择了这样的道德标准。康德认为人们以前企图找到道德原则的行为都是失败的,因为他们把道德建立在他律的基础上,没有意识到只有自律才能产生道德律令。康德曾说:"已经看出人通过义务受法则束缚,但没有看到他所服从的只是自己制定的法则,尽管它们同时是普遍的,没有看到他只是按照他自己的意志来行动,而自然指定这个意志来制定普遍法则。"康德指出,如果只看到了服从的必要性,而看不到服从的律令是出自自己的意志,那么这种强迫性的行为不是真正的道德行为。

与道德自律相联系的另一概念是目的王国。康德曾这样描绘目的王国:"因为所有的理性存在者懂得这条法则,他们中的每一个都必须不仅仅是当作手段来对待自己和所有其他人,而是在每种情况下都同时把每个人自身当

---

① 安培能成:《康德的实践哲学》,于凤梧、王宏文译,福州:福建人民出版社,1984年,第3页。

作目的。"目的王国中的人之所以可以成为自己的目的,关键就在于他们是意志自律的,而不是被动地服从道德律令。康德说:"当在其中给出了普遍法则,他自己也服从这些法则时,一个理性存在物作为成员属于目的王国。在给出法则时,他不服从任何其他人的意志,这时他作为统治者属于目的王国。"只有自己服从自己的意志,人才是自己的目的,才能拥有真正的尊严。康德把这种尊严看作不可替代的绝对价值,他说:"和人类的一般爱好和需求有关的东西具有**市场价值**;不包含需求、符合某种趣味的东西具有**情感价值**,这里的情趣指的是我们的官能的无目的性的游戏所产生的快乐;然而构成了任何事物都能够成为自身目的的全部条件的东西不仅仅具有相对的价值,而且具有内在价值,那就是**尊严**。"

康德认为,道德律令不仅仅是自己给自己下的命令,这个命令还必然具有普遍意义。怎样达到普遍意义呢?那就是去掉具体的内容,回到纯粹的理性主体,完全先验地判断什么是道德。如果不这样做,而是从主体本身走出来,在任何对象的特性中寻求法则,就总会产生他律。可见要使道德律令达到绝对而普遍的境界,必须从理性的思考中得到,而不能被具体的实践经验所左右,否则就不可能有什么标准。他在《实践理性批判》中曾指出:"同一个人能够将一部不可再得的富有教益的书,不经阅读而还给他人,以免耽误打猎;能够中途离开一场绝妙演讲;能够从自己平时相当赞赏的话语澄明的谈局中抽身出来,去参加牌局;甚至能够因为他当时手头的钱仅够用来买一张喜剧门票,而斥退自己原本乐意周济的穷人。"[①]这就是说,道德律令应当先天地来自理性本身,不能因为具体的情况而随便动摇。否则每个人都有理由,不按照道德准则行动。

康德所提出的道德自律、目的王国非常有意义,使人成为超越于物理世界之上的理性动物,具有特别的尊严和自由。康德的观点属于典型的理性主义伦理观,与经验主义伦理观针锋相对。许多经验主义者认为,善和有利是一致的,在有利之外无所谓善。假如我们问他们,为什么在食堂吃饭要排队?经验主义者会说,排队有利于大家方便地打到饭;而康德会说,我的理性告诉我,只有排队才是道德的。经验主义者的观点较容易为一般的大众所接受,但其麻烦在于,这样的道德命令不是绝对的,人们总能够找到理由不遵守道德。康德的观点更加体现了道德的尊严和绝对性,但有些人可能偏偏要说,我不想要那种尊严,你能拿我怎么办?而且,康德的所谓道德的普遍性和绝对性,在现实中也会遇到难题。在纯粹的实践理性中,人是不能撒谎的。但一个不幸落入敌人手中的人,是否为了不撒谎就该把秘密告诉敌人呢?所以哪一种理论都有自身的长

---

① 康德:《实践理性批判》,韩水法译,北京:商务印书馆,1999年,第22页。

处和不足。

Foundations of the Metaphysics of Morals

If we now look back upon all previous attempts which have ever been undertaken to discover the principle of morality, it is not to be wondered at that they all had to fail. Man was seen to be bound to laws by his duty, but it was not seen that he is subject only to his own, yet universal, legislation, and that he is only bound to act in accordance with his own will, which is, however, designed by nature to be a will giving universal laws. For if one thought of him as subject only to a law (whatever it may be), this necessarily implied some interest as a stimulus or compulsion to obedience because the law did not arise from his will. Rather, his will was constrained by something else according to a law to act in a certain way. By this strictly necessary consequence, however, all the labor of finding a supreme ground for duty was irrevocably lost, and one never arrived at duty but only at the necessity of action from a certain interest. This might be his own interest or that of another, but in either case the imperative always had to be conditional and could not at all serve as a moral command. This principle I will call the principle of *autonomy* of the will in contrast to all other principles which I accordingly count under *heteronomy*.

The concept of each rational being as a being that must regard itself as giving universal law through all the maxims of its will, so that it may judge itself and its actions from this standpoint, leads to a very fruitful concept, namely, that of *a realm of ends*.

By "realm" I understand the systematic union of different rational beings through common laws. Because laws determine ends with regard to their universal validity, if we abstract from the personal difference of rational beings and thus from all content of their private ends, we can think of a whole of all ends in systematic connection, a whole of rational beings as ends in themselves as well as of the particular ends which each may set for himself. This is a realm of ends, which is possible on the aforesaid principles. For all rational beings stand under the law that each of them should treat himself and all others never merely as means but in every case also as an end in himself. Thus there arises a systematic union of rational beings through common objective laws. This is a realm which may be called a realm of ends (certainly only an ideal), because what these laws have in view is just the relation of these beings to each other as ends and means.

A rational being belongs to the realm of ends as a member when he gives universal laws in it while also himself subject to these laws. He belongs to it as sovereign when he, as legislating, is subject to the will of no other. The rational being must regard himself always as legislative in a realm of ends possible through the freedom of the will, whether he belongs to it as member or as sovereign. He cannot maintain the latter position merely through the maxims of his will but only when he is a completely independent being without need and with power adequate to his will.

Morality, therefore, consists in the relation of every action to that legislation through which alone a realm of ends is possible. This legislation, however, must be found in every rational being. It must be able to arise from his will, whose principle then is to take no action according to any maxim which would be inconsistent with its being a universal law and thus to act only so that the will through its maxims could regard itself at the same time as universally lawgiving. If now the maxims do not by their nature already necessarily conform to this objective principle of rational beings as universally lawgiving, the necessity of acting according to that principle is called practical constraint, i. e., duty. Duty pertains not to the sovereign in the realm of ends, but rather to each member, and to each in the same degree.

The practical necessity of acting according to this principle, i. e., duty, does not rest at all on feelings, impulses, and inclinations; it rests merely on the relation of rational beings to one another, in which the will of a rational being must always be regarded as legislative, for otherwise it could not be thought of as an end in itself. Reason, therefore, relates every maxim of the will as giving universal laws to every other will and also to every action toward itself; it does so not for the sake of any other practical motive or future advantage but rather from the idea of the dignity of a rational being who obeys no law except that which he himself also gives.

In the realm of ends everything has either a *price* or a *dignity*. Whatever has a price can be replaced by something else as its equivalent; on the other hand, whatever is above all price, and therefore admits of no equivalent, has a dignity.

That which is related to general human inclinations and needs has a *market price*. That which, without presupposing any need, accords with a certain taste, i. e., with pleasure in the mere purposeless play of our faculties, has an *affective price*. But that which constitutes the condition under which alone something can be an end in itself does not have mere relative worth, i. e., a price, but an intrinsic worth, i. e., *dignity*.

Now morality is the condition under which alone a rational being can be an end in itself, because only through it is it possible to be a legislative member in the realm of ends. Thus morality and humanity, so far as it is capable of morality, alone have dignity. Skill and diligence in work have a market value; wit, lively imagination, and humor have an affective price; but fidelity in promises and benevolence on principle (not from instinct) have intrinsic worth, Nature and likewise art contain nothing which could replace their lack, for their worth consists not in effects which flow from them, nor in advantage and utility which they procure; it consists only in intentions, i. e., maxims of the will which are ready to reveal themselves in this manner through actions even though success does not favor them. These actions need no recommendation from any subjective disposition or taste in order that they may be looked upon with immediate favor and satisfaction, nor do they have need of any immediate propensity or feeling directed to them. They exhibit the will which performs them as the object of an immediate respect, since nothing but reason is required in order to impose them on the will. The will is not to be cajoled into them, for this, in the case of duties, would be a contradiction. This esteem lets the worth of such a turn of mind be recognized as dignity and puts it infinitely beyond any price, with which it cannot in the least be brought into competition or comparison without, as it were, violating its holiness.

And what is it that justifies the morally good disposition or virtue in making such lofty claims? It is nothing less than the participation it affords the rational being in giving universal laws. He is thus fitted to be a member in a possible realm of ends to which his own nature already destined him. For, as an end in himself, he is destined to be legislative in the realm of ends, free from all laws of nature and obedient only to those which he himself gives. Accordingly, his maxims can belong to a universal legislation to which he is at the same time also subject. A thing has no worth other than that determined for it by the law. The legislation which determines all worth must therefore have a dignity, i. e., unconditional and incomparable worth. For the esteem which a rational being must have for it, only the word "respect" is a suitable expression. Autonomy is thus the basis of the dignity of both human nature and every rational nature.

The three aforementioned ways of presenting the principle of morality are fundamentally only so many formulas of the very same law, and each of them unites the others in itself. There is, nevertheless, a difference in them, but the difference is more subjectively than objectively practical, for it is intended to bring an idea of reason closer to intuition (by means of a certain analogy) and thus nearer to feeling. All maxims have:

1. A form, which consists in universality; and in this respect the formula of the moral imperative requires that the maxims be chosen as though they should hold as universal laws of nature.

2. A material, i. e., an end; in this respect the formula says that the rational being, as by its nature an end and thus as an end in itself, must serve in every maxim as the condition restricting all merely relative and arbitrary ends.

3. A complete determination of all maxims by the formula that all maxims which stem from autonomous legislation ought to harmonize with a possible realm of ends as with a realm of nature.

There is a progression here like that through the categories of the unity of the form of the will (its universality), the plurality of material (the objects, i.e., the ends), and the all-comprehensiveness or totality of the system of ends. But it is better in moral evaluation to follow the rigorous method and to make the universal formula of the categorical imperative the basis: Act according to the maxim which can at the same time make itself a universal law. But if one wishes to gain a hearing for the moral law, it is very useful to bring one and the same action under the three stated principles and thus, so far as possible, to bring it nearer to intuition.

We can now end where we started, with the concept of an unconditionally good will. That will is absolutely good which cannot be bad, and thus it is a will whose maxim, when made a universal law, can never conflict with itself. Thus this principle is also its supreme law: Always act according to that maxim whose universality as a law you can at the same time will. This is the only condition under which a will can never come into conflict with itself, and such an imperative is categorical①. Because the validity of the will, as a universal law for possible actions, has an analogy with the universal connection of the existence of things under universal laws, which is the formal element of nature in general, the categorical imperative can also be expressed as follows. Act according to maxims which can at the same time have themselves as universal laws of nature as their object. Such, then, is the formula of an absolutely good will.

Rational nature is distinguished from others in that it proposes an end to itself. This end would be the material of every good will. Since, however, in the idea of an absolutely good will without any limiting condition of the attainment of this or that end, every end to be effected must be completely abstracted (as any particular end would make each will only relatively good), the end here is not conceived as one to be effected but as an independent end, and thus merely negatively. It is that which must never be acted against, and which must consequently never be valued as merely a means but in every volition also as an end. Now this end can never be other than the subject of all possible ends themselves, because this is at the same time the subject of a possible will which is absolutely good; for the latter cannot be made secondary to any other object without contradiction. The principle: Act with reference to every rational being (whether yourself or another) so that it is an end in itself in your maxim. It is thus basically identical with the principle: Act by a maxim which involves its own universal validity for every rational being.

That in the use of means to every end I should restrict my maxim to the condition of its universal validity as a law for every subject is tantamount to saying that the subject of ends, i. e., the rational being itself, must be made

---

① categorical, 绝对的, 无条件的, 指这种命令先天地来自理性, 不能因为具体的情况而变化。

the basis of all maxims of actions and must thus be treated never as a mere means but as the supreme limiting condition in the use of all means, i. e. , as an end at the same time.

It follows incontestably that every rational being must be able to regard himself as an end in himself with reference to all laws to which he may be subject, whatever they may be, and thus as giving universal laws. For it is just the fitness of his maxims to a universal legislation that indicates that he is an end in himself. It also follows that his dignity (his prerogative) over all merely natural beings entails that he must take his maxims from the point of view which regards himself, and hence also every other rational being, as legislative. (The rational beings are, on this account, called persons.) In this way, a world of rational beings (*mundus intelligibilis*) is possible as a realm of ends, because of the legislation belonging to all persons as members. Consequently, every rational being must act as if he, by his maxims, were at all times a legislative member in the universal realm of ends. The formal principle of these maxims is: So act as if your maxims should serve at the same time as the universal law (of all rational beings). A realm of ends is thus possible only by analogy with a realm of nature. The former, however, is possible only by maxims, i. e. , self-imposed rules, while the latter is possible by laws of efficient causes of things externally necessitated. Regardless of this difference, by analogy we call the natural whole a realm of nature so far as it is related to rational beings as its end; we do so even though the natural whole is looked at as a machine. Such a realm of ends would actually be realized through maxims whose rule is prescribed to all rational beings by the categorical imperative, if they were universally obeyed. But a rational being, though he scrupulously follow this maxim, cannot for that reason expect every other rational being to be true to it; nor can he expect the realm of nature and its orderly design to harmonize with him as a fitting member of a realm of ends which is possible through himself. That is, he cannot count on its favoring his expectation of happiness. Still the law: Act according to the maxims of a universally legislative member of a merely potential realm of ends, remains in full force, because it commands categorically. And just in this lies the paradox that merely the dignity of humanity as rational nature without any end or advantage to be gained by it, and thus respect for a mere idea, should serve as the inflexible precept of the will. There is the further paradox that the sublimity of the maxims and the worthiness of every rational subject to be a legislative member in the realm of ends consist precisely in independence of the maxims from all such incentives. Otherwise he would have to be viewed as subject only to the natural law of his needs. Although the realm of nature as well as that of ends would be thought of as united under a sovereign so that the latter would no longer remain a mere idea but would receive true reality, the realm of ends would undoubtedly gain a strong urge in its favor, but its intrinsic worth would not be augmented. Regardless of this, even the one and only absolute legislator would still have to be conceived as judging the worth of rational beings only by the disinterested① conduct which they prescribe to themselves merely from the idea [of dignity]. The essence of things is not changed by their external relations, and without reference to these relations a man must be judged only by what constitutes his absolute worth; and this is true whoever his judge is, even if it be the Supreme Being. Morality is thus the relation of actions to the autonomy of the will, i. e. , to possible universal lawgiving by maxims of the will. The action which can be compatible with the autonomy of the will is permitted; that which does not agree with it is prohibited. The will whose maxims necessarily are in harmony with the laws of autonomy is a holy will or an absolutely good will. The dependence of a will not absolutely good on the principle of autonomy (moral constraint) is *obligation*. Hence obligation cannot be applied to a holy will. The objective necessity of an action from obligation is called *duty*.

From what has just been said, it can easily be explained how it happens that, although in the concept of duty we think of subjection to law, we do nevertheless ascribe a certain sublimity and dignity to the person who fulfills all his duties. For though there is no sublimity in him in so far as he is subject to the moral law, yet he is sublime in so far as he is legislative with reference to the law and subject to it only for this reason. We have also shown above how neither fear of nor inclination to the law is the incentive which can give a moral worth to action; only respect for it can do so. Our own will, so far as it would act only under the condition of a universal legislation rendered possible by its maxims—

---

① disinterested,超功利的。

this will, ideally possible for us, is the proper object of respect, and the dignity of humanity consists just in its capacity of giving universal laws, although with the condition that it is itself subject to this same legislation.

THE AUTONOMY OF THE WILL AS THE SUPREME PRINCIPLE OF MORALITY

Autonomy of the will is that property of it by which it is a law to itself independently of any property of objects of volition. Hence the principle of autonomy is: Never choose except in such a way that the maxims of the choice are comprehended in the same volition as a universal law. That this practical rule is an imperative, that is, that the will of every rational being is necessarily bound to it as a condition, cannot be proved by a mere analysis of the concepts occurring in it, because it is a synthetical proposition. To prove it, we would have to go beyond the knowledge of objects to a critical examination of the subject, i. e., of the pure practical reason, for this synthetical proposition which commands apodictically[①] must be susceptible of being known completely *a priori*[②]. This matter, however, does not belong in the present section. But that the principle of autonomy, which is now in question, is the sole principle of morals can be readily shown by mere analysis of concepts of morality; for by this analysis we find that its principle must be a categorical imperative and that the imperative commands neither more nor less than this very autonomy.

THE HETERONOMY OF THE WILL AS THE SOURCE OF ALL SPURIOUS PRINCIPLES OF MORALITY

If the will seeks the law which is to determine it any where else than in the fitness of its maxims to its own universal legislation, and if it thus goes outside itself and seeks this law in the property of any of its objects, heteronomy always results. For then the will does not give itself the law, but the object through its relation to the will gives the law to it. This relation,

---

① apodictically,必然真实地,绝对肯定地。
② a priori,先验的,与经验的相对。

whether it rests on inclination or on conceptions of reason, only admits of hypothetical imperatives: I should do something for the reason that I will something else. The moral, and therewith categorical, imperative, on the other hand, says I should act this or that way even though I will nothing else. For example, the former says I should not lie if I wish to keep my reputation. The latter says I should not lie even though it would not cause me the least injury. The latter, therefore, must disregard every object to such an extent that it has absolutely no influence on the will, so that practical reason (will) may not merely minister to an interest not its own but rather may show its commanding authority as the supreme legislation. Thus, for instance, I should seek to further the happiness of others, not as though its realization was any concern of mine (whether because of direct inclination or of some satisfaction related to it indirectly through reason); I should do so merely because the maxim which excludes it from my duty cannot be comprehended as a universal law in one and the same volition.

 选文出处

Immanuel Kant. *Foundations of the Metaphysics of Morals*. Translated by Lewis White Beck, Beijing: China Social Sciences Publishing House (reprinted from the English Edition by The Macmillan Publishing company, 1989), 1999, pp. 51—60.

 思考题

1. 能否在现实中建立起"目的王国"？为什么？
2. 康德的伦理观在现实中行得通吗？

 阅读 参考书目

1. 郑昕:《康德学述》,北京:商务印书馆,2001年。
2. 李泽厚:《批判哲学的批判——康德述评》,天津:天津社会科学院出版社,2003年。

叔本华

叔本华（Arthur Schopenhauer，1788—1860）是著名的德国哲学家。1788年，他出生于但泽（今波兰境内）一个大银行家的家庭中，母亲是一位有才气的作家。小时候，他接受漫游式教育，游览过欧洲许多著名的地方，曾在巴黎和伦敦长期居住。所以，他的法语和英语都很流利。后来他在哥廷根大学、柏林大学和耶拿大学学习过，获博士学位。在柏林大学任教期间，他把自己的课与黑格尔的课排在相同的时间段，试图与当时处于顶峰期的黑格尔一比高下。结果黑格尔的课堂人满为患，叔本华的教室中几乎没有人。也许正是由于这一打击，他非常憎恨黑格尔，曾攻击他说："当今一代学者的头脑被黑格尔的胡说搅乱了：他们不会反思，既粗俗又糊涂，完全沦为一种从蛇妖的蛋里爬出来的浅薄的物质主义的牺牲品。"[①] 叔本华的思想深受康德、柏拉图以及古印度哲学的影响。他的主要著作有《作为意志和表象的世界》(The World as Will and Representation)、《伦理学的两个基本问题》(The Two Fundamental Problems of Ethics)、《充足理由律的四重根》(The Fourfold Root of the Principle of Sufficient Reason)、《论自然界的意志》(On the Will in Nature)等。叔本华对后人产生了深远的影响，尼采、弗洛伊德、瓦格纳、D. H. 劳伦斯、托马斯·曼、约瑟夫·康拉德、列夫·托尔斯泰、马歇尔·普鲁斯特、路德维希·维特根斯坦等都从叔本华的哲学中吸取了有用的东西。

---

① 叔本华：《充足理由律的四重根·序言》，陈晓希译，北京：商务印书馆，1996年，第2页。

《作为意志和表象的世界》是叔本华的代表作,集中反映了他的思想。叔本华认为,世界仅仅为主体而存在,只是纯粹的表象。他曾说:"于是,他就会清楚而确切地明白,他不认识什么是太阳,什么是地球,而永远只是眼睛,是眼睛看见太阳;永远只是手,是手感触着地球;就会明白围绕着他的这世界只是作为表象而存在着的;也就是说这世界的存在完全只是就它对一个其他事物的,一个进行'表象者'的关系来说的。"①这个只能作为表象出现在主体面前的世界,就其本质而言,是意志的客体化。至于什么是意志,不是一个非常清楚的问题。杰克·奥德尔曾这样界定叔本华的意志:"它是一种力,在外部世界中,它把自己显现为能量;从内在意识或内省的角度来看,它是一种难以抗拒的欲求或'驱动力'。"②在叔本华看来,意志这种能量或者驱动力不是人类所特有的,而是动物、植物,乃至无生命的万物存在的根本原因。人类的意志达到了最为自觉化的水平,有着无穷的欲望、需求等,永远无法满足,所以处于最痛苦的状态。人要解脱出来,只有否定生命意志,通过禁欲的办法达到清心寡欲的境界,才有幸福可言。叔本华的意志不再是德国古典哲学中的绝对理性,而是非理性的原创力。黄前文先生对叔本华的创造性给予了很高的评价:"他同当时的主流哲学格格不入,但又无疑指出了新的哲学发展方向,是西方现代哲学的先驱和开拓者。"③由此可见叔本华在西方哲学史上的地位。

这篇选文出自《作为意志和表象的世界》的第 57 章,集中探讨了人生的痛苦状态。在叔本华看来,人生是非常短暂的,最大的痛苦就是死亡。死神时时刻刻都威胁着人们,生命只是被延期的死亡。就算暂时显得充满活力,但丝毫不能改变死亡的结局,"因为诞生就意味着死亡是我们的命运,它不过是在吞噬自己的猎物之前,逗着玩耍一会儿罢了"。生命在死神面前显得非常可怜,就像被猫捕获的老鼠一样,虽然暂时还能跳几下,但只是猫的玩物,注定了要成为猫的口中之物。然而人们还是对生活乐此不疲,"就好像吹肥皂泡,尽管明知一定要破灭,还是要尽可能吹下去,吹大些"。

人由于受意志的控制,总是充满着痛苦。可以说,人的欲望是一切痛苦的根源:欲望不能得到满足时,就会陷入痛苦之中;即便得到了满足,快乐也只是非常短暂的。因为,人接着就会产生更多的欲望,从而产生出新的痛苦。但是如果没有了欲望,人又会陷入空虚和无聊之中,"所以人生在痛苦和无聊之间像钟摆一样来回摆动着,事实上痛苦和无聊就是构成人生的最终成分"。即不管

---

① 叔本华:《作为意志和表象的世界》,石冲白译,北京:商务印书馆,1995 年,第 25 页。
② 杰克·奥德尔:《叔本华》,王德岩译,北京:中华书局,2002 年,第 64 页。
③ 黄前文:《叔本华》,《西方哲学史》第 7 卷,谢地坤主编,南京:凤凰出版社,2005 年,第 35 页。

有没有欲望,人都不会快乐。所以说,人生常常处于矛盾之中:一方面,人生的痛苦和烦恼是这样容易激增,以致死亡有时竟然变为人所祈求的东西;另一方面,欲望和痛苦一旦予人以喘息,无聊就会马上来临,致使人们又必然需要消遣和娱乐。不过,相对较幸福的生活还是存在的,对于这种生活叔本华是这样定义的:"愿望和满足相交替,间隔不太长也不太短,把两者各自产生的痛苦缩小到最低程度,构成最幸福的生活。"当然,就是所谓的幸福生活,也是以痛苦为主体的,即所谓的幸福只是一个相对的概念。

由于痛苦是人生的本质,所以那些企图消灭痛苦的行为是注定不会成功的。叔本华说:"消除痛苦的不懈努力除了改变痛苦的形态外,一事无成。"在人的一生中,痛苦从不会中断,只不过形式不同而已:好不容易消除了这一形态的痛苦,立刻又有其他形态的痛苦接踵而来,如性冲动、狂热的爱情、醋意、嫉妒、仇恨、担忧、好名、爱财、疾病等,根据年龄和不同情况而交替出现。就算没有这些痛苦,可怕的空虚也会袭来。叔本华提出了一个有意思的假设:"每一个体在本质上少不了痛苦,不管形式是如何变换,痛苦的量已经一次性地被他的天性决定了,既不会空缺,也不会超额。"也就是说,一个人是忧郁还是乐观决定于他的性情,与外在的得失没有多少联系,从这个角度看痛苦是定量的。叔本华还观察到,有的巨大不幸似乎是根本无法接受的,但果真发生了,只要忍过第一阵创痛后,生活还会慢慢地恢复正常,即新增的痛苦又会被整合到可以接受的范围之内,总体的量并没有增加。如果突然遇到了惊喜,人们也会同样地调整过来。所以叔本华把痛苦看作是内心欲望的必然结果,外在的得失都是偶然的诱因。他说:"对于这一定额来说,引起烦恼的外在原因只是一张疮泡膏药,原来分散开来的脓毒现在都往膏药上集结了。"可见,痛苦已经先天地存在于我们心中,外在的遭遇所引起的痛苦,不管以什么样的形状和多大的体积出现,都最终会被整合到那个必然的定额中去。

与绝大多数抽象、难懂的德国哲学著作相比,叔本华的著作充满着形象的比喻和诗性的想象,读起来让人感到非常愉快。杰克·奥德尔在评论黑格尔和其他德国哲学家时说:"他的沉闷的绕来绕去折磨人的写作风格,足以使大多数读者相信,德国作家是一些专门寻找有受虐癖读者的虐待狂。在这种令人不快的写作风气中,尼采和叔本华却是例外。"[①]仔细阅读以下的选文就可知道,叔本华的文体的确与别的哲学家不一样,能够给人带来美好的享受。

---

① 杰克·奥德尔:《叔本华》,王德岩译,北京:中华书局,2002年,第3页。

The World as Will and Representation

At every stage illuminated by knowledge, the will appears as individual. The human individual finds himself in endless space and time as finite, and consequently as a vanishing quantity compared with these. He is projected into them, and on account of their boundlessness has always only a relative, never an absolute, *when* and *where* of his existence, for his place and duration are finite parts of what is infinite and boundless. His real existence is only in the present, whose unimpeded flight into the past is a constant transition into death, a constant dying. For his past life, apart from its eventual consequences for the present, and also apart from the testimony regarding his will that is impressed in it, is entirely finished and done with, dead, and no longer anything. Therefore, as a matter of reason, it must be indifferent to him whether the contents of that past were pains or pleasures. But the present in his hands is constantly becoming the past; the future is quite uncertain and always short. Thus his existence, even considered from the formal side alone, is a continual rushing of the present into the dead past, a constant dying. And if we look at it also from the physical side, it is evident that, just as we know our walking to be only a constantly prevented falling, so is the life of our body only a constantly prevented dying, an ever-deferred death. Finally, the alertness and activity of our mind are also a continuously postponed boredom. Every breath we draw wards off the death that constantly impinges on us. In this way, we struggle with it every second, and again at longer intervals through every meal we eat, every sleep we take, every time we warm ourselves, and so on. Ultimately death must triumph, for by birth it has already become our lot, and it plays with its prey only for a while before swallowing it up. However, we continue our life with great interest and much solicitude as long as possible, just as we blow out a soap-bubble as long and as large as possible, although with the perfect certainty that it will burst.

We have already seen in nature-without-knowledge her inner being as a constant striving without aim and without rest, and this stands out much more distinctly when we consider the animal or man. Willing and striving are its whole essence, and can be fully compared to an unquenchable thirst. The basis of all willing, however, is need, lack, and hence pain, and by its very nature and origin it is therefore destined to pain. If, on the other hand, it lacks objects of willing, because it is at once deprived of them again by too easy a satisfaction, a fearful emptiness and boredom come over it; in other words, its being and its existence itself become an intolerable burden for it. Hence its life swings like a pendulum to and fro between pain and boredom, and these two are in fact its ultimate constituents. This has been expressed very quaintly by saying that, after man had placed all pains and torments in hell, there was nothing left for heaven but boredom.

But the constant striving, which constitutes the inner nature of every phenomenon of the will, obtains at the higher grades of objectification its first and most universal foundation from the fact that the will here appears as a living body with the iron command to nourish it. What gives force to this command is just that this body is nothing but the objectified will-to-live[①] itself. Man, as the most complete objectification of this will, is accordingly the most necessitous of all beings. He is concrete willing and needing through and through; he is a concretion of a thousand wants and needs. With these he stands on the earth, left to his own devices, in uncertainty about everything except his own need and misery. Accordingly, care for the maintenance of this existence, in the face of demands that are so heavy and proclaim themselves anew every day, occupies, as a rule, the whole of human life. With this is directly connected the second demand, that for the propagation of the race. At the same time dangers of the most varied kinds threaten him from all sides, and to escape from them calls for constant vigilance. With cautious step and anxious glance around he pursues his path, for a thousand accidents and a thousand enemies lie in wait for him. Thus he went in the savage state, and thus he goes in civilized life; there is no security for him:

Qualibus in tenebris vitae, quantisque periclis

---

① will-to-live,生存意志。在叔本华的哲学中,生存意志不仅为人类所具有,也是万物存在的根本。

Degitur hocc'aevi, quodcunque est!

Lucretius, ii, 15.

The life of the great majority is only a constant struggle for this same existence, with the certainty of ultimately losing it. What enables them to endure this wearisome battle is not so much the love of life as the fear of death, which nevertheless stands in the background as inevitable, and which may come on the scene at any moment. Life itself is a sea full of rocks and whirlpools that man avoids with the greatest caution and care, although he knows that, even when he succeeds with all his efforts and ingenuity in struggling through, at every step he comes nearer to the greatest, the total, the inevitable and irremediable shipwreck, indeed even steers right on to it, namely death. This is the final goal of the wearisome voyage, and is worse for him than all the rocks that he has avoided.

Now it is at once well worth noting that, on the one hand, the sufferings and afflictions of life can easily grow to such an extent that even death, in the flight from which the whole of life consists, becomes desirable, and a man voluntarily hastens to it. Again, on the other hand, it is worth noting that, as soon as want and suffering give man a relaxation, boredom is at once so near that he necessarily requires diversion and amusement. The striving after existence is what occupies all living things, and keeps them in motion. When existence is assured to them, they do not know what to do with it. Therefore the second thing that sets them in motion is the effort to get rid of the burden of existence, to make it no longer felt, "to kill time," in other words, to escape from boredom. Accordingly we see that almost all men, secure from want and cares, are now a burden to themselves, after having finally cast off all other burdens. They regard as a gain every hour that is got through, and hence every deduction from that very life, whose maintenance as long as possible has till then been the object of all their efforts. Boredom is anything but an evil to be thought of lightly; ultimately it depicts on the countenance real despair. It causes beings who love one another as little as men do, to seek one another so much, and thus becomes the source of sociability. From political prudence public measures are taken against it everywhere, as against other universal calamities, since this evil, like its opposite extreme, famine, can drive people to the greatest excesses and anarchy; the people need *panem* et circenses①. The strict penitentiary system of Philadelphia makes mere boredom an instrument of punishment through loneliness and idleness. It is so terrible an instrument, that it has brought convicts to suicide. Just as need and want are the constant scourge of the people, so is boredom that of the world of fashion. In middle-class life boredom is represented by the Sunday, just as want is represented by the six weekdays.

Now absolutely every human life continues to flow on between willing and attainment. Of its nature the wish is pain; attainment quickly begets satiety. The goal was only apparent; possession takes away its charm. The wish, the need, appears again on the scene under a new form; if it does not, then dreariness, emptiness, and boredom follow, the struggle against which is just as painful as is that against want. For desire and satisfaction to follow each other at not too short and not too long intervals, reduces the suffering occasioned by both to the smallest amount, and constitutes the happiest life. What might otherwise be called the finest part of life, its purest joy, just because it lifts us out of real existence, and transforms us into disinterested spectators of it, is pure knowledge which remains foreign to all willing, pleasure in the beautiful, genuine delight in art. But because this requires rare talents, it is granted only to extremely few, and even to those only as a fleeting dream. Then again higher intellectual power makes those very few susceptible to much greater sufferings than duller men can ever feel. Moreover, it makes them feel lonely among beings that are noticeably different from them, and in this way also matters are made even. But purely intellectual pleasures are not accessible to the vast majority of men. They are almost wholly incapable of the pleasure to be found in pure knowledge; they are entirely given over to willing. Therefore. if anything is to win their sympathy, to be *interesting* to them, it must (and this is to be found already in the meaning of the word) in some way excite their *will*, even if it be only through a remote relation to it which is merely within the bounds of possibility. The will must never be left entirely out of question, since their existence lies far more in willing than in knowing; action and reaction are their only element. The naïve expressions of this quality can be seen in trifles and

---

① panem et circenses,(拉丁语)面包和马戏,指生存和娱乐。

everyday phenomena; thus, for example, they write their names up at places worth seeing which they visit, in order thus to react on, to affect the place, since it does not affect them. Further, they cannot easily just contemplate a rare and strange animal, but must excite it, tease it, play with it, just to experience action and reaction. But this need for exciting the will shows itself particularly in the invention and maintenance of card-playing, which is in the truest sense an expression of the wretched side of humanity.

But whatever nature and good fortune may have done, whoever a person may be and whatever he may possess, the pain essential to life cannot be thrown off:

Πηλείδης δ'ᾤμωξεν, ἰδὼν εἰς οὐρχνὸν εὐρύν.
(*pelides autem ejulavit, intuitus in coelum latum*).

And again:

Ζηνὸς μὲν παῖς ἦχ Κρονίονος, αὐτὰρ ὀϊζύν
Εἶχον ἀπειρεσίην.
(*Jovis quidem filius eram Saturnii; verum aerumnam Habebam infinitam.*)

The ceaseless efforts to banish suffering achieve nothing more than a change in its form. This is essentially want, lack, care for the maintenance of life. If, which is very difficult, we have succeeded in removing pain in this form, it at once appears on the scene in a thousand others, varying according to age and circumstances, such as sexual impulse, passionate love, jealousy, envy, hatred, anxiety, ambition, avarice, sickness, and so on. Finally, if it cannot find entry in any other shape, it comes in the sad, grey garment of weariness, satiety, and boredom, against which many different attempts are made. Even if we ultimately succeed in driving these away, it will hardly be done without letting pain in again in one of the previous forms, and thus starting the dance once more at the beginning; for every human life is tossed backwards and forwards between pain and boredom. Depressing as this discussion is, I will, however, draw attention in passing to one aspect of it from which a consolation can be derived, and perhaps even a stoical indifference to our own present ills may be attained. For our impatience at these arises for the most part from the fact that we recognize them as accidental, as brought about by a chain of causes that might easily be different. We are not usually distressed at evils that are inescapably necessary and quite universal, for example, the necessity of old age and death, and of many daily inconveniences. It is rather a consideration of the accidental nature of the circumstances that have brought suffering precisely on us which gives this suffering its sting. Now we have recognized that pain as such is inevitable and essential to life; that nothing but the mere form in which it manifests itself depends on chance; that therefore our present suffering fills a place which without it would be at once occupied by some other suffering which the one now present excludes; and that, accordingly, fate can affect us little in what is essential. If such a reflection were to become a living conviction, it might produce a considerable degree of stoical equanimity, and greatly reduce our anxious concern about our own welfare. But such a powerful control of the faculty of reason over directly felt suffering is seldom or never found in fact.

Moreover, through this consideration of the inevitability of pain, of the supplanting of one pain by another, of the dragging in of a fresh pain by the departure of the preceding one, we might be led to the paradoxical but not absurd hypothesis that in every individual the measure of the pain essential to him has been determined once for all by his nature, a measure that could not remain empty or be filled to excess, however much the form of the suffering might change. Accordingly, his suffering and well-being would not be determined at all from without, but only by that measure, that disposition, which might in fact through the physical condition experience some increase and decrease at different times, but which on the whole would remain the same. and would be nothing but what is called his temperament. More accurately, this is called the degree in which he might be εὔχολος or δύσχολος, as Plato puts it in the first book of the *Republic*, in other words, of an easy or difficult nature. In support of this hypothesis is the well-known experience that great sufferings render lesser ones quite incapable of being felt, and conversely, that in the absence of great sufferings even the smallest vexations and annoyances torment us, and put us in a bad mood. But experience also teaches us that if a great misfortune, at the mere thought of which we shuddered, has now actually happened, our frame of mind remains on the whole much the same as soon as we have overcome the first pain. Conversely, experience also teaches us that, after the appearance of a long-desired happiness, we do not feel ourselves on the whole and permanently much better off or more comfortable than before. Only the moment of appearance of these changes moves us with unusual strength, as deep distress or shouts of joy; but both of these soon disappear, because they rested on illusion. For they do not spring from the immediately present pleasure or pain, but only from the opening up of a new future that is anticipated in them. Only by pain or pleasure borrowing from the future could they be heightened so abnormally, and consequently not for any length of time. The following remarks may be put in evidence in support of the hypothesis we advanced, by which, in knowing as well as in feeling suffering or well-being, a very large part would be subjective and determined *a priori*. Human cheerfulness or dejection is obviously not determined by external circumstances, by wealth or position, for we come across at least as many cheerful faces among the poor as among the rich. Further, the motives that induce suicide are so very different, that we cannot mention any misfortune which would be great enough to bring it about in any character with a high degree of probability, and few that would be so small that those like them would not at some time have caused it. Now although the degree of our cheerfulness or sadness is not at all times the same, yet in consequence of this view we shall attribute it not to the change of external circumstances, but to that of the internal state, the physical condition. For when an actual, though always only temporary, enhancement of our cheerfulness takes place, even to the extent of joy, it usually appears without any external occasion. It is true that we often see our pain result only from a definite external relation, and that we are visibly oppressed and saddened merely by this. We then believe that, if only this were removed, the greatest contentment would necessarily ensue. But this is a delusion. The measure of our pain and our well-being is, on the whole, subjectively determined for each point of time according to our hypothesis; and in reference to this, that external motive for sadness is only what a blister is for the body, to which are drawn all the bad humours that would otherwise be spread throughout it. The pain to be found in our nature for this period of time, which therefore cannot be shaken off, would be distributed at a hundred points were it not for that definite external cause of our suffering. It would appear in the form of a hundred little annoyances and worries over things we now entirely overlook, because our capacity for pain is already filled up by that principal evil that has concentrated at a point all the suffering otherwise dispersed. In keeping with this is also the observation that, if a great and pressing care is finally lifted from our breast by a fortunate issue, another immediately takes its place. The whole material of this already existed previously, yet it could not enter consciousness as care, because the consciousness had no capacity left for it. This material for care, therefore, remained merely as a dark and unobserved misty form on the extreme horizon of consciousness. But now, as there is room, this ready material at once comes forward and occupies the throne of the reigning care of the day (πρυτανε ὐουσα). If so far as its matter is concerned it is very much lighter than the material of the care that has vanished, it knows how to blow itself out, so that it apparently equals it in size, and thus, as the chief care of the day, completely fills the throne.

Excessive joy and very severe pain occur always only in the same person, for they reciprocally condition each other, and are also conditioned in common by great mental activity. As we have just now found, both are brought about not by what is actually present, but by anticipation of the future. But as pain is essential to life, and is also determined as regards its degree by the nature of the subject, sudden changes, since they are always external, cannot really change its degree. Thus an error and delusion are at the root of immoderate joy or pain; consequently, these two excessive strains of the mind could be avoided by insight. Every immoderate joy (*exultatio, insolens laetitia*[①]) always rests on the delusion that we have found something in life that is not to be met with at all, namely permanent satisfaction of the tormenting desires or cares that constantly breed new ones. From each particular delusion of this kind we must inevitably later be brought back; and then, when it vanishes, we must pay for it with pains just as bitter as the joy caused by its entry was keen. To this extent it is exactly like a height from which we can descend again only by a fall; we should therefore avoid them; and every sudden,

---

① exultatio, insolens laetitia,（拉丁语）狂欢,乐而忘形。

excessive grief is just a fall from such a height, the vanishing of such a delusion, and is thus conditioned by it. Consequently, we could avoid both, if we could bring ourselves always to survey things with perfect clearness as a whole and in their connexion, and resolutely to guard against actually lending them the colour we should like them to have. The Stoic① ethics aimed principally at freeing the mind from all such delusion and its consequences, and at giving it an unshakable equanimity instead. Horace② is imbued with this insight in the well-known ode:

> *Aequam memento rebus in arduis*
> *Servare mentem, non secus in bonis*
> *Ab insolenti temperatam*
> *Laetitia.* —

But we frequently shut our eyes to the truth, comparable to a bitter medicine, that suffering is essential to life, and therefore does not flow in upon us from outside, but that everyone carries around within himself its perennial source. On the contrary, we are constantly looking for a particular external cause, as it were a pretext for the pain that never leaves us, just as the free man makes for himself an idol, in order to have a master. For we untiringly strive from desire to desire, and although every attained satisfaction, however much it promised, does not really satisfy us, but often stands before us as a mortifying error, we still do not see that we are drawing water with the vessel of the Danaides③, and we hastea to ever fresh desires:

> *Sed, dum abest quod avemus, id exsuperare videtur*
> *Caetera; post aliud, quum contigit illud, avemus;*
> *Et sitis aequa tenet vitai semper hiantes.*
>
> (Lucretius, iii, 1082.)

Thus it goes on either *ad infinitum*④, or, what is rarer and already presupposes a certain strength of character, till we come to a wish that is not

---

① Stoic,斯多葛派学者,禁欲者。
② Horace,贺拉斯(前65—前8),古罗马诗人,著有《诗艺》等。
③ the Danaides,达那伊得斯姐妹,犯杀夫之罪,所遭到的惩罚,是在地狱中永远用筛取水。
④ ad infinitum(拉丁语),无限地,无止境地。

fulfilled, and yet cannot be given up. We then have, so to speak, what we were looking for, namely something that we can denounce at any moment, instead of our own inner nature, as the source of our sufferings. Thus, although at variance with our fate, we become reconciled to our existence in return for this, since the knowledge that suffering is essential to this existence itself and that true satisfaction is impossible, is again withdrawn from us. The consequence of this last kind of development is a somewhat melancholy disposition, the constant bearing of a single, great pain, and the resultant disdain for all lesser joys and sorrows. This is in consequence a worthier phenomenon than the constant hunting for ever different deceptive forms which is much more usual.

 选文出处

Arthur Schopenhauer. *The World as Will and Representation*. Translated by E. F. J. Payne, Beijing: China Social Sciences Publishing House (reprinted from the English Edition by Dover Publication, Inc., 1966), 1999, pp. 311—319.

思考题

1. 人生真的只能在痛苦和无聊之间徘徊吗？为什么？
2. 如何评价叔本华的痛苦定量说？

阅读

参考书目

1. 成海鹰、成芳：《唯意志论哲学在中国》，北京：首都师范大学出版社，2002年。
2. Michael Fox, *Schopenhauer: His Philosophical Achievements*, Oxford: Oxford University Press, 1980.

尼　采

曾被鲁迅赞誉为20世纪最具革命性的思想家尼采,是一位悲剧性的英雄人物。活着时默默无闻,忍受着无人理解、赏识与沟通的痛苦。死后,幸运之光才降临到他的身上。时至今日,他不但登上了西方哲学史经典人物的排行榜,而且还被认为是后现代主义哲学的开创者。然而,由于尼采的哲学总是高蹈着一种强烈的主观征服欲,故而又被屡屡牵涉到他并不喜欢的政治之中。

1844年10月15日,尼采(Friedrich Nietzsche,1844—1900)出生于德国普鲁士萨克森州(Sachsen)的洛肯镇(Lutzen)的一个新教牧师家庭。1864年,20岁的尼采进波昂大学读书,专修神学与古典文献学。1865年,他由波昂大学转入莱比锡大学,并在这一年接触到对其后来的哲学思想有很大影响的一本书,即叔本华的《作为意志和表象的世界》。1869年,尼采担任了巴塞尔大学古典文献学的副教授,并于第二年转为教授。自1871年开始,尼采进入了作为一个哲学家的写作历程。1879年,由于病魔对身体的侵蚀和对所谓学问的怀疑,尼采给10年的书斋生涯画上了一个句号,背着行囊孤身一人在欧洲各地漂泊、流浪。这十年尼采在生活、情感上都异常艰苦,值得欣慰的是,他迎来了创作的高峰期,几乎所有的主要著作都完成于该历史时段中。1889年,中风后的尼采在精神上出现了障碍,神智始终处于麻痹状态。1900年,历尽精神煎熬与疾病折磨的尼采终于撒手人寰,葬于故乡洛肯镇。

尼采一生的主要哲学著作有《悲剧的诞生》(*The Birth of*

Tragedy，1872)、《人性的，太人性的》(Human，All Too Human，1877—1879)、《漂泊者及其影子》(The Wander and His Shadow，1880)、《曙光》(The Dawn，1881)、《快乐的科学》(The Gay Science，1881—1882)、《查拉图斯特拉如是说》(Thus Spake Zarathustra，1883—1885)、《善与恶的超越》(Beyond Good and Evil，1885)、《道德的系谱》(On the Genealogy of Morals，1886)、《偶像的黄昏》(Twilight of the Idols，1889)等。《反基督》(The Antichrist，Curse on Christianity，1888)、《瞧！这个人》(Ecce Homo，1888)、《尼采反对瓦格纳》(Nietzsche Contra Wagner，1888)等著作，是尼采去世后收于全集中出版的。

尼采的哲学以标新立异、横空出世而著称，但这不意味着他的哲学找不到思想渊源。在尼采的哲学生涯中，曾有两个人给他带来巨大的启发与冲击：一个是当时已去世了的哲学家叔本华；另一个是还活着的德国作曲家瓦格纳。尼采喜欢、倾心瓦格纳，实际还是源于叔本华。因为，他从瓦格纳的音乐旋律中仿若看到了叔本华的哲学。乔治·勃兰兑斯曾说："作为一个思想家，尼采是以叔本华的理论为出发点的。就其最初的著作而言，他实际上不过是叔本华的门徒。"①叔本华哲学中所表达出的那种强烈的生存意志的痛苦，深深震撼了尼采的心灵。但是，生性勇猛、豪迈，并有过两次从军经历(1867、1870)的尼采②是一位大胆、彪悍的行动主义者，他虽被叔本华的深邃思考所陶醉，但却不满意于其哲学中对生命意志的彻底否定的消极情绪。因此，他开始着手改造叔本华的哲学，即在继承了叔本华的非理性主义传统的同时，把其生存意志发展、转换成了以不断进取、超越自我为特征的权力意志。这种权力意志不但成为尼采哲学的独特标示，也成为尼采哲学的出发点与归宿。

由于尼采的哲学主要是建立在重估一切价值基础上的，所以，尼采哲学的最大贡献表现在对西方传统文化的抨击与瓦解上。(一)他解构了基督教中的"上帝"观念。在西方传统文化中，"上帝"一直占据、端坐于神圣偶像的座椅。而如今上帝死了，人便拥有了自我管理、发展和抉择的权力；(二)他解构了西方的理性主义传统。自柏拉图以来，西方的哲学家们就把世界分成了"表象世界"(The world of appearance)和"理式世界"(The world of idea)两部分。对人类而言，肉眼所看到的生活和情感所触摸到的东西，只是关乎于世界的一些表象(假象)，而世界的真实面貌和人生的真正价值则只能在"理式世界"中得以裸露

---

① 乔治·勃兰兑斯：《尼采》，安延明译，北京：工人出版社，1985年，第27页。
② 尼采外表看上去忧郁、瘦弱、孤僻、多愁善感，但其灵魂却异常彪悍、勇猛，这种内外反差构成了其哲学的独特魅力。

与实现。作为一种理论探讨,上述这种真、假"二元论"还是颇有哲理深度的,但是如果作为一种指导人生的价值准则,实际是对现实人生的彻底否定。尼采在其哲学中,把肉眼所看到的这个世界定义为最真实、可信的唯一世界,一方面把人从虚无、缥缈的虚构世界中解放了出来,另一方面对后来的存在主义哲学家海德格尔也有极大的影响。

"超人"学说是尼采哲学中的另一个重要的关键性内容。这个学说源于尼采的一本哲学专著《查拉斯特拉如是说》。不管是尼采本人还是其他研究者,均把该书视为最能代表尼采的本真想法和影响最大的一部哲学著作。

《查拉斯特拉如是说》共有9卷构成。由于这部哲学著作在写法上采用了寓言、象征性的文体框架,而在语言上,又有大量抒情、隽永的警句、格言穿插于其中,因而读起来像诗歌一样地酣畅淋漓。尼采在这部书中塑造了一个生动、形象而又充满争议的人物形象——"超人"。这里所选取的片段是出自该书的第9卷,即表达了"上帝已死:现在我们热望着——超人生存!"的信念。

何谓"超人"?在学术界历来有不同的看法与解释。由于"超人"是诞生于上帝死后,所以"超人"不应该等同于上帝。由于"超人"在作品中不但不等同于"今日之支配者",而且还把他们称为"一种贱氓的族类"。而所谓的"贱氓",是指一种"不知道什么是伟大,什么是渺小,什么是无枉,什么是正直,贱氓永远是无知的歪曲,他们永远是说谎话的人"。所以说,"超人"是一种既不同于"上帝"又区别于普通人的更高贵的人。其实,这种人在现实生活中是难以找到的,他不过是尼采理想世界的象征,正如乔治·勃兰兑斯在分析其哲学时所说:"所谓伟大的、真正的进步在于,培养起一个比今天我们周围的人更聪明、更强壮的人种(超人)。"[①]显然,"超人"是对现有人种的否定与超越。这说明尼采把拯救世界和人类的希望寄托在了"超人"的身上。

值得说明的是,尽管尼采是一位无神论和强烈的反基督教者,但是"超人"在其哲学中还是具有"神"的意味。一方面,这部书的中心人物查拉斯特拉,即"超人"本来就是从波斯的《阿维斯陀》(Avesta)中借鉴来的,而这个人物本身就是一种纯洁宗教的创建人;[②]另一方面,"超人"在书中的言谈举止始终都是以一种万物创造、主宰者的身份出现的,他与"民众""凡夫俗子"的关系是一种教化与被教化的关系。也就是说,尼采实际是用一种新型的"神"代替了耶稣这个衰老的神。

尼采的哲学有时又被称为生命哲学。这表明他的哲学思想主要不是来自

[①] 乔治·勃兰兑斯:《尼采》,安延明译,第85页。
[②] 同上书,第97—98页。

书本上的推理与考据,而是源于生命和意志的涌动与喷发。他在自传《瞧!这个人》中曾说:"我是第一个反道德者,因此,我是根本的破坏者。"①尼采哲学所呈现出的这种血肉相连的特征,在使他的哲学贴近生命和人生的同时,可能会使某些观点过于激进而不够缜密与统一。

Thus Spake Zarathustra

1

When I came unto men for the first time, then did I commit the anchorite folly, the great folly: I appeared on the market-place.

And when I spake unto all, I spake unto none. In the evening, however, rope-dancers were my companions, and corpses; and I myself almost a corpse.

With the new morning, however, there came unto me a new truth: then did I learn to say: "Of what account to me are market-place and populace and populace-noise and long populace-ears!"

Ye higher men, learn *this* from me: On the market-place no one believeth in higher men. But if ye will speak there, very well! The populace, however, blinketh: "We are all equal."

"Ye higher men," —so blinketh the populace— "there are no higher men, we are all equal; man is man, before God—we are all equal!"

Before God! —Now, however, this God hath died. Before the populace, however, we will not be equal. Ye higher men, away from the market-place!

2

Before God! —Now however this God hath died! Ye higher men, this God was your greatest danger.

Only since he lay in the grave have ye again arisen. Now only cometh the

---

① 尼采:《瞧! 这个人》,刘崎译,北京:中国和平出版社,1986年,第109页。

great noontide, now only doth the higher man become—master!

Have ye understood this word, O my brethren? Ye are frightened: do your hearts turn giddy? Doth the abyss here yawn for you? Doth the hellhound here yelp at you?

Well! Take heart! ye higher men! Now only travaileth the mountain of the human future. God hath died: now do *we* desire—the Superman to live.

3

The most careful ask to-day: "How is man to be maintained?" Zarathustra however asketh, as the first and only one: "How is man to be *surpassed*?"

The Superman, I have at heart; *that* is the first and only thing to me—and *not* man: not the neighbour, not the poorest, not the sorriest, not the best. —

O my brethren, what I can love in man is that he is an over-going and a down-going. And also in you there is much that maketh me love and hope.

In that ye have despised, ye higher men, that maketh me hope. For the great despisers are the great reverers.

In that ye have despaired, there is much to honour. For ye have not learned to submit yourselves, ye have not learned petty policy.

For to-day have the petty people become master: they all preach submission and humility and policy and diligence and consideration and the long *et cetera* of petty virtues.

Whatever is of the effeminate type, whatever originateth from the servile type, ana especially the populace-mishmast: —*that* wisheth now to be master of all human destiny—O disgust! Disgust! Disgust!

That asketh and asketh and never tireth: "How is man to maintain himself best, longest, most pleasantly?" Thereby—are they the masters of to-day.

These masters of to-day—surpass them, O my brethenthese petty people: *they* are the Superman's greatest danger!

Surpass, ye higher men, the petty virtues, the petty policy, the sand-grain considerateness, the ant-hill trumpery, the pitiable comfortableness, the "happiness of the greatest number"—!

And rather despair than submit yourselves. And verily, I love you, because ye know not to-day how to live, ye higher men! For thus do *ye* live—best!

4

Have ye courage, O my brethren? Are ye stout-hearted? *Not* the courage before witnesses, but anchorite and eagle courage, which not even a God any longer beholdeth?

Cold souls, mules, the blind and the drunken, I do not call stout-hearted. He hath heart who knoweth fear, But *vanquisheth* it; who seeth the abyss, but with *pride*.

He who seeth the abyss, but with eagle's eyes,— he who with eagle's talons *graspeth* the abyss: he hath courage. — —

5

"Man is evil" —so said to me for consolation, all the wisest ones. Ah, if only it be still true to-day! For the evil is man's best force.

"Man must become better and eviler" —so do *I* teach. The evilest is necessary for the Superman's best.

It may have been well for the preacher of the petty people to suffer and be burdened by men's sin. I, However, rejoice in great sin as my great *consolation*. —

Such things, however, are not said for long ears. Every word, also, is not suited for every mouth. These are fine, far-away things: at them sheep's claws shall not grasp!

6

Ye higher men, think ye that I am here to put right what ye have put wrong?

Or that I wished henceforth to make snugger couches for you sufferers?

Or show you restless, miswandering, misclimbing ones, new and easier footpaths?

Nay! Nay! Three times Nay! Always more, always better ones of your type shall succumb, —for ye shall always have it worse and harder. Thus only—

—Thus only groweth man aloft to the height where the lightning striketh and shattereth him: high enough for the lightning!

Towards the few, the long, the remote go forth my soul and my seeking: of what account to me are your many little, short miseries!

Ye do not yet suffer enough for me! For ye suffer from yourselves, ye have not yet suffered *from man*. Ye would lie if ye spake otherwise! None of you suffereth from what *I* have suffered. — —

7

It is not enough for me that the lightning no longer doeth harm. I do not wish to conduct it away: it shall learn—to work for *me*. —

My wisdom hath accumulated long like a cloud, it becometh stiller and darker. So doeth all wisdom which shall one day bear *lightnings*. —

Unto these men of to-day will I not be *light*, nor be called light. *Them*— will I blind: lightning of my wisdom! put out their eyes!

8

Do not will anything beyond your power: there is a bad falseness in those who will beyond their power.

Especially when they will great things! For they awaken distrust in great things, these subtle false-coiners and stage-players: —

—Until at last they are false towards themselves, squint-eyed, whited cankers, glossed over with strong words, parade virtues and brilliant false deeds.

Take good care there, ye higher men! For nothing is more precious to me, and rarer, than honesty.

Is this to-day not that of the populace? The populace however knoweth not what is great and what is small, what is straight and what is honest: it is innocently crooked, it ever lieth.

9

Have a good distrust to-day, ye higher men, ye enheartened ones! Ye open-hearted ones! And keep your reasons secret! For this to-day is that of the populace.

What the populace once learned to believe without reasons, who could—refute it to them by means of reasons?

And on the market-place one convinceth with gestures. But reasons make the populace distrustful.

And when truth hath once triumphed there, then ask yourselves with good distrust: "What strong error hath fought for it?"

Be on your guard also against the learned! They hate you, because they are unproductive! They have cold, withered eyes before which every bird is unplumed.

Such persons vaunt about not lying: but inability to lie is still far from being love to truth. Be on your guard!

Freedom from fever is still far from being knowledge! Refrigerated spirits I do not believe in. He who cannot lie, doth not know what truth is.

10

If ye would go up high, then use your owm legs! Do not get yourselves *carried* alolt; do not seat yourselves on other people's backs and heads!

Thou hast mounted, however, on horseback? Thou now ridest briskly up to thy goal? Well, my friend! But thy lame foot is also with thee on horseback!

When thou reachest thy goal, when thou alightest from thy horse: precisely on thy *height*, thou higher man,—then wilt thou stumble!

11

Ye creating ones, ye higher men! One is only pregnant with one's own child.

Do not let yourselves be imposed upon or put upon! Who then is *your* neighbour? Even if ye act "for your neighbour" —ye still do not create for him!

Unlearn, I pray you, this "for," ye creating ones: your very virtue wisheth you to have naught to do with "for" and "on account of" and "because." Against these false little words shall ye stop your ears.

"For one's neighbour," is the virtue only of the petty people: there it is said "like and like," and "hand washeth hand": —they have neither the right nor the power for *your* self-seeking!

In your self-seeking, ye creating ones, there is the foresight and foreseeing of the pregnant! What no one's eye hath yet seen, namely, the fruit—this, sheltereth and saveth and nourisheth your entire love.

Where your entire love is, namely, with your child, there is also your entire virtue! Your work, your will is *your* "neighbour": let no false values impose upon you!

12

Ye creating ones, ye higher men! Whoever hath to give birth is sick; whoever hath given birth, however, is unclean.

Ask women: one giveth birth, not because it giveth pleasure. The pain maketh hens and poets cackle.

Ye creating ones, in you there is much uncleanness. That is because ye have had to be mothers.

A new child: oh, how much new filth hath also come into the world! Go apart! He who hath given birth shall wash his soul!

13

Be not virtuous beyond your powers! And seek nothing from yourselves opposed to probability!

Walk in the footsteps in which your fathers' virtue hath already walked! How would ye rise high, if your fathers' will should not rise with you?

He, however, who would be a firstling, let him take care lest he also become a lastling! And where the vices of your fathers are, there should ye not set up as saints!

He whose fathers were inclined for women, and for strong wine and flesh of wildboar swine; what would it be if he demanded chastity of himself?

A folly would it be! Much, verily, doth it seem to me for such a one, if he should be the husband of one or of two or of three women.

And if he founded monasteries, and inscribed over their portals: "The way to holiness," —I should still say: What good is it! it is a new folly!

He hath founded for himself a penance-house and refuge-house: much good may it do! But I do not believe in it.

In solitude there groweth what any one bringeth into it—also the brute in one's nature. Thus is solitude inadvisable unto many.

Hath there ever been anything filthier on earth than the saints of the wilderness? *Around them* was not only the devil loose—but also the swine.

14

Shy, ashamed, awkward, like the tiger whose spring hath failed—thus, ye higner men, have I often seen you slink aside. A *cast* which ye made had failed.

But what doth it matter, ye dice-players! Ye had not learned to play and mock, as one must play and mock! Do we not ever sit at a great table of mocking and playing?

And if great things have been a failure with you, have ye yourselves therefore—been a failure? And if ye yourselves have been a failure, hath man therefore—been a failure? If man, however, hath been a failure: well then!

never mind!

15

The higher its type, always the seldomer doth a thing succeed. Ye higher men here, have ye not all—been failures?

Be of good cheer; what doth it matter? How much is still possible! Learn to laugh at yourselves, as ye ought to laugh!

What wonder even that ye have failed and only half-succeeded, ye half-shattered ones! Doth not—man's *future* strive and struggle in you?

Man's furthest, profoundest, star-highest issues, his prodigious powers—do not all these foam through one another in your vessel?

What wonder that many a vessel shattereth! Learn to laugh at yourselves, as ye ought to laugh! Ye higher men, Oh, how much is still possible!

And verily, how much hath already succeeded! How rich is this earth in small, good, perfect things, in well-constituted things!

Set around you small, good, perfect things, ye higher men. Their golden maturity healeth the heart. The perfect teacheth one to hope.

16

What hath hitherto been the greatest sin here on earth? Was it not the word of him who said: "Woe unto them that laugh now!"

Did he himself find no cause for laughter on the earth? Then he sought badly. A child even findeth cause for it.

He—did not love sufficiently: otherwise would he also have loved us, the laughing ones! But he hated and hooted us; wailing and teeth-gnashing did he promise us.

Must one then curse immediately, when one doth not love? That—seemeth to me bad taste. Thus did he, however, this absolute one. He sprang from the populace.

And he himself just did not love sufficiently; otherwise would he have raged less because people did not love him. All great love doth not *seek* love:

—it seeketh more.

Go out of the way of all such absolute ones! They are a poor sickly type, a populace-type: they look at this life with ill-will, they have an evil eye for this earth.

Go out of the way of all such absolute ones! They have heavy feet and sultry hearts:—they do not know how to dance. How could the earth be light to such ones!

17

Tortuously do all good things come nigh to their goal. Like cats they curve their backs, they purr inwardly with their approaching happiness,—all good things laugh.

His step betrayeth whether a person already walketh on *his own* path: just see me walk! He, however, who cometh nigh to his goal, danceth.

And verily, a statue have I not become, not yet do I stand there still, stupid and stony, like a pillar; I love fast racing.

And though there be on earth fens and dense afflictions, he who hath light feet runneth even across the mud, and danceth, as upon well-swept ice.

Lift up your hearts, my brethren, high, higher! And do not forget your legs! Lift up also your legs, ye good dancers, and better still, if ye stand upon your heads!

18

This crown of the laughter, this rose-garland crown: I myself have put on this crown, I myself have consecrated my laughter. No one else have I found to-day potent enough for this.

Zarathustra the dancer, Zarathustra the light one, who beckoneth with his pinions, one ready for flight, beckoning unto all birds, ready and prepared, a blissfully light-spirited one:—

Zarathustra the sooth-sayer, Zarathustra the sooth-laugher, no impatient one, no absolute one, one who loveth leaps and side-leaps; I myself have put on this crown!

19

Lift up your hearts, my brethren, high, higher! And do not forget your legs! Lift up also your legs, ye good danccrs, and better still if ye stand upon your heads!

There are also heavy animals in a state of happiness, there are club-footed ones from the beginning. Curiously do they exert themselves, like an elephant which endeavoureth to stand upon its head.

Better, however, to be foolish with happiness than foolish with misfortune, better to dance awkwardly than walk lamely. So learn, I pray you, my wisdom, ye higher men: even the worst thing hath two good reverse sides,—

—Even the worst thing hath good dancing-legs: so learn, I pray you, ye higher men, to put yourselves on your proper legs!

So unlearn, I pray you, the sorrow-sighing, and all the populace-sadness! Oh, how sad the buffoons of the populace seem to me to-day! This to-day, however, is that of the populace.

20

Do like unto the wind when it rusheth forth from its mountain-caves: unto its own piping will it dance; the seas tremble and leap under its footsteps.

That which giveth wings to asses, that which milketh the lionesses: —praised be that good, unruly spirit, which cometh like a hurricane unto all the present and unto all the populace,—

—Which is hostile to thistle-heads and puzzle-heads, and to all withered leaves and weeds: —praised be this wild, good, free spirit of the storm, which danceth upon fens and afflictions, as upon meadows!

Which hateth the consumptive populace-dogs, and all the ill-constituted, sullen brood: —praised be this spirit of all free spirits, the laughing storm, which bloweth dust into the eyes of all the melanopic and melancholic!

Ye higher men, the worst thing in you is that ye have none of you learned to dance as ye ought to dance—to dance beyond yourselves! What doth it matter that ye have failed!

How many things are still possible! So *learn* to laugh beyond yourselves! Lift up your hearts, ye good dancers, high! higher! And do not forget the good laughter!

This crown of the laugher, this rose-garland crown: to you my brethren do I cast this crown! Laughing have I consecrated; ye higher men, *learn*, I pray you—to laugh!

 选文出处

Friedrich Nietzsche. *Thus Spake Zarathustra*. Translated by Thomas Common, Beijing: China Social Sciences Publishing House (reprinted from the English Edition by Boni and Liveright, Inc., 1917), 1999, pp. 285—295.

思考题

1. 分析、总结尼采的哲学思想与叔本华哲学的关系。
2. "超人"是上帝吗？应该怎样理解《查拉图斯特拉如是说》中的"超人"形象？
3. 尼采的哲学对分解、推进西方文化传统起到哪些积极的作用？

参考书目

1. 乔治·勃兰兑斯：《尼采》，安延明译，北京：工人出版社，1985年。
2. 尼采：《瞧！这个人》，刘崎译，北京：中国和平出版社，1986年。
3. Magnus, Bernd and Higgins, K. Marie. (eds.), *The Cambridge Companion to Nietzsche*, Cambridge: University of Cambridge Press, 1996.
4. Danto, A. Coleman, *Nietzsche as Philosopher*, Columbia: Columbia University Press, 1965.

克尔凯郭尔

索伦·阿拜·克尔凯郭尔（Soren Aabye Kierkegaard，1813—1855）是丹麦著名的哲学家、诗人、文学批评家以及宗教思想家。克尔凯郭尔出生于哥本哈根一个笃信基督教的富裕的牧师家庭，父亲强暴家中女佣生下了他。其父马可·克尔凯郭尔一方面强迫子女从小接受基督教信仰，同时又为早年咒骂过上帝以及有过通奸行为而自认有罪，担心上帝惩罚，惶惶不可终日。克尔凯郭尔由于受到父亲情绪的影响，从小就为有罪和受惩的宗教情感所支配。另外，由于先天驼背跛足的生理缺陷以及体弱多病等原因，更加剧了他悲观颓废的情绪。1830年，克尔凯郭尔进入哥本哈根大学学习神学。其间，他阅读了大量哲学和文化学著作，并对戏剧、音乐产生了浓厚兴趣。但这些都不足以改变他悲观颓废的反常心理，直到与一位名叫雷吉娜的姑娘交往，克尔凯郭尔才燃起了追求新生活的热情。然而，1840年在与雷吉娜订婚后不久，克尔凯郭尔又重新为恐惧、颤栗、悲观、绝望等消极情绪所支配。他自以为在上帝与婚姻之间只能二者择一，于是在矛盾和痛苦中解除了婚约。此后，他的生活更为孤僻，心理状态近乎疯狂。正是在这种痛苦的状态下，他使自己潜心于哲学、文学等的创作。1841年，他完成了硕士论文《论讽刺概念》，同年10月去柏林继续上学，曾听过谢林反黑格尔的课。1842年3月，他回到哥本哈根，靠所获巨额遗产生活。在其后的十多年间，他的作品如急流汹涌，源源而来，形成世界文学及哲学史上的奇观。晚年，他几乎将全部精力转向宗教领域，写了大量关于宗教的论著，直至1855年病逝。

克尔凯郭尔最主要的哲学著作有:《非此即彼》(Either—Or，1843)、《畏惧与战栗》(Fear and Trembling，1843)、《恐惧的概念》(The Concept of Anxiety，1844)、《人生道路上的各个阶段》(Stages On Life's Way，1845)、《〈哲学片断〉一书最后的非科学性附言》(Philosophical Fragments：A Mimetic-Pathetic-Dialectic Compilation，An Existential Plea，1846)等,其著作充满着思辨和个性。

19世纪40年代,克尔凯郭尔处于创作的高峰期。那时,曾在德国占统治地位的黑格尔哲学迅速衰落,受到了来自不同方面的批判,其中就有叔本华、后期谢林等人从非理性主义立场进行的批判。克尔凯郭尔对谢林把"实在当作个人伦理上的实在"的论述十分欣赏,对德国浪漫主义者主张"在孤独的个人主观体验中去把握真正的实在和内在无限性"的观点极为赞同,并努力把它们与基督教传统中的非理性主义结合起来。因此,他的哲学是欧洲哲学和宗教中的非理性主义思潮发展的产物。

克尔凯郭尔被认为是使欧洲哲学发生方向性转折的重要人物之一。他所推进的转折,主要内容是以孤独的、非理性的个人存在取代客观物质和理性意识的存在,并以此作为全部哲学的出发点;以个人的非理性情感,特别是厌烦、忧郁、绝望等悲观情绪,代替对外部世界和人的理智认识的研究,特别是代替黑格尔主义对纯思维、理性和逻辑的研究,作为其哲学的主要内容。

作为存在主义的先驱者,克尔凯郭尔在西方哲学界享有盛名。一般说来,他的存在主义有两大要义:其一,存在先于本质的理念。他认为人的生存是被动的、命定的,可是人可以利用自己命定的这种存在,去创造自己的本质。换言之,人之所以可贵,并非由于他有一个命定的存在,并非由于他的历史背景、家世,而在于人如何改造自己的本质的自由,这就是人的本质;其二,将存在分为三个阶段。他认为,第一阶段是感性存在(又称为审美阶段):感性存在通常是追求自己的快乐,追求轻薄的人生,追求自己自私的一面,是一种从维持生命到享乐方面的存在;第二阶段是理性存在(又称为伦理阶段):是一种比较严肃的、尽责的人生,以理性和哲学的方法解决自己的问题,使自己对别人尽到伦理责任,合于社会道德的存在;第三阶段是宗教性存在(又称为宗教阶段):是一种祈祷和爱的生活,是对神的自觉和崇敬,从而使精神有所寄托的存在。

克尔凯郭尔所提倡的存在主义,强调哲学家应探讨现实中人生问题,认为人生最主要的是如何具体地把握住个人的存在。克尔凯郭尔个人对"孤独"与"例外"的感受,促使其创造出关心自己的哲学——存在主义。他指出,语言、理性和逻辑无法揭示每一个人独特的个性,无法揭示人的真正存在。对于后者,只能依靠每一个人本身内在的独特的主观体验。作为一个存在主义思想家,克尔凯郭尔试图将一切与个体自身的情况相联系，而不是从中提取本质的东西，以此来理解生活。他的第一本著作《非此即彼》，集中论述了自由与奴役之间的选择，这一论题几乎可以在他的所有著述中找到。他坚持认为责任和宿命论在人类中互相缠绕，由此蕴藏了心理学中的去个性化和意志危机等课题。

克尔凯郭尔题为《轮作方法》①的论文，节选自《非此即彼》这部经典著作，为我们理解其深奥的哲学思想提供了一把灵验的钥匙。文章分为三个部分。第一部分，克尔凯郭尔从一个具有可驳斥性的命题开始切入——"所有的人都是厌烦的"。此命题认为，厌烦作为个人处于审美阶段的基本情绪，并不是对这样或那样东西感到厌烦，而是一种基于无对象的自我厌烦，对一切和每一样东西，全觉得无聊透顶。厌烦对于人的存在来说是一种自身的空虚，这种空虚虽然可以通过工作和消遣被充实和驱散，但却无法被消除。针对这种无聊、空虚的存在，克尔凯郭尔推出了他关于讽刺、无聊的神话，指出，无聊是"构成生存色彩的虚无的主观相应物"，揭示了存在自身的无根据性和无意义性。由此，他将个人的存在置于决定之前，存在之后才是人的情绪，或信仰或绝望或厌烦。克尔凯郭尔对"所有厌烦的人"做了一个有趣的划分（厌人者和厌己者），并辨证地指出："不厌己者通常厌烦别人，厌己者通常使人愉悦。"前者大多是些平凡人，终日碌碌无为，自己无趣，亦让他人难受；后者为少数优秀分子，能使人愉悦。他们越是厌己，转化出的能量便越大；当他们的厌烦达到顶点时，爆发出的必然是求变之心，这时，社会变革的时代便不远了。

克尔凯郭尔在第二部分中引出了文章的主题：怎么排解这个厌烦的"万恶之源"？他提出了被称为"轮作方法"的观点："我的方法不在于换田地，而在于换耕作的农作物和耕作方式。"换言之，需要有一种不断否定自我，超越自我的态度。在生活中，很多事物是不能改变的，可以改变的是我们看待事物的眼光。在具体说明的时候，作者首先引导我们看待"受限"问题："你限制自己的程度越大，你在创造上就越强。"他还举出了许多例子加以说明，如：一个囚犯因为孤独的牢狱生活而变成了发明家；蜘蛛因为禁闭而更能娱乐自己等。他还将"轮作方法"细化成相对"记忆和遗忘"，一个人的遗忘程度决定其精神的弹性。当然，这里的"遗忘"不等于彻底忘记，而是一种移除不快，解除苦痛的艺术和技能，即在记忆的指引下，剪掉没有用的那一部分。

克尔凯郭尔在第三部分探讨如何将"轮作方法"运用于伦理生活中。文中对"友谊""婚姻"和"工作"的论述，实际上映射出克尔凯郭尔本人对伦理生活的态度。对伦理主义者来说，这些范畴具有至关重要的意义。因为只有借助它

---

① 原文题名为"Rotation"，本篇中译作"轮作方法"。

们，个人才能在自己伦理生活中实现特殊与普遍的伦理综合：人必须结婚，必须有朋友，必须珍视自己的工作和职业。然而，克尔凯郭尔的哲学却有点"反其道而行之"："必须提防友谊"、"最好不要和婚姻扯上关系"、"不要接受对任何一个职位的指派"。甚至还"危言耸听"地说："友谊是危险的，婚姻更为危险，所以当需要和她绑定一份永恒的关系的时候，女人对男人来说，意味着一种毁灭。""如果你接受了指派，就注定沦为国家工具上的一个小的齿轮；你将注定丧失主宰自己行为的能力。"

克尔凯郭尔的这些哲学观点，可以说是得自其个人反常的、非理性的经验，甚至带有自传色彩。1840 年，克尔凯郭尔在与 17 岁的雷吉娜订婚以后，把内心的感受，包括自己的两个原罪告诉了她，而雷吉娜不能接受如此古怪的、颓丧的思想，对此一笑置之。克尔凯郭尔认为不该也无法把自己内心的痛苦分担给这位未来的太太，因此断然与她解除了婚约。之后，他感到更痛苦，直到去世。在他的日记和著作中，他和雷吉娜的关系一直都是他自我折磨式思虑的主题之一。克尔凯郭尔的另一个重大经历是，早年曾发表文章反对法国资产阶级革命理论和"群众的统治"。他在政治上一直保守，晚年更与当时丹麦的官方教会发生过激烈的冲突。正是由于有这些经历，他才深刻地认识到人无法以感性的方法解除内心的苦闷，亦无法以感性的方法来实现自己的存在，排除心中苦闷的出路应该是属于思想的层次。克尔凯郭尔曾在日记中写道：我的感觉是，你只能投入狂乱放荡的生活，或者选择绝对的宗教虔诚。结果他选择了献身于绝对的宗教激情，这是一个极为重大的"非此即彼"的选择，他一生的成就和身后的英名都系于此。

《轮作方法》着力论述了在面对"厌烦"这一人类特有的消极特质的时候，人类该如何采取"轮作方法"做出积极的伦理选择。针对伦理生活相关的三个重要组成部分，即"友谊""婚姻"和"工作"，克尔凯郭尔关于"轮作"合乎逻辑的论述，无疑是一种"社会智慧学"，从中不难透视出这位"孤独的信仰骑士"的思想嬗变过程。

Either—Or

Starting from a principle is affirmed by people of experience to be a very reasonable procedure; I am willing to humor them, and so begin with the principle that all men are bores.① Surely no one will prove himself so great a bore as to contradict me in this. This principle possesses the quality of being② in the highest degree repellent, an essential requirement in the case of negative principles, which are in the last analysis the principles of all motion. It is not merely repellent, but infinitely forbidding; and whoever has this principle back of him cannot but receive an infinite impetus forward, to help him make new discoveries. For if my principle is true, one need only consider how ruinous boredom is for humanity, and by properly adjusting the intensity of one's concentration upon this fundamental truth, attain any desired degree of momentum. Should one wish to attain the maximum momentum, even to the point of almost endangering the driving power, one need only say to oneself: Boredom is the root of all evil.③ Strange that boredom, in itself so staid and stolid, should have such power to set in motion. The influence it exerts is altogether magical, except that it is not the influence of attraction, but of repulsion.

In the case of children, the ruinous character of boredom is universally acknowledged. Children are always well-behaved as long as they are enjoying themselves. This is true in the strictest sense; for if they sometimes become unruly in their play, it is because they are already beginning to be bored—boredom is already approaching, though from a different direction. In choosing a governess one, therefore, takes into account not only her sobriety, her faithfulness, and her competence, but also her aesthetic qualifications for amusing the children; and there would be no hesitancy in dismissing a governess who was lacking in this respect, even if she had all the other desirable virtues. Here, then, the principle is clearly acknowledged; but so strange is the way of the world, so pervasive the influence of habit and boredom, that this is practically the only case in which the science of aesthetics receives its just dues. If one were to ask for a divorce because his

---

① "人类都是厌烦的"——该命题是本文阐述"轮作方法"的前提。个人的非理性的情感，包括厌烦、忧郁、绝望等悲观情绪，是克尔凯郭尔哲学的主要内容之一，就是以孤独的、非理性的个人存在取代客观物质和理性意识(感性经验和理性思维)的存在并当作全部哲学的出发点。

② 克尔凯郭尔的思考活动不断深入"存在"的问题，克尔凯郭尔哲学活动的内在系统都基于"人是什么?"和"人成为了什么?"厌烦被克尔凯郭尔认为是"存在"的特质，从属于人的审美阶段。

③ "厌烦是万恶之根源。"克尔凯郭尔追溯了圣经中有关上帝造人、巴别塔的历史，阐述人类由第一阶段审美阶段过渡到第二阶段伦理阶段的过程——厌烦促使人去追求另一种较高的生活方式，即伦理的生活。

wife was tiresome, or demand the abdication of a king because he was boring to look at, or the banishment of a preacher because he was tiresome to listen to, or the dismissal of a prime minister, or the execution of a journalist, because he was terribly tiresome, one would find it impossible to force it through. What wonder, then, that the world goes from bad to worse, and that its evils increase more and more, as boredom increases, and boredom is the root of all evil.

The history of this can be traced from the very beginning of the world. The gods were bored, and so they created man. Adam was bored because he was alone, and so Eve was created. Thus boredom entered the world, and increased in proportion to the increase of population. Adam was bored alone; then Adam and Eve were bored together; then Adam and Eve and Cain and Abel① were bored *en familler*; then the population of the world increased, and the peoples were bored *en masse*. To divert themselves they conceived the idea of constructing a tower high enough to reach the heavens. This idea is itself as boring as the tower was high, and constitutes a terrible proof of how boredom gained the upper hand. The nations were scattered over the earth, just as people now travel abroad, but they continued to be bored. Consider the consequences of this boredom. Humanity fell from its lofty height first because of Eve, and then from the Tower of Babel②. What was it, on the other hand, that delayed the fall of Rome, was it not *panis and circenses*? And is anything being done now? Is anyone concerned about planning some means of diversion? Quite the contrary, the impending ruin is being accelerated. It is proposed to call a constitutional assembly. Can anything more tiresome be imagined, both for the participants themselves, and for those who have to hear and read about it? It is proposed to improve the financial condition of the state by practicing economy. What could be more tiresome? Instead of increasing the national debt, it is proposed to pay it off. As I understand the political situation, it would be an easy matter for Denmark to negotiate a loan of fifteen million dollars. Why not consider this plan? Every once in a while

---

① 该隐(Cain)、亚伯(Abel),为亚当和夏娃之子。该隐种地,亚伯牧羊。后该隐杀死弟弟亚伯遭上帝流放。见《旧约·创世记》。

② Tower of Babel,巴别塔,古巴比伦人建筑未成的通天塔。上帝因他们狂妄,责罚他们各操不同的语言,彼此不相了解,结果该塔无法完成。见《旧约·创世记》。

we hear of a man who is a genius, and therefore neglects to pay his debts—why should not a nation do the same, if we were all agreed? Let us then borrow fifteen millions, and let us use the proceeds, not to pay our debts, but for public entertainment. Let us celebrate the millennium in a riot of merriment. Let us place boxes everywhere, not, as at present, for the deposit of money, but for the free distribution of money. Everything would become gratis; theaters gratis, women of easy virtue gratis, one would drive to the park gratis, be buried gratis, one's eulogy would be gratis; I say gratis, for when one always has money at hand, everything is in a certain sense free. No one should be permitted to own any property. Only in my own case would there be an exception. I reserve to myself securities in the Bank of London to the value of one hundred dollars a day, partly because I cannot do with less, partly because the idea is mine, and finally because I may not be able to hit upon a new idea when the fifteen millions are gone.

What would be the consequences of all this prosperity? Everything great would gravitate toward Copenhagen, the greatest artists, the greatest dancers, the greatest actors. Copenhagen would become a second Athens. What then? All rich men would establish their homes in this city. Among others would come the Shah of Persia[①], and the King of England would also come. Here is my second idea. Let us kidnap the Shah of Persia. Perhaps you say an insurrection might take place in Persia and a new ruler be placed on the throne, as has often happened before, the consequence being a fall in price for the old Shah. Very well then, I propose that we sell him to the Turks; they will doubtless know how to turn him into money. Then there is another circumstance which our politicians seem entirely to have overlooked. Denmark holds the balance of power in Europe. It is impossible to imagine a more fortunate lot. I know that from my own experience; I once held the balance of power in a family and could do as I pleased; the blame never fell on me, but always on the others. O that my words might reach your ears, all you who sit in high places to advise and rule, you king's men and men of the people, wise and understanding citizens of all classes! Consider the crisis! Old Denmark is on the brink of ruin; what a calamity! it will be destroyed by boredom. Of all

---

① the shah of persia,波斯国王。

calamities the most calamitous! In ancient times they made him king who extolled most beautifully the praises of the deceased king; in our times we ought to make him king who utters the best witticism, and make him crown prince who gives occasion for the utterance of the best witticism.

O beautiful, emotional sentimentality, how you carry me away! Should I trouble to speak to my contemporaries, to initiate them into my wisdom? By no means. My wisdom is not exactly *zum Gebrauch für Jedermann*, and it is always more prudent to keep one's maxims of prudence to oneself. I desire no disciples; but if there happened to be someone present at my deathbed, and I was sure that the end had come, then I might in an attack of phthropic delirium, whisper my theory in his ear, uncertain whether I had done him a service or not. People talk so much about man being a social animal; at bottom, he is a beast of prey, and the evidence for this is not confined to the shape of his teeth. All this talk about society and the social is partly inherited hypocrisy, partly calculated cunning.

All men are bores. The word itself suggests the possibility of a subdivision. It may just as well indicate a man who bores others as one who bores himself. Those who bore others are the mob, the crowd, the infinite multitude of men in general. Those who bore themselves are the elect, the aristocracy; and it is a curious fact that those who do not bore themselves usually bore others, while those who bore themselves entertain others. Those who do not bore themselves are generally people who, in one way or another, keep themselves extremely busy; these people are precisely on this account the most tiresome, the most utterly unendurable. This species of animal life is surely not the fruit of man's desire and woman's lust. Like all lower forms of life, it is marked by a high degree of fertility, and multiplies endlessly. It is inconceivable that nature should require nine months to produce such beings; they ought rather to be turned out by the score. The second class, the aristocrats, are those who bore themselves. As noted above, they generally entertain others—in a certain external sense sometimes the mob, in a deeper sense only their fellow initiates. The more profoundly they bore themselves, the more powerfully do they serve to divert these latter, even when their boredom reaches its zenith, as when they either die of boredom (the passive form) or shoot themselves out of curiosity (the active form).

It is usual to say that idleness is a root of all evil. To prevent this evil one is advised to work. However, it is easy to see, both from the nature of the evil that is feared and the remedy proposed, that this entire view is of a very plebeian extraction. Idleness is by no means as such a root of evil; on the contrary, it is a truly divine life, provided one is not himself bored. Idleness may indeed cause the loss of one's fortune, and so on, but the high-minded man does not fear such dangers; he fears only boredom. The Olympian gods were not bored, they lived happily in happy idleness. A beautiful woman, who neither sews nor spins nor bakes nor reads nor plays the piano, is happy in her idleness, for she is not bored. So far from idleness being the root of all evil, it is rather the only true good. Boredom is the root of all evil, and it is this which must be kept at a distance. Idleness is not an evil; indeed one may say that every human being who lacks a sense for idleness proves that his consciousness has not yet been elevated to the level of the humane. There is a restless activity which excludes a man from the world of the spirit, setting him in a class with the brutes, whose instincts impel them always to be on the move. There are men who have an extraordinary talent for transforming everything into a matter of business, whose whole life is business, who fall in love, marry, listen to a joke, and admire a picture with the same industrious zeal with which they labor during business hours. The Latin proverb, *otium est pulvinar diaboli*[①], is true enough, but the devil gets no time to lay his head on this pillow when one is not bored. But since some people believe that the end and aim of life is work, the disjunction, idleness-work, is quite correct. I assume that it is the end and aim of every man to enjoy himself, and hence my disjunction is no less correct.

Boredom is the daemonic side of pantheism[②]. If we remain in boredom as such, it becomes the evil principle; if we annul it, we posit it in its truth; but

---

① "otium est pulvinar diaboli" (Idleness is the devil's pillow) 意为"懒惰是恶魔的枕头",此处引用的拉丁谚语用作说明段首处"懒惰是万恶之根源"的命题。

② 泛神论,把神和整个宇宙或自然视为同一的哲学理论。最早提出并使用"泛神论"一词的是17世纪英国哲学家 J. 托兰德(J. Tolland,1670—1722)。该理论认为整个宇宙本身具有神性,万物存在于神内,神是万物的内因。这个神不同于基督教信奉的人格神,也不同于自然神论者所主张的第一因的神,它没有类似人的属性,不是凌驾于世界之上,而是存在于世界之内。欧洲哲学史上的泛神论大体上可归结为两类:一类是具有自然主义倾向的泛神论,它把神融化于自然之中;另一类是具有宗教神秘主义倾向的泛神论,它把自然消解于神中。这两类泛神论在反对正统神学的斗争中曾起过一定的积极作用。

we can only annul boredom by enjoying ourselves—*ergo*, it is our duty to enjoy ourselves. To say that boredom is annulled by work betrays a confusion of thought; for idleness can certainly be annulled by work, since it is its opposite, but not boredom, and experience shows that the busiest workers, whose constant buzzing most resembles an insect's hum, are the most tiresome of creatures; if they do not bore themselves, it is because they have no true conception of what boredom is; but then it can scarcely be said that they have overcome boredom.

Boredom is partly an inborn talent, partly an acquired immediacy. The English are in general the paradigmatic nation. A true talent for indolence is very rare; it is never met with in nature, but belongs to the world of the spirit. Occasionally, however, you meet a traveling Englishman who is, as it were, the incarnation of this talent—a heavy, immovable animal, whose entire language exhausts its riches in a single word of one syllable, an interjection by which he signifies his deepest admiration and his supreme indifference, admiration and indifference having been neutralized in the unity of boredom. No other nation produces such miracles of nature; every other nation I will always show himself a little more vivacious, not so absolutely stillborn. The only analogy I know of is the apostle of the empty enthusiasm, who also makes his way through life on an interjection. This is the man who everywhere makes a profession of euthusiasm, who cries Ah! or Oh! whether the event be significant or insignificant, the difference having been lost for him in the emptiness of a blind and noisy enthusiasm. The second form of boredom is usually the result of a mistaken effort to find diversion. The fact that the remedy against boredom may also serve to produce boredom, might appear to be a suspicious circumstance; but it has this effect only in so far as it is incorrectly employed. A misdirected search for diversion, one which is eccentric in its direction, conceals boredom within its own depths and gradually works it out toward the surface, thus revealing itself as that which it immediately is. In the case of horses, we distinguish between blind staggers and sleepy staggers, but call both staggers; and so we can also make a distinction between two kinds of boredom, though uniting both under the common designation of being tiresome.

Pantheism is, in general, characterized by fullness; in the case of boredom we find the precise opposite, since it is characterized by emptiness; but it is just this which makes boredom a pantheistic conception. Boredom depends on the nothingness which pervades reality; it causes a dizziness like that produced by looking down into a yawning chasm, and this dizziness is infinite. The eccentric form of diversion noted above sounds forth without producing an echo, which proves it to be based on boredom; for in nothingness not even an echo can be produced.

Now since boredom as shown above is the root of all evil, what can be more natural than the effort to overcome it? Here, as everywhere, however, it is necessary to give the problem calm consideration; otherwise one may find oneself driven by the daemonic spirit of boredom deeper and deeper into the mire in the very effort to escape. Everyone who feels bored cries out for change. With this demand I am in complete sympathy, but it is necessary to act in accordance with some settled principle.

My own dissent from the ordinary view is sufficiently expressed in the use I make of the word, "rotation."① This word might seem to conceal an ambiguity, and if I wished to use it so as to find room in it for the ordinary method, I should have to define it as a change of field. But the farmer does not use the word in this sense. I shall, however, adopt this meaning for a moment, in order to speak of the rotation which depends on change in its boundless infinity, its extensive dimension, so to speak.

This is the vulgar and inartistic method, and needs to be supported by illusion. One tires of living in the country, and moves to the city; one tires of one's native land, and travels abroad; one is *europamude*, and goes to America, and so on; finally one indulges in a sentimental hope of endless journeyings from star to star. Or the movement is different but still extensive. One tires of porcelain dishes and eats on silver; one tires of silver and turns to gold; one burns half of Rome to get an idea of the burning of Troy. This method defeats itself; it is plain endlessness. And what did Nero② gain by it? Antonine was wiser; he says: "It is in your power to review your life, to look

---

① ratation,轮作,通常为农业术语,指同一块地上有计划地按顺序轮种不同类型的作物的复种形式。文中的"轮作方法"换一个角度看待生活和经历的事物,反映了克尔凯郭尔本人对伦理生活的态度。

② Nero,尼禄(37—68),罗马帝国第五位皇帝,杀害母亲和妻子、迫害基督教徒、恶行昭著的暴君。

at things you saw before, from another point of view."

My method does not consist in change of field, but resembles the true rotation method in changing the crop and the mode of cultivation. Here we have at once the principle of limitation, the only saving principle in the world. The more you limit yourself, the more fertile you become in invention. A prisoner in solitary confinement for life becomes very inventive, and a spider may furnish him with much entertainment. One need only hark back to one's schooldays. We were at an age when aesthetic considerations were ignored in the choice of one's instructors, most of whom were for that reason very tiresome; how fertile in invention one then proved to be! How entertaining to catch a fly and hold it imprisoned under a nut shell and to watch how it pushed the shell around; what pleasure from cutting a hole in the desk, putting a fly in it, and then peeping down at it through a piece of paper! How entertaining sometimes to listen to the monotonous drip of water from the roof! How close an observer one becomes under such circumstances, when not the least noise nor movement escapes one's attention! Here we have the extreme application of the method which seeks to achieve results intensively, not extensively.

The more resourceful in changing the mode of cultivation one can be, the better; but every particular change will always come under the general categories of *remembering* and *forgetting*. Life in its entirety moves in these two currents, and hence it is essential to have them under control. It is impossible to live artistically before one has made up one's mind to abandon hope; for hope precludes self-limitation. It is a very beautiful sight to see a man put out to sea with the fair wind of hope, and one may even use the opportunity to be taken in tow, but one should never permit hope to be taken aboard one's own ship, least of all as a pilot; for hope is a faithless shipmaster. Hope was one of the dubious gifts of Prometheus[①]; instead of giving men the foreknowledge of the immortals, he gave them hope.

To forget—all men wish to forget, and when something unpleasant happens, they always say: Oh, that one might forget! But forgetting is an art that must be practiced beforehand. The ability to forget is conditioned upon

---

① Prometheus,普罗米修斯,因从天上盗取火种给人类而触怒主神宙斯,被锁在高加索山崖受神鹰折磨,但他始终坚毅不屈。

the method of remembering, but this again depends upon the mode of experiencing reality. Whoever plunges into his experiences with the momentum of hope will remember in such wise that he is unable to forget. *Nil admirari* is therefore the real philosophy. No moment must be permitted so great a significance that it cannot be forgotten when convenient; each moment ought, however, to have so much significance that it can be recollected at will. Childhood, which is the age which remembers best, is at the same time most forgetful. The more poetically one remembers, the more easily one forgets; for remembering poetically is really only another expression for forgetting. In a poetic memory the experience has undergone a transformation, by which it has lost all its painful aspects. To remember in this manner, one must be careful how one lives, how one enjoys. Enjoying an experience to its full intensity to the last minute will make it impossible either to remember or to forget. For there is then nothing to remember except a certain satiety, which one desires to forget, but which now comes back to plague the mind with an involuntary remembrance. Hence, when you begin to notice that a certain pleasure or experience is acquiring too strong a hold upon the mind, you stop a moment for the purpose of remembering. No other method can better create a distaste for continuing the experience too long. From the beginning one should keep the enjoyment under control, never spreading every sail to the wind in any resolve; one ought to devote oneself to pleasure with a certain suspicion, a certain wariness, if one desires to give the lie to the proverb which says that no one can have his cake and eat it too. The carrying of concealed weapons is usually forbidden, but no weapon is so dangerous as the art of remembering. It gives one a very peculiar feeling in the midst of one's enjoyment to look back upon it for the purpose of remembering it.

One who has perfected himself in the twin arts of remembering and forgetting is in a position to play at battledore and shuttlecock with the whole of existence.

The extent of one's power to forget is the final measure of one's elasticity of spirit. If a man cannot forget he will never amount to much. Whether there be somewhere a Lethe gushing forth, I do not know; but this I know, that the art of forgetting can be developed. However, this art does not consist in permitting the impressions to vanish completely; forgetfulness is one thing and the art of forgetting is something quite different. It is easy to see that most people have a very meager understanding of this art, for they ordinarily wish to forget only what is unpleasant, not what is pleasant. This betrays a complete one-sidedness. Forgetting is the true expression for an ideal process of assimilation by which the experience is reduced to a sounding-board for the soul's own music. Nature is great because it has forgotten that it was chaos; but this thought is subject to revival at any time. As a result of attempting to forget only what is unpleasant, most people have a conception of oblivion as an untamable force which drowns out the past. But forgetting is really a tranquil and quiet occupation, and one which should be exercised quite as much in connection with the pleasant as with the unpleasant. A pleasant experience has as past something unpleasant about it, by which it stirs a sense of privation; this unpleasantness is taken away by an act of forgetfulness. The unpleasant has a sting, as all admit. This, too, can be removed by the art of forgetting. But if one attempts to dismiss the unpleasant absolutely from mind, as many do who dabble in the art of forgetting, one soon learns how little that helps. In an unguarded moment it pays a surprise visit, and it is then invested with all the forcibleness of the unexpected. This is absolutely contrary to every orderly arrangement in a reasonable mind. No misfortune or difficulty is so devoid of affability, so deaf to all appeals, but that it may be flattered a little; even Cerberus① accepted bribes of honey-cakes, and it is not only the lassies who are beguiled. The art in dealing with such experiences consists in talking them over, thereby depriving them of their bitterness; not forgetting them absolutely, but forgetting them for the sake of remembering them. Even in the case of memories such that one might suppose an eternal oblivion to be the only safeguard, one need permit oneself only a little trickery, and the deception will succeed for the skillful. Forgetting is the shears with which you cut away what you cannot use, doing it under the supreme direction of memory. Forgetting and remembering are thus identical

---

① Cerberus,古希腊神话中,守护冥府入口的长有三头的狗。

arts, and the artistic achievement of this identity is the Archimedean point[①] from which one lifts the whole world. When we say that we *consign* something to oblivion, we suggest simultaneously that it is to be forgotten and yet also remembered.

The art of remembering and forgetting will also insure against sticking fast in some relationship of life, and make possible the realization of a complete freedom.

One must guard against *friendship*. How is a friend defined? He is not what philosophy calls the necessary other, but the superfluous third. What are friendship's ceremonies? You drink each other's health, you open an artery and mingle your blood with that of the friend. It is difficult to say when the proper moment for this arrives, but it announces itself mysteriously; you feel some way that you can no longer address one another formally. When once you have had this feeling, then it can never appear that you have made a mistake, like Geert Vestphaler, who discovered that he had been drinking to friendship with the public hangman. What are the infallible marks of friendship? Let antiquity answer: *idem velle*, *idem nolle*, *ea demum firma amicitia*, and also extremely tiresome. What are the infallible marks of friendship? Mutual assistance in word and deed. Two friends form a close association in order to be everything to one another, and that although it is impossible for one human being to be anything to another human being except to be in his way. To be sure one may help him with money, assist him in and out of his coat, be his humble servant, and tender him congratulations on New Year's Day, on the day of his wedding, on the birth of a child, on the occasion of a funeral.

But because you abstain from friendship it does not follow that you abstain from social contacts. On the contrary, these social relationships may at times be permitted to take on a deeper character, provided you always have so much more momentum in yourself that you can sheer off at will, in spite of sharing for a time in the momentum of the common movement. It is believed that such conduct leaves unpleasant memories, the unpleasantness being due

---

① Archimedean point,阿基米德的支点,古希腊著名的物理学家阿基米德(Archimedes,前287—前212)曾经说过,"给我一个支点,我可以撬动整个地球"。

to the fact that a relationship which has meant something now vanishes and becomes as nothing. But this is misunderstanding. The unpleasant is merely a piquant ingredient in the sullenness of life. Besides, it is possible for the same relationship again to play a significant role, though in another manner. The essential thing is never to stick fast, and for this it is necessary to have oblivion back of one. The experienced farmer lets his land lie fallow now and then, and the theory of social prudence recommends the same. Everything will doubtless return, though in a different form; that which has once been present in the rotation will remain in it, but the mode of cultivation will be varied. You therefore quite consistently hope to meet your friends and acquaintances in a better world, but you do not share the fear of the crowd that they will be altered so that you cannot recognize them; your fear is rather lest they be wholly unaltered. It is remarkable how much significance even the most insignificant person can gain from a rational mode of cultivation.

One must never enter into the relation of *marriage*. Husband and wife promise to love one another for eternity. This is all very fine, but it does not mean very much; for if their love comes to an end in time, it will surely be ended in eternity. If, instead of promising forever, the parties would say: until Easter, or until May-day comes, there might be some meaning in what they say; for then they would have said something definite, and also something that they might be able to keep. And how does a marriage usually work out? In a little while one party begins to perceive that there is something wrong, then the other party complains, and cries to heaven: faithless! faithless! A little later the second party reaches the same standpoint, and a neutrality is established in which the mutual faithlessness is mutually canceled, to the satisfaction and contentment of both parties. But it is now too late, for there are great difficulties connected with divorce.

Such being the case with marriage, it is not surprising that the attempt should be made in so many ways to bolster it up with moral supports. When a man seeks separation from his wife, the cry is at once raised that he is depraved, a scoundrel, etc. How silly, and what an indirect attack upon marriage! If marriage has reality, then he is sufficiently punished by forfeiting this happiness; if it has no reality, it is absurd to abuse him because he is wiser than the rest. When a man grows tired of his money and throws it out of the window, we do not call him a scoundrel; for either money has reality, and so he is sufficiently punished by depriving himself of it, or it has none, and then he is, of course, a wise man.

One must always take care not to enter into any relationship in which there is a possibility of many members. For this reason friendship is dangerous, to say nothing of marriage. Husband and wife are indeed said to become one, but this is a very dark and mystic saying. When you are one of several, then you have lost your freedom; you cannot send for your traveling boots whenever you wish, you cannot move aimlessly about in the world. If you have a wife it is difficult; if you have a wife and perhaps a child, it is troublesome; if you have a wife and children, it is impossible. True, it has happened that a gypsy woman has carried her husband through life on her back, but for one thing this is very rare, and for another, it is likely to be tiresome in the long run-for the husband. Marriage brings one into fatal connection with custom and tradition, and traditions and customs are like the wind and weather, altogether incalculable. In Japan, I have been told, it is the custom for husbands to lie in childbed. Who knows but the time will come when the customs of foreign countries will obtain a foothold in Europe?

Friendship is dangerous, marriage still more so; for woman is and ever will be the ruin of a man, as soon as he contracts a permanent relation with her. Take a young man who is fiery as an Arabian courser, let him marry, he is lost. Woman is first proud, then is she weak, then she swoons, then he swoons, then the whole family swoons. A woman's love is nothing but dissimulation and weakness.

But because a man does not marry, it does not follow that his life need be wholly deprived of the erotic element. And the erotic ought also to have infinitude; but poetic infinitude, which can just as well be limited to an hour as to a month. When two beings fall in love with one another and begin to suspect that they were made for each other, it is time to have the courage to break it off; for by going on they have everything to lose and nothing to gain. This seems a paradox, and it is so for the feeling, but not for the understanding. In this sphere it is particularly necessary that one should make use of one's moods; through them one may realize an inexhaustible variety of combinations.

One should never accept appointment to an official position. If you do, you will become a mere Richard Roe①, a tiny little cog in the machinery of the body politic; you even cease to be master of your own conduct, and in that case your theories are of little help. You receive a title, and this brings in its train every sin and evil. The law under which you have become a slave is equally tiresome, whether your advancement is fast or slow. A title can never be got rid of except by the commission of some crime which draws down on you a public whipping; even then you are not certain, for you may have it restored to you by royal pardon.

Even if one abstains from involvement in official business, one ought not to be inactive, but should pursue such occupations as are compatible with a sort of leisure; one should engage in all sorts of breadless arts. In this connection the self-development should be intensive rather than extensive, and one should, in spite of mature years, be able to prove the truth of the proverb that children are pleased with a rattle and tickled with a straw.

If one now, according to the theory of social jurisprudence, varies the soil—for if he had contact with one person only, the rotation method would fail as badly as if a farmer had only one acre of land, which would make it impossible for him to fallow, something which is of extreme importance—then one must also constantly vary himself, and this is the essential secret. For this purpose one must necessarily have control over one's moods. To control them in the sense of producing them at will is impossible, but prudence teaches how to utilize the moment. As an experienced sailor always looks out over the water and sees a squall coming from far away, so one ought always to see the mood a little in advance. One should know how the mood affects one's own mind and the mind of others, before putting it on. You first strike a note or two to evoke pure tones, and see what there is in a man; the intermediate tones follow later. The more experience, you have, the more readily you will be convinced that there is often much in a man which is not suspected. When sentimental people, who as such are extremely tiresome, become angry, they are often very entertaining. Badgering a man is a particularly effective method

---

① Richard Roe,理查德·罗,某甲,用在法律程序中以指示一个虚构的或未验明的名字,诉讼中不知名的当事人称呼。此处,意为一个不知名、不重要的小人物。

of exploration.

The whole secret lies in arbitrariness. People usually think it easy to be arbitrary, but it requires much study to succeed in being arbitrary so as not to lose oneself in it, but so as to derive satisfaction from it. One does not enjoy the immediate but something quite different which he arbitrarily imports into it. You go to see the middle of a play, you read the third part of a book. By this means you insure yourself a very different kind of enjoyment from that which the author has been so kind as to plan for you. You enjoy something entirely accidental; you consider the whole of existence from this standpoint; let its reality be stranded thereon. I will cite an example. There was a man whose chatter certain circumstances made it necessary for me to listen to. At every opportunity he was ready with a little philosophical lecture, a very tiresome harangue. Almost in despair, I suddenly discovered that he perspired copiously when talking. I saw the pearls of sweat gather on his brow, unite to form a stream, glide down his nose, and hang at the extreme point of his nose in a drop-shaped body. From the moment of making this discovery, all was changed. I even took pleasure in inciting him to begin his philosophical instruction, merely to observe the perspiration on his brow and at the end of his nose.

The poet Baggesen[①] says somewhere of someonse that he was doubtless a good man, but that there was one insuperable objection against him, that there was no word that rhymed with his name. It is extremely wholesome thus to let the realities of life split upon an arbitrary interest. You transform something accidental into the absolute, and, as such, into the object of your admiration. This has an excellent effect, especially when one is excited. This method is an excellent stimulus for many persons. You look at everything in life from the standpoint of a wager, and so forth. The more rigidly consistent you are in holding fast to your arbitrariness, the more amusing the ensuing combinations will be. The degree of consistency shows whether you are an artist or a bungler; for to a certain extent all men do the same. The eye with

---

① Baggesen,柏格森(1764—1826),丹麦诗人,善于用德文和丹麦文写作讽刺诗歌和抒情爱情诗歌。著有《迷路》(*The Labyrinth*, 1792—1793)。

which you look at reality must constantly be changed. The Neo-Platonists① assumed that human beings who had been less perfect on earth became after death more or less perfect animals, all according to their deserts. For example, those who had exercised the civic virtues on a lower scale (retail dealers) were transformed into busy animals, like bees. Such a view of life, which here in this world sees all men transformed into animals or plants (Plotinus also thought that some would become plants), suggests rich and varied possibilities. The painter Tischbein② sought to idealize every human being into an animal. His method has the fault of being too serious, in that it endeavors to discover a real resemblance.

The arbitrariness in oneself corresponds to the accidental in the external world. One should therefore always have an eye open for the accidental, always be *expeditus*, if anything should offer. The so-called social pleasures for which we prepare a week or two in advance amount to so little; on the other hand, even the most insignificant thing may accidentally offer rich material for amusement. It is impossible here to go into detail, for no theory can adequately embrace the concrete. Even the most completely developed theory is poverty-stricken compared with the fullness which the man of genius easily discovers in his ubiquity.

 选文出处

Soren Kierkegaard. *Either/Or* (Vol. 2). Translated by Howard A. Johnson, Beijing: China Social Sciences Publishing House (reprinted from the English Edition by Princeton University Press, 1959), 1999, pp. 281—296.

---

① Neo-platonists,新柏拉图派,公元3—6世纪流行于古罗马的哲学流派,是古希腊罗马哲学史上最后一个有影响的学派。开创者是亚历山大里亚的阿蒙尼阿·萨卡(约175—约242)。著名代表是普罗提诺、波菲利。529年,东罗马皇帝查士丁尼下令封闭雅典新柏拉图派的学园,该派在组织上趋于瓦解。这个学派在理论上以柏拉图哲学为基础。吸取了毕达哥拉斯学派、亚里士多德派、斯多葛学派和东方宗教哲学的部分内容,具有浓厚的宗教神秘主义成分。其中以普罗提诺的学说最为系统和典型,他提出"太一说""流溢说"和灵魂解脱说,认为"太一"即神,是宇宙之本原,从中流溢出"逻各斯"(理性),又从理性流溢出灵魂,再由灵魂流溢出物质世界。人生目的是要返回"太一",为此人的灵魂须从肉体中超脱,在"忘我""出神"状态中与"太一",与神合为一体。

② Tischbein,铁旭白(1751—1829),德国画家。著有歌德、席勒等人的肖像。

思考题

1. 试论述克尔凯郭尔哲学观点的形成因素。
2. 结合克尔凯郭尔存在主义中的"跨跃",比较黑格尔"量的辩证法"和克尔凯郭尔"质的辩证法"。

阅读参考书目

1. 克尔凯郭尔:《克尔凯郭尔文集》,汤晨溪译,中国社会科学出版社,2005年。
2. Susan Leigh Anderson, *On Kierkegaard*, Belmont, Calif:Wadsworth, 2000.
3. Patrick Gardiner, *Kierkegaard*, New York:Oxford University Press, 1998.
4. David J. Gouwens, *Kierkegaard as religious thinker*, New York: Cambridge University Press, 1996.

克罗齐

B. 克罗齐(Benedetto Croce，1866—1952)是20世纪意大利著名哲学家、美学家、文学批评家、政治家，更是享誉西方的历史学家和史学理论家。他出生于阿奎拉城邦的佩斯卡塞罗利，不久便移居那不勒斯，在当地天主教学校接受初等和中等教育。1883年，他的父母不幸死于地震。克罗齐随叔父迁居罗马，进入罗马大学学习，结识了意大利马克思主义哲学家拉布里奥拉(Antonio Labriola，1843—1904)和唯意志主义哲学家乔万尼·詹蒂莱(Giovanni Gentile，1875—1944)。在他们的影响下，克罗齐开始深入研究黑格尔哲学和马克思主义。1896年至1900年，他发表的一系列讨论马克思主义经济学说问题的文章被收入《历史唯物主义和卡尔·马克思的经济学》(*Historical Materialism and the Economics of Karl Marx*，1900)一书中。1910年，克罗齐担任终身参议员。1920年至1921年，在乔万尼·乔利蒂内阁中任教育部长。1922年墨索里尼上台后，他拒绝宣誓效忠法西斯政权，被撤去教育部长职务，并被意大利学院除名。他在1925年发表了著名的《反法西斯知识分子宣言》，公开与法西斯分子决裂。在法西斯统治时期，克罗齐在其所撰写的《意大利史》(*A History of Italy*，1929)和《十九世纪欧洲史》(*History of Europe in the Nineteenth Century*，1932)两书中表达自己的自由主义观点。1934年，他积极活动重建自由党，并担任主席，成为现代西方自由派的一个代表人物。1947年，他在那不勒斯建立了意大利历史研究院，1952年11月20日在那不勒斯去世。

克罗齐是西方美学界最有影响的学者之一。他继承了维柯（Giambattista Vico）、黑格尔（G. W. F. Hegel）和德·桑克蒂斯（Francesco De Sanctis）等人的思想。克罗齐著有四部哲学著作：《美学，作为表现的科学和一般语言学》（Aesthetic as Science of Expression and General Linguistic，1902）、《逻辑学，作为纯粹概念的科学》（Logic as the Science of Pure Concept，1909）、《实践活动的哲学》（Philosophy of the Practical，1913）以及《历史学的理论与实践》（History: Its Theory and Practice，1915）。他将此统称为"精神哲学"。克罗齐把精神活动分为认识和实践两类，指出认识活动是美学和逻辑学的对象，实践活动是经济和伦理学的对象。克罗齐的哲学著作以《美学》影响最大，在听取了多方意见后，他将原有观点略作改变，撰写了《美学要素》（The Essence of Aesthetics，1920），使其哲学体系更为完整。此外，克罗齐还是重要的评论家。在1903年至1944年间，他主编《批评》（Critics）杂志达41年之久，这是当时欧洲影响最大的文艺批评刊物。另外，他还发表了评论当时欧洲许多重要的哲学、历史和文学著作的作品。

克罗齐的美学自成体系。其一，强调直觉的重要。他认为，直觉即艺术。直觉是认识的起点，是最基本的感性方式。直觉的功用是给本无形式的情感以形式，使它因成为意象而形象化。如果情感能恰如其分地被意象表现出来，这种表现就是成功的，而美就是成功的表现。克罗齐关于直觉的观点一方面把文学艺术看作人的情感的反映，强调文学艺术有特殊的属性和规律；另一方面，又认为感觉先于观念、行动，否认文学作品对社会生活的艺术概括和作家世界观对创作的指导作用。其二，强调美学的普遍意义。克罗齐把艺术活动看作尽人皆有的一种最基本、最普通的活动。他认为，人人都有几分艺术家的才能。大艺术家和平常人在这一点上只有量的分别，没有质的区别。在这个问题上，克罗齐继承了维柯的传统，抛弃了"精神贵族"的观点。其三，强调创造与欣赏统一。他认为，欣赏者必须既要置身于作者的历史情境，又要结合自己当前的历史情境，只有这样才能正确理解一部艺术作品。

克罗齐对近代欧洲文化的贡献，还在于他对史学理论和历史哲学的深入研究。历史哲学是对历史和历史学的哲学反思，杰出的历史哲学家往往兼有历史学家和哲学家的双重身份，同时具备历史研究实践和哲学思维的能力，克罗齐就是其中的典型。克罗齐的历史观点有两个突出的表现：一是历史唯心主义，把精神活动作为历史过程的决定力量；二是所谓"历史唯今主义"，认为历史的发展有如滚雪球，愈滚愈大，现存的历史就包括了过去的全部历史，而且历史事件经现代历史学家分析、判断，已是现代人思想的产物；它不仅是简单地记录史实，而且也为当前的现实需要服务。本章节选自《历史学的理论与实践》的开篇之作——《编年史理论》——是克罗齐在探索历史哲学过程中所迈出的坚实之步。

他在文章的第一部分中列举了人们对于"当代史"和"历史(非当代史)"的常规理解:"'当代史'通常是指被视为最近过去的一段时间的历史,不论它是过去五十年的、十年的、一年的、一个月的、一天的、还是过去一小时或一分钟的","反之,'非当代史','过去史'则是面对着一种已成历史的,因而是作为对那种历史的批判而出现的历史,不论那种历史是几千年前还是不到一小时前的。"诚然,历史科学的特点之一是以"过去"为研究对象和素材。而人们则逐渐形成了一种错觉,以为历史就是凝固僵死的过去。这种错觉和静态的研究方法,极大地限制了历史科学的进步。继而,克罗齐提出了一个看似突兀却让人耳目一新的命题——"一切历史都是当代史"。这个独特的论断,揭示了历史认识的另一面,颠覆了传统思维对"当代史"和"过去史"的划分,在历史和现实之间架起了桥梁。克罗齐在论证和发挥这一命题时,打破了主观与客观、历史与现实、历史与哲学这三种界限,可谓独树一帜。他在文中写道:"当代史来源于现实生活,历史(非当代史)同样来源于生活,唯有当前活生生的兴趣才能推动我们去寻求对于过去事实的知识,因此那种过去的事实,就其是被当前的兴趣所引发出来的而言,就是在响应着一种对当前的兴趣,而非对过去的兴趣。"也就是说,人总是从当前的兴趣和面临的现实关切出发,来考察过往的历史。一段详述密特拉教战争的历史,假若不具有任何的现实意义,就无法让人产生兴趣,它们充其量只是一些著作的名称而已;相反,如果和一个雅典人做生意或者谈恋爱,自然会引发了解对方所根植的文化土壤,习俗渊源的意愿和需求。有了此般现实意义,这段历史便"重生"了,活起来了,其被记录和被阅读的意义不言自明。

有人曾指责克罗齐赋予一切历史以当代性的历史观是一种实用主义的历史观,这其实是对克罗齐"一切历史都是当代史"命题的歪曲。历史学中的实用主义者相信史料本身会说话,会给研究者呈现出其希望有的意义来,实用主义史学更是为了现实的需要对历史进行有意识的篡改或解说。与此相反,克罗齐认为,史料本身并不会说话,使史料发挥作用的只能是历史学家的学识水平,历史学家的学识水平越高,越具有创造性,所揭示的历史意义就越深刻;历史学家不是被动接受、考订和阐释史料,而是发挥巨大的主动性和创造力。所以说,克罗齐的"一切历史都是当代史"并不是实用主义史学,相反,这是其历史哲学所揭示的历史研究的特性之一。

文章的第二部分,克罗齐重点论证了编年史和历史的区别和辩证关系。他归纳了以往探究"编年史"和"历史"的性质差别时常见的几种谬误:一、有人从"兴趣"上来判断二者的本质区别。有关个人的事实以编年史方式记录,有关大众的事实以历史方式记录;私事以编年史方式记录,公众之事以历史方式记录;

重要的事以历史方式记录,不重要的事以编年史方式记录;二、有人主观地从"形式"上对二者加以区分。认为历史是由相互结合紧密的事件构成的,编年史是由不连贯的事件构成的;历史遵循逻辑顺序,编年史遵循时间顺序;历史是对事件本质和核心的穿透,编年史局限于肤浅外围的叙述。剖析至此,克罗齐提出了其对历史和编年史的性质的精辟论述。他说:"两者区别不在于一种史的两种不同形式,相互不足,也不在于一个从属于另一个,而是两种不同的精神态度:历史是生动有活力有现实意义的编年史,编年史是死板的历史;历史是当代的历史,编年史是过去的历史;历史是一种思考行为,编年史是一种意识行为"。尤为难能可贵的是,克罗齐还指出了二者之间的辩证关系,肯定了二者有转换的前提:当不懂哲学的人阅读哲学史的时候,可以说他是在阅读一本编年史;一段具有表现力的有形的历史,当其不再是思想而是用抽象的字句记录下来时,就变成了编年史。最后,克罗齐指出了"历史"和"编年史"的意义和作用。

克罗齐在《编年史理论》中所着力阐发的命题"一切历史都是当代史",生动地概括了关于精神的绝对本质理论。一旦死的历史被赋予了新的精神,它就会活过来成为活的历史。正因为历史内在于精神,在克罗齐的历史哲学体系中,历史学家的主动性才可能得以凸现。如果说,历史学有高下之分,那么历史学家的思想观念便决定了历史学的高下。可见,克罗齐本人,无论在历史哲学领域,还是在传统史学领域,都是一位为人类自由发展和创造力进行论证和辩护的卓越思想家。

History: Its Theory and Practice

I

"Contemporary history" is wont to be called the history of a passage of time, looked upon as a most recent past, whether it be that of the last fifty years, a decade, a year, a month, a day, or indeed of the last hour or of the last minute. But if we think and speak rigorously, the term "contemporaneous" can be applied only to that history which comes into being immediately after the act which is being accomplished, as consciousness of that act: it is, for instance, the history that I make of myself while I am in the act of composing these pages; it is the thought of my composition, linked of necessity to the work of composition. "Contemporary" would be well employed in this case, just because this, like every act of the spirit, is outside time (of the first and after) and is formed "at the same time" as the act to which it is linked, and from which it is distinguished by means of a distinction not chronological but ideal. "Non-contemporary history," "past history," would, on the other hand, be that which finds itself in the presence of a history already formed, and which thus comes into being as a criticism of that history, whether it be thousands of years or hardly an hour old.

But if we look more closely, we perceive that this history already formed, which is called or which we would like to call "non-contemporary" or "past" history, if it really is history, that is to say, if it mean something and is not an empty echo, is also *contemporary*, and does not in any way differ from the other. As in the former case, the condition of its existence is that the deed of which the history is told must vibrate in the soul of the historian, or (to employ the expression of professed historians) that the documents are before the historian and that they are intelligible. That a narrative or a series of narratives of the fact is united and mingled with it merely means that the fact has proved more rich, not that it has lost its quality of being present: what were narratives or judgments before are now themselves facts, "documents" to be interpreted and judged. History is never constructed from narratives, but always from documents, or from narratives that have been reduced to documents and treated as such. Thus if contemporary history springs straight from life, so too does that history which is called non-contemporary, for it is evident that only an interest in the life of the present can move one to investigate past fact. Therefore this past fact does not answer to a past interest, but to a present interest, in so far as it is unified with an interest of the present life. This has been said again and again in a hundred ways by historians in their empirical formulas, and constitutes the reason, if not the deeper content, of the success of the very trite saying that history is *magister vitae*.①

I have recalled these forms or historical technique in order to remove the

---

① magister vitae 为拉丁语,意思是"生活的教师"(teacher of life)。magister 意为古罗马或中世纪的教师。

aspect of paradox from the proposition that "every true history is contemporany history."① But the justice of this proposition is easily confirmed and copiously and perspicuously exemplified in the reality of historiographical work, provided always that we do not fall into the error of taking the works of the historians all together, or certain groups of them confusedly, and of applying them to an abstract man or to ourselves considered abstractly, and of then asking what present interest leads to the writing or reading of such histories: for instance, what is the present interest of the history which recounts the Peloponnesian② or the Mithradatic war③, of the events connected with Mexican art, or with Arabic philosophy. For me at the present moment they are without interest, and therefore for me at this present moment those histories are not histories, but at the most simply titles of historical works. They have been or will be histories in those that have thought or will think them, and in me too when I have thought or shall think them, reelaborating them according to my spiritual needs. If, on the other hand, we limit ourselves to real history, to the history that one really thinks in the act of thinking, it will be easily seen that this is perfectly identical with the most personal and contemporary of histories. When the development of the culture of my historical moment presents to me(it would be superfluous and perhaps also inexact to add to myself as an individual)the problem of Greek civilization or of Platonic philosophy④ or of a particular mode of Attic manners⑤, that problem is related to my being in the same way as the history of a bit of business in which I am engaged, or of a love affair in which I am indulging, or of a danger that threatens me. I examine it with the same anxiety and am

---

① "一切历史都是当代史",此为克罗齐于1915年出版的《历史学的理论与实践》著作中关于历史定义的重要命题。

② Peloponnesian,伯罗奔尼撒战争,公元前431—前404年,雅典及其同盟者与以斯巴达为首的伯罗奔尼撒同盟之间的战争。

③ Mithradatic war,米特拉达梯战争,公元前89—前65年,古代本都王国与罗马间的三次战争。

④ Platonic philosophy,柏拉图哲学。柏拉图(Plato,前427—前347),是古希腊最著名的唯心论哲学家和思想家,是西方哲学史上第一个使唯心论哲学体系化的人。《理想国》是其中的代表作,涉及柏拉图思想体系的各个方面,包括哲学、伦理、教育等内容,主要是探讨理想国家的问题。理念论是柏拉图哲学体系的核心。他认为物质世界之外还有一个非物质的观念世界。理念世界是真实的,而物质世界是不真实的,是理念世界的模糊反映。

⑤ Attic manners,阿提卡习俗。因雅典是阿提卡(Attic)地区历史最悠久的城市,即概指雅典的风俗习惯。

troubled with the same sense of unhappiness until I have succeeded in solving it. Hellenic life is on that occasion present in me; it solicits, it attracts and torments me, in the same way as the appearance of the adversary, of the loved one, or of the beloved son for whom one trembles. Thus too it happens or has happened or will happen in the case of the Mithradatic War, of Mexican art, and of all the other things that I have mentioned above by way of example.

Having laid it down that contemporaneity is not the characteristic of a class of histories (as is held with good reason in empirical classifications), but an intrinsic characteristic of every history, we must conceive the relation of history to life as that of *unity*; certainly not in the sense of abstract identity, but of synthetic unity, which implies both the distinction and the unity of the terms. Thus to talk of a history of which the documents are lacking would appear to be as extravagant as to talk of the existence of something as to which it is also affirmed that it is without one of the essential conditions of existence. A history without relation to the document would be an unverifiable history; and since the reality of history lies in this verifiability, and the narrative in which it is given concrete form is historical narrative only in so far as it is a *critical exposition of* the document (intuition and reflection, consciousness and auto-consciousness, etc.), a history of that sort, being without meaning and without truth, would be inexistent as history. How could a history of painting be composed by one who had not seen and enjoyed the works of which he proposed to describe the genesis critically? And how far could anyone understand the works in question who was without the artistic experience assumed by the narrator? How could there be a history of philosophy without the works or at least fragments of the works of the philosophers? How could there be a history of a sentiment or of a custom, for example that of Christian humility or of knightly chivalry, without the capacity for living again, or rather without an actual living again of these particular states of the individual soul?

On the other hand, once the indissoluble link between life and thought in history has been effected, the doubts that have been expressed as to the *certainty* and the *utility* of history disappear altogether in a moment. How could that which is a *present* producing of our spirit ever be *uncertain*? How could that knowledge be *useless* which solves a problem that has come forth from the bosom of *life*?

II

But can the link between document and narrative, between life and history, ever be broken? An affirmative answer to this has been given when referring to those histories of which the documents have been lost, or, to put the case in a more general and fundamental manner, those histories whose documents are no longer alive in the human spirit. And this has also been implied when saying that we all of us in turn find ourselves thus placed with respect to this or that part of history. The history of Hellenic painting is in great part a history without documents for us, as are all histories of peoples concerning whom one does not know exactly where they lived, the thoughts and feelings that they experienced, or the individual appearance of the works that they accomplished; those literatures and philosophies, too, as to which we do not know their theses, or even when we possess these and are able to read them through, yet fail to grasp their intimate spirit, either owing to the lack of complementary knowledge or because of our obstinate temperamental reluctance, or owing to our momentary distraction.

If, in these cases, when that connexion is broken, we can no longer call what remains history (because history was nothing but that connexion), and it can henceforth only be called history in the sense that we call a man the corpse of a man, what remains is not for that reason nothing (not even the corpse is really nothing). Were it nothing, it would be the same as saying that the connexion is indissoluble, because nothingness is never effectual. And if it be not nothing, if it be something, what is narrative without the document?

A history of Hellenic painting, according to the accounts that have been handed down or have been constructed by the learned of our times, when closely inspected, resolves itself into a series of names of painters (Apollodorus, Polygnotus, Zeuxis, Apelles,[①] etc.), surrounded with

---

[①] 阿波罗多罗斯(Apollodorus),波律诺托司(Polygnotus),杰乌克西司(Zeuxis),阿佩列斯(Apelles)。画家名。其中,《不列颠百科全书》有"阿波罗多罗斯"一条:"阿波罗多罗斯(雅典的)(活动时期,前140)希腊著名学者,以所著《希腊编年史》闻名。阿佩列斯曾将诽谤、妒忌、阴谋、欺骗、忏悔、真理、无知、迷信,拟人化作为画题。"

biographical anecdotes, and into a series of subjects for painting (the burning of Troy, the contest of the Amazons, the battle of Marathon, Achilles, Calumny, etc.),① of which certain particulars are given in the descriptions that have reached us; or a graduated series, going from praise to blame, of these painters and their works, together with names, anecdotes, subjects, judgments, arranged more or less chronologically. But the names of painters separated from the direct knowledge of their works are empty names; the anecdotes are empty, as are the descriptions of subjects, the judgment of approval or of disapproval, and the chronological arrangement, because merely arithmetical and lacking real development; and the reason why we do not realize it in thought is that the elements which should constitute it are wanting. If those verbal forms possess any significance, we owe it to what little we know of antique paintings from fragments, from secondary works that have come down to us in copies, or in analogous works in the other arts, or in poetry. With the exception, however, of that little, the history of Hellenic art is, as such, a tissue of empty words.

We can, if we like, say that it is "empty of determinate content," because we do not deny that when we pronounce the name of a painter we think of some painter, and indeed of a painter who is an Athenian, and that when we utter the word "battle," or "Helen," we think of a battle, indeed of a battle of hoplites, or of a beautiful woman, similar to those familiar to us in Hellenic sculpture. But we can think indifferently of any one of the numerous facts that those names recall. For this reason their content is indeterminate, and this indetermination of content is their emptiness.

All histories separated from their living documents resemble these examples and are empty narratives, and since they are empty they are without truth. Is it true or not that there existed a painter named Polygnotus② and that he painted a portrait of Miltiades③ in the poecile? We shall be told that it is true, because one person or several people, who knew him and saw the work

---

① 特洛伊的焚毁(the burning of Troy),亚马逊人的斗争(the contest of the Amazons),马拉松战役(the battle of Marathon),阿基里斯(Achilles),诽谤(Calumny)等。画题名。
② Polygnotus,波依启列,公元前5世纪的希腊画家。
③ Miltiades,米尔提亚戴斯(559—556),为色雷斯·凯尔索涅索斯的僭主。

in question, bear witness to its existence. But we must reply that it was true for this or that witness, and that for us it is neither true nor false, or (which comes to the same thing) that it is true only on the evidence of those witnesses—that is to say, for an extrinsic reason, whereas truth always requires intrinsic reasons. And since that proposition is not true (neither true nor false), it is not useful either, because where there is nothing the king loses his rights, and where the elements of a problem are wanting the effective will and the effective need to solve it are also wanting, along with the possibility of its solution. Thus to quote those empty judgments is quite useless for our actual lives. Life is a present, and that history which has become an empty narration is a past: it is an irrevocable past, if not absolutely so, $\kappa\alpha\theta'\alpha\upsilon\rho\acute{o}$, then certainly for the present moment.

The empty words remain, and the empty words are sounds, or the graphic signs which represent them, and they hold together and maintain themselves, not by an act of thought that thinks them (in which case they would soon be filled), but by an act of will, which thinks it useful for certain ends of its own to presence those words, however empty or half empty they may be. Mere narrative, then, is nothing but a complex of empty words or formulas asserted by an act of the will.

Now with this definition we have succeeded in giving neither more nor less than the true distinction hitherto sought in vain, between *history* and *chronicle*. It has been sought in vain, because it has generally been sought in a difference in the *quality* of the facts which each difference took as its object. Thus, for instance, the record of *individual* facts has been attributed to chronicle, to history that of *general* facts; to chronicle the record of *private*, to history that of *public* facts: as though the general were not always individual and the individual general, and the public were not always also private and the private public! Or else the record of *important* facts (memorable things) has been attributed to history, to chronicle that of the *unimportant*: as though the importance of facts were not relative to the situation in which we find ourselves, and as though for a man annoyed by a mosquito the evolutions of the minute insect were not of greater importance than the expedition of Xerxes①! Certainly, we are sensible of a just sentiment in these fallacious distinctions—namely, that of placing the difference between history and chronicle in the conception of what *interests* and of what does not *interest* (the general interests and not the particular, the great interests and not the little, etc.). A just sentiment is also to be noted in other considerastions that are wont to be adduced, such as the close bond between events that there is in history and the *disconnectedness* that appears on the other hand in chronicle, the *logical* order of the first, the purely *chronological* order of the second, the penetration of the first into the *core* of events and the limitation of the second to the superficial or *external*, and the like. But the differential character is here rather metaphorized than thought, and when metaphors are not employed as simple forms expressive of thought we lose a moment after what has just been gained. The truth is that chronicle and history are not distinguishable as two forms of history, mutually complementary, or as one subordinate to the other, but as two different spiritual *attitudes*. History is living chronicle, chronicle is dead history; history is contemporary history, chronicle is past history; history is principally an act of thought, chronicle an act of will. Every history becomes chronicle when it is no longer thought, but only recorded in abstract words, which were once upon a time concrete and expressive. the history of philosophy even is chronicle, when written or read by those who do not understand philosophy: history would even be what we are now disposed to read as chronicle, as when, for instance, the monk of Monte Cassino② notes: 1001. *Beatus Dominicus migravit ad Christum.*③ 1002. *Hoc anno venerunt Saraceni super Capuam.*④ 1004. *Terremotus ingens hunc montem exagitavit*,⑤ etc.; for those facts were present to him when he wept over the

---

① expedition of Xerxes,克谢尔克谢斯远征。克谢尔克谢斯(Xerxes),大流士的儿子,波斯的国王,曾率领波斯历史上最大的一支远征军向希腊进军。
② Monte Cassino,卡西诺山寺院。有 1400 年历史,位于意大利中部的蒙特卡西诺(Monte Cassino)。圣·本笃(St. Benedict,480—547) 529 年前往卡西诺山,建立了规模宏大的修道院,成为中世纪最重要的基督教中心之一。
③ 1001 年,有福的多密尼库斯到基督那里去了(1001, Beatus Dominicus migravit ad Christum)。
④ 1002 年,今年萨拉森人越过了卡普阿城。
⑤ 1004 年,卡西诺山大为地震所苦。

death of the departed Dominic①, or was terrified by the natural human scourges that convulsed his native land, seeing the hand of God in that succession of events. This does not prevent that history from assuming the form of chronicle when that same monk of Monte Cassino wrote down cold formulas, without representing to himself or thinking their content, with the sole intention of not allowing those memories to be lost and of handing them down to those who should inhabit Monte Cassino after him.

But the discovery of the real distinction between chronicle and history, which is a formal distinction (that is to say, a truly real distinction), not only frees us from the sterile and fatiguing search after material distinctions (that is to say, imaginary distinctions), but it also enables us to reject a very common presupposition—namely, that of the *priority* of chronicle in respect to history. *Primo annales* [chronicles] *fuere, post historiæ factæ sunt*,② the saying of the old grammarian, Mario Vittorino, has been repeated, generalized, and universalized. But precisely the opposite of this is the outcome of the inquiry into the character and therefore into the genesis of the two operations or attitudes: *first comes history, then chronicle*. First comes the living being, then the corpse; and to make history the child of chronicle is the same thing as to make the living be born from the corpse, which is the residue of life, as chronicle is the residue of history.

 选文出处

Benedetto Croce. *History: Its Theory and Practice*. Translated by Douglas Ainslie, Beijing: China Social Sciences Publishing House (reprinted from the English Edition by Harcourt, Brace and Company, 1923), 1999, pp. 11—26.

---

① Dominic,指 St. Dominic,圣道明:创立道明托钵僧兄弟会的西班牙神父,讲道反对所谓异端的阿尔比派。
② "编年史,先有年代史,然后才写成历史。"——意大利文法学家马里奥·维托里诺的观点。

思考题

1. 克罗齐"一切历史都是当代史"的观点是否可以归结为一种实用主义历史观?
2. 试论述编年史和历史的根本区别和辩证关系。

阅读参考书目

1. 彭刚:《精神、自由与历史:克罗齐历史哲学研究》,北京:清华大学出版社,1999年。
2. Jack D'Amico, *The Legacy of Benedetto Croce: Contemporary Critical Views*, University of Toronto Press, 1999.
3. Fabio Fernando Rizi, *Benedetto Croce and Italian Fascism*, University of Toronto Press, 2003.
4. Michael Bentley, *Modern Historiography: An Introduction*, London: Routledge, 1999.
5. De Gennaro, *The Philosophy of Benedetto Croce*, New York: Philosophical library, Inc. 1961.

韦 伯

马克斯·韦伯(Max Weber,1864—1920)出生于德国埃尔福特,毕业于海德堡大学法律系,先后任教于柏林大学、弗莱堡大学、海德堡大学、慕尼黑大学。1897年,韦伯精神崩溃,不得不暂时离开教职。1918年,他重登讲坛两年后在慕尼黑去世。韦伯的主要著作有《新教伦理与资本主义精神》(The Protestant Ethic and the Spirit of Capitalism)、《社会学和社会政治知识的客观性》(The Objectivity of the Sociological and Social-Political Knowledge)、《经济与社会》(Economy and Society)、《作为职业的政治》(Politics as Vocation)、《普通经济史》(General Economic History)、《社会科学方法论》(The Methodology of the Social Science)等。

韦伯是现代著名的历史学家,也是十分重要的社会学家之一。他对社会学学科性质的理解和他所提出的一系列概念至今影响着社会学的研究,与迪尔凯姆(Emile Durkheim)、齐美尔(Georg Simmel)一起被公认为社会学三大"奠基人"。他以宗教社会学的成就而闻名,其"新教伦理"理论将"新教"与"资本主义精神"进行巧妙关联。在方法论领域,韦伯创导了"理想型"概念,归纳、概括出一些可用来相互比较的历史的模式;在政治社会学方面,韦伯的研究涉及社会阶层和官僚政治,认为西方现代文明最有意义的发展是生活的理性化。当然,我们不能把韦伯的学问单纯地当作社会学进行理解,那时的社会学(或者说是社会学的前身)带有明显的跨学科特征,涉及经济学、法理学、历史学以及社会学,因此韦伯更应该是社会科学大师。尤其值得注意的是,他早期的历史学积淀使得他的研究有了洞穿时空的深邃。

韦伯的《新教伦理与资本主义精神》于 1904 年和 1905 年分两次发表。在该书中,韦伯致力于分析和解释什么是"合理的资本主义",并试图阐明新教改革对西方近代资本主义发展所起的重大作用。该书着眼于探讨资本主义经济兴起过程中非经济因素的重要意义,"寻求基督教新教伦理和资本主义精神之间的关联"①,揭示新教伦理与近代理性资本主义发展之间明显存在的共生关系。当然,韦伯并不否认高度发达的资本主义企业在加尔文教之前早已存在,且社会上也存在着发展资本主义所必备的其他物质的和心理的先决条件,但是,他强调了在加尔文教出现以前,资本主义的兴业精神一直是受教会流行观念的敌视与排挤,而后来宗教伦理的广泛传播成为资本主义发展的内在推动力量。

节选部分是《新教伦理与资本主义精神》中的第 2 章《资本主义精神》。尽管标题是"资本主义精神",但在原文中难以找到对资本主义精神,甚至"资本主义"的确切定义。不过,我们在通读之后却又可以隐约感受到一种倾向或独特的"精神"意蕴。韦伯坚持认为,"最终的定义性概念不能放在研究开端,而必须在研究结尾得到"②,也就是说,在他看来,必须在阐述过程中,作为阐述的最重要的结果,才能找出对所理解的资本主义精神的最佳概念。

韦伯对富兰克林等的论述,看起来似乎无关乎宗教及其所研究的主题。但是,这些看似简单的论述却蕴含了资本主义精神的本质。韦伯解释道:"这种贪财哲学之所以奇特,就在于它竟成为具有公共诚信之人的理想,而且成为一种观念:认为个人有增加自己资本的责任,而增加资本本身就是目的。"这看似宣扬发迹的方法,其实在本质上是一种伦理道德规范。这种伦理道德规范不仅仅表现了从商的精明,更蕴含了一种精神气质。违反这种伦理道德规范就会被认为是渎职。

毫无疑问,"精神气质"不同于"市侩气",其道德教化功能带有某种功利的气息。例如,诚实是上策,因为它能确保信用;守时、勤勉是美德,因为有益于事业。可以看出,在这类训勉背后有某种"情操"的支持,蕴含着伦理道德气味的特殊作风。从中也可以看出韦伯的一种倾向,即"从人身上赚钱"并非坏事,只要正当地赚钱,都可以看作是职业上的美德。这也恰好符合现代经济活动的"职业责任"思想。韦伯论述的重点体现了他对世俗职业持有责任观念的看法。

---

① 周伯戡:《社会思想的皇冠——韦伯》,上海:上海书店,1987 年,第 3—7 页。
② 韦伯:《新教伦理与资本主义精神》,彭强、黄晓京译,西安:陕西师范大学出版社,2001 年,第 18 页。

在他看来，这种思想最能表现资本主义社会文化的特征。

韦伯从三个维度对宗教伦理与资本主义精神进行了论述。一是文化维度。他认为，商业活动也许是单纯的赚钱行为，但韦伯从资本主义的社会伦理角度来论述，强调在资本主义经济环境中，任何参与商业活动的个体都要遵循市场秩序，这是规范的体现，"个人只要介入市场关系体系，那个秩序就会迫使他服从资本主义的行动规则"。二是时间维度。他认为，这种观念不单是在资本主义条件下出现，可以"上溯到资本主义出现之前去追寻它的起源"。三是空间维度。他认为，对于资本主义的群体和个体，遵循规则就是主动适应的经济过程，这种适应并不是在孤立的个人中间发生，"而应是整个人类群体的共同生活方式。这才是真正需要说明的起源"。谋利或者"金钱欲"在不同的宗教背景有着不同的特征，必然产生差别迥异的资本主义发展特征和效率。比如说，意大利之所以不同于德国，就在于前者的劳动者缺乏必要的"良心"（coscienziosita），造成"在一定程度上至今仍然是其资本主义发展的一个主要障碍"。显然，这里所说的良心就是指一种职业责任以及对工作的奉献精神。

现代资本主义精神代表着合乎伦理道德的生活准则，而传统或传统主义则与这种现代资本主义精神格格不入。其直接表现是，这种传统阻碍了资本主义企业中的工人对新生产方法、经营管理的理解和接受，而那些具有特殊宗教背景的人则不然。对企业家或新兴资产阶级而言，新教传播的"天职观"有助于他们以更加合理和系统的方式追求"正当"的经济利益，掌握大量市场的经济机会，并始终保持冷静和自我克制，避免道德上和经济上的破产。在韦伯看来，新兴资产阶级带领下的自由经济企业的充分发展与新教教育产生的效果有着直接的关系。

韦伯的资本主义精神是特指西欧和美国的，与中国、印度等国家的早期资本主义精神气质有所不同。历史学家休斯（H. Stuart Hughes）认为："韦伯并不是要追溯某一种单纯的因果关系，他所要完成的工作远比这复杂——他要描述资本主义与基督新教之间具有选择性的亲和力。"[①]韦伯要揭示的是，一个宗教所设定的伦理行为是如何被转化成一种非常有效的物质动机的，新教伦理道德规范与资本主义精神有着怎样的一种天然而又内在的因果关系。

---

① 斯图亚特·休斯：《意识与社会》，李丰斌译，台北：联经出版事业公司，1981年，第328页。

The Protestant Ethic and the Spirit of Capitalism

"Remember, that *time* is money. He that can earn ten shillings a day by his labour, and goes abroad, or sits idle, one half of that day, though he spends but sixpence during his diversion or idleness, ought not to reckon *that* the only expense; he has really spent, or rather thrown away, five shillings besides.

"Remember, that *credit* is money. If a man lets his money lie in my hands after it is due, he gives me the interest, or so much as I can make of it during that time. This amounts to a considerable sum where a man has good and large credit, and makes good use of it.

"Remember, that money is of the prolific, generating nature. Money can beget money, and its offspring can beget more, and so on. Five shillings turned is six, turned again it is seven and threepence, and so on, till it becomes a hundred pounds. The more there is of it, the more it produces every turning, so that the profits rise quicker and quicker. He that kills a breeding-sow, destroys all her offspring to the thousandth generation. He that murders a crown, destroys all that it might have produced, even scores of pounds."

"Remember this saying, *The good paymaster is lord of another man's purse*. He that is known to pay punctually and exactly to the time he promises, may at any time, and on any occasion, raise all the money his friends can spare. This is sometimes of great use. After industry and frugality, nothing contributes more to the raising of a young man in the world than punctuality and justice in all his dealings; therefore never keep borrowed money an hour beyond the time you promised, lest a disappointment shut up your friend's purse for ever.

"The most trifling actions that affect a man's credit are to be regarded. The sound of your hammer at five in the morning, or eight at night, heard by a creditor, makes him easy six months longer; but if he sees you at a billiard-table, or hears your voice at a tavern, when you should be at work, he sends for his money the next day; demands it, before he can receive it, in a lump.

"It shows, besides, that you are mindful of what you owe; it makes you appear a careful as well as an honest man, and that still increases your credit.

"Beware of thinking all your own that you possess, and of living accordingly. It is a mistake that many people who have credit fall into. To prevent this, keep an exact account for some time both of your expenses and your income. If you take the pains at first to mention particulars, it will have this good effect: you will discover how wonderfully small, trifling expenses mount up to large sums, and will discern what might have been, and may for the future be saved, without occasioning any great inconvenience."

"For six pounds a year you may have the use of one hundred pounds, provided you are a man of known prudence and honesty.

"He that spends a groat a day idly, spends idly above six pounds a year, which is the price for the use of one hundred pounds.

"He that wastes idly a groat's worth of his time per day, one day with another, wastes the privilege of using one hundred pounds each day.

"He that idly loses five shillings' worth of time, loses five shillings, and might as prudently throw five shillings into the sea.

"He that loses five shillings, not only loses that sum, but all the advantage that might be made by turning it in dealing, which by the time that a young man becomes old, will amount to a considerable sum of money."

It is Benjamin Franklin[①] who preaches to us in these sentences, the same which Ferdinand Kurnberger satirizes in his clever and malicious *Picture of American Culture*[②] as the supposed confession or faith of the Yankee. That it is the spirit of capitalism which here speaks in characteristic fashion, no one

---

① Benjamin Franklin, 本杰明·富兰克林(1706—1790), 美国科学家、发明家和政治活动家。引文中富兰克林的话, 出自他 1748 年《给年轻商人的忠告》一书。

② 《美国文化览胜》, 作者为费迪南德·古恩伯格(Ferdinand Kurnberger)。这本书因为在韦伯的《新教伦理与资本主义精神》中的出现和他对美国人哲学的精辟概括, 即"从牛身上刮油, 从人身上刮钱", 而广为人知。

will doubt, however little we may wish to claim that everything which could be understood as pertaining to that spirit is contained in it. Let us pause a moment to consider this passage, the philosophy of which Kürnberger sums up in the words, "They make tallow out of cattle and money out of men". The peculiarity of this philosophy of avarice appears to be the ideal of the honest man of recognized credit, and above all the idea of a duty of the individual toward the increase of his capital, which is assumed as an end in itself. Truly what is here preached is not simply a means of making one's way in the world, but a peculiar ethic. The infraction of its rules is treated not as foolishness but as forgetfulness of duty. That is the essence of the matter. It is not mere business astuteness, that sort of thing is common enough, it is an ethos. *This* is the quality which interests us.

When Jacob Fugger①, in speaking to a business associate who had retired and who wanted to persuade him to do the same, since he had made enough money and should let others have a chance, rejected that as pusillanimity and answered that "he (Fugger) thought otherwise, he wanted to make money as long as he could", the spirit of his statement is evidently quite different from that of Franklin. What in the former case was an expression of commercial daring and a personal inclination morally neutral, in the latter takes on the character of an ethically coloured maxim for the conduct of life. The concept spirit of capitalism is here used in this specific sense, it is the spirit of modern capitalism. For that we are here dealing only with Western European and American capitalism is obvious from the way in which the problem was stated. Capitalism existed in India, Babylon, in the classic world, and in the Middle Ages. But in all these cases, as we shall see, this particular ethos was lacking.

Now, all Franklin's moral attitudes are coloured with utilitarianism②. Honesty is useful, because it assures credit; so are punctuality, industry, frugality, and that is the reason they are virtues. A logical deduction from this would be that where, for instance, the appearance of honesty serves the same

---

① Jacob Fugger,雅各布·福格(1459—1525),德国成功的清教徒企业家、商人、银行家。
② utilitarianism,功利主义,是由边沁(J. Bentham)、密尔(J. S. Mill)和西奇威克(H. Sidgwick)等人发展起来的现代伦理学理论,认为一个行为的正当与错误取决于它所产生的善的、好的或坏的、恶的后果。在现代英美社会中,这种主张作为道德和立法的基本原则起到了重大作用。

purpose, that would suffice, and an unnecessary surplus of this virtue would evidently appear to Franklin's eyes as unproductive waste. And as a matter of fact, the story in his autobiography of his conversion to those virtues, or the discussion of the value of a strict maintenance of the appearance of modesty, the assiduous belittlement of one's own deserts in order to gain general recognition later, confirms this impression. According to Franklin, those virtues, like all others, are only in so far virtues as they are actually useful to the individual, and the surrogate of mere appearance is always sufficient when it accomplishes the end in view. It is a conclusion which is inevitable for strict utilitarianism. The impression of many Germans that the virtues professed by Americanism are pure hypocrisy seems to have been confirmed by this striking case. But in fact the matter is not by any means so simple. Benjamin Franklin's own character, as it appears in the really unusual candidness of his autobiography, belies that suspicion. The circumstance that he ascribes his recognition of the utility of virtue to a divine revelation which was intended to lead him in the path of righteousness, shows that something more than mere garnishing for purely egocentric motives is involved.

In fact, the *summum bonum*① of this ethic, the earning of more and more money, combined with the strict avoidance of all spontaneous enjoyment of life, is above all completely devoid of any eudaemonistic, not to say hedonistic②, admixture. It is thought of so purely as an end in itself, that from the point of view of the happiness of, or utility to, the single individual, it appears entirely transcendental and absolutely irrational. Man is dominated by the making of money, by acquisition as the ultimate purpose of his life. Economic acquisition is no longer subordinated to man as the means for the satisfaction of his material needs. This reversal of what we should call the natural relationship, so irrational from a naïve point of view, is evidently as

---

① summum bonum,至善,拉丁文中最高的或至上的善,是一种没有任何条件的善,是绝对目的自身,是一切善的缘起。伦理学上则是道德的理想,有可能是愉快、幸福、自我实现、履行职责或服从上帝。

② eudaemonistic 和 hedonistic 分别指幸福论和快乐论。其中幸福论认为应该把幸福作为最终的生活目标去追求,并为了幸福而从事其他一切事情,这是伦理学上的意义,而心理学上的幸福论则主张一个人的所有意向行为,目的都在于他自己的幸福;快乐论认为人们应该追求尽可能多的愉快和尽可能少的痛苦,愉快是生活中最高的和最内在的善,这个理论的支持者包括希腊哲学家亚里斯提卜(Aristippus)、伊壁鸠鲁(Epicurus)、经验主义者霍布斯(T. Hobbs)、洛克(J. Locke)、休谟(D. Hume)等,以及功利主义者,当然他们对快乐论的理解也有差异。

definitely a leading principle of capitalism as it is foreign to all peoples not under capitalistic influence. At the same time it expresses a type of feeling which is closely connected with certain religious ideas. If we thus ask, *why* should "money be made out of men", Benjamin Franklin himself, although he was a colourless deist, answers in his autobiography with a quotation from the Bible, which his strict Calvinistic father drummed into him again and again in his youth: "Seest thou a man diligent in his business? He shall stand before kings" (Prov. xxii 29). The earning of money within the modern economic order is, so long as it is done legally, the result and the expression of virtue and proficiency in a calling①, and this virtue and proficiency are, as it is now not difficult to see, the real Alpha and Omega of Franklin's ethic, as expressed in the passages we have quoted, as well as in all his works without exception.

And in truth this peculiar idea, so familiar to us to-day, but in reality so little a matter of course, of one's duty in a calling, is what is most characteristic of the social ethic of capitalistic culture, and is in a sense the fundamental basis of it. It is an obligation which the individual is supposed to feel and does feel towards the content of his professional activity, no matter in what it consists, in particular no matter whether it appears on the surface as a utilization of his personal powers, or only of his material possessions (as capital).

Of course, this conception has not appeared only under capitalistic conditions. On the contrary, we shall later trace its origins back to a time previous to the advent of capitalism. Still less, naturally, do we maintain that a conscious acceptance of these ethical maxims on the part of the individuals, entrepreneurs or labourers, in modern capitalistic enterprises, is a condition of the further existence of present-day capitalism. The capitalistic economy of the present day is an immense cosmos into which the individual is born, and which presents itself to him, at least as an individual, as an unalterable order of things in which he must live. It forces the individual, in so far as he is

---

① calling,在《圣经》中有两个含义,最常用的是"蒙召",一种来自神的救赎;第二种是"身份",张汉裕先生译为"天职",当然这种身份不是一般的身份,而是指某个人的命运或上帝指定的工作。身为奴隶,也要顺服地把上帝指定的工作,即奴隶的工作做好,以显示上帝的荣耀。后来马丁·路德在翻译《圣经》时,赋予了一种新的、世俗的意义,即"职业"。

involved in the system of market relationships, to conform to capitalistic rules of action. The manufacturer who in the long run acts counter to these norms, will just as inevitably be eliminated from the economic scene as the worker who cannot or will not adapt himself to them will be thrown into the streets without a job.

Thus the capitalism of to-day, which has come to dominate economic life, educates and selects the economic subjects which it needs through a process of economic survival of the fittest. But here one can easily see the limits of the concept of selection as a means of historical explanation. In order that a manner of life so well adapted to the peculiarities of capitalism could be selected at all, i. e. should come to dominate others, it had to originate somewhere, and not in isolated individuals alone, but as a way of life common to whole groups of men. This origin is what really needs explanation. Concerning the doctrine of the more naïve historical materialism, that such ideas originate as a reflection or superstructure of economic situations, we shall speak more in detail below. At this point it will suffice for our purpose to call attention to the fact that without doubt, in the country of Benjamin Franklin's birth (Massachusetts), the spirit of capitalism (in the sense we have attached to it) was present before the capitalistic order. There were complaints of a peculiarly calculating sort of profit-seeking in New England, as distinguished from other parts of America, as early as 1632. It is further undoubted that capitalism remained far less developed in some of the neighbouring colonies, the later Southern States of the United States of America, in spite of the fact that these latter were founded by large capitalists for business motives, while the New England colonies were founded by preachers and seminary graduates with the help of small bourgeois, craftsmen and yoemen, for religious reasons. In this case the causal relation is certainly the reverse of that suggested by the materialistic standpoint.

But the origin and history of such ideas is much more complex than the theorists of the superstructure suppose. The spirit of capitalism, in the sense in which we are using the term, had to fight its way to supremacy against a whole world of hostile forces. A state of mind such as that expressed in the passages we have quoted from Franklin, and which called forth the applause of a whole people, would both in ancient times and in the Middle Ages have been proscribed as the lowest sort of avarice and as an attitude entirely lacking in self-respect. It is, in fact, still regularly thus looked upon by all those social groups which are least involved in or adapted to modern capitalistic conditions. This is not wholly because the instinct of acquisition was in those times unknown or undeveloped, as has often been said. Nor because the *auri sacra fames*, the greed for gold, was then, or now, less powerful outside of bourgeois capitalism than within its peculiar sphere, as the illusions of modern romanticists are wont to believe. The difference between the capitalistic and precapitalistic spirits is not to be found at this point. The greed of the Chinese Mandarin, the old Roman aristocrat, or the modern peasant, can stand up to any comparison. And the *auri sacra fames* of a Neapolitan cab-driver or *barcaiuolo*, and certainly of Asiatic representatives of similar trades, as well as of the craftsmen of southern European or Asiatic countries, is, as anyone can find out for himself, very much more intense, and especially more unscrupulous than that of, say, an Englishman in similar circumstances.

The universal reign of absolute unscrupulousness in the pursuit of selfish interests by the making of money has been a specific characteristic of precisely those countries whose bourgeois-capitalistic development, measured according to Occidental standards, has remained backward. As every employer knows, the lack of *coscienziosità* of the labourers of such countries, for instance Italy as compared with Germany, has been, and to a certain extent still is, one of the principal obstacles to their capitalistic development. Capitalism cannot make use of the labour of those who practise the doctrine of undisciplined *liberum arbitrium*, any more than it can make use of the business man who seems absolutely unscrupulous in his dealings with others, as we can learn from Franklin. Hence the difference does not lie in the degree of development of any impulse to make money. The *auri sacra fames* is as old as the history of man. But we shall see that those who submitted to it without reserve as an uncontrolled impulse, such as the Dutch sea-captain who "would go through hell for gain, even though he scorched his sails", were by no means the representatives of that attitude of mind from which the specifically modern capitalistic spirit as a mass phenomenon is derived, and that is what matters. At all periods of history, wherever it was possible, there has been ruthless acquisition, bound to no ethical norms whatever. Like war and piracy, trade has often been unrestrained in its relations with foreigners and those outside the group. The double ethic has permitted here what was forbidden in dealings among brothers.

Capitalistic acquisition as an adventure has been at home in all types of economic society which have known trade with the use of money and which have offered it opportunities, through *commenda*①, farming of taxes, State loans, financing or wars, ducal courts and office-holders. Likewise the inner attitude of the adventurer, which laughs at all ethical limitations, has been universal. Absolute and conscious ruthlessness in acquisition has often stood in the closest connection with the strictest conformity to tradition. Moreover, with the breakdown of tradition and the more or less complete extension of free economic enterprise, even to within the social group, the new thing has not generally been ethically justified and encouraged, but only tolerated as a fact. And this fact has been treated either as ethically indifferent or as reprehensible, but unfortunately unavoidable. This has not only been the normal attitude of all ethical teachings, but, what is more important, also that expressed in the practical action of the average man of pre-capitalistic times, pre-capitalistic in the sense that the rational utilization of capital in a permanent enterprise and the rational capitalistic organization of labour had not yet become dominant forces in the determination of economic activity. Now just this attitude was one of the strongest inner obstacles which the adaptation of men to the conditions of an ordered bourgeois-capitalistic economy has encountered everywhere.

 选文出处

Max Weber. *The Protestant Ethic and the Spirit of Capitalism*. Translated by Talcott Parsons, Beijing: China Social Sciences Publishing House (reprinted from the English Edition by Charles Schribner, 1958), 1999, pp.48—58.

---

① Commenda,有人译作克门达,实际上指的是一种"委托交易"。

思考题

1. 在富兰克林的"生意经"的基础上,韦伯是如何将它们运用到新教伦理和资本主义精神之中进行解析的?你认为富兰克林的"生意经"如何?
2. 在资本主义精神出现过程中,宗教或新教所产生的影响是怎样的?
3. 简单评述韦伯的资本主义精神。

阅读参考书目

1. 周伯戡:《社会思想的冠冕——韦伯》,上海:上海书店,1987年。
2. 玛丽安妮·韦伯:《马克斯·韦伯传》,南京:江苏人民出版社,2002年。

柯林武德

柯林武德(Robin George Collingwood，1889—1943)，英国哲学家，历史学家。柯林武德4岁开始学习拉丁文，6岁学习希腊文，13岁以前一直在家接受其父亲的家庭教育。父亲 W. G. 柯林武德在考古学方面的兴趣与研究对他影响颇深。1908年柯林武德进入牛津大学，1912年被任命为牛津大学导师。不久第一次世界大战爆发，他被征入伍，参加了战时工作，战后他重返牛津任崎布鲁克学院研究院，1934年被选入皇家学会，1935年任牛津教授，1941年退休。柯林武德一生短暂，但著作颇丰。主要作品有《宗教与哲学》(Religion and Philosophy)、《知识的地图》(The Map of Knowledge)、《艺术原理》(The Principle of Art)、《艺术哲学大观》(Outline of a Philosophy of Art)、《历史哲学》(Philosophy of History)、《新利维坦》(The New Leviathan)、《自然的观念》(The Idea of Nature)、《历史的观念》(The Idea of History)等。

柯林武德一生致力于在历史学和哲学之间寻找一种联系，尤其在他的晚年，特别侧重探讨历史哲学。柯林武德是实证主义历史思潮的批判者。他反对用自然科学家研究自然事件的方法来研究历史事件，认为历史学家只有摆脱实证主义的束缚，寻求适合历史学研究的途径，才能推动史学的发展。他的这一思想在他晚年的著作中得到了集中的表达。

《历史的观念》由两个部分组成。第一编至第四编是柯林武德本人对历史哲学发展的梳理，覆盖了从希腊、罗马到20世纪历史学家及哲学家的历史哲学思想；导论和第五编"后论"阐述的是柯林武德本人的历史哲学思想。这里所选的片段来自第五篇"后论"的第一节。其中心目的是界定历史研究的范畴，尤其是阐述历史学与自然科学之区分。

为了阐明自己的观点，柯林武德提出了两组概念："外部"（outside）与"内在"（inside）以及"事件"（event）与"行动"（action）。他认为事件由"外部"与"内在"两部分构成。所谓事件的"外部"是指"可以用身体和它们的运动来加以描述的一切事物；如恺撒（Caesar）带着某些人在某个时刻渡过了一条叫作卢比康（Rubicon）的河流，或者恺撒的血在某一时刻流在了元老院的地面上"。而所谓的"内在"是指"其中只能用思想来加以描述的东西：如恺撒对共和国法律的蔑视，或者他本人和他的谋杀者之间有关宪法政策的冲突"等。柯林武德将"外部"与"内在"兼具的事件称为"行动"，而将仅有"外部"，而无"内在"的事件称为"单纯的事件"。他提出科学家研究的对象是单纯的事件，而历史学家研究的对象则是行动。在柯林武德看来两者的不同就在于自然现象仅仅是现象，而历史现象的背后则有思想。自然科学家研究自然现象时，没有必要研究自然是怎么想的，但历史学家研究历史事件时，他的主要任务是渗透到事件内部去探究事件行动者的思想。自然过程是单纯事件的序列，而历史过程则有一个由思想的过程所构成的内在方面。历史学家所要做的就是寻求这些思想过程。所以柯林武德说："一切历史都是思想史。"

柯林武德认为要想寻求这些思想过程，唯一的途径就是"在自己的心灵中重新思想它们"。他认为，"思想史以及一切的历史，都是在历史学家自己的心灵中重演（reenact）过去的思想。"但是，柯林武德同时又强调，所谓的重演并不是指"消极地屈服于别人的心灵之下"，重演应该是积极的，历史学家需要在自己的知识结构中去重演它。"重演的同时，历史学家也就批判了它，并形成了对它的价值判断。"柯林武德认为对思想的评判是历史学家的职责。他强烈反对"历史学家只是确定'某某人思想着什么'，而把决定'它是否真确'留给别人"。

柯林武德通过阐述自然过程与历史过程的区别，最终将历史知识的领域限定在"人类的行动"上，但也并非一切的人类行动都是历史学的题材。对于何为历史范畴内的人类行动，何为非历史的人类行为，柯林武德是如此划分的："只要人的行为是由可以称之为他的动物本性，他的冲动和嗜欲所决定的，他就是非历史的……历史学家感兴趣的是人们用自己的思想所创立的社会习惯，作为使这些嗜欲在其中以习俗和道德所认可的方式而得到满足的一种结构。"说到底，还是思想。我们不妨这样理解：历史研究的对象应该是人类在其思想支配下所做出的一切行动。

柯林武德的《历史的观念》一书，被1995年的《泰晤士报文学副刊》评为第二次世界大战后一百本最有影响的书之一。他在其中提出的"一切历史都是思想史"以及"思想重演"的观点，对于历史学摆脱自然科学、实证主义的影响和确立历史科学的独立地位都有重要意义。但其中也不乏可商榷之处，正如何兆武先生在译序中所评论的那样，"即使思想是历史的主要内容，也没有理由可以引申出思想就是历史的决定因素和唯一的因素的结论。……而实际物质力量往往有如海水之下的冰山，而至于思想则不过是水面上浮露出来的那一小部分顶尖罢了"。思想可以是历史的重要部分，但没有理由将历史全部归为思想史。根据柯林武德的"思想重演理论"，假如每个史学家都在自己思想里重演古人的思想，那结果将是有多少史学家在思维，就会有多少种不同的历史世界，每个人各以自己的思想方式在重演古代的历史。那样一来，客观历史作为一个统一体也就不复存在而被分裂为无数的单子，那就非但没有史学，甚至也没有历史了。因此，我们在阅读柯林武德的这篇选文时，应辩证地看待他所提出的史学观点。

The Idea of History

The field of historical thought

I must begin by attempting to delimit the proper sphere of historical knowledge as against those who, maintaining the historicity of all things, would resolve all knowledge into historical knowledge. Their argument runs in some such way as this.

The methods of historical research have, no doubt, been developed in application to the history of human affairs: but is that the limit of their applicability? They have already before now undergone important extensions: for example, at one time historians had worked out their methods of critical interpretation only as applied to written sources containing narrative material, and it was a new thing when they learnt to apply them to the unwritten data provided by archaeology. Might not a similar but even more revolutionary extension sweep into the historian's net the entire world of nature? In other words, are not natural processes really historical processes, and is not the being of nature a historical being?

Since the time of Heraclitus and Plato, it has been a commonplace that things natural, no less than things human, are in constant change, and that the entire world of nature is a world of "process" or "becoming". But this is not what is meant by the historicity of things; for change and history are not at all the same. According to this old-established conception, the specific forms of natural things constitute a changeless repertory of fixed types, and the process of nature is a process by which instances of these forms (or quasi-instances of them, things approximating to the embodiment of them) come into existence and pass out of it again. Now in human affairs, as historical research had clearly demonstrated by the eighteenth century, there is no such fixed repertory of specific forms. Here, the process of becoming was already by that time recognized as involving not only the instances or quasi-instances of the forms, but the forms themselves. The political philosophy of Plato and Aristotle teaches in effect that city-states come and go, but the idea of the city-state remains for ever as the one social and political form towards whose realization human intellect, so far as it is really intelligent, strives. According to modern ideas, the city-state itself is as transitory a thing as Miletus or Sybaris①. It is not an eternal ideal, it was merely the political ideal of the ancient Greeks. Other civilizations have had before them other political ideals, and human history shows a change not only in the individual cases in which these ideals are realized or partially realized, but in the ideals themselves. Specific types of human organization, the city-state, the feudal system, representative government, capitalistic industry, are characteristic of certain historical ages.

At first, this transience of specific forms was imagined to be a peculiarity of human life. When Hegel said that nature has no history, he meant that whereas the specific forms of human organization change as time goes on, the forms of natural organization do not. There is, he grants, a distinction of higher and lower in the specific forms of nature, and the higher forms are a development out of the lower; but this development is only a logical one, not a

---

① Sybaris,锡巴里斯,意大利南部一古希腊城,位于塔兰托海湾,曾因其富饶与奢靡而著名。公元前510年在与科洛托那战争中被毁。

temporal, and in time all the "strata" of nature exist simultaneously. But this view of nature has been overthrown by the doctrine of evolution. Biology has decided that living organisms are not divided into kinds each permanently distinct from the rest, but have developed their present specific forms through a process of evolution in time. Nor is this conception limited to the field of biology. It appeared simultaneously, the two applications being closely connected through the study of fossils, in geology. To-day even the stars are divided into kinds which can be described as older and younger; and the specific forms of matter, no longer conceived in the Daltonian manner, as elements eternally distinct like the living species of pre-Darwinian biology, are regarded as subject to a similar change, so that the chemical constitution of our present world is only a phase in a process leading from a very different past to a very different future.

This evolutionary conception of nature, whose implications have been impressively worked out by philosophers like M. Bergson, Mr. Alexander① and Mr. Whitehead②, might seem at first sight to have abolished the difference between natural process and historical process, and to have resolved nature into history. And if a further step in the same resolution were needed, it might seem to be provided by Mr. Whitehead's doctrine that the very possession of its attributes by a natural thing takes time. Just as Aristotle argued that a man cannot be happy at an instant, but that the possession of happiness takes a lifetime, so Mr. Whitehead argues that to be an atom of hydrogen takes time—the time necessary for establishing the peculiar rhythm of movements which distinguishes it from other atoms—so that there is no such thing as "nature at an instant".

These modern views of nature do, no doubt, "take time seriously". But just as history is not the same thing as change, so it is not the same thing as "timefulness", whether that means evolution or an existence which takes time. Such views have certainly narrowed the gulf between nature and history

---

① Mr. Alexander(1859—1938),英国哲学家。柯林武德的这篇文章是针对他的作品《事物的历史性》中提到的"世界即由事件构成的世界"而写的。柯林武德认为这句话的意思即"世界上所有的一切都是历史的",所以提出了异议。

② Mr. Whitehead,即 Alfred North Whitehead(1861—1947),A. N. 怀特海,英国数学家及哲学家,是逻辑数学的创建者,与伯特兰·罗素合著了《数学原理》。

of which early nineteenth-century thinkers were so conscious; they have made it impossible to state the distinction any longer in the way in which Hegel stated it; but in order to decide whether the gulf has been really closed and the distinction annulled, we must turn to the conception of history and see whether it coincides in essentials with this modern conception of nature.

If we put this question to the ordinary historian, he will answer it in the negative. According to him, all history properly so called is the history of human affairs. His special technique, depending as it does on the interpretation of documents in which human beings of the past have expressed or betrayed their thoughts, cannot be applied just as it stands to the study of natural processes; and the more this technique is elaborated in its details, the farther it is from being so applicable. There is a certain analogy between the archaeologist's interpretation of a stratified site and the geologist's interpretation of rock-horizons with their associated fossils; but the difference is no less clear than the similarity. The archaeologist's use of his stratified relics depends on his conceiving them as artifacts serving human purposes and thus expressing a particular way in which men have thought about their own life; and from his point of view the palaeontologist, arranging his fossils in a time-series, is not working as an historian, but only as a scientist thinking in a way which can at most be described as quasi-historical.

Upholders of the doctrine under examination would say that here the historian is making an arbitrary distinction between things that are really the same, and that his conception of history is an unphilosophically narrow one, restricted by the imperfect development of his technique; very much as some historians, because their equipment was inadequate to studying the history of art or science or economic life, have mistakenly restricted the field of historical thought to the history of politics. The question must therefore be raised, why do historians habitually identify history with the history of human affairs? In order to answer this question, it is not enough to consider the characteristics of historical method as it actually exists, for the question at issue is whether, as it actually exists, it covers the whole field which properly belongs to it. We must ask what is the general nature of the problems which this method is designed to solve. When we have done so, it will appear that the special problem of the historian is one which does not arise in the case of natural science.

The historian, investigating any event in the past, makes a distinction between what may be called the outside and the inside of an event. By the outside of the event I mean everything belonging to it which can be described in terms of bodies and their movements: the passage of Caesar, accompanied by certain men, across a river called the Rubicon at one date, or the spilling of his blood on the floor of the senate-house at another. By the inside of the event I mean that in it which can only be described in terms of thought: Caesar's defiance of Republican law, or the clash of constitutional policy between himself and his assassins. The historian is never concerned with either of these to the exclusion of the other. He is investigating not mere events (where by a mere event I mean one which has only an outside and no inside) but actions, and an action is the unity of the outside and inside of an event. He is interested in the crossing of the Rubicon only in its relation to Republican law, and in the spilling of Caesar's blood only in its relation to a constitutional conflict. His work may begin by discovering the outside of an event, but it can never end there; he must always remember that the event was action, and that his main task is to think himself into this action, to discern the thought of its agent.

In the case of nature, this distinction between the outside and the inside of an event does not arise. The events of nature are mere events, not the acts of agents whose thought the scientist endeavours to trace. It is true that the scientist, like the historian, has to go beyond the mere discovery of events; but the direction in which he moves is very different. Instead of conceiving the event as an action and attempting to rediscover the thought of its agent, penetrating from the outside of the event to its inside, the scientist goes beyond the event, observes its relation to others, and thus brings it under a general formula or law of nature. To the scientist, nature is always and merely a "phenomenon", not in the sense of being defective in reality, but in the sense of being a spectacle presented to his intelligent observation; whereas the events of history are never mere phenomena, never mere spectacles for contemplation, but things which the historian looks, not at, but through, to discern the thought within them.

In thus penetrating to the inside of events and detecting the thought which they express, the historian is doing something which the scientist need not and cannot do. In this way the task of the historian is more complex than that of the scientist. In another way it is simpler: the historian need not and cannot (without ceasing to be an historian) emulate the scientist in searching for the causes or laws of events. For science, the event is discovered by perceiving it, and the further search for its cause is conducted by assigning it to its class and determining the relation between that class and others. For history, the object to be discovered is not the mere event, but the thought expressed in it. To discover that thought is already to understand it. After the historian has ascertained the facts, there is no further process of inquiring into their causes. When he knows what happened, he already knows why it happened.

This does not mean that words like "cause" are necessarily out of place in reference to history; it only means that they are used there in a special sense. When a scientist asks "Why did that piece of litmus paper turn pink?" he means "On what kinds of occasions do pieces of litmus paper turn pink?" When an historian asks "Why did Brutus stab Caesar?" he means "What did Brutus think, which made him decide to stab Caesar?" The cause of the event, for him, means the thought in the mind of the person by whose agency the event came about: and this is not something other than the event, it is the inside of the event itself.

The processes of nature can therefore be properly described as sequences of mere events, but those of history cannot. They are not processes of mere events but processes of actions, which have an inner side, consisting of processes of thought; and what the historian is looking for is these processes of thought. All history is the history of thought.

But how does the historian discern the thoughts which he is trying to discover? There is only one way in which it can be done: by re-thinking them in his own mind. The historian of philosophy, reacting Plato, is trying to know what Plato thought when he expressed himself in certain words. The only way in which he can do this is by thinking it for himself. This, in fact, is what we mean when we speak of "understanding" the words. So the historian of politics or warfare, presented with an account of certain actions done by Julius Caesar, tries to understand these actions, that is, to discover what thoughts in Caesar's mind determined him to do them. This implies envisaging for himself the situation in which Caesar stood, and thinking for himself what Caesar thought about the situation and the possible ways of dealing with it. The history of thought, and therefore all history, is the re-enactment of past thought in the historian's own mind.

This re-enactment is only accomplished, in the case of Plato and Caesar respectively, so far as the historian brings to bear on the problem all the powers of his own mind and all his knowledge of philosophy and politics. It is not a passive surrender to the spell of another's mind; it is a labour of active and therefore critical thinking. The historian not only re-enacts past thought, he re-enacts it in the context of his own knowledge and therefore, in re-enacting it, criticizes it, forms his own judgement of its value, corrects whatever errors he can discern in it. This criticism of the thought whose history he traces is not someting secondary to tracing the history of it. It is an indispensable condition of the historical knowledge itself. Nothing could be a completer error concerning the history of thought than to suppose that the historian as such merely ascertains "what so-and-so thought", leaving it to some one else to decide "whether it was true". All thinking is critical thinking; the thought which re-enacts past thoughts, therefore, criticizes them in re-enacting them.

It is now clear why historians habitually restrict the field of historical knowledge to human affairs. A natural process is a process of events, an historical process is a process of thoughts. Man is regarded as the only subject of historical process, because man is regarded as the only animal that thinks, or thinks enough, and clearly enough, to render his actions the expressions of his thoughts. The belief that man is the only animal that thinks at all is no doubt a superstition; but the belief that man thinks more, and more continuously and effectively, than any other animal, and is the only animal whose conduct is to any great extent determined by thought instead of by mere impulse and appetite, is probably well enough founded to justify the historian's rule of thumb.

It does not follow that all human actions are subject-matter for history; and indeed historians are agreed that they are not. But when they are asked how the distinction is to be made between historical and non-historical human actions, they are somewhat at a loss how to reply. From our present point of view we can offer an answer: so far as man's conduct is determined by what may be called his animal nature, his impulses and appetites, it is non-historical; the process of those activities is a natural process. Thus, the historian is not interested in the fact that men eat and sleep and make love and thus satisfy their natural appetites; but he is interested in the social customs which they create by their thought as a framework within which these appetites find satisfaction in ways sanctioned by convention and morality.

Consequently, although the conception of evolution has revolutionized our idea of nature by substituting for the old conception of natural process as a change within the limits of a fixed system of specific forms the new conception of that process as involving a change in these forms themselves, it has by no means identified the idea of natural process with that of historical process; and the fashion, current not long ago, of using the word "evolution" in a historical context, and talking of the evolution of parliament or the like, though natural in an age when the science of nature was regarded as the only true form of knowledge, and when other forms of knowledge, in order to justify their existence, felt bound to assimilate themselves to that model, was the result of confused thinking and a source of further confusions.

There is only one hypothesis on which natural processes could be regarded as ultimately historical in character: namely, that these processes are in reality processes of action determined by a thought which is their own inner side. This would imply that natural events are expressions of thoughts, whether the thoughts of God, or of angelic or demonic finite intelligences, or of minds somewhat like our own inhabiting the organic and inorganic bodies of nature as our minds inhabit our bodies. Setting aside mere flights of metaphysical fancy, such an hypothesis could claim our serious attention only if it led to a better understanding of the natural world. In fact, however, the scientist can reasonably say of it "je n'ai pas eu besoin de cette hypothèse", and the theologian will recoil from any suggestion that God's action in the natural world resembles the action of a finite human mind under the conditions of historical life. This at least is certain: that, so far as our scientific and historical knowledge goes, the processes of events which constitute the world of nature are altogether different in kind from the processes of thought which constitute the world of history.

 选文出处

R. G. Collingwood. *The Idea of History*. Beijing: China Social Sciences Publishing House (reprinted from the English Edition by Oxford University Press, 1966), 1999, pp. 210—217.

思考题

1. 柯林武德认为"一切历史都是思想史",你同意他的观点吗?为什么?
2. 柯林武德认为寻找历史的思想过程的唯一途径就是"在心灵中重演过去的思想",你觉得可行吗?

参考书目

1. 何兆武、陈启能主编:《当代西方史学理论》,上海:上海社会科学院出版社,2003年。
2. 柯林武德:《柯林武德自传》,陈静译,北京:北京大学出版社,2005年。

道金斯

克林顿·理查德·道金斯(Clinton Richard Dawkins,1941—)出生于第二次世界大战时期英属东非殖民地首府内罗毕市的一个基督教家庭,于1949年随父母回迁英国,是英国著名的动物行为学家、科普作家以及英国皇家科学院院士和牛津大学教授,是全世界最具争议的进化生物学家。尽管道金斯从小在基督教家庭文化的熏陶下长大,但在身为农业专家的父亲的影响下,他对自然更为着迷。因为在东非大草原上对自然的好奇、观察和思考,幼小的道金斯在回英国后不久便开始对基督教思想心存疑惑,但懵懂的直觉认知还不足以使之全然摆脱基督教信仰。当道金斯在青年时遇到了达尔文的进化论之后,他脑海中先前萌发的无神论思想便渐渐有了理论框架。在进化论思想的激发和学术研究的锤炼下,道金斯不仅持续收获了丰硕的研究成果,同时也让他自己在论证中越发表现为一个坚定的无神论信仰者。正因为如此,道金斯被称为"达尔文的罗威纳犬(Darwin's Rottweiler)",且是当今最著名、最直言不讳的无神论者和进化论拥护者之一。

道金斯著作等身,声名远播,影响深广。自从发掘用进化论去理解生命的复杂性更具合理性后,道金斯一直笔耕不辍。自《自私的基因》(*The Selfish Gene*)于1976年出版以来,道金斯的新作迭出。他此后的主要著作有:《延伸的表现型》(*The Extended Phenotype*,1982)、《盲眼钟表匠》(*The Blind Watchmaker*,1986)、《伊甸园之河》(*River Out of Eden*,1995)、《攀登不可能山峰》(*Climbing Mount*

Improbable，1996)、《解析彩虹》(*Unweaving the Rainbow*，1998)、《恶魔的教士》(*A Devil's Chaplain*，2003)、《祖先的故事》(*The Ancestor's Tale*，2004)、《上帝错觉》(*The God Delusion*，2006)、《地球上最伟大的表演：演化的证据》(*The Greatest Show on Earth：The Evidence for Evolution*，2009)等等。近年来,已逾古稀之年的道金斯依然创作力惊人,又连续出版了《自然的魔法：我们如何知道什么是真的》(*The Magic of Reality：How We Know What's Really True*，2011)和《玄妙的诱惑：一个科学家的产生》(*An Appetite for Wonder：The Making of a Scientist*，2013)两部力作。此外,道金斯是一位极其活跃的科普教授,先后录制的文献片有十几部之多,如《好人吃香》(*Nice Guys Finish First*，1987)、《信仰学校之威胁》(*Faith School Menace*，2010)和《不信教者》(*The Unbelievers*，2013)等等。正因为道金斯笃信达尔文的进化论,且倾毕生精力于基因选择的理论建构中,对宗教思想极具否定性,所以他与美国哲学家丹尼尔·丹尼特(Daniel Dennett)、神经科学家山姆·哈里斯(Sam Harris)和英裔美国作家克里斯托弗·希钦斯(Christopher Hitchens)一起被称为"新无神论的四骑士"。尽管道金斯的思想颇受争议,但其影响力无疑已是颠覆性的和国际性的。截至目前,道金斯的著作和文献片已被翻译成了几十种语言,在全球各地广泛传播。更引人关注的是,道金斯不仅在周游列国时积极传讲自己的学说思想,还不断地与各流派宗教领袖进行公开辩论,在相关领域引起了巨大的反响,也让世界各国的各类哲学家、生物学家和宗教人士为之恼怒不已,解构或重构了人们的许多传统认知。

《自私的基因》无疑是道金斯所有著作中影响力最为强劲和持久的一部。无论在生物学等自然科学领域,还是在哲学、宗教等人文学科,抑或在非学术研究的普通读者中,《自私的基因》都因对达尔文的自然选择理论的重新阐释引起读者们极大的震惊、欣喜和兴趣。它不仅系统性地改变了社会生物学的原有本质,也使芸芸众生以一种新的视角重新审视生命的存在和信仰的存在。正因为如此,《自私的基因》一书受到了世界各地读者的狂热追捧,成了长盛不衰的经典畅销著作。道金斯认为,自然选择发生于基因层面,基因借助生物机体得以持续存在,即便是那些利他主义的行为也是为了最大化地确保基因的存续。《自私的基因》不仅是道金斯的处女作和成名作,也是其学术思想的精髓所在,他后来相继出版的系列著作是就相关论题的进一步拓展和挖掘。所以,要想真正了解道金斯在西方思想史激起的思想浪花,我们不仅有必要细细研读《自私的基因》,也有必要阅读他的相关著作。下面摘选的文字出自《自私的基因》的第十二章"好人终有好报",展现了自私的基因如何在"囚徒困境"中以利他主义行为确保其生存的最大机率。

为了存活下去，基因始终在展现自私的本质特性。然而，生物界却同时普遍存在利他主义行为，如饱餐的吸血鬼蝙蝠通过返流血液与饥饿的同伴分享自己腹中的一部分血液。那么，在自私基因主导下的生物群落中，行善举的生物个体的命运到底如何？为此，道金斯充分利用"囚徒博弈"理论进行论证。道金斯认为，如果两个共同犯罪的囚犯被分别关在独立的牢房里，最理想的状态是，两者都选择相互信任，不向警方告发对方，使彼此都免于确凿证据下的法律诉讼。如果其中一人先告发了另一人，便可使对方承担主要法律责任，而让自己仅仅受到较轻的惩罚。信任和背叛之间的博弈正与惩罚的大小相联系。由于基因的自私性，每一个生物体都想最大化地获取资源，且最小化地为此付出代价，在短期内选择背叛同伴无疑是利大于弊，但生物的进化是物种在大自然中的长期选择。显然，长期背叛必然遭到同伴的抛弃和报复，使自己陷于生存窘境，所以生物在连续复杂的合作和背叛之中不断上演极其繁杂的"囚徒博弈"。通过计算机对"重复博弈"中种种情况的梳理和分析，道金斯认为，"我们算出了赢家策略的两个特点：善良与宽容。这几乎是一个乌托邦式的结论：善良与宽容能得到好报"。[①] 在复杂的社会性群落中，其稳定性状是善良和宽容，还是邪恶和刻薄，取决于"针锋相对"和"永远背叛"两种策略在社会中累积的数量优势。道金斯认为，"'针锋相对'是可以超越决胜点的，它所需的只是这些个体的聚合，这一点在自然选择里可以很自然地发生。这个与生俱来的优点使得'针锋相对'即使在数目稀少的时候，还可以成功跨越决胜点而获得成功"；相反，"'永远背叛'个体的聚合，不仅不能彼此互助而获得群体繁荣，还会使各自的生存环境更加恶劣。它们无法暗自帮助对方获得银行家的奖赏，而只能把对方也拖下水"。道金斯通过描述和阐析细菌、无花果树和榕小蜂、海鲈鱼、吸血鬼蝙蝠等层面的利他主义生物行为，最终将论点指向了"一个善良的思想：即使我们都由自私的基因掌舵，好人终有好报"。

Nice Guys Finish First

Nice guys finish last. The phrase seems to have originated in the world of baseball, although some authorities claim priority for an alternative

---

[①] 引自理查德·道金斯：《自私的基因》，卢允中等译，北京：中信出版社，2012年。

connotation. The American biologist Garrett Hardin used it to summarize the message of what may be called "sociobiology" or "selfish genery". It is easy to see its aptness. If we translate the colloquial meaning of "nice guy" into its Darwinian equivalent, a nice guy is an individual that assists other members of its species, at its own expense, to pass their genes on to the next generation. Nice guys, then, seem bound to decrease in numbers: niceness dies a Darwinian death. But there is another, technical, interpretation of the colloquial word "nice". If we adopt this definition, which is not too far from the colloquial meaning, nice guys can *finish first*. This more optimistic conclusion is what this chapter is about.

Remember the Grudgers of Chapter 10. These were birds that helped each other in an apparently altruistic way, but refused to help—bore a grudge against—individuals that had previously refused to help them. Grudgers came to dominate the population because they passed on more genes to future generations than either Suckers (who helped others indiscriminately, and were exploited) or Cheats (who tried ruthlessly to exploit everybody and ended up doing each other down). The story of the Grudgers illustrated an important general principle, which Robert Trivers[①] called "reciprocal altruism". As we saw in the example of the cleaner fish (pages 186—187), reciprocal altruism is not confined to members of a single species. It is at work in all relationships that are called symbiotic—for instance the ants milking their aphid "cattle" (page 181). Since Chapter 10 was written, the American political scientist Robert Axelrod[②] (working partly in collaboration with W. D. Hamilton, whose name has cropped up on so many pages of this book), has taken the idea of reciprocal altruism on in exciting new directions. It was Axelrod who coined the technical meaning of the word "nice" to which I alluded in my opening paragraph.

Axelrod, like many political scientists, economists, mathematicians and

---

① Robert Trivers, 罗伯特·特里弗斯(1943—)是罗格斯大学的人类学和生物科学教授,因其在社会进化、冲突和合作方面的原创性阐析而于2007年获得了生物科学领域的克拉福德奖(the Crafoord Prize)。

② Robert Axelrod, 罗伯特·阿克塞尔罗德(1949—)是密歇根大学的沃尔格林教授,主要研究方向为人类认知,2006—2007年任美国政治科学协会主席,并于2015年荣获哈佛大学荣誉法学博士学位。

psychologists, was fascinated by a simple gambling game called Prisoner's Dilemma. It is so simple that I have known clever men misunderstand it completely, thinking that there must be more to it! But its simplicity is deceptive. Whole shelves in libraries are devoted to the ramifications of this beguiling game. Many influential people think it holds the key to strategic defence planning, and that we should study it to prevent a third world war. As a biologist, I agree with Axelrod and Hamilton that many wild animals and plants are engaged in ceaseless games of Prisoner's Dilemma, played out in evolutionary time.

...

"Prisoner" comes from one particular imaginary example. The currency in this case is not money but prison sentences. Two men—call them Peterson and Moriarty—are in jail, suspected of collaborating in a crime. Each prisoner, in his separate cell, is invited to betray his colleague (DEFECT) by turning King's Evidence against him. What happens depends upon what both prisoners do, and neither knows what the other has done. If Peterson throws the blame entirely on Moriarty, and Moriarty renders the story plausible by remaining silent (cooperating with his erstwhile and, as it turns out, treacherous friend), Moriarty gets a heavy jail sentence while Peterson gets off scot-free, having yielded to the Temptation to defect. If each betrays the other, both are convicted of the crime, but receive some credit for giving evidence and get a somewhat reduced, though still stiff, sentence, the Punishment for mutual defection. If both cooperate (with each other, not with the authorities) by refusing to speak, there is not enough evidence to convict either of them of the main crime, and they receive a small sentence for a lesser offence, the Reward for mutual cooperation. Although it may seem odd to call a jail sentence a "reward", that is how the men would see it if the alternative was a longer spell behind bars. You will notice that, although the "payoffs" are not in dollars but in jail sentences, the essential features of the game are preserved (look at the rank order of desirability of the four outcomes). If you put yourself in each prisoner's place, assuming both to be motivated by rational self interest and remembering that they cannot talk to one another to make a pact, you will see that neither has any choice but to betray the other, thereby condemning both to heavy sentences.

Is there any way out of the dilemma? Both players know that, whatever their opponent does, they themselves cannot do better than DEFECT; yet both also know that, if only both had cooperated, each one would have done better. If only … if only … if only there could be some way of reaching agreement, some way of reassuring each player that the other can be trusted not to go for the selfish jackpot, some way of policing the agreement.

In the simple game of Prisoner's Dilemma, there is no way of ensuring trust. Unless at least one of the players is a really saintly sucker, too good for this world, the game is doomed to end in mutual defection with its paradoxically poor result for both players. But there is another version of the game. It is called the "Iterated" or "Repeated" Prisoner's Dilemma. The iterated game is more complicated, and in its complication lies hope.

The iterated game is simply the ordinary game repeated an indefinite number of times with the same players. Once again you and I face each other, with a banker sitting between. Once again we each have a hand of just two cards, labelled COOPERATE and DEFECT. Once again we move by each playing one or other of these cards and the banker shells out, or levies fines, according to the rules given above. But now, instead of that being the end of the game, we pick up our cards and prepare for another round. The successive rounds of the game give us the opportunity to build up trust or mistrust, to reciprocate or placate, forgive or avenge. In an indefinitely long game, the important point is that we can both win at the expense of the banker, rather than at the expense of one another.

…

But although Tit for Tat is strictly speaking not a true ESS, it is probably fair to treat some sort of mixture of basically nice but retaliatory "tit for Tat-like" strategies as roughly equivalent to an ESS in practice. Such a mixture might include a small admixture of nastiness. Robert Boyd and Jeffrey Lorberbaum, in one of the more interesting follow-ups to Axelrod's work, looked at a mixture of Tit for Two Tats and a strategy called Suspicious Tit for Tat. Suspicious Tit for Tat is technically nasty, but it is not very nasty. It behaves just like Tit for Tat itself after the first move, but—this is what makes it technically nasty—it does defect on the very first move of the game. In a climate entirely dominated by Tit for Tat, Suspicious Tit for Tat does not prosper, because its initial defection triggers an unbroken run of mutual recrimination. When it meets a Tit for Two Tats player, on the other hand, Tit for Two Tats's greater forgivingness nips this recrimination in the bud. Both players end the game with at least the "benchmark", all C, score and with Suspicious Tit for Tat scoring a bonus for its initial defection. Boyd and Lorberbaum showed that a population of Tit for Tat could be invaded, evolutionarily speaking, by a mixture of Tit for Two Tats and Suspicious Tit for Tat, the two prospering in each other's company. This combination is almost certainly not the only combination that could invade in this kind of way. There are probably lots of mixtures of slightly nasty strategies with nice and very forgiving strategies that are together capable of invading. Some might see this as a mirror for familiar aspects of human life.

Axelrod recognized that Tit for Tat is not strictly an ESS[①], and he therefore coined the phrase "collectively stable strategy" to describe it. As in the case of true ESSs, it is possible for more than one strategy to be collectively stable at the same time. And again, it is a matter of luck which one comes to dominate a population. Always Defect is also stable, as well as Tit for Tat. In a population that has already come to be dominated by Always Defect, no other strategy does better. We can treat the system as bistable, with Always Defect being one of the stable points, Tit for Tat (or some mixture of mostly nice, retaliatory strategies) the other stable point. Whichever stable point comes to dominate the population first will tend to stay dominant.

But what does "dominate" mean, in quantitative terms? How many Tit for Tats must there be in order for Tit for Tat to do better than Always Defect? That depends upon the detailed payoffs that the banker has agreed to shell out in this particular game. All we can say in general is that there is a critical frequency, a knife-edge. On one side of the knife-edge the critical frequency of Tit for Tat is exceeded, and selection will favour more and more Tit for Tats. On the other side of the knife-edge the critical frequency of Always Defect is exceeded, and selection will favour more and more Always Defects. We met the equivalent of this knife-edge, you will remember, in the

---

① ESS 是 Evolutionary Stable Strategy 的缩写形式,即进化稳定策略。

story of the Grudgers and Cheats in Chapter 10.

It obviously matters, therefore, on which side of the knife-edge a population happens to start. And we need to know how it might happen that a population could occasionally cross from one side of the knife-edge to the other. Suppose we start with a population already sitting on the Always Defect side. The few Tit for Tat individuals don't meet each other often enough to be of mutual benefit. So natural selection pushes the population even further towards the Always Defect extreme. If only the population could just manage, by random drift, to get itself over the knife-edge, it could coast down the slope to the Tit for Tat side, and everyone would do much better at the banker's (or "nature's") expense. But of course populations have no group will, no group intention or purpose. They cannot strive to leap the knife-edge. They will cross it only if the undirected forces of nature happen to lead them across.

...

Coming back to our knife-edge, then, Tit for Tat could surmount it. All that is required is a little local clustering, of a sort that will naturally tend to arise in natural populations. Tit for Tat has a built-in gift, even when rare, for crossing the knife-edge over to its own side. It is as though there were a secret passage underneath the knife-edge. But that secret passage contains a one-way valve: there is an asymmetry. Unlike Tit for Tat, Always Defect, though a true ESS, cannot use local clustering to cross the knife-edge. On the contrary. Local clusters of Always Defect individuals, far from prospering by each other's presence, do especially badly in each other's presence. Far from quietly helping one another at the expense of the banker, they do one another down. Always Defect, then, unlike Tit for Tat, gets no help from kinship or viscosity in the population.

So, although Tit for Tat may be only dubiously an ESS, it has a sort of higher-order stability. What can this mean? Surely, stable is stable. Well, here we are taking a longer view. Always Defect resists invasion for a long time. But if we wait long enough, perhaps thousands of years, Tit for Tat will eventually muster the numbers required to tip it over the knife-edge, and the population will flip. But the reverse will not happen. Always Defect, as we have seen, cannot benefit from clustering, and so does not enjoy this higher-order stability.

Tit for Tat, as we have seen, is "nice", meaning never the first to defect, and "forgiving", meaning that it has a short memory for past misdeeds. I now introduce another of Axelrod's evocative technical terms. Tit for Tat is also "not envious". To be envious, in Axelrod's terminology, means to strive for more money than the other player, rather than for an absolutely large quantity of the banker's money. To be non-envious means to be quite happy if the other player wins just as much money as you do, so long as you both thereby win more from the banker. Tit for Tat never actually "wins" a game. Think about it and you'll see that it cannot score more than its "opponent" in any particular game because it never defects except in retaliation. The most it can do is draw with its opponent. But it tends to achieve each draw with a high, shared score. Where Tit for Tat and other nice strategies are concerned, the very word "opponent" is inappropriate. Sadly, however, when psychologists set up games of Iterated Prisoner's Dilemma between real humans, nearly all players succumb to envy and therefore do relatively poorly in terms of money. It seems that many people, perhaps without even thinking about it, would rather do down the other player than cooperate with the other player to do down the banker. Axelrod's work has shown what a mistake this is.

It is only a mistake in certain kinds of game. Games theorists divide games into "zero sum" and "nonzero sum". A zero sum game is one in which a win for one player is a loss for the other. Chess is zero sum, because the aim of each player is to win, and this means to make the other player lose. Prisoner's Dilemma, however, is a nonzero sum game. There is a banker paying out money, and it is possible for the two players to link arms and laugh all the way to the bank.

...

Football is a zero sum game. At least, it usually is. Occasionally it can become a nonzero sum game. This happened in 1977 in the English Football League (Association Football or "soccer"; the other games called football—Rugby Football, Australian Football, American Football, Irish Football, etc., are also normally zero sum games). Teams in the Football League are split into four divisions. Clubs play against other clubs within their own division, accumulating points for each win or draw throughout the season. To be in the First Division is prestigious, and also lucrative for a club since it ensures large crowds. At the end of each season, the bottom three clubs in the First Division are relegated to the Second Division for the next season. Relegation seems to be regarded as a terrible fate, worth going to great efforts to avoid.

May 18th 1977 was the last day of that year's football season. Two of the three relegations from the First Division had already been determined, but the third relegation was still in contention. It would definitely be one of three teams, Sunderland, Bristol, or Coventry. These three teams, then, had everything to play for on that Saturday. Sunderland were playing against a fourth team (whose tenure in the First Division was not in doubt). Bristol and Coventry happened to be playing against each other. It was known that, if Sunderland lost their game, then Bristol and Coventry needed only to draw against each other in order to stay in the First Division. But if Sunderland won, then the team relegated would be either Bristol or Coventry, depending on the outcome of their game against each other. The two crucial games were theoretically simultaneous. As a matter of fact, however, the Bristol-Coventry game happened to be running five minutes late. Because of this, the result of the Sunderland game became known before the end of the Bristol-Coventry game. Thereby hangs this whole complicated tale.

For most of the game between Bristol and Coventry the play was, to quote one contemporary news report, "fast and often furious", an exciting (if you like that sort of thing) ding-dong battle. Some brilliant goals from both sides had seen to it that the score was 2-all by the eightieth minute of the match. Then, two minutes before the end of the game, the news came through from the other ground that Sunderland had lost. Immediately, the Coventry team manager had the news flashed up on the giant electronic message board at the end of the ground. Apparently all 22 players could read, and they all realized that they needn't bother to play hard anymore. A draw was all that either team needed in order to avoid relegation. Indeed, to put effort into scoring goals was now positively bad policy since, by taking players away from defence, it carried the risk of actually losing—and being relegated after all. Both sides became intent on securing a draw. To quote the same news report: "supporters who had been fierce rivals seconds before when Don

Gillies fired in an 80th minute equaliser for Bristol, suddenly joined in a combined celebration. Referee Ron Challis watched helpless as the players pushed the ball around with little or no challenge to the man in possession." What had previously been a zero sum game had suddenly, because of a piece of news from the outside world, become a nonzero sum game. In the terms of our earlier discussion, it is as if an external "banker" had magically appeared, making it possible for both Bristol and Coventry to benefit from the same outcome, a draw.

Spectator sports like football are normally zero sum games for a good reason. It is more exciting for crowds to watch players striving mightily against one another than to watch them conniving amicably. But real life, both human life and plant and animal life, is not set up for the benefit of spectators. Many situations in real life are, as a matter of fact, equivalent to nonzero sum games. Nature often plays the role of "banker", and individuals can therefore benefit from one another's success. They do not have to do down rivals in order to benefit themselves. Without departing from the fundamental laws of the selfish gene, we can see how cooperation and mutual assistance can flourish even in a basically selfish world. We can see how, in Axelrod's meaning of the term, nice guys may finish first.

But none of this works unless the game is iterated. The players must know that the present game is not the last one between them. In Axelrod's haunting phrase, the "shadow of the future" must be long. But how long must it be? It can't be infinitely long. From a theoretical point of view it doesn't matter how long the game is; the important thing is that neither player should know when the game is going to end. Suppose you and I were playing against each other, and suppose we both knew that the number of rounds in the game was to be exactly 100. Now we both understand that the 100th round, being the last, will be equivalent to a simple one-off game of Prisoner's Dilemma. Therefore the only rational strategy for either of us to play on the 100th round will be DEFECT, and we can each assume that the other player will work that out and be fully resolved to defect on the last round. The last round can therefore be written off as predictable. But now the 99th round will be the equivalent of a one-off game, and the only rational choice for each player on this last but one game is also DEFECT. The 98th round succumbs to the same reasoning, and so on back. Two strictly rational players, each of whom assumes that the other is strictly rational, can do nothing but defect if they both know how many rounds the game is destined to run. For this reason, when games theorists talk about the Iterated or Repeated Prisoner's Dilemma game, they always assume that the end of the game is unpredictable, or known only to the banker.

Even if the exact number of rounds in the game is not known for certain, in real life it is often possible to make a statistical guess as to how much longer the game is likely to last. This assessment may become an important part of strategy. If I notice the banker fidget and look at his watch, I may well conjecture that the game is about to be brought to an end, and I may therefore feel tempted to defect. If I suspect that you too have noticed the banker fidgeting, I may fear that you too may be contemplating defection. I will probably be anxious to get my defection in first. Especially since I may fear that you are fearing that I...

The mathematician's simple distinction between the one-off Prisoner's Dilemma game and the Iterated Prisoner's Dilemma game is too simple. Each player can be expected to behave as if he possessed a continuously updated estimate of how long the game is likely to go on. The longer his estimate, the more he will play according to the mathematician's expectations for the true iterated game: in other words, the nicer, more forgiving, less envious he will be. The shorter his estimate of the future of the game, the more he will be inclined to play according to the mathematician's expectations for the one-off game: the nastier, and less forgiving will he be.

...

The live-and-let-live system could have been worked out by verbal negotiation, by conscious strategists bargaining round a table. In fact it was not. It grew up as a series of local conventions, through people responding to one another's behaviour; the individual soldiers were probably hardly aware that the growing up was going on. This need not surprise us. The strategies in Axelrod's computer were definitely unconscious. It was their behaviour that defined them as nice or nasty, as forgiving or unforgiving, envious or the reverse. The programmers who designed them may have been any of these things, but that is irrelevant. A nice, forgiving, non-envious strategy could easily be programmed into a computer by a very nasty man. And vice versa. A strategy's niceness is recognized by its behaviour, not by its motives (for it has none) nor by the personality of its author (who has faded into the background by the time the program is running in the computer). A computer program can behave in a strategic manner, without being aware of its strategy or, indeed, of anything at all.

We are, of course, entirely familiar with the idea of unconscious strategists, or at least of strategists whose consciousness, if any, is irrelevant. Unconscious strategists abound in the pages of this book. Axelrod's programs are an excellent model for the way we, throughout the book, have been thinking of animals and plants, and indeed of genes. So it is natural to ask whether his optimistic conclusions—about the success of non-envious, forgiving niceness—also apply in the world of nature. The answer is yes, of course they do. The only conditions are that nature should sometimes set up games of Prisoner's Dilemma, that the shadow of the future should be long, and that the games should be nonzero sum games. These conditions are certainly met, all round the living kingdoms.

...

Vampires, as is well known, feed on blood at night. It is not easy for them to get a meal, but if they do it is likely to be a big one. When dawn comes, some individuals will have been unlucky and return completely empty, while those individuals that have managed to find a victim are likely to have sucked a surplus of blood. On a subsequent night the luck may run the other way. So, it looks like a promising case for a bit of reciprocal altruism. Wilkinson found that those individuals who struck lucky on any one night did indeed sometimes donate blood, by regurgitation, to their less fortunate comrades. Out of 110 regurgitations dial Wilkinson witnessed, 77 could easily be understood as cases of mothers feeding their children, and many other instances of blood-sharing involved other kinds of genetic relatives. There still remained, however, some examples of blood sharing among unrelated bats, cases where the "blood is thicker than water" explanation would not fit the facts. Significantly the individuals involved here tended to be frequent roostmates—they had every opportunity to interact with one another repeatedly, as is required for an Iterated Prisoner's Dilemma. But were the other requirements for a Prisoner's Dilemma met? The payoff matrix in Figure

D is what we should expect if they were.

		What you do	
		Cooperate	Defect
What I do	Cooperate	Fairly good REWARD I get blood on my unlucky nights, which saves me from starving. I have to give blood on my lucky nights, which doesn't cost me too much	Very bad SUCKER's PAYOFF I pay the cost of saving your life on my good night. But on my bad night you don't feed me and I run a real risk of starving to death.
	Defect	Very good TEMPTATION You save my life on my poor night. But then I get the added benefit of not having to pay the slight cost of feeding you on my good night.	Fairly bad PUNISHMENT I don't have to pay the slight costs of feeding you on my good nights. But I run a real risk of starving on my poor nights.

FIGURE D. Vampire bat blood-donor scheme: payoffs to me from various outcomes

Do vampire economics really conform to this table? Wilkinson looked at the rate at which starved vampires lose weight. From this he calculated the time it would take a sated bat to starve to death, the time it would take an empty bat to starve to death, and all intermediates. This enabled him to cash out blood in the currency of hours of prolonged life. He found, not really surprisingly, that the exchange rate is different, depending upon how starved a bat is. A given amount of blood adds more hours to the life of a highly starved bat than to a less starved one. In other words, although the act of donating blood would increase the chances of the donor dying, this increase was small compared with the increase in the recipient's chances of surviving. Economically speaking, then, it seems plausible that vampire economics conform to the rules of a Prisoner's Dilemma. The blood that the donor gives up is less precious to her (social groups in vampires are female groups) than the same quantity of blood is to the recipient. On her unlucky nights she really would benefit enormously from a gift of blood. But on her lucky nights she would benefit slightly, if she could get away with it, from defecting—refusing to donate blood. "Getting away with it", of course, means something only if the bats are adopting some kind of Tit for Tat strategy. So, are the other conditions for the evolution of Tit for Tat reciprocation met?

In particular, can these bats recognize one another as individuals? Wilkinson did an experiment with captive bats, proving that they can. The basic idea was to take one bat away for a night and starve it while the others were all fed. The unfortunate starved bat was then returned to the roost, and Wilkinson watched to see who, if anyone, gave it food. The experiment was repeated many times, with the bats taking turns to be the starved victim. The key point was that this population of captive bats was a mixture of two separate groups, taken from caves many miles apart. If vampires are capable of recognizing their friends, the experimentally starved bat should turn out to be fed only by those from its own original cave.

That is pretty much what happened. Thirteen cases of donation were observed. In twelve out of these thirteen, the donor bat was an "old friend" of the starved victim, taken from the same cave; in only one out of the thirteen cases was the starved victim fed by a "new friend", not taken from the same cave. Of course this could be a coincidence but we can calculate the odds against this. They come to less than one in 500. It is pretty safe to conclude that the bats really were biased in favour of feeding old friends rather than strangers from a different cave.

Vampires are great mythmakers. To devotees of Victorian Gothic they are dark forces that terrorize by night, sapping vital fluids, sacrificing an innocent life merely to gratify a thirst. Combine this with that other Victorian myth, nature red in tooth and claw, and aren't vampires the very incarnation of deepest fears about the world of the selfish gene? As for me, I am sceptical of all myths. If we want to know where the truth lies in particular cases, we have to look. What the Darwinian corpus gives us is not detailed expectations about particular organisms. It gives us something subtler and more valuable: understanding of principle. But if we must have myths, the real facts about vampires could tell a different moral tale. To the bats themselves, not only is blood thicker than water. They rise above the bonds of kinship, forming their own lasting ties of loyal blood brotherhood. Vampires could form the vanguard of a comfortable new myth, a myth of sharing, mutualistic cooperation. They could herald the benignant idea that, even with selfish genes at the helm, nice guys can finish first.

选文出处

Clinton Richard Dawkins. *The Selfish Gene*. Oxford: Oxford University Press, 2006, pp. 202—233.

思考题

1. 利他行为是由自私的基因决定的吗？为什么？
2. 你觉得自然选择是发生在个体上，还是集体上，抑或是发生在基因上？为什么？
3. 请结合自私的基因来谈谈你生活中的"囚徒困境"和"零和博弈"。

阅读参考书目

1. 理查德·道金斯：《上帝的错觉》，陈蓉霞译，海口：海南出版社，2017年。
2. 理查德·道金斯：《盲眼钟表匠：生命自然选择的秘密》，王道还译，北京：中信出版社，2016年。
3. 理查德·道金斯：《魔鬼的牧师：关于希望、谎言、科学和爱的思考》，马岩、刘丹、齐东峰译，北京：中信出版社，2016年。

伊格尔顿

特里·伊格尔顿(Terry Eagleton)于1943年出生于英国西北部的一个海港城市索尔福德(Salford)的一个贫困工人家庭里。他的父亲信奉社会主义,曾经对他说:"我觉得耶稣基督是位社会主义者"[①]。或许是深受父亲言行的影响,或许真如伊格尔顿所说:"伊格尔顿家族有着激进的基因"[②],伊格尔顿自小就显露出非常激进的一面。他七岁时对爱尔兰的共和主义感兴趣,写下一些爱尔兰共和军歌曲。他就读教会中学时便开始阅读社会主义思想方面的书籍。他十八岁那年进入剑桥大学学习。在这所以贵族气息著称的英国高等学府里,一直在贫困、简陋,甚至受欺压环境中长大的伊格尔顿,处处觉得不自在。正如他说:"索尔福德甚至连个中产阶级都没有。虽然我没有见过统治阶级的真身,但我对他们充满深深的反感。当我还在读高中的时候,一说到统治阶级,我就会有种愤懑不平感。见到他们,只会强化我的偏见。"[③]"见到他们"就是指他进入剑桥大学以后,这里的生活环境和所接触到的人与他之前的经验完全不一样。就在落落寡欢之际,他被学校中的一位同样出身于工人家庭,名叫雷蒙德·威廉斯(Raymond Williams,1921—1988)的老师所吸引。

[①] 特里·伊格尔顿、马修·博蒙特:《批评家的任务——与特里·伊格尔顿的对话》,王杰、贾洁译,北京:北京大学出版社,2014年,第3页。
[②] 同上。
[③] 同上书,第19页。

威廉斯也是一位与剑桥的文化体制格格不入的人。他或许也是"受阶级情感的影响"①，推崇马克思主义，是一位马克思主义理论家，对社会主义运动和马克思主义思潮有着深刻而系统的研究。在他的引领下，伊格尔顿系统地阅读了有关马克思主义的书籍，并把其一生的研究目标，包括人生选择都定位在了马克思主义这个大的思想框架中。2008年前后，马克思主义在西方陷入低潮，不少西方的马克思主义研究者纷纷调整其研究策略，以便适应汹涌而来的后现代主义思潮。就在这时，伊格尔顿郑重宣布："我不把自己看作是'后马克思主义者'，我是马克思主义者。在我看来，'后马克思主义者'是指那些在某些方面保留着马克思主义、但总体上已经从马克思主义转向了其他学说的人们。"②他不愿让其学说与"后"字粘连上关系，依旧以正宗的马克思主义者身份而感到自豪。确实，伊格尔顿是西方20世纪70年代以来最令人瞩目的马克思主义文论家，与詹姆逊、哈贝马斯一起被誉为该领域中的"三巨头"。

伊格尔顿的学术生涯起始于20世纪的60年代。他是一位勤奋而高产的文学理论批评家，截至2017年，他已出版的美学理论与文学批评专著多达46部。其中，被翻译成中文的约有10余种，如《批评与意识形态》（*Criticism & Ideology*，1976）、《马克思主义与文学批评》（*Marxism and Literary Criticism*，1976）、《瓦尔特·本雅明或革命的批评》（*Walter Benjamin, or Towards a Revolutionary Criticism*，1981）、《克拉丽莎被强暴》（*The Rape of Clarissa: Writing, Sexuality, and Class Struggle in Samuel Richardson*，1982）、《文学理论引论》（*Literary Theory: An Introduction*，1983）、《审美意识形态》（*The Ideology of the Aesthetic*，1990）、《后现代主义的幻象》（*The Illusions of Postmodernism*，1996）、《甜蜜的暴力：悲剧的观念》（*Sweet Violence: The Idea of the Tragic*，2002）、《理论之后》（*After Theory*，2003）等。

以上所罗列的这些专著或多或少地都被国内的研究者涉猎过，成为国内研究和论述伊格尔顿美学思想与文学批评的理论依据。遗憾的是，出版于1984年的《批评的功能》，由于一直没有被翻译过来，故而迄今没有得到学术界的普遍关注，只有个别研究者在介绍伊格尔顿的美学思想时偶尔提及一笔。其实，这本看上去略显单薄的书，对从总体上理解伊格尔顿的文学批评理论有着重要的参考价值；往前，它承接了伊格尔顿前期美学的诸多思考；往后，它开启了伊格尔顿90年代以后的研究大门，对我们全面理解、把握伊格尔顿的美学思想、

---

① 特里·伊格尔顿、马修·博蒙特：《批评家的任务——与特里·伊格尔顿的对话》，王杰、贾洁译，北京：北京大学出版社，2014年，第19页。

② 王杰、徐方赋：《我不是后马克思主义者，我是马克思主义者》——特里·伊格尔顿访谈录》，见《文艺研究》，2008年第12期，第87页。

文学批评的发展脉络有着不可忽视的作用。

纵观《批评的功能》全书可以感觉到,伊格尔顿对以英国为代表的欧洲现代批评现状很不满意。他认为,现有的批评已经走上了非批评的道路,丧失了批评的原有功能。他把在书中所批判的"批评"分成了两大类别:商业化的批评和纯粹的学院化批评。他对其不满的原因是,前一种批评模式使批评家丧失了独立的批评立场,落入了文学产业的公共关系网中。在这个商业化市场的体系中,批评家说什么和不说什么均由"市场说了算",批评家的身份就是"雇佣写手"的身份;后一种批评模式则把文学批评放置到了"一个制度基础和职业架构上"。在伊格尔顿看来,这种放置意味着"批评最终脱离公共领域被封存起来了。批评通过政治自杀保证了自己的安全:其学术制度化的那一刻,也是其作为一个社会活动力有效消亡的那一刻"。换句话说,在他看来,文学批评作为一种批评之所以能保存下来,就是因为它借助了"学术制度化",即变成了一种"学术制度化"的批评。这种批评的特征就是,与"政治"和"社会或动力"等分裂开来,成为一门"'纯'文学理论"[1]。这是伊格尔顿所断然不可接受的,因为他一贯认为文学理论是"一个非学科"[2]。而且还始终坚持:"一切艺术都产生于某种关于世界的意识形态观念。"[3] 没有了"意识形态观念"的批评,自然算不上是批评。在对以上这两种批评展开质疑和批判的基础上,伊格尔顿提出了《批评的功能》的写作宗旨:"本书的论点即批评在今天缺乏实质性的社会功能。"

"实质性的社会功能"到底是指什么样的一种功能?商业化的批评不是,纯粹的学院派批评也不是,那么到底怎样的批评才是能体现出"实质性的社会功能"的批评?

伊格尔顿在书中没有直接回答这个问题,而是通过借用尤尔根·哈贝马斯的"公共领域"(public sphere)概念,来隐喻他言说语境中的文学批评所应该发挥出的功能。既然是"隐喻",自然说的有些含混和模糊。纵览全书,可以知道,伊格尔顿借用的这个"公共领域",就是他以往的那些理论专著中所反复提及的"意识形态"。换句话说,伊格尔顿在此孜孜以求的"实质性的社会功能",就是政治意识形态功能。事实也的确如此,正如他在书中所说的那样,"只有当'文化'成为一个紧迫的政治项目,'诗歌'成为社会生活质量的一个隐喻,语言从整体来看成为社会实践的一种典范时,批评才可能获得任何严肃的名头而存在"。显然,在他看来,真正的批评都是与"政治""社会实践"等相联系在一起的。否

---

[1] 特里·伊格尔顿:《文学原理引论》,何百华译,北京:文化艺术出版社,1987年,第229页。
[2] 特雷·伊格尔顿:《二十世纪西方文学理论》,伍晓明译,北京:北京大学出版社,2007年,第199页。
[3] 特里·伊格尔顿:《马克思主义与文学批评》,文宝译,北京:人民文学出版社,1980年,第81页。

则,批评的价值和意义就要大打折扣了。

对伊格尔顿而言,这一逻辑理路是顺理成章的。因为他一直坚守着文学批评是从属于政治意识形态这样的一个观念。他曾这样表达他的这一看法:"与其说文学理论本身就有权作为理智探究的一个对象,还不如说它是由以观察我们时代的历史的一个特殊角度。"①这话的言外之意是,文学理论本身是无权作为理智探究的对象的,它的作用就是为我们认识"时代的历史"提供一种方法。

毋庸置疑,伊格尔顿语境中的这个"实质性的社会功能",就是指文学批评对社会、政治和时代进行批判的功能。当然,该处的社会、政治和时代并非笼统地所指,而是有着特殊的含义,指无产阶级对资产阶级的取代,即倡导的是无产阶级革命政权。正是基于这一前提,他才在书中反复强调大众文化和大众文学。同样,该处的大众文化和大众文学也有着特定的价值所指,即这种文化和文学是面向广大民众的,也就是无产者阶层的——这个群体的文化程度不高,需要通俗易懂。

正是由于伊格尔顿坚定地立足于无产阶级和大众文化(文学)的立场,才致使他在书中不但对以审美为上的新批评、结构主义予以批判,就是对与其批评理论有暗合之处的解构主义也有诸多不满,斥责它是"一种理论话语而不是一种政治话语"。与此同时,他旗帜鲜明地反对纯理论、纯学术研究和自由人文主义,几乎一切不把批评与政治紧密相关联的流派、学者,都在他的抨击之内,包括艾略特、詹姆斯、福斯特以及福柯、德里达等这些大名鼎鼎的批评家,说他们是"残废的""边缘化的""自我反讽的人文主义者"和"反人文主义者"等。

从上述分析中不难看出,伊格尔顿的文学批评是建立在现实社会基础之上的,主要着眼于社会文化中的政治意识形态,体现的是一种面向群体的和大众的政治运动式的文化批评实践。这种以政治权力为核心的批评理论,优势是使文学批评,包括知识分子从封闭的书斋里投入到社会实践中去,成为社会中一股强大的力量。当然,作为一种文学批评理论而言,其弊端也是显而易见的。最大的问题是,这种把文学批评与时事政治完全契合到一起,即认为唯有"实用批评"才能与"将'生活'拒之门外的学术机构"相抗衡,进而"为精神救赎提供了一条路径"的功利化批评模式,遮蔽了文学批评功能的多样性。

诚如我们所知,无论是文学还是文学批评,其功能都应该是多样化的,伊格尔顿独尊其中的一种——政治性,而对其他的功能统统不予肯定的批评姿态,容易使文学批评,包括文学创作失去自身所固有的那种审美特性,而沦落成意识形态的传声筒。显然,假如从更高的层面要求,这种紧紧攀附着意识形态的

---

① 特雷·伊格尔顿:《二十世纪西方文学理论》,伍晓明译,北京:北京大学出版社,2007年,第170页。

批评,缺乏了一些哲学层面上思考。事实上,伊格尔顿也深知这点,伊格尔顿的文学批评就是用来解决社会生活中的具体问题的。这种问题一旦解决,它的历史作用也就完结了。

相比之下,《批评的功能》中更有价值的部分是伊格尔顿关于资本对文学生产的渗透和影响的那部分论述;特别是他所提出的"市场力量渐渐开始决定文学产品的命运"的观点,即文学创作越来越变得生产化和商品化以及批评已经被纳入文化产业,文学的评定"被置于市民社会的商品生产法则之中"的观点,对认识和评判中国当下的文学创作、文学批评以及文学出版都具有一定的参考价值与启发意义。

Preface

Perhaps I could best describe the impulse behind this book by imagining the moment in which a critic, sitting down to begin a study of some theme or author, is suddenly arrested by a set of disturbing questions. What is the point of such a study? Who is it intended to reach, influence, impress? What functions are ascribed to such a critical act by society as a whole? A critic may write with assurance as long as the critical institution itself is thought to be unproblematical. Once that institution is thrown into radical question, then one would expect individual acts of criticism to become troubled and self-doubting. The fact that such acts continue today, apparently in all their traditional confidence, is doubtless a sign that the crisis of the critical institution has either not been deeply enough registered, or is being actively evaded.

The argument of this book is that criticism today lacks all substantive social function. It is either part of the public relations branch of the literary industry, or a matter wholly internal to the academies. That this has not always been the case, and that it need not even today be the case, I try to show by a drastically selective history of the institution of criticism in England since the early eighteenth century. The guiding concept of this brief survey is that of the "public sphere", first developed by Jürgen Habermas in his *Structural Transformation of the Public Sphere* (1962). This concept has proved by no means uncontroversial: it hovers indecisively between ideal model and historical description, suffers from severe problems of historical periodization, and in Habermas's own work is not easily dissociable from a certain view of socialism which is deeply debatable. The "public sphere" is a notion difficult to rid of nostalgic, idealizing connotations; like the "organic society", it sometimes seems to have been disintegrating since its inception. It is not my intention here, however, to enter into these theoretical contentions; I am concerned rather to deploy aspects of the concept, flexibly and opportunistically, to shed light on a particular history. It goes without saying that this historical retrospect is by no means politically disinterested: I examine this history as a way of raising the question of what substantive social functions criticism might once again fulfil in our own time, beyond its crucial role of maintaining from within the academies a critique of ruling-class culture.

I must thank in particular Perry Anderson, John Barrell, Neil Belton, Norman Feltes, Toril Moi, Francis Mulhern, Graham Pechey and Bernard Sharratt, all of whom have given me valuable assistance with this book. I am also deeply indebted to the warmth and comradeship of Terry Collits and David Bennett of the University of Melbourme, in whose company I first rehearsed some of these ideas.

The Function of Criticism

I

Modern European criticism was born of a struggle against the absolutist state. Within that repressive regime, in the seventeenth and eighteenth centuries, the European bourgeoisie begins to carve out for itself a distinct discursive space, one of rational judgement and enlightened critique rather than of the brutal ukases of an authoritarian politics. Poised between state and civil society, this bourgeois "public sphere", as Jürgen Habermas has termed it, comprises a realm of social institutions—clubs, journals, coffee houses, periodicals—in which private individuals assemble for the free, equal interchange of reasonable discourse, thus welding themselves into a relatively cohesive body whose deliberations may assume the form of a powerful political force. A polite, informed public opinion pits itself against the arbitrary diktats of autocracy; within the translucent space of the public sphere it is supposedly no longer social power, privilege and tradition which confer upon individuals the title to speak and judge, but the degree to which they are constituted as discoursing subjects by sharing in a consensus of universal reason. The norms of such reason, while in their own way absolute, turn their backs upon the insolence of aristocratic authority; the rules, as Dryden remarks, are founded upon good sense, and sound reason, rather than on authority.

"In the Age of Enlightenment, writes Peter Hohendahl," "the concept of criticism cannot be separated from the institution of the public sphere. Every judgement is designed to be directed toward a public; communication with the reader is an integral part of the system. Through its relationship with the reading public, critical reflection loses its private character. Criticism opens itself to debate, it attempts to convince, it invites contradiction. It becomes a part of the public exchange of opinions. Seen historically, the modern concept of literary criticism is closely tied to the rise of the liberal, bourgeois public sphere in the early eighteenth century. Literature served the emancipation movement of the middle class as an instrument to gain self-esteem and to articulate its human demands against the absolutist state and a hierarchical society. Literary discussion, which had previously served as a form of legitimation of court society in the aristocratic salons, became an arena to pave the way for political discussion in the middle classes." This process, Hohendahl goes on to remark, happened first in England; but one should stress that, given the peculiarities of the English, the bourgeois public sphere was consolidated more in the wake of political absolutism than as a resistance to it from within. The English bourgeois public sphere of the early eighteenth century, of which Steele's *Tatler* and Addison's *Spectator* are central institutions, is indeed animated by moral correction and satiric ridicule of a licentious, socially regressive aristocracy; but its major impulse is one of class-consolidation, a codifying of the norms and regulating of the practices whereby the English bourgeoisie may negotiate an historic alliance with its social superiors. When Macaulay remarks that Joseph Addison "knew how to use ridicule without abusing it", he means in effect that Addison knew how to upbraid the traditional ruling class while keeping in with it, avoiding the divisive vituperation of a Pope or Swift. Jürgen Habermas points out that the public sphere develops earlier in England than elsewhere because the English gentry and aristocracy, traditionally involved in questions of cultural taste, also shared economic interests with the emergent mercantile class, unlike, say, their French counterparts. The intimacy of cultural, political and economic preoccupations is thus more marked in England than elsewhere. The hallmark of the English public sphere is its consensual character: the *Tatler* and *Spectator* are catalysts in the creation of a new ruling bloc in English society, cultivating the mercantile class and uplifting the profligate aristocracy. The single daily or thrice-weekly sheets of these journals, with their hundreds of lesser imitators, bear witness to the birth of a new discursive formation in post-Restoration England—an intensive intercourse of class-values which "fuse(d) the best qualities of Puritan and Cavalier" (A. J. Beljame) and fashioned "an idiom for common standards of taste and conduct" (Q. D. Leavis). Samuel Johnson was to trace this ideological osmosis in Addison's very literary style, "familiar, but not coarse" as he found it. The moderate Whiggism of Addison and Steele, the unbuttoned, affably non-sectarian quality of a politics which could indulge the backwoods Tory Sir Roger de Coverley even as it admired the Whig merchant Sir Andrew Freeport, underlay this cultural consensus. Addison himself had both city investments and a country estate, reconciling landed and monied interests in his own person; he was, according to one of his commentators, "his party's most eloquent apologist for English mercantile success and the Exchange", but the Spectator club is deliberately designed to reflect all respectable social ranks (*Spectator* 34). Addison, Beljame effuses, "fixed his eyes not on the Court alone, but on society as a whole, and he sought to open Everyman's eyes to literature; better still, to open his mind, form his judgement, teach him to think and provide him with general ideas on art and life. He made it his business to conduct a course on literature and aesthetics." What will help to unify the English ruling bloc, in short, is culture; and the critic is the chief bearer of this historic task.

One might claim, then, that modern criticism in England was born ironically of political consensus. It is not, of course, that the eighteenth century was any stranger to strife and rancour, or that we should imagine the bourgeois public sphere as an organic society of universal agreement. But the ferocious contentions of essayists and pamphleteers took place within the gradual crystallization of an increasingly self-confident ruling bloc in English society, which defined the limits of the acceptably sayable. Leslie Stephen contrasts the oppositional character of such French eighteenth-century men of letters as Voltaire and Rousseau with such critics as Samuel Johnson, who largely shared and articulated the views of the public for whom they wrote. This, indeed, is the irony of Enlightenment criticism, that while its appeal to standards of universal reason signifies a resistance to absolutism, the critical gesture itself is typically conservative and corrective, revising and adjusting particular phenomena to its implacable model of discourse. Criticism is a reformative apparatus, scourging deviation and repressing the transgressive; yet this juridical technology is deployed in the name of a certain historical emancipation. The classical public sphere involves a discursive reorganization of social power, redrawing the boundaries between social classes as divisions between those who engage in rational argument, and those who do not. The sphere of cultural discourse and the realm of social power are closely related but not homologous: the former cuts across and suspends the distinctions of the latter, deconstructing and reconstituting it in a new form, temporarily transposing its "vertical" gradations onto a "horizontal" plane. In principle, Hohendahl comments, "social privileges were not acknowledged whenever private citizens gathered together as a public body. In the reading societies and clubs, status was suspended so that a discussion among equals could take place. Authoritarian, aristocratic art judgements were replaced by a discourse among educated laymen." A new cultural formation is mapped on to the traditional power-structure of English society, momentarily dissolving its distinctions in order the more thoroughly to buttress its hegemony. In the coffee houses of eighteenth-century England (and there were over three thousand of them in London alone), "the writers rubbed shoulders, in an egalitarian context, with their patrons, whether they were noblemen or squires or parsons or merchants or professional men... It is a mark of the literary societies of the age that membership was entirely heterogeneous, including politicians, diplomats, lawyers, theologians, scientists, physicians, surgeons, actors, and so on, besides the poets and other writers." "The coffee houses," Beljame writes, "provided rallying points. People met, exchanged opinions, formed groups, gathered number. It was through them, in short, that a public opinion began to evolve, which thereafter had to be reckoned with." Addison, according to his Victorian biographer, was the "chief architect of Public Opinion in the eighteenth century". Discourse becomes a political force: "The spread of general culture in every direction," remarks the enraptured Beljame, "united all classes of society. Readers were no longer segregated into water-tight compartments of Puritan and Cavalier, Court and City, the metropolis and province: *all the English were now readers.*" He exaggerates a little, no doubt: the Spectator sold around three thousand copies in a total population of some five and a half million, the book-buying public of the time can be measured in tens of thousands, and a great many of the English were illiterate or barely literate. It does not seem that the emulsive space of the public sphere extended beyond parsons and surgeons to farm labourers or domestic servants, despite Defoe's surely exaggerated claim that "you'll find very few Coffee-houses in this opulent City(London), without an illiterate Mechanick, Commenting upon the most material Occurrences, and Judging the Actions of the greatest in Europe, and rarely a Victualing House but you meet with a *Tinker*, *a Cobbler*, or a *Porter*, Criticizing upon the Speeches of Majesty, or the writings of the most celebrated Men of the Age." Nevertheless, Beljame has in his own way grasped the essential point: what is at stake, in this ceaseless circulation of polite discourse among rational subjects, is the cementing of a new power bloc at the level of the sign. The "advocating of good Literature in the World", according to John Clarke, "is not only highly subservient to the Ends of Religion and Virtue, but likewise to those of Good Policy and Civil Government." "Promotion of good Taste in poetical Compositions," wrote Thomas Cooke, "is the Promotion likewise of good Manners. Nothing can more nearly concern a State than the Encouragement of good Writers."

What is spoken or written, within this rational space, pays due deference to the niceties of class and rank; but the speech act itself, the *énonciation* as opposed to the *énoncé*, figures in its very form an equality, autonomy and reciprocity at odds with its class-bound content. The very act of utterance discloses a quasi-transcendental community of subjects, a universal model of rational exchange, which threatens to contradict the hierarchies and exclusions of which it speaks. The public sphere in some sense resolves the contradictions of mercantile society by boldly inverting its terms: if what is embarrassing for bourgeois liberal theory is the process by which an abstract equality at the level of natural rights becomes transmuted into a system of actual differential rights, the bourgeois public sphere will take those differential rights as its starting-point and convert them back, in the region of discourse, to an abstract equality. The truly free market is that of cultural discourse itself, within, of course, certain normative regulations; the role of the critic is to adminster those norms, in a double refusal of absolutism and anarchy. What is said derives its legitimacy neither from itself as message nor from the social title of the utterer, but from its conformity as a statement with a certain paradigm of reason inscribed in the very event of saying. One's title as a speaker is derived from the formal character of one's discourse, rather than the authority of that discourse derived from one's social title. Discursive identities are not pre-given, but constructed by the very act of participation in polite conversation; and this, one might claim, is to some degree at odds with Lockeian wisdom, for which pre-established propertied subjects then enter into contractual relations with one another. The public sphere, by contrast, acknowledges no given rational identity beyond its own bounds, for what counts as rationality is precisely the capacity to articulate within its constraints; the rational are those capable of a certain mode of discourse, but this cannot be judged other than in the act of deploying it. To collaborate in the public sphere thus becomes the criterion of one's right to do so, though it is of course inconceivable that those without property without, in the eighteenth-century sense, an "interest" could participate in this realm. It is not, however, that the public sphere exists for the direct discussion of those interests; on the contrary, such interests become its very concealed problematic, the very enabling structure of its disinterested enquiry. Only those with an interest can be disinterested. Shadowing all particular utterances within this space, delivered inseparably along with them as the very guarantee of their authority, is the form and event of universal reason itself, ceaselessly reproduced in a style of enunciation and exchange which rises above and sits in judgement upon the partial, local messages it communicates. All utterances thus move within a regime which raises them at the very point of production to universal status, inscribes within them a legitimacy which neither wholly pre-exists the particular statement nor is exactly reducible to it, but which, like the elusive concept of "capacity", is at once identical with and in excess of whatever is spoken. The very rule-governed form of utterance and exchange is what regulates the relation between individual statements and the discursive formation as a whole; and this form is neither extermally imposed by some extrinsic centre, as the state might regulate commodity production, nor wholly organic to the statement itself. The bourgeoisie thus discovers in discourse an idealized image of its own social relations: the "Literati of the Country", D'Israeli remarks in his *Periodical Essays* (1780), "are set of independent *Free Burghers*, among whom there is a natural and political equality." It is not for nothing that Goldsmith noted the significance of the phrase "republic of letters"; for what could better correspond to the bourgeoisie's dream of freedom than a society of petty producers whose endlessly available, utterly inexhaustible commodity is discourse itself, equitably exchanged in a mode which reconfirms the autonomy of each producer? Only in this ideal discursive sphere is exchange without domination possible; for to persuade is not to dominate, and to carry one's opinion is more an act of collaboration than of competition. Circulation can proceed here without a breath of exploitation, for there are no subordinate social classes within the public sphere—indeed in principle, as we have seen, no social classes at all. What is at stake in the public sphere, according to its own ideological self-image, is not power but reason. Truth, not authority, is its ground, and rationality, not domination, its daily currency. It is on this radical dissociation of politics and knowledge that its entire discourse is founded; and it is when this dissociation becomes less plausible that the public sphere will begin to crumble.

The periodicals of the early eighteenth century were a primary constituent of the emergent bourgeois public sphere. They were, as A. S. Collins writes, "a very powerful educative influence, affecting politics as well by the formation of a broad, national public opinion". Jane Jack views the periodicals, with their "high-class popularization", as the dominant literary form of the first half of the century, and Leslie Stephen described them as "the most successful innovation of the day". The *Tatler* and *Spectator* marked a qualitative development from what had come before: "A number of earlier periodicals," reports Richard P. Bond, "had been heavily committed tolearmed works, using abstracts and extracts more than original criticism, and a few papers had admitted bellelettristic features, but no journal had attempted to elevate taste by giving large attention to the arts, mainly literary, in a way both serious and genial. The *Tatler* was the first English periodical to do this." It was still not, of course, "professional" criticism in the modern sense. Steele's own literary comments are ad hoc and impressionistic, lacking any theoretical structure or goverming principles; Addison is somewhat more analytical, but his criticism, like his thought in general, is essentially empiricist and affective in the mould of Hobbes and Locke, concerned with the pragmatic psychological effect of literary works— does this please, and how? —rather than with more technical or theoretical questions. Literary criticism as a whole, at this point, is not yet an autonomous specialist discourse, even though more technical forms of it exist; it is rather one sector of a general ethical humanism, indissociable from moral, cultural and religious reflection. The *Tatler* and *Spectator* are projects of a bourgeois cultural politics whose capacious, blandly homogenizing language is able to encompass art, ethics, religion, philosophy and everyday life; there is here no question of a "literary critical" response which is not wholly determined by an entire social and cultural ideology. Criticism here is not yet "literary" but "cultural": the examination of literary texts is one relatively marginal moment of a broader enterprise which explores attitudes to servants and the rules of gallantry, the status of women and familial affections, the purity of the English language, the character of conjugal love, the psychology of the sentiments and the laws of the toilet. A parallel range is discernibe in Defoe's contemporaneous, vastly influential *Review*, the "first eminent essay periodical in England to treat politics, economics, ecclesiastical, social and ethical themes". The critic, as cultural strategist rather than literary expert, must resist specialization: The Truth of it is, "Addison remarks in *Spectator* 291, 'there is nothing more absurd, than for a Man to set himself up as a

Critick, without a good Insight into all the Parts of Learning..." The polite is at war with the pedantic: though Addison was an enthusiast for scientific experiment and the new philosophy, he espoused such pursuits only because he considered them fit study for a gentleman. The critic as cultural commentator acknowledges no inviolable boundary between one idiom and another, one field of social practice and the next; his role is to ramble or idle among them all, testing each against the norms of that general humanism of which he is the bearer. The flexible, heterogeneous forms of the magazine and periodical reflect this relaxed capaciousness: fictional and non-fictional materials equably co-exist, moral essays slip easily into anecdote and allegory, and the collaboration of the readership is actively solicited in the writing. (In danger of running out of material, Steele at one point warns his audience that unless they write in the journal, it will have to close.) The frontiers between literary genres, as between authors and readers, or genuine and fictitious correspondents, are comfortably indeterminate; the *Tatler* and *Spectator* are themselves complex refinements and recyclings of previous periodical forms, borrowing a device here, polishing or discarding a style there, artfully recombining elements from a number of discrete sources. The digest or abstract of learned books carried for busy readers by some seventeenth-century periodicals(the earliest "literary criticism" in England, no doubt) has now become elaborated into the full-blown literary critical essay; the bawdy and doggerel of such earlier publications is soberly expunged, but their efforts to disseminate knowledge become in the hands of Addison and Steele a more obliquely informative portrayal of the *beau monde*. The collaborative gambits of such influential journals as John Dunton's *Athenian Mercury*, supplying quasi-scientific answers to readers' inquiries, are modulated to the inclusion of readers' real or fictive correspondence. The seventeenth-century popular press's canny responsiveness to audience demand, feeding its appetite for scientific knowledge, moral solace and social orientation, is preserved, but sublimed to a sophisticated idiom which flatters its readers' *savoir faire* even as it fosters it. Writer and reader, fact and fiction, documentation and didacticism, suavity and sobriety:a single, scrupulously standardised language is constructed to articulate all of these together, blurring the boundaries between production and consumption, reflection and reportage, moral theory and social practice. What emerges from this melting pot of literary sub-genres, class styles and ideological motifs is a new brand of cultural politics, at once broadly dispersed, instantly available and socially closed.

The critic as *flâneur* or *bricoleur*, rambling and idling among diverse social landscapes where he is everywhere at home, is still the critic as judge; but such judgement should not be mistaken for the censorious verdicts of an Olympian authority. "It is a particular Observation I have always made," writes Steele in *Tatler* 29, "That of all Mortals, a Critick is the silliest; for by inuring himself to examine all Things, whether they are of Consequence or not, he never looks upon any Thing but with a Design of passing Sentence upon it; by which means, he is never a Companion, but always a Censor... A thorough Critick is a Sort of Puritan in the polite World..." The very act of criticism, in short, poses a pressing ideological problem: for how is one to criticize without lapsing into exactly that sullen sectarianism which has lain waste the English social order, and which it is part of Steele's project genially to reform? How can the ineluctably negative movement of criticism celebrate an ideological compact with the object of its disapprobation? The very business of criticism, with its minatory overtones of conflict and dissension, offers to disrupt the consensualism of the public sphere; and the critic himself, who stands at the nub of that sphere's great circuits of exchange, disseminating, gathering in and recirculating its discourse, represents a potentially fractious element within it. Steele's comforting response to this dilemma is "companionship": the critic is less the castigator of his fellows than their clubbable, co-discoursing equal, spokesman rather than scourge. As passing symbolic representative of the public realm, the merefold of its self-knowledge, he must chide and correct from within a primordial social pact with his readership, laying claim to no status or subject position which is not spontaneously precipitated by those intimate social elations.

Periodical literature, William Hazlitt remarks, is "in morals and manners what the experimental is in natural philosophy, as opposed to the dogmatical method." The distinctive tones of the *Tatler* and *Spectator*, light, eirenic and urbane at the very point of satiric ridicule, are the sign of this solution. "In principle," writes Hohendahl, "everyone has a basic judgemental capacity, although individual circumstances may cause each person to develop that capacity to a different degree. This means that everyone is called upon to participate in criticism; it is not the privilege of a certain social class or professional clique. It follows that the critic, even a professional one, is merely a speaker from the general audience and formulates ideas that could be thought by anyone. His special task vis-à-vis the public is to conduct the general discussion." Pope treated the same problem a little more succinctly: "Men must be taught as if you taught them not, And things unknown propos'd as things forgot"(Essay on Criticism). What makes criticism's tacit assumption of superiority tolerable, as what makes the accumulation of power and property tolerable, is the fact that all men possess the capacity for it. If such a capacity involves the most civilized skills, it is also incurably amateur: criticism belongs with a traditional English conception of gentility which troubles the distinction between innate and acquired, art and Nature, specialist and spontaneous. Such amateurism is not ignorance or half-capacity, but the casual polymorphous expertise of one to whom no sector of cultural life is alien—who passes from writer to reader, moralist to mercantilist, Tory to Whig and back, offering himself as little more than the vacant space within which these diverse elements may congregate and interbreed. The drawing together of writer and reader, critic and citizen, multiple literary modes and dispersed realms of enquiry, all folded into a language at once mannerly and pellucid, is the mark of a non-specialism which is perhaps only in part intelligible to us today, predating as it does that intellectual division of labour to which our own amateurisms are inevitably reactive. The critic, anyway, as functionary, mediator, chairperson, locus of languages he receives rather than invents; the *Spectator*, as T. H. Green remarked, as a kind of literature which "consists in talking to the public about itself", and the critic as the mirror in which this fascinated self-imaging takes shape. Regulator and dispensor of a general humanism, guardian and instructor of public taste, the critic must fulfil these tasks from within a more fundamental responsibility as reporter and informer, a mere mechanism or occasion by which the public may enter into deeper imaginary unity with itself. The *Tatler* and *Spectator* are consciously educating a socially heterogeneous public into the universal forms of reason, taste and morality, but their judgements are not to be whimsically authoritarian, the diktats of a technocratic caste.

On the contrary, they must be moulded and constrained from within by the very public consensus they seek to nurture. The critic is not in our sense an intellectual: in the eighteenth century, as Richard Rorty comments, "there were witty men and learned men and pious men, but there were no highbrows". If, like the silent Mr. Spectator, the critic stands a little apart from the bustle of the metropolis, this is no mark of alienation: it is only so as the more keenly to observe, and so the more effectively to report what he learns of that world to its more preoccupied participants. Valid critical judgement is the fruit not of spiritual dissociation but of an energetic collusion with everyday life. It is in intimate empirical engagement with the social text of early-bourgeois England that modern criticism first makes its a ppearance; and the line from this vigorous empiricism to F. R. Leavis, along which such criticism will at a certain point mutate into the "literary", remains relatively unbroken.

Such "spontaneous" engagements were made possible only by a peculiarly close interaction between the cultural, political and economic. The early eighteenth-century coffee houses were not only forums where, as one commentator puts it, "a sort of communal reading became the rage"; they were also nubs of finance and insurance, where the stockjobbers set up in business and the South Sea Bubble débacle was to reach its climax. In the clubs based on these ambivalently cultural and pragmatic institutions, what Leslie Stephen calls a "characteristic fraternization of the politicians and the authors" was daily current. Such men, Stephen notes, would congregate at the coffee houses "in a kind of tacit confederation of clubs to compare notes and form the whole public opinion of the day". "Cultural" and political idioms continuously interpenetrated: Addison himself was a functionary of the state apparatus as well as a journalist, and Steele also held government office. Relations between the literary and political castes were probably closer than at any other point in modern English history, and Thomas Macaulay suggests one plausible reason why this was so. In the early eighteenth century, before the advent of free parliamentary reporting, the effects of parliamentary oratory were limited to its immediate audience; to disseminate ideas beyond this forum thus demanded that intensive political polemicizing and pamphleteering which absorbs so much of the period's literary production. "It may well be doubted," Macaulay comments, "whether St John did so much for the Tories as Swift and whether Cowper did so much for the Whigs as Addison." If the *Tatler* and *Spectator* are not themselves especially "political", the cultural project they represent could nevertheless be sustained only through a close traffic with political power; and if they were not especially political, it is in part because, as I have argued, what the political moment demanded was precisely "cultural".

"Addison," writes Macaulay in a celebrated comment, "reconciled wit with virtue, after a long and disastrous separation, during which wit had been led astray by profligacy and virtue by fanaticism." The names of Addison and Steele signify the very essence of English compromise: that adroit blending of grace and *gravitas*, urbanity and morality, correction and consolidation could not fail to seduce a later bourgeois intelligentsia, now spiritually severed from the industrial capitalism which had produced them. To return in spirit to a *pre-industrial* bourgeoisie, whose moral fervour has not yet been struck leaden by industrial philistinism, and which sounds the aristocratic note at the same time as it refuses its frivolity: such a fantasy solution, one suspects, would probably have been invented if it had not been historically available. "There is nothing here as yet," comment Legouis and Cazamian, "of that Philistinism with which the English middle classes will be charged later, and not without some reason." In these early periodicalists, English criticism is able to glimpse its own glorious origins, seize the fragile moment at which the bourgeoisie entered into respectability before passing out of it again. Most literary critics, Raymond Williams once remarked, are natural cavaliers; but since most of them are also products of the middle class, the image of Addison and Steele allows them to indulge their antibourgeois animus on gratifyingly familiar, impeccably "moral" terrain. If Addison and Steele mark the moment of bourgeois respectability, they also signify the point at which the hitherto disreputable genre of journalism becomes legitimate. Previous periodicals, writes Walter Graham, "suffered from the ills of partisan truculence, rampant sectarianism, crude taste, and personal rancour... Thanks to Addison and Steele, the 'literary' periodical becomes respectable, and with essay writing, journalism begins to lose its stigma." The respite from sectarian truculence—one which, as we shall see, was destined to be brief—is identical with the rebirth of the periodical as Literature: it is when writing succeeds in transmuting the sordidly political into "style", replacing rancour with reconciliation, that it qualifies for the canon. It is for this reason that the eighteenth-century Tory satirists have often proved something of an embarrassment, in their "extremist" violence, to the later custodians of the literary: are not Swift's prose and *The Dunciad* marred as artefacts by their pathological spleen? The literary is the vanishing point of the political, its dissolution and reconstitution into polite letters. The irony of such a judgement on the eighteenth century is surely plain: the transition from sectarian polemic to cultural consensus which marks the polite periodicals is precisely their most politically essential function.

In the early eighteenth century, then, the bourgeois principle of abstract free and equal exchange is elevated from the market-place to the sphere of discourse, to mystify and idealize real bourgeois social relations. The petty proprietors of a commodity known as "opinion" assemble together for its regulated interchange, at once miming in purer, non-dominative form the exchanges of bourgeois economy, and contributing to the political apparatus which sustains it. The public sphere thereby constructed is at once universal and class-specific: all may in principle participate in it, but only because the class-determined criteria of what counts as significant participation are always unlodgeably in place. The currency of this realm is neither title nor property but rationality—a rationality in fact articulable only by those with the social interests which property generates. But because that rationality is not the possession of a single class within the hegemonic social bloc—because it is the product of an intensive conversation *between* those dominant classes, a discourse for which the *Tatler* and *Spectator* are particular names—it is possible to view it as universal, and hence to prise the definition of the gentleman free of any too rigidly genetic or class-specific determinants. The possession of power and property inserts you into certain forms of polite discourse, but that discourse is by no means merely instrumental to the furtherance of material ends. On the contrary, the communication into which you enter with your equally propertied interlocutors is in an important sense "phatic": a deployment of the appropriate forms and conventions of discourse which has as its goal nothing more than the delightful exercise of taste and reason. Culture, in this sense, is autonomous of material interests; where it interlocks with them is visible in the very form of the discursive community itself, in the freedom, autonomy and equality of the speech acts appropriate to bourgeois subjects.

 选文出处

Terry Eagleton. *The Function of Criticism*. New York: Verso Books, 2005, pp. 9—27.

思考题

1. 你是怎样理解文学批评多样化的?
2. 你是怎样理解"公共领域"在文学批评中的作用的?
3. 在现阶段,资本是如何渗透和影响文学生产的?

参考书目

1. Terry Eagleton, *After Theory*, Londan: Penguin Books, 2003.
2. Terry Eagleton and Matthew Beaumont, *The Task of the Critic: Terry Eagleton in Dialogue*, London: Verso, 2009.
3. Harold Bloom, *The Anxiety of Influence*, Oxford: Oxford University Press, 1973.

达马西奥

安东尼奥·达马西奥（Antonio Damasio,1944—　）现为美国南加州大学神经科学教授、脑与创造力研究中心主任。达马西奥曾在葡萄牙的里斯本大学医学院就读并完成博士学业。作为神经科学家,达马西奥致力于探究情感、感觉与意识在大脑运作中所起的作用。他的研究阐明了情感在人类决策中起的重要作用,对身心二元论提出质疑,给神经科学、心理学和哲学领域带来了深刻的影响和启示。达马西奥的作品并非抽象术语和研究数据的堆砌,而是利用富有文学性的文字对人类的日常关切以及经久不衰的哲学问题做出实证的解答,颠覆了以往哲学家们对于身体、心灵与决策的认知。人类的推理从何而来？自我意识如何产生？我们的情感有何意义？如何实现更好的生存？达马西奥将从神经科学的视角对这些问题做出解答。

达马西奥著述颇丰,主要包括《笛卡尔的错误:情绪、推理和人脑》(*Descartes' Error*：*Emotion，Reason and the Human Brain*)、《感受发生的一切:意识产生中的身体和情绪》(*The Feeling of What Happens*：*Body and Emotion in the Making Of Consciousness*)、《寻找斯宾诺莎:快乐、悲伤和感受着的脑》(*Looking for Spinoza*：*Joy，Sorrow，and the Feeling Brain*)、《当自我来敲门:构建意识大脑》(*Self Comes to Mind*：*Constructing the Conscious Brain*)等。

《笛卡尔的错误》是达马西奥的代表作,主要阐述了情绪对于决策以及社会行为的意义。法国哲学家笛卡尔是唯心主义哲学观的代表人物,强调人的主体性与身心二元论。笛卡尔认为身体拥有运动的特性,但是却是被动的,而精神代表了纯粹的思维,是主动的。笛卡尔与康德皆认为人类依靠理性做出最佳决策,理性决策须将情绪排除在外。《笛卡尔的错误》一书否定了二人的观点,认为理性本身存在诸多缺陷,并且重新审视了情感的作用。该书颠覆了身心二元论以及与之相关的理性情感二元论,阐明了三个有力的观点:情绪与推理网络相互交织;情绪和感受是生物的调节机制;身体是脑形成表征的基础。书中提出了著名的"躯体标识器假设"(Somatic-marker Hypothesis),指出人的推理过程是理性和情绪相互交织的。所谓"躯体标识器"就是内脏和非内脏感受,它迫使人们将注意力集中在某种选择可能带来的风险,并且做出相应的躯体反应。例如,在决策的过程中,当某个不利结果出现在脑海时,我们会即刻体验到非常不愉快的内脏感受,这便是来自躯体标识器的信号,它对我们的决策至关重要。那我们的躯体标识器又来自何处?达马西奥认为,人类天生具有相关的神经机制,可以对某些刺激产生躯体反应。同时,这一机制也需要通过后天的学习和文化逐渐完善。这便意味着如果大脑或者后天的文化存在缺陷,躯体标识器便无法健康形成,导致人们无法做出良好的决策,甚至形成反社会人格与精神疾病。

为了更好地论述他的观点,达马西奥在《笛卡尔的错误》一书中介绍了铁路工人盖奇的案例。1848年的夏天,25岁的铁路工人盖奇在爆破行动中遭遇意外,一根铁棒从他脑部穿过。他虽然奇迹般地活了下来,但这一事故带来的脑部损伤使他性情大变。原本平和友好的他变得喜怒无常,最后悲惨地度过余生。神经科学家们对死去的盖奇的颅骨进行研究,发现"盖奇的前额叶皮层的选择性损伤破坏了他计划未来的能力、遵循既已习得的社会规则做出行为的能力,以及根据自己最终生存利益进行最有利的行动选择的能力"[1]。但是,从事故发生到郁郁而终,盖奇的心理究竟是如何运作的则随着盖奇的逝去永远无法得到解答。为了更好地认识这一点,达马西奥对"现代的盖奇们",即与盖奇有着相似病症的人们进行了研究,并在书中的第三章"一个现代的菲尼亚斯·盖奇"阐述了其研究成果。

在这一章中,达马西奥研究了一个与盖奇一样由于前额叶损伤导致人格转变的病人埃利奥特。埃利奥特曾经是个模范同事和模范丈夫,拥有令人艳羡的家庭生活和社会地位。但自从患上脑瘤后,他性情大变。虽然肿瘤以及被损伤的前额叶组织被成功切除,但他的性格也随之发生了剧变。他因此失去工作、家庭破裂。埃利奥特就是现代的盖奇,经历了脑损伤之后,再也无法做出对自

---

[1] 达马西奥:《笛卡尔的错误:情绪、推理和人脑》,毛彩凤译,北京:教育科学出版社,2007年,第33页。

身有利的决策。但是埃利奥特并非疯癫之人,达马西奥与之交谈发现他智力正常,"是一个令人感到愉快和有趣的人,非常有魅力,从容不迫"①。大量的测验证明埃利奥特拥有完善的理智,甚至智商偏高,但他却为何无法做出有利的决策?达马西奥转而观察他的情绪,发现了症结所在——他的情绪过于镇定,可以超然平静地叙述自己的悲惨遭遇,如同一名旁观者。在心理实验中,面对具有强烈视觉刺激的图片,如地震坍塌建筑的图片和鲜血淋漓的伤者的图片时,埃利奥特也无法产生任何正面或负面的情绪。达马西奥将这样的情况归结为"知道但没有感受到"②,并指出衰减的情绪和感受在埃利奥特的决策失败中扮演了至关重要的角色。为了佐证这一观点,达马西奥对埃利奥特进行了大量的测验以排除可能存在的理智缺陷。实验证明,埃利奥特仍然具备相关的社会行为知识,并且推理机制正常,但就是无法生成良好的决策。达马西奥总结了盖奇和埃利奥特的相似之处,即都具有正常的社会知识和推理能力,但是出现了社会行为缺陷和决策失败,并依此提出了一个想法——不健全的情绪造成了这一系列的问题。

在后续的章节中,达马西奥肯定了情感在决策中的重要作用,同时也指出情感对决策的作用有利有弊。冷静的推理需要情感的参与,但是某些躯体信号引起的过度情感反应也可能会降低推理的质量。毫无疑问,达马西奥在探索理性与情感的属性上开辟了一条以神经生物学为基础的入口。达马希奥对以笛卡尔与康德为代表的理性主义提出质疑的同时,与大卫·休谟的观点不谋而合。休谟认为道德来源于情感——德行使人产生愉快的感觉,恶行令人感到不快。这一研究无疑是对以往哲学思想的巨大挑战,从实证科学的视角重新审视了理性主义和经验主义哲学。达马西奥的研究同样指向人类的现实关切。他认为,笛卡尔的错误在于他在身体和心灵之间划定了一条鸿沟,没有认识到身体与心灵之间互相影响和作用的复杂关系。对于理性的高度推崇,使人们无法意识到隐含在身体和情绪中的利弊因素。人类的身体并不是被动的、机械的存在,而是我们的精神家园,对我们的生存和福祉影响颇深。有时候人的悲剧就是来自个体生物机制上的缺陷。如果我们无法意识到隐含在我们有机体里的悲剧性因素,"就很少会想到如何将其最小化,从而对生命的价值也不那么尊重"③。

---

① 达马西奥:《笛卡尔的错误:情绪、推理和人脑》,毛彩凤译,北京:教育科学出版社,2007年,第34页。
② 同上书,第42页。
③ 同上书,第194页。

A Modern Phineas Gage

A NEW MIND

I remember being impressed by Elliot's intellectual soundness, but I remember also thinking that other patients with frontal lobe damage seemed sound when they had in fact subtle changes in intellect, detectable only by special neuropsychological tests. Their altered behavior often had been attributed to defects in memory or attention. Elliot would disabuse me of that notion.

He had been evaluated previously at another institution where the opinion had been that there was no evidence of "organic brain syndrome." In other words, he showed no sign of impairment when he was given standard intelligence tests. His intelligence quotient (the so-called IQ) was in the superior range, and his standing on the Wechsler Adult Intelligence Scale indicated no abnormality. His problems were found not to result from "organic disease" or "neurological dysfunction"—in other words, brain disease—but instead to reflect "emotional" and "psychological" adjustment problems—in other words, mental trouble—and would be thus amenable to psychotherapy. Only after a series of therapy sessions proved unsuccessful was Elliot referred to our unit. (The distinction between diseases of "brain" and "mind," between "neurological" problems and "psychological" or "psychiatric" ones, is an unfortunate cultural inheritance that permeates society and medicine. It reflects a basic ignorance of the relation between brain and mind. Diseases of the brain are seen as tragedies visited on people who cannot be blamed for their condition, while diseases of the mind, especially those that affect conduct and emotion, are seen as social inconveniences for which sufferers have much to answer. Individuals are to be blamed for their character flaws, defective emotional modulation, and so on; lack of willpower is supposed to be the primary problem.

The reader may well ask whether the previous medical evaluation was in error. Is it conceivable that somebody as impaired as Elliot would perform well on psychological tests? In fact it is: patients with marked abnormalities of social behavior can perform normally on many and even most intelligence tests, and clinicians and investigators have struggled for decades with this frustrating reality. There may be brain disease, but laboratory tests fail to measure significant impairments. The problem here lies with the tests, not with the patients. The tests simply do not address properly the particular functions that are compromised and thus fail to measure any decline. Knowing of Elliot's condition and his lesion, I predicted that he would be found normal on most psychological tests but abnormal on a small number of tests which are sensitive to malfunction in frontal cortices. As you will see, Elliot would surprise me.

The standardized psychological and neuropsychological tests revealed a superior intellect.① On every subtest of the Wechsler Adult Intelligence Scale, Elliot showed abilities that were either superior or average. His immediate memory for digits was superior, as were his short-term verbal memory and visual memory for geometric designs. His delayed recall of Rey's word list and complex figures were in the normal range. His performance on the Multilingual Aphasia Examination, a battery of tests which assesses various aspects of language comprehension and production, was normal. His visual perception and construction skills were normal on Benton's standardized tests of facial discrimination, judgment of line orientation, tests of geographic orientation, and two- and three-dimensional block construction. The copy of the Rey-Osterrieth complex figure was also normal.

Elliot performed normally on memory tests employing interference procedures. One test involved the recall of consonant trigrams after three-, nine-, and eighteen-second delays, with the distraction of counting backward; another, the recall of items after a fifteen-second delay spent in calculations. Most patients with frontal lobe damage test abnormally; Elliot performed well in both tasks, with 100 and 95 percent accuracy, respectively.

---

① 在此节中提及的许多神经心理测试在以下文献中可以找到: M. Lezak, *Neuropsychological Assessment*, New York: Oxford University Press; and A. L., Benton, *Contributions to Neuropsychological Assessment*, New York: Oxford University Press.

In short, perceptual ability, past memory, short-term memory, new learning, language, and the ability to do arithmetic were intact. Attention, the ability to focus on a particular mental content to the exclusion of others, was also intact; and so was working memory, which is the ability to hold information in mind over a period of many seconds and to operate on it mentally. Working memory is usually tested in the domains of words or numbers, objects or their features. For example, after being told of a telephone number, the subject will be asked to repeat it immediately afterward in backward direction, skipping the odd digits.

My prediction that Elliot would fail on tests known to detect frontal lobe dysfunction was not correct. He turned out to be so intact intellectually that even the special tests were a breeze for him. The task to be given was the Wisconsin Card Sorting Test, the workhorse of the small group of so-called frontal lobe tests, which involves sorting through a long series of cards whose face image can be categorized according to color (e. g. , red or green), shape (stars, circles, squares), and number (one, two, or three elements). When the examiner shifts the criterion according to which the subject is sorting, the subject must realize the change quickly and switch to the new criterion. In the 1960s the psychologist Brenda Milner showed that patients with damage to prefrontal cortices often are impaired in this task, and this finding has been confirmed repeatedly by other investigators.① Patients tend to stick to one criterion rather than shift gears appropriately. Elliot achieved six categories in seventy sorts—something that most patients with frontal lobe damage cannot do. He sailed through the task, seemingly no different from unimpaired people. Through the years he has maintained this type of performance on the Wisconsin test and on comparable tasks. Implicit in Elliot's normal performance in this test are the ability to attend and operate on a working memory, as well as an essential logical competence and the ability to change mental set.

The ability to make estimates on the basis of incomplete knowledge is another index of superior intellectual function that is often compromised in

---

① B. Milner, Some Effects of Frontal Lobectomy in Man, in J. M. Warren and K. Akert, eds. , *The Frontal Granular Cortex and Behavior*, New York: McGraw-Hill.

patients with frontal lobe damage. Two researchers, Tim Shallice and M. Evans, have devised a task to assess this ability consisting of questions for which you will not have a precise answer (unless, perhaps, you are a collector of trivia), and which can be answered only by conjuring up a variety of unconnected facts, and operating on them with logical competence so as to arrive at a valid inference.① Imagine being asked, for example, how many giraffes there are in New York City, or how many elephants in the state of Iowa. You must consider that neither species is indigenous to North America, and that zoos and wild life parks are thus the only place where they can be found; you must also consider the overall map of New York City or the state of Iowa, and plot how many such facilities are likely to exist in each space; and from another bank of your knowledge you may estimate the probable number of giraffes and elephants in each such facility; and eventually add it all up and come up with a number. (I hope you answer with a reasonable ballpark figure; but I would be surprised—and worried—if you know the exact number). In essence you have to generate an acceptable estimate based on bits and pieces of unrelated knowledge; and you must have normal logical competence, normal attention, and normal working memory. It is of interest to know, then, that the often unreasonable Elliot produced cognitive estimates in the normal range.

By then Elliot had passed through most of the hoops set up for him. He had not taken a personality test yet, and this would be it, I thought. What was the chance that he would fare well in the prime personality test, the Minnesota Multiphasic Personality Inventory, also known as MMPI②. As you may have guessed by now, Elliot was normal in that one too. He generated a valid profile; his performance was genuine.

After all these tests, Elliot emerged as a man with a normal intellect who was unable to decide properly, especially when the decision involved personal or social matters. Could it be that reasoning and decision making in the personal and social domain were different from reasoning and thinking in

---

① T. Shallice and M. E. Evans, The Involvement of the Frontal Lobes in Cognitive Estimation, *Cortex*, 14: 294—303.

② S. R. Hathaway and J. C. McKinley, *The Minnesota Multi-phasic Personality Inventory Manual* (rev. ed.), New York: Psychological Corporation.

domains concerning objects, space, numbers, and words? Might they depend on different neural systems and processes? I had to accept the fact that despite the major changes that had followed his brain damage, nothing much could be measured in the laboratory with the traditional neuropsychological instruments. Other patients had shown this sort of dissociation, but none so devastatingly, as far as we investigators were concerned. If we were to measure any impairment, we had to develop new approaches. And if we wanted to explain Elliot's behavior defects satisfactorily, we should desist from the traditional accounts; Elliot's impeccable performances meant that the usual suspects could not be blamed.

RESPONDING TO THE CHALLENGE

Few things can be as salutary, once you find an intellectual hurdle, as giving yourself a vacation from the problem. So I took some time off from the problem of Elliot, and when I returned, I found that my perspective on the case had begun to change. I realized I had been overly concerned with the state of Elliot's intelligence and the instruments of his rationality, and had not paid much attention to his emotions, for various reasons. At first glance, there was nothing out of the ordinary about Elliot's emotions. He was, as I said earlier, an emotionally contained sort, but many illustrious and socially exemplary people have been emotionally contained. He certainly was not overemotional; he did not laugh or cry inappropriately, and he seemed neither sad nor joyful. He was not facetious, just quietly humorous (his wit was far more engaging and socially acceptable than that of some people I know). On a more probing analysis, however, something was missing, and I had overlooked much of the prime evidence for this: Elliot was able to recount the tragedy of his life with a detachment that was out of step with the magnitude of the events. He was always controlled, always describing scenes as a dispassionate, uninvolved spectator. Nowhere was there a sense of his own suffering, even though he was the protagonist. Mind you, restraint of this sort is often most welcome, from the point of view of a physician listener, since it does reduce one's emotional expense. But as I talked to Elliot again for hours on end, it became clear that the magnitude of his distance was unusual.

Elliot was exerting no restraint whatsoever on his affect. He was calm. He was relaxed. His narratives flowed effortlessly. He was not inhibiting the expression of internal emotional resonance or hushing inner turmoil. He simply did not have any turmoil to hush. This was not a culturally acquired stiff upper lip. In some curious, unwittingly protective way, he was not pained by his tragedy. I found myself suffering more when listening to Elliot's stories than Elliot himself seemed to be suffering. In fact, I felt that I suffered more than he did just by thinking of those stories.

Bit by bit the picture of this disaffection came together, partly from my observations, partly from the patient's own account, partly from the testimony of his relatives. Elliot was far more mellow in his emotional display now than he had been before his illness. He seemed to approach life on the same neutral note. I never saw a tinge of emotion in my many hours of conversation with him: no sadness, no impatience, no frustration with my incessant and repetitious questioning. I learned that his behavior was the same in his own daily environment. He tended not to display anger, and on the rare occasions when he did, the outburst was swift; in no time he would be his usual new self, calm and without grudges.

Later, and quite spontaneously, I would obtain directly from him the evidence I needed. My colleague Daniel Tranel had been conducting a psychophysiological experiment in which he showed subjects emotionally charged visual stimuli—for instance, pictures of buildings collapsing in earthquakes, houses burning, people injured in gory accidents or about to drown in floods. As we debriefed Elliot from one of many sessions of viewing these images, he told me without equivocation that his own feelings had changed from before his illness. He could sense how topics that once had evoked a strong emotion no longer caused any reaction, positive or negative.

This was astounding. Try to imagine it. Try to imagine not feeling pleasure when you contemplate a painting you love or hear a favorite piece of music. Try to imagine yourself forever robbed of that possibility and yet aware of the intellectual contents of the visual or musical stimulus, and also aware that once it did give you pleasure. We might summarize Elliot's predicament as to *know but not to feel*.

I became intrigued with the possibility that reduced emotion and feeling might play a role in Elliot's decision-making failures. But further studies, of Elliot and other patients, were necessary to support this idea. I needed, first of all, to exclude beyond the shadow of a doubt that I had not missed detecting any primary intellectual difficulty, one that might explain Elliot's problems independently of any other defect.

REASONING AND DECIDING

The continued exclusion of subtle intellectual defects took many paths. It was important to establish whether Elliot still knew the rules and principles of behavior that he neglected to use day after day. In other words, had he lost knowledge concerning social behavior, so that even with his normal reasoning mechanisms he would not be able to solve a problem? Or was he still in possession of the knowledge but no longer able to conjure it up and manipulate it? Or was he able to gain access to the knowledge but unable to operate on it and make a choice?

I was helped in this investigation by my then student Paul Eslinger. We began by presenting Elliot with a series of problems, centered on ethical dilemmas and financial questions. Say he needed cash, for example; would he steal if given the opportunity and the virtual guarantee that he would not be discovered? Or: If he knew the performance of company X's stock over the past month, would he sell any stock he owned or buy more of it? Elliot responded no differently from how any of us in the laboratory would have. His ethical judgments followed principles we all shared. He was aware of how social conventions applied to the problems. His financial decisions sounded reasonable. There was nothing especially sophisticated about the problems we set, but it was remarkable to discover, nonetheless, that Elliot did not perform abnormally. His real-life performance, after all, was a catalogue of violations in the domains covered by the problems. This dissociation between real-life failure and laboratory normalcy presented yet another challenge.

My colleague Jeffrey Saver would later respond to this challenge by studying Elliot's behavior in a series of controlled laboratory tasks having to do with social convention and moral value. Let me describe the tasks.

The first concerned the generation of options for action. This instrument was designed to measure the ability to devise alternative solutions to hypothetical social problems. Four social situations (predicaments, in fact) are presented verbally in the test, and the subject is asked to produce different verbal response options to each (which he is supposed to describe verbally). In one situation, the protagonist breaks a spouse's flower pot; the subject is asked to come up with actions the protagonist might take to prevent the spouse from becoming angry. A standardized set of questions such as "What else can he do?" is employed to elicit alternative solutions. The number of relevant and discrete solutions conceptualized by the subject are scored before and after prompting. Elliot exhibited no deficit in performance relative to that of a control group in number of relevant solutions generated prior to prompting, total number of relevant solutions, or relevance score.

The second task concerned awareness of consequences. This measure was constructed to sample a subject's spontaneous inclination to consider the consequences of actions. The subject is presented with four hypothetical situations in which there arises a temptation to transgress ordinary social convention. In one segment, the protagonist cashes a check at a bank and is given too much money by the teller. The subject is asked to describe how the scenario might evolve, and indicate the protagonist's thoughts prior to an action and any subsequent thoughts or events. The subject's score reflects the frequency with which his or her replies include a consideration of the consequences of choosing a particular option. On this task Elliot's performance was even superior to that of the control group.

The third task, the Means-Ends Problem-Solving Procedure, concerned the ability to conceptualize efficacious means of achieving a social goal. The subject is given ten different scenarios and is to conceive appropriate and effective measures to reach a specified goal in order to satisfy a social need—for instance, forming a friendship, maintaining a romantic relationship, or resolving an occupational difficulty. The subject might be told about someone who moves to a new neighborhood, and develops many good friends and feels at home there. The subject then is asked to elaborate a story describing the events that led to this successful outcome. The score is the number of effective acts leading to the outcome. Elliot performed impeccably.

The fourth task concerned the ability to predict the social consequences of events. In each of the thirty test items, the subject views a cartoon panel showing an interpersonal situation, and is asked to choose from among three other panels the one that depicts the most likely outcome of the initial panel. Scoring reflects the number of correct choices. Elliot was no different from normal control subjects.

The fifth and final task, the Standard Issue Moral Judgment Interview (a modified version of the Heinz dilemma as designed by L. Kohlberg and colleagues)[①], concerned the developmental stage of moral reasoning. Presented with a social situation that poses a conflict between two moral imperatives, the subject is asked to indicate a solution to the dilemma and to provide a detailed ethical justification for that solution. In one such situation, for instance, the subject must decide, and explain, whether or not a character should steal a drug to prevent his wife from dying. Scoring employs explicit staging criteria to assign each interview judgment to a specific level of moral development.

The Standard Issue Moral Judgment Interview score ranks a subject in one of five successively more complex stages of moral reasoning. These modes of moral reasoning include preconventional levels (stage 1, obedience and punishment orientation; stage 2, instrumental purpose and exchange); conventional levels (stage 3, interpersonal accord and conformity; stage 4, social accord and system maintenance); and a postconventional level (stage 5, social contract, utility, individual rights). Studies suggest that by age thirty-six, 89 percent of middle-class American males have developed to the conventional stage of moral reasoning and 11 percent to the postconventional stage. Elliot attained a global score of 4/5, indicating a late-conventional, early-postconventional mode of moral thought. This is an excellent result.

In brief, Elliot had a normal ability to generate response options to social situations and to consider spontaneously the consequences of particular response options. He also had a capacity to conceptualize means to achieve social objectives, to predict the likely outcome of social situations, and to perform moral reasoning at an advanced developmental level. The findings

---

① L. Kohlberg, *The Measurement of Moral Judgment*, Cambridge, Massachusetts: Cambridge University Press.

indicated clearly that damage to the ventromedial sector of the frontal lobe did not destroy the records of social knowledge as retrieved under the conditions of the experiment[①].

While Elliot's preserved performance was consonant with his superior scoring on conventional tests of memory and intellect, it contrasted sharply with the defective decision-making he exhibited in real life. How could this be explained? We accounted for the dramatic dissociation on the basis of several differences between the conditions and demands of these tasks and the conditions and demands of real life. Let us analyze those differences.

Except for the last task, there was no requirement to make a choice among options. It was sufficient to conjure up options and likely consequences. In other words, it was sufficient to reason through the problem, but not necessary for reasoning to abut a decision. Normal performance in this task demonstrated the existence of social knowledge and access to it, but said nothing about the process or choice itself. Real life has a way of forcing you into choices. If you do not succumb to the forcing, you can be just as undecided as Elliot.

The above distinction is illustrated best in Elliot's own words. At the end of one session, after he had produced an abundant quantity of options for action, all of which were valid and implementable, Elliot smiled, apparently satisfied with his rich imagination, but added: "And after all this, I still wouldn't know what to do!"

Even if we had used tests that required Elliot to make a choice on every item, the conditions still would have differed from real-life circumstances; he would have been dealing only with the original set of constraints, and not with new constraints resulting from an initial response. If it had been "real life," for every option Elliot offered in a given situation there would have been a response from the other side, which would have changed the situation and required an additional set of options from Elliot, which would have led to yet another response, and in turn to another set of options required from him, and

---

① J. L. Saver and A. R. Damasio, Preserved Access and Processing of Social Knowledge in a Patient with Acquired Sociopathy Due to Ventromedial Frontal Damage, *Neuropsychologia*, 29: 1241—1249.

so on. In other words, the ongoing, open-ended, uncertain evolution of real-life situations was missing from the laboratory tasks. The purpose of Jeffrey Saver's study, however, was to assess the status and accessibility of the knowledge base itself, not the reasoning and deciding process.

I should point out other differences between real life and the laboratory tasks. The time frame of the events under consideration in the tasks was compacted rather than real. In some circumstances, real-time processing may require holding information—representations of persons, objects, or scenes, for instance—in mind for longer periods, especially if new options or consequences surface and require comparison. Furthermore, in our tasks, the situations and questions about them were presented almost entirely through language. More often than not, real life faces us with a greater mix of pictorial and linguistic material. We are confronted with people and objects; with sights, sounds, smells, and so on; with scenes of varying intensities; and with whatever narratives, verbal and or pictorial, we create to accompany them.

These shortcomings aside, we had made progress. The results strongly suggested that we should not attribute Elliot's decision making defect to lack of social knowledge, or to deficient access to such knowledge, or to an elementary impairment of reasoning, or, even less, to an elementary defect in attention or working memory concerning the processing of the factual knowledge needed to make decisions in the personal and social domains. The defect appeared to set in at the late stages of reasoning, close to or at the point at which choice making or response selection must occur. In other words, whatever went wrong went wrong late in the process. Elliot was unable to choose effectively, or he might not choose at all, or choose badly. Remember how he would drift from a given task and spend hours sidetracked? As we are confronted by a task, a number of options open themselves in front of us and we must select our path correctly, time after time, if we are to keep on target. Elliot could no longer select that path. Why he could not is what we needed to discover.

I was now certain that Elliot had a lot in common with Phineas Gage. Their social behavior and decision-making defect were compatible with a normal social-knowledge base, and with preserved higher-order neuropsychological functions such as conventional memory, language, basic attention, basic working memory and basic reasoning. Moreover, I was certain that in Elliot the defect was accompanied by a reduction in emotional reactivity and feeling. (In all likelihood the emotional defect was also present in Gage, but the record does not allow us to be certain. We can infer at least that he lacked the feeling of embarrassment, given his use of foul language and his parading of self-misery.) I also had a strong suspicion that the defect in emotion and feeling was not an innocent bystander next to the defect in social behavior. Troubled emotions probably contributed to the problem. I began to think that the cold-bloodedness of Elliot's reasoning prevented him from assigning different values to different options, and made his decision-making landscape hopelessly flat. It might also be that the same cold-bloodedness made his mental landscape too shifty and unsustained for the time required to make response selections, in other words, a subtle rather than basic defect in working memory which might alter the remainder of the reasoning process required for a decision to emerge. Be that as it may, the attempt to understand both Elliot and Gage promised an entry into the neurobiology of rationality.

 选文出处

Antonio Damasio. *Descartes' Error: Emotion, Reason and the Human Brain*. New York: Avon Books, 1994, pp. 34—51.

思考题

1. 达马西奥认为情绪和感受的衰减使人们无法做出良好的决策,生活中有哪些例子可以佐证这一点?
2. 若我们的决策深受身体与情感的影响,这是否意味着我们缺乏自由意志? 谈谈你的看法。

阅读参考书目

1. 安东尼奥·达马西奥:《寻找斯宾诺莎:快乐、悲伤和感受着的脑》,孙延军译,北京:教育科学出版社,2009年。
2. 安东尼奥·达马西奥:《感受发生的一切:意识产生中的身体和情绪》,杨韶刚译,北京:教育科学出版社,2007年。
3. Joseph Ledoux: *The Emotional Brain: The Mysterious Underpinnings of Emotional Life*, New York: Simon & Schuster, 1998.